IDEAS IN CONTEXT

FACES OF DEGENERATION
A European Disorder, c. 1848–c. 1918

IDEAS IN CONTEXT

Edited by Richard Rorty, J. B. Schneewind, Quentin Skinner and Wolf Lepenies

The books in this series will discuss the emergence of intellectual traditions and of related new disciplines. The procedures, aims and vocabularies that were generated will be set in the context of the alternatives available within the contemporary frameworks of ideas and institutions. Through detailed studies of the evolution of such traditions, and their modification by different audiences, it is hoped that a new picture will form of the development of ideas in their concrete contexts. By this means, artificial distinctions between the history of philosophy, of the various sciences, of society and politics, and of literature, may be seen to dissolve.

Forthcoming titles include works by Keith Baker, Martin Dzelzainis, Mark Goldie, Ian Hacking, Noel Malcolm, Roger Mason, James Moore, Dorothy Ross, Nicolai Rubinstein, Quentin Skinner, Martin Warnke and Robert Wokler.

FACES OF DEGENERATION

A European Disorder, c. 1848 – c. 1918

DANIEL PICK

Research Fellow of Christ's College, Cambridge

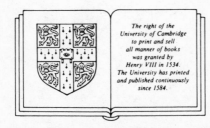

The right of the
University of Cambridge
to print and sell
all manner of books
was granted by
Henry VIII in 1534.
The University has printed
and published continuously
since 1584.

CAMBRIDGE UNIVERSITY PRESS

CAMBRIDGE

NEW YORK   PORT CHESTER   MELBOURNE   SYDNEY

Published by the Press Syndicate of the University of Cambridge
The Pitt Building, Trumpington Street, Cambridge CB2 1RP
40 West 20th Street, New York, NY 10011, USA
10 Stamford Road, Oakleigh, Melbourne 3166, Australia

First published 1989

Printed in Great Britain by
Redwood Burn Limited, Trowbridge, Wiltshire

British Library cataloguing in publication data

Pick, Daniel
Faces of degeneration: a European disorder,
c. 1848–c. 1918. – (Ideas in context)
1. Society. Degeneration. Theories, 1848–1918
I. Title   II. Series
303.4'5

Library of Congress cataloguing in publication data

Pick, Daniel.
Faces of degeneration : a European disorder, c. 1848–c. 1918 / Daniel
Pick.
p.   cm. – (Ideas in context)
Bibliography.
Includes index.
ISBN 0–521–36021–8
1. Degeneration – History – 19th century.   2. Europe – Social
conditions – 1789–1900.   I. Title.   II. Series.
HM111.P54   1989   89–31452 CIP
306'.094—dc20

ISBN 0 521 36021 8

CONTENTS

PLATES

PREFACE

Amongst those who have advised and helped me during my research, I would particularly like to thank Gareth Stedman Jones, who as supervisor of the thesis on which this book is based provided invaluable guidance and insight; in addition, I am greatly indebted to Tony Tanner for patiently reading and discussing my work at various stages and giving so much support. I would also especially like to acknowledge Isobel Banks, Eric Brenman, Roy Porter, Jennifer Davis, Simon Schaffer, Gillian Beer, Quentin Skinner, Michael Neve, Paul Ginsborg, Stephen Heath and David Feldman, all of whom have generously given up time at some stage of this project to make specific comments on the material or to offer encouragement and observations. But no one, needless to say, can bear responsibility for the limitations and deficiencies which remain except myself. I would like to express thanks to Sylvia Sylvester for her kind and efficient help with the production of the final text. The Economic and Social Research Council, the Political Science Fund (Cambridge University), the British Academy and Christ's College, Cambridge have provided grants which enabled me to carry out various research visits to France and Italy. I must also record my gratitude to the Master and Fellows of Christ's for electing me to a Research Fellowship in 1986.

It is, however, to my mother that I owe the most; and it is to her that I dedicate this book.

NOTES ON THE TEXT

Where the footnotes to quotations rendered in English refer to a foreign language source, the translation is mine. For the sake of clarity, I have also frequently translated foreign titles in the main text whilst indicating the original in both the accompanying reference and in the bibliography. I leave the term 'dégénérescence' in the French, since, as will be emphasised below, it often carries quite specific connotations and resonances which are important in my argument. Footnote entries qualified by '(per.)' and '(diss.)' refer the reader to the periodical and dissertation sections of the bibliography. Italics are in the passages I quote unless otherwise stated. I have tried whenever possible to refer to easily accessible editions of the novels which are discussed below. An earlier version of my account of Lombroso and Italian criminal anthropology in part II was published in *History Workshop Journal*, issue 21 (Spring 1986) and the discussion of Bram Stoker's *Dracula* in part III has appeared in a slightly more extended form in *Critical Quarterly*, 30 no. 4 (Winter 1988).

1

◁ ══════════════════════════════════ ▷

Contexts

INTRODUCTION

Pécuchet takes a gloomy view of the future of mankind.
Modern man had been diminished and has become a machine.
Final anarchy of the human race (Buchner, I, ii).
Impossibility of peace (id).
Barbarity caused by excessive individualism and ravings of science.
Three hypotheses: 1. Pantheistic radicalism will break every link with the past, and inhuman despotism will result; 2. if theistic absolutism triumphs, the liberalism which has pervaded mankind since the Reformation will collapse, everything is overturned; 3. if the convulsions existing since the Revolution of 1789 continue endlessly between two outcomes, these oscillations will carry us away with their own strength. There will be no more ideal, religion, morality.
America will have conquered the world.
Future of literature.
Universal vulgarity. There will be nothing left but a vast working-class spree.
End of the world because heat runs out.

Bouvard takes rosy view of future of mankind. Modern man is progressing.
Europe will be regenerated by Asia. The law of history being that civilization goes from East to West – role of China – two branches of mankind will finally be merged.
Future inventions; means of travel. Balloon. Submarine boat with windows; always in calm waters, as the sea is only disturbed on the surface – It will be possible to see fish go by and landscapes at the bottom of the ocean. – Animals tamed – All kinds of cultivation. Future of literature (other side of industrial literature).
Future sciences – Control magnetic pull.
Paris is a winter-garden – fruit espaliers on the boulevards.
The Seine filtered and warm – abundance of artificial precious stones – lavish gilding – house lighting – light will be stored, because certain bodies have this property, like sugar, the flesh of certain molluscs and Bologna phosphorous. House façades will be compulsorily painted with the phosphorescent substance and their radiation will light up the streets.
Evil will disappear as want disappears. Philosophy will be a religion.
Communion of all peoples. Public holidays.
There will be travel to the stars – and when the earth is used up mankind will move over to the stars.[1]

[1] Flaubert, *Bouvard and Pécuchet*, pp. 286–7.

1

The plan for the ending of *Bouvard and Pécuchet*, the novel left unfinished by Flaubert on his death in 1880, includes that passage counterposing the evidence for and against 'progress', or rather, setting each up as the object of laughter and derision. What these notes, indeed, may suggest in the context of the novel, is the symbiotic fatuity and futility of either such given gloomy or rosy view of human history. If the passage had been drawn out by Flaubert, the hapless Bouvard and Pécuchet would no doubt have sought to flatten all contradictions and difficulties as they proceeded in their advocacy of absolute optimism or pessimism, ransacking the encyclopaedia and the newspaper, conflating a miscellany of historical and cultural images in the quest for a singular, definitive vision of change.

This study is an attempt to bring into focus and analyse key elements in the immense dictionary of received and contested ideas about degeneration in and beyond the mid nineteenth century. Although referring at various points to the nineteenth-century novel, the discussion is not primarily of fiction. The aim is to trace something of the culture, politics and language of degeneration across disciplines and forms. At the very moment of publication of *Madame Bovary* (1856), another writer in Rouen, Dr Bénédict Augustin Morel, had been completing a *Traité des dégénérescences physiques, intellectuelles et morales de l'espèce humaine*. Published in 1857, it recorded a much wider unease at the direction of French history during the previous decade, but was in its turn to have a powerful influence in later-nineteenth-century psychiatry, criminology and anthropology, and across a very large range of social commentaries and debates. New discourses of degeneration, it will be argued, emerged during the nineteenth century and powerfully appealed to the natural sciences, particularly to evolutionary theory. The research offered here maps out various conceptions of atavism, regression, relapse, transgression and decline within a European context so often identified as the quintessential age of evolution, progress, optimism, reform or improvement.

My exposition is not centrally concerned with Literary Decadence and its innumerable lyrical laments and aesthetic discontents, nor twentieth-century modernist representations of culture as a wasteland or as a world which 'is, was and will be writing its own wrunes for ever',[2] but rather with the formation and dissemination of a medico-psychiatric and natural-scientific language of degeneration. What is attempted, in this necessarily highly selective study, is a recognition of the political complexity of the idea of degeneration, its over-determination and irreducibility to a single cause or origin. At the same time, I stress the historical specificity of the model of degeneration which, in the shadows of evolutionary naturalism,

[2] Joyce, *Finnegans Wake*, p. 19.

inflected so much writing of the period. Contemporary fiction registered that wider social, scientific debate, sometimes challenging, sometimes simply assuming the stock assumptions of its language.

To take one example; even a socialist novel as critical of dominant ideologies and rationales for inequality as Robert Tressell's *The Ragged Trousered Philanthropists*, published posthumously in 1914, assumed the socio-biological reality of degeneration: 'Under existing circumstances the community is degenerating mentally and physically because the majority cannot afford to have decent houses to live in.' Revolutionary transformation was indispensable, we are told, 'if we are to keep our old place in the van of human progress. A nation of ignorant, unintelligent, half-starved, broken-spirited degenerates cannot hope to lead humanity in its never-ceasing march onward to the conquest of the future.'[3] It is easy now to read over that reference, to miss the specific image of degeneration or to take it as an innocuous euphemism for poverty, disease, destitution, degradation and misery in general. Certainly the political solutions proposed for the problems of contemporary society by the speaker in the novel are in no way a fatalistic acceptance of the arrest of progress; nonetheless he has taken for granted notions about the degenerate and the process of degeneration which in themselves have complex and arguably ominous political implications. Part of the aim in this study is indeed to draw attention to the political, ideological and historiographical implications of that 'taken for granted' language.

I have subjected certain figures to especially close scrutiny: most notably Bénédict Augustin Morel (1809–73) and Cesare Lombroso (1835–1909). Each forms a point of focus in my survey of the interlocking languages of progress and degeneration. Both were doctors who wrote influentially on French and Italian society respectively. Lombroso appears on the face of it to have followed the direction of investigation into crime and madness opened up by Morel in the 1850s and his successor Magnan in the 1870s and 1880s, but there were important differences in nuance and emphasis which were not only the effect of the vagaries of each personal intellectual evolution (interesting though that was), but a consequence of the strikingly different discursive contexts in each country. The work of an English doctor, Henry Maudsley (1835–1918), is also discussed at some length and again I seek to suggest the specificity of the immediate socio-political concerns it addressed and symptomatised, as well as to indicate its place within wider shifts across late-nineteenth-century European thought.

The work which follows is divided into three sections. Part 1 looks in some detail at the intellectual career of Morel and then considers the

[3] *The Ragged Trousered Philanthropists*, p. 472.

importance of hereditarian theory and *dégénérescence* in a variety of French writers such as Buchez, Taine, Le Bon, Sorel and Zola. It shows how Buchez's endorsement of *dégénérescence* in the 1850s related to the crisis of his Catholic-socialist faith in revolution and progress after 1848. But this is not to suggest the doctrine was the exclusive preserve of Catholics, progressives or disillusioned utopian socialists, and most especially not by the 1870s. Taine's history of the Revolution is used to consider the deployment of *dégénérescence* in an explicitly counter-revolutionary historiography after the crisis of France's military defeat in 1870–1871. The notion of inherited criminality and endemic social pathology can be found across the political spectrum in the troubled climate of the Third Republic. From Durkheim to Sorel the resonances of a medical model of degeneration and pathology can be felt, although in each case with a rather different inflection. I argue in my chapter on Zola that the great novelist of heredity and degeneration not only disseminates but also interrogates ideas about *dégénérescence* and medical authority. Zola declared that his writing 'mirrored' science. Too often, however, critics have simply accepted that view unreservedly. Thus the Rougon-Macquart cycle is seen as naively and narrowly faithful to a facile determinism and positivism. Instead, one can show how *Dr Pascal*, the final novel in the cycle, dramatises the contradictions, indeed even the disintegration, of the positivism which had hitherto partially structured Zola's own project.

My discussion describes a late nineteenth-century fascination with the ancestry and atavism of the crowd in Zola and Gustave Le Bon. It focusses on their common graphic representations of the mob as sexually degenerate 'avenger'. The dominant scene of degeneration, I suggest, was displaced from the individual (specific cretins, criminals, the insane and so on) and even the family (whose neuropathic strains were explored by Féré and Magnan) to society itself – crowds, masses, cities, modernity. But the nuances of the medico-psychiatric theory were still present and sometimes significantly productive in the social visions of new sciences of the crowd and elitist theories of 'civilisation and its discontents'.

Part II considers Cesare Lombroso and the formation of criminal anthropology in Italy. Concepts of atavism and degeneration articulated the horror of a largely northern Italian medical and scientific intelligentsia in the face of a fragmented and 'backward' countryside on the one hand, and, increasingly, by the perceived volatility and delinquency of urban populations. Again the politics of the Lombrosian school are complex and plural, as my account endeavours to suggest. The discussion of the international congresses of criminal anthropology which were held in Europe in the late nineteenth and early twentieth centuries analyses some discursive relations between Italian and French sciences of crime, and traces some of the differences between their respective conceptions of degeneration.

Part III begins with a brief discussion of certain late-nineteenth-century English fictions of crime and degeneration. I then consider the influence of, and the resistance to, criminological and psychiatric notions of degeneration and atavism in some key English social debates. The image of the 'habitual criminal' both in England and on the Continent was increasingly conceived through the language of degeneration. I argue that texts such as Goring's *The English Convict* (1913) which are often seen as the definitive environmentalist refutation of Lombrosianism in particular and Continental positivism in general, in fact opt only for a different brand of hereditarian theory. Existing work on degeneration in England has often focussed the question specifically with regard to institutional developments (there is no shortage of histories of the formation of the eugenics movement[4]) and the effects (or non-effects) of Continental positivism in English social theory and law.[5] These usually end by conceding that England was far more guarded in its response to the supposed need for 'social defence', perhaps because the state was so rarely decisively threatened. I discuss that point here, but also shift the ground by emphasising how a language of degeneration in fact informed much wider representations of culture in the late nineteenth and early twentieth centuries. The debate then appears more diffuse than on the Continent, less easily specified. But from the fear of 'Outcast London' in the 1880s to the disenchanted new-liberal perception of democracy, mass society and urban life around the turn of the century, social critique was powerfully inflected by biological theories of decline. The shared emphasis was on degeneration more than the degenerate, hence the difficulty of changing the law, imprisoning or institutionalising the 'problem'.

The constitution of a language of degeneration in and beyond the metropolitan crises of the 1880s was not simply a reflection of changes in London society, labour and politics. By describing certain aspects of the descent of evolutionary thought across the Victorian period, and emphasising the European-wide context of anxiety about degeneration, my argument suggests that the perception of urban 'pathology' was powerfully enhanced and shaped by a discourse which went much wider than the alarmist debate on the capital and its poor. Of course that language interacted with, and was inflected by, the particular economic and political situation of London society, but was not only a consequence of the immediate sense of crisis in the 1880s. My aim is to locate a shift in the very

[4] See, for instance, Kevles, *In the Name of Eugenics*.
[5] See, for instance, Radzinowicz and Hood, *Penal Policy*, pts. 1 and 4.

terms of social criticism from the early to the late-Victorian period, and, more specifically, the move towards a central preoccupation with the economy of the body and the social effects of its reproduction.

Each part offers a somewhat different chronology of degeneration, and traces specific features of its discursive rise, critique and apparent demise. To deal with the complex later-twentieth-century history and politics of socio-biology and evolutionism would involve different intellectual and social contexts from those which are here under discussion. This is not to say, however, that the images of *dégénérescence*, atavism, regression, do not have their resonances within the politics of science and the sciences of politics today.

There is now a significant and rapidly growing body of work on the politics of Darwinism.[6] Evolutionary theory, it has been made plain, must be understood historically; we can trace in Darwin's metaphors and narrative patterns, wider Victorian social concerns and fears. Darwinism was undoubtedly social, inextricably enmeshed in the language, politics, culture of a past.[7] We have now been convincingly shown that evolution has an extremely complex discursive genealogy irreducible to 'two family trees' (say, Darwin versus Spencer, Huxley versus Galton, good against bad, true against false, pure against impure).[8]

But whilst evolution is widely explored, very little critical historical attention has been paid until recently to the related nineteenth-century theme of degeneration. Somewhere along the line, degeneration had receded from view; it had slipped out of focus in the mainstream history of ideas, perhaps relegated to a footnote in literary criticism or brief mention in specialist histories of biology, psychiatry and criminology. Degeneration, once such a 'key word', became something of a lost word. Where discussed at all, it was characteristically confined within a narrowly defined exegesis of nineteenth-century psychiatry,[9] or else distanced from British culture and portrayed as primarily part of the history of Nazism.

In the last few years, however, several books have been published in the

---

[6] See, for instance, many of the contributions to Kohn (ed.), *Darwinian Heritage*, an important recent collection of essays with extensive bibliographical notes.
[7] See Young, *Darwin's Metaphor*; 'Darwinism is social'; Beer, 'Plot and analogy'; *Darwin's Plots*; 'Darwin's reading'.
[8] See Kohn (ed.), *Darwinian Heritage*; Moore, 'Socialising Darwinism', (per.); Helfand, 'Huxley's "Evolution and ethics"'; Durant, 'Meaning of evolution', (diss.); 'Roots of sociobiology', (per.).
[9] See, for instance, the useful but entirely internalist discussion of degeneration in Ackerknecht's *Short History of Psychiatry*, pp. 47–8.

United States which begin to address the question of degenera[tion] provide a great deal of interesting material and discussion. T[o this] instance, Robert Nye has looked in considerable detail at French on 'national decline' during the Third Republic.[10] Gilman and Ch[amberlin] have edited a collection of essays which document, albeit rather com- partmentally, the fear of degeneration in a variety of fields: theatre, fiction, sociology, anthropology, biology, and so on.[11] What is offered in the present study is not only an exposition of figures and contexts inadequately dealt with in or largely beyond the scope of such existing work (Lombroso's criminal anthropology in Italy for example), but also a more sustained attempt to compare and contrast the language of degeneration in several different national contexts of debate. The aim is to focus more sharply than hitherto the terms of the language of degeneration; to provide some sense of historical periodisation; to trace important shifts in this conception during the second half of the nineteenth century and early part of the twentieth century. This research has involved the excavation and analysis of a large primary literature, but it also draws on the existing studies, biographical material, social histories of crime and madness, criminology and psychiatry in the period, and aims to draw out some of the available archival research of others into a wider discussion.

Degeneration was never successfully reduced to a fixed axiom or theory in the nineteenth century despite the expressed desire to resolve the con- ceptual questions once and for all in definitive texts. Rather it was a shifting term produced, inflected, refined, and re-constituted in the movement between human sciences, fictional narratives and socio-political commen- taries. It is not possible to trace it to one ideological conclusion, or to locate its identification with a single political message. But it is perhaps possible to suggest something of the political range of its connotations.

Issues of language will be important in the present study; it will not be a matter of searching for the pure essence of a theory shorn of its figurative veils, but of seeking out the forms, oppositions and denials of a language inextricably bound up in metaphors and analogies, a language whose real, material 'objects' were variable and numerous, if never arbitrarily chosen. The term *dégénérescence*, after all, developed in a later-nineteenth-century European psychiatry 'obsessed' with the naming and fixing of conditions: disorders such as agoraphobia, claustrophobia, astrophobia, thastophobia, dipsomania, aboulia, kleptomania, algophilia, algophobia, satyriasis, nym- phomania, necrophilia, onomatomania, coprolalia, *folie du doute*, arith- momania, pyromania, pyrophobia, exhibitionism, syphilophobia,

[10] Nye, *Crime*.   [11] Gilman and Chamberlin (eds.), *Dark Side*.

nosophilia, nosophobia, necrophobia, thanatophobia,[12] might all embellish an expert diagnosis at the time. But although deployed by medical authorities, the terms were always slipping out of focus, leading into one another, crossing borderlines, signifying only another signifier. Nevertheless the experts on degeneration were remarkably united in their own self-exclusion from the field of pathology; they invariably seemed to position themselves beyond its reach.

Many of these terms were first coined or brought to prominence in late-nineteenth-century Vienna by Richard Krafft-Ebing,[13] a famous contemporary of the young Freud and a keen admirer of Morel. But *dégénérescence* was more than just another mental condition to set alongside the others in an interminable *psychopathia sexualis*; it became indeed the condition of conditions, the ultimate signifier of pathology. *Dégénérescence* was thus perceived as the resolution to a felt imprecision of language and diagnosis. It served to anchor meaning, but paradoxically its own could never be fully stabilised, indeed was in doubt more than all the others; it explained everything and nothing as it moved back and forth between the clinic, the novel, the newspaper and the government investigation. It suggested at once a technical diagnosis and a racial prophecy. In short, it was a complex term. As Dr Cullèrre complained in the *Annales médico-psychologiques* in 1895, the word was widely used but nobody was able to agree precisely on what it meant:

Dégénérescence is one of the most divisive problems amongst contemporary alienists ... is it useful in the understanding of mental illnesses? ... At the present time, such questions preoccupy not only congresses, but also books, the press, clinics ... the quarrel turns as much on the words as on their contents; nobody agrees to speak the same language.[14]

But despite the sense of confusion and division about the scientific validity of degeneration which reached something of a crescendo in the 1890s, the term continued to be widely used or presumed as a virtual orthodoxy. The late nineteenth century was after all the age when, as Henri Ellenberger argues in his classic work, *The Discovery of the Unconscious*,

[12] For such terms and many others see the index to Féré, *Pathologie*, and Nordau, *Degeneration*.
[13] See Krafft-Ebing, *Psychopathia Sexualis*.
[14] Cullèrre, *Difformités*, (per.), p. 52; see Tuke, *Dictionary*, I, p. 332, 'There seems to be a danger of employing the term degeneration in so comprehensive a sense as to comprise forms of mental disorder under one head which differ widely in their form, their prognosis, and their treatment.' Also see Maudsley, 'Criminal Responsibility' (per.), p. 663: 'Has not the theory of degeneracy been somewhat abused of late? As used by Morel the term had scientific meaning and value; but of late much has been done to rob it of all definite meaning by stretching it out to cover all sorts and degrees of deviation from an ideal standard of feeling and thinking'.

'almost all diagnostic certificates in French mental hospitals began with words *dégénérescence mentale avec . . .*'.[15] In the decades after the Franco-Prussian War (1870–1), *dégénérescence* was indeed a fundamental term in the world of French psychiatry. And certainly by contrast, Ellenberger could never have written that there came a time when almost all diagnostic certificates in English mental hospitals began with the words 'mental degeneration with . . .'. But the term degeneration was picked up in Victorian psychiatry and in many other fields. I suggest below that the medico-psychiatric discourse inaugurated by Morel continually invoked some notion of the degenerate, a given individual whose physiognomic contours could be traced out and distinguished from the healthy. But degeneration also connoted invisibility and ubiquity – thus suggesting the inadequacy of traditional phrenology and physiognomy; it was a process which could usurp all boundaries of discernible identity, threatening the very overthrow of civilisation and progress. There were two overlapping conceptions at issue: one concerned with the degenerate and another with degeneration. English culture in the later nineteenth century, I suggest, did not question the possibility of degeneration, so much as the legal and political implications of distinguishing the degenerate outside society and the polity.

It will not be part of my aim to engage in any extended discussion of my theoretical approach and methodology – its efficacy and its limitations should be apparent in the course of the specific historical exposition and argument. Nevertheless, the word 'discourse' should be briefly situated at the outset. As a common term in modern critical theory, it has come to stress the idea of a movement to and fro of a given mode of language within historically specific boundaries. This is to emphasise the etymological root of the word, *discurrere*. Discourse here means more than the articulation of an argument, or the deployment of a set of rhetorical figures. It suggests rather the sense of a discursive space and thus of confines, horizons. There will inevitably be, as it were, 'blind-spots' in any discourse, places assumed or incorporated whilst in fact remaining unseen. Moreover, to persist with the optical metaphor, there will be areas of what is seen and of the process of seeing, which are so taken for granted at a given time as to be barely perceptible. The history which a discourse 'sites' (the pun is not superfluous for this certainly includes a selective process of seeing, positioning and referencing the past) will bear the traces of antecedents, but will also be founded upon the rejection and dissolution of other conceptions and narratives. Discourses are historical but generate different versions of what

---

[15] Ellenberger, *Discovery*, p. 281.

history means. This prompts certain questions in what follows here. When did degeneration become a social-scientific term? How can it be period-ised? Above all, in the pursuit of whose desire or interests and in response to what historical contingencies, did the nineteenth-century discourse of degeneration seek to de-politicise itself altogether, through the signifi-cation of a stern and unyielding 'Nature'?

This study seeks to trace a particular cluster of themes, a crack, as it were, 'which runs zig-zag across the front of the House of Usher'.[16] It shows the common terms of a debate about degeneration and stresses simultaneously the irreducibility of the various discussions: hence in tracing the consti-tution of the language of degeneration, I emphasise wider perceptions about revolutionary and counter-revolutionary inheritance in France, post-unification politics in Italy, and, in the case of England, the con-vergence of a supposed crisis of the city as a viable system, with deep conservative and liberal fears of socialism, democracy and 'mass society'. These did not constitute exclusive preoccupations; moreover there were many overlaps between them. My claim is not that, in some simple way, these alone can be proved to have been determining 'in the final instance', but rather that these are crucial, and in some cases now crucially neglected, emphases. I describe how certain narratives of history were construed in the development of each theory of degeneration. Clearly my analysis seeks to trace not simply what the authors declared to be the subject-matter of their discourse (too often the limitation imposed by traditional 'histories of ideas'), but also the images and narrative sequences which haunted their writing – the skeletons in the cupboard as well as the skulls on the laboratory table. Or rather something of the terrors and desires which in part produced this 'science' of skulls, bodies and ancestors. Lombroso after all was actually to 'see' his mother return from the dead, conjured by a spiritualist medium, as though to challenge the naturalist terms in which decade after decade he had studied the problem of heredity in his motherland.[17]

There were always 'ghosts' in the writing of our authors, to be glimpsed not only in the margins of their 'formal' ideas, but in the constant and anxious displacement and merging of conceptions one into another, even as the texts insisted on their scrupulous singularity, objectivity and detached-ness. There were unconscious levels of the discourse never successfully repressed in this Victorian construction of 'impersonality'; degeneration constituted an impossible endeavour to 'scientise', objectify and cast off whole underworlds of political and social anxiety. Is not *Dr Jekyll and Mr*

16 I take the phrase from Praz, *Romantic Agony*, p. xi. Praz in turn is referring to Poe's tale.
17 See the concluding pages to part II below.

Hyde (1886) exactly the fictional representation and exploration of that impossibility?[18] The doctors of degeneration took it for granted that their work was impersonal. Within the terms of this ritual disavowal, social commentary was transformed into 'scientific truth'.

PROGRESS AND DEGENERATION

My argument returns briefly to certain debates in the Enlightenment, but the focus here is specifically on the conceptualisation of degeneration in the language and culture of later-nineteenth-century evolutionary naturalism. Evolutionary scientists, criminal anthropologists and medical psychiatrists confronted themselves with the apparent paradox that civilisation, science and economic progress might be the catalyst of, as much as the defence against, physical and social pathology. In the words of the pioneering German psychiatrist, Griesinger,[19] European science was faced by 'the much discussed and ambiguous question, whether *the progress of civilisation* has increased the number of [certain] ... diseases'.[20] Numerous investigations and commentaries surrounded the 'almost universally remarked'[21] increase in the number of the insane. Industry, capitalism and social mobility appeared to produce a feverish political and physiological unrest.[22]

There was sustained discussion about increasing crime and insanity rates, but, as we are frequently reminded, evolutionary theories, as expounded by Chambers, Spencer and Darwin were often explicitly progressivist, even if they popularly and outrageously could arouse, despite themselves,[23] images of a simian humanity. Robert Chambers for instance insisted that 'there have been, in the progress of time, strong appearances of a progress of forms, from the more simple to the more complex, from the more general to the more special, the highest and most

---

[18] See ch. 6 below.

[19] On Griesinger see Ackerknecht, *History*; Doerner, *Madmen*; Verwey, *Psychiatry*.

[20] Griesinger, *Pathology*, p. 138.

[21] Griesinger, *Pathology*, p. 138. For some discussions of these general questions in *The Fortnightly Review*, see Cobb, 'Progress', (per.); Bridges, 'Influence', (per.); Corbet, 'Increase', (per.); Drapes, 'Insanity', (per.).

[22] 'Industrial, political, and social agitations work destructively on individuals, as they do on the masses; all live faster – a feverish pursuit of gain and pleasure, and great discussions upon political and social questions keep the world in constant commotion. We may say ... that the present state of society in Europe and America keeps up a general half-intoxicating state of cerebral irritation which is far removed from a natural and healthy condition, and must predispose to mental disorder' (Griesinger, *Pathology*, pp. 138–9). Cf. Maudsley, *Pathology of Mind* (1985), pp. 27–30.

[23] It was really the post-Darwinian evolutionists, like Thomas Huxley who set out to confront head on, exactly, *Man's Place in Nature*, the title of Huxley's controversial work in 1863. See Bowler, *Theories*, pp. 63–4.

typical forms, being always attained last ... the general fact of a progress in all the orders is not to be doubted'.[24]

Progress has indeed proved a key term in the characterisation of the nineteenth century. As one intellectual historian has typically put it: 'progress was the religion of the nineteenth century, just as Catholicism was of the Middle Ages'.[25] Or as the article on progress in the Larousse dictionary in 1875 defined the term:

Humanity is perfectible and it moves incessantly from less good to better, from ignorance to science, from barbarism to civilisation ... The idea that humanity becomes day by day better and happier is particularly dear to our century. Faith in the law of progress is the true faith of our century.[26]

There are many histories of the idea of progress,[27] and often they move between the citation of the idea of advance in nineteenth-century intellectual history, and the interrogation of its factual basis, hence the explication of whether the trends of the society and economy really did signify improvement. The expressed optimism of certain nineteenth-century writers is all too easily taken as axiomatic of the individual in question and by extension of the age (hence very quickly, for example, Macaulay is equated with absolute optimism and a supposed general spirit of the epoch[28]).

---

[24] Chambers, *Vestiges*, p. 180.

[25] Martin, *French Liberal Thought*, p. 299.

[26] Larousse, *Dictionnaire*, XIII, pp. 224–5. Note, however, the articles on degeneration and *dégénérescence*, *Dictionnaire*, VI, p. 302.

[27] See for instance Bury, *Idea of Progress*; Pollard, *Idea*; Nisbet, *History of Idea of Progress*.

[28] ' ... the history of our country during the last hundred and sixty years', said Macaulay, 'is eminently the history of physical, of moral, and of intellectual improvement.' (*History of England*, I, p. 1.) Macaulay's optimism, however, was not absolute. He celebrated Britain's difference from the Continent; moments of crisis abroad highlighted England's triumph, but also intimated its potential fragility. As though to off-set the danger of foreign infiltration, he appealed blithely to unique Anglo-Saxon virtues. 'All around us', he wrote in November 1848, 'the world is convulsed by the agonies of great nations. Governments which lately seemed likely to stand during ages have been on a sudden shaken and overthrown'. By contrast, he went on, 'in our island the regular course of governments has never been for a day interrupted. The few bad men who longed for licence and plunder have not had the courage to confront for one moment the strength of a loyal nation, rallied in firm array round a parental throne' (*History of England*, III, pp. 1,311–12). As he looked back to the seventeenth century, Macaulay's patriotic confidence was not without its alarmist aspect; his account seemed to suggest a potential lesson for the (albeit more advanced) nineteenth century. Describing the flight of James II, he saw the spectre of a vulgar multitude always ready to rise up: 'All those evil passions which it is the office of government to restrain, and which the best governments restrain but imperfectly, were on a sudden emancipated from control ... On such occasions it will ever be found that the human vermin, which neglected by ministers of state and ministers of religion, barbarous in the midst of civilisation, heathen in the midst of Christianity ... will at once rise into a terrible importance' (*History of England*, III, p. 1,206); cf. Hamburger, *Macaulay*, pp. 33, 36. On Macaulay's fear of revolution and the return of irrationalism, see Burrow, *Liberal Descent*, pp. 84–5.

Contemporary society was of course frequently counterposed by Victorian commentators to a putatively barbarous past, or to the current tribulations of another country. In 1851, the *Economist* in a piece on 'progress in political, civil and religious freedom' could apparently rejoice in the 'entire failure of the French Revolution' and at home celebrate the 'vast elevation of public men' and 'the destruction of Feudalism'. Now 'the middle ranks, including all that is educated, sensible, and respectable, are the real rulers of society' but they acted on behalf of 'the greatness of the community – the whole PEOPLE in short'. 'We are', they decided, 'as sanguine of our Future Progress as we are satisfied with our recent steps.'[29] That expression of optimism in the year of the Great Exhibition no doubt coalesced with a sense of relief. The words perhaps connote an aura of manic triumph over, and rhetorical defence against, a vanquished Chartism, the economic crises of the 1840s and the massive political vicissitudes of 1848 on the Continent. But to some it seemed that triumphalist celebrations of progress risked *hubris*, a dangerous tempting of fate. Thus in subsequent decades even the most ebullient ambassadors of progress sometimes spoke of the need for caution, the recognition of the difficulties threatening from outside or the recalcitrance of the primitive within. 'Only a few nations', warned Bagehot in 1872, 'and these of European origin, advance; and yet these think – seem irresistibly compelled to think – such advance to be inevitable, natural, and eternal.'[30]

The judgement of subsequent social and intellectual historians has frequently endorsed the view that the last century (or some portion of it) was, if not 'the age of progress', at least 'the age of improvement'. Historians often blur the question of whether they are citing or endorsing such an epithet. Thus Norman Stone observes that '[t]he years from 1870 to 1900 were the classic age of Progress, a time when the history of the world appeared to be as H. G. Wells was later to see it in his *History*: a matter of enlightened people using science to promote the cause of "Up and Up and Up and On and On and On" (in the expression of Ramsay MacDonald, a characteristic pre-war progressive)'.[31] Stone's own description mimics uncannily that faith in advance, caught up in a celebration of remorseless technological triumphs:

One spectacular discovery or invention succeeded another. Medicine improved almost beyond recognition. In earlier times, most people died if they underwent an operation – not, usually, from a cause any more complicated than the simple shock of the pain. Now, hospitals became hygienic; people survived, rather than died, in

---

[29] *The Economist*, 8 February 1851, 138–9.
[30] Bagehot, *Physics*, p. 42.   [31] Stone, *Europe*, p. 15.

them; and death-rates were cut in half in most countries. There seemed to be no end to this process of improvement. In 1895 the novelist Henry James acquired electric lighting; in 1896 he rode a bicycle; in 1897 he wrote on a typewriter; in 1898 he saw a cinematograph. Within very few years, he could have had a Freudian analysis, travelled in an aircraft, understood the principles of the jet-engine or even of space-travel. (pp. 14–15)

The classic age of progress? To answer that question would involve close and scrupulous analysis of the very meaning and limits of such a phrase. A case can be made for seeing virtually any portion of the second half of the eighteenth and the whole of the nineteenth century in those terms, if we wish to. But it is always a partial and arguable case. Moreover we would need to consider what ideological function such description serves in our own culture and discourse, what kind of comparative statement is being made about the present. Nevertheless, Stone's emphasis is a useful one, serving as a backdrop against the multiple voices and plural emphases of degeneration, decadence and disappointment to be explored below. There is no direct and simple connection between 'the objective state' of the economy and society, and its literary articulations, because there is indeed no 'objective state' – no statistic or fact – which is wholly outside contemporary discourses. Progressivism was not directly caused by economic 'growth' (itself a problematic concept), nor was Literary Decadence the effect of economic 'depression'. Metaphors and models mediated the very reading of the economy. This is not to argue against economic determinants of language, but against economic determinism. Was there a classic age of degeneration and decadence? If so, did it begin with Baudelaire, Flaubert and Morel in the 1850s? Or was its locus 1880–1914, when, no doubt relevantly, but still not necessarily causatively, the very patterns of disease were undergoing a major transition? 'The years between 1880 and 1914 are the crucial ones in the great transition from the age-old pattern of mass morbidity and mortality occasioned by infectious diseases, poor nutrition and heavy labour, to the contemporary assemblage of functional disorders, viral diseases and bodily decay associated with old age.'[32] It is tempting to try to coordinate 'literary depression' directly with economic depression, or contemporary fears about population increase or decline

[32] Smith, 'Health', p. 38; cf. the view of Enrico Ferri, one of the figures discussed below (see part II): 'The nineteenth century has won a great victory over mortality and infectious diseases by means of the masterful progress of physiology and natural science. But while contagious diseases have gradually diminished, we see on the other hand that moral diseases are growing more numerous in our so-called civilisation. While typhoid fever, smallpox, cholera, and diphtheria retreated before the remedies which enlightened science applied by means of the experimental method, removing their concrete causes, we see on the other hand that insanity, suicide, and crime, that painful trinity, are growing apace.' (Ferri, in Grupp (ed.), *Positive School*, pp. 44–5)

with 'actual' demographic facts.[33] As they looked anxiously at Bismarck's Germany, with its 'alarmingly' rapid increase in population, French commentators perceived disaster looming in their own 'slow' national birth rate. Modern demographic history may confirm that France's population was rising more slowly than Germany's which, the naive historian too quickly argues, simply 'explains' why the French were so worried.

There were always 'actual', material referents at issue in the pronouncement of degeneration. To see the mythological dimensions of this language should not blind us to the reality of many of the social problems and human ...ings with which it engaged; this was not some free-floating realm of ...aphor completely unrelated to society. But nevertheless the 'reality' of ...n issue like cretinism (one of Morel's major concerns) was inextricably bound up with, and fundamentally transformed by, the pathologising language in which it was conceived. And crucially, there was no one stable referent to which degeneration applied; instead a fantastic kaleidoscope of concerns and objects through the second half of the century, from cretinism to alcoholism to syphilis, from peasantry to urban working class, bourgeoisie to aristocracy, madness to theft, individual to crowd, anarchism to feminism, population decline to population increase. My aim is not to affirm or dispute progress or degeneration, but to explore and examine the forces which played a part in the construction of such views. I am not concerned here to argue whether society really was progressing in the Victorian age, as Ruskin was when he insisted that 'all evidences of progress or decline have ... to be collected in mass, – then analyzed with extreme care – then weighed in the balance of the Ages, before we can judge the meaning of any one';[34] or even to insist that in reality they are simultaneous (as in Tennyson: 'Evolution ever climbing after some idea good,/ And reversion ever dragging Evolution in the mud'[35]) but to ask what themes, anxieties, politics were brought together in these terms in and beyond the second half of the nineteenth century and to trace the forms in which progress and decline were pre-supposed and counterposed to one another.

'The history of England', wrote Seeley in 1883, 'ought to end with something that might be called a moral.'[36] What was the meaning and the conclusion, he mused: 'What is [the] general drift or goal of English history?' (p. 7). 'No one', he insisted, 'can long study history without being haunted by the idea of development, of progress' (p. 3). The insistence of

---

[33] Disputes raged in France between pro- and anti-natalists in the decades before 1914; see: Donzelot, *Policing*; Nye, *Crime*, p. 166; Gay, *Bourgeois Experience*, 266–8; Winter and Teitelbaum, *Fear*.
[34] *Fors Clavigera*, letter 82 (October 1877), Ruskin, *Works*, XXIX, p. 224.
[35] 'Locksley Hall Sixty Years After' (lines 199–200), Tennyson, *Poems*, p. 1,367.
[36] Seeley, *Expansion*, p. 1.

the present study is that no *singular* conclusion as to contemporary social evolution or degeneration was simply impelled or determined by 'objective' factors from which we can now directly extrapolate – say from the 'bed-rock' of medical history, demography or economics. Nevertheless the choice of 'morals' drawn in the period, the versions of progress which 'haunted' contemporaries and their naturalisation as the definitive 'truth' of society, are themselves historically interesting and important.

The failure to look critically at the language of nineteenth-century ideas has produced some singularly questionable results in the recent historiography of progress. In Nisbet's *History of the Idea of Progress* (1980), for instance, an encyclopaedic-style survey of the intellectual past from ancient Greece onwards leads into a consideration of progress today. The decline of belief in progress in the West, argues Nisbet, has brought about 'our' degeneration. Conversely, the East has risen to power partly through the theft of the West's once dominant progressivism.[37] Nisbet argues that only through 'the authority of some kind of class or elite'[38] can the spirit on which progress depends be re-constituted in the West.

The ideology of progress is perceived as a key weapon in the Cold War – a Cold War in which the text itself is hopelessly implicated and marooned:

The tragedy is that today there is a great deal more conviction of the reality of progress in some of the unfree nations of the world, beginning with the Soviet Union, than there is in the free Western nations ... Such [faith in progress], one must record in melancholy tones, is not the case in Western civilization at the present time. Disbelief, doubt, disillusionment, and despair have taken over – or so it would seem from our literature, art, philosophy, theology, even our scholarship and science. (p. 318)

But if one analyses the discussions of progress and degeneration in the past, one must surely also be provoked to hesitate in the face of such political nomenclature today, to question the meaning of these and other related terms ('growth', 'development', 'evolution', 'crisis') and see what weight they carry, and what complexity they may elide, in any particular context.

Nisbet's text falls outside my historical period, but nevertheless it could be placed together with the primary material in certain of its discursive concerns. It is limited by its inability to call into question the opposition progress/decline, and ask what it means to speak thus globally of the

[37] '[T]he dogma of progress is today strong in the official philosophies or religions of those nations which are the most formidable threats to Western culture and its historical, moral and spiritual values – one more instance of the capacity for Western skills and values to be exported, corrupted, and then turned against the very West that gave them birth.' (Nisbet, *History of Idea of Progress*, p. 9.)

[38] *History of Idea of Progress*, p. 334.

(moral? economic? ecological? political?) direction of societies. For Nisbet, the present is nothing but the apotheosis of degeneration, the realisation of all those old Spenglerian fears of the decline of the West:

What Spengler referred to in the title of his famous work is already well under way ... what is in all ways most devastating, however, is the signal decline in *America and Europe themselves* of faith in the values of Western civilization. (p. 331)

The First World War, it can be argued, put paid to the dominance of *dégénérescence* within psychiatry and shifted the language of debate. Certainly in England it seemed obvious to many commentators that the nation had not degenerated, despite all the fears. 'We may well be surprised', a report on the health of recruits concluded in 1920, 'that with human material of such physique, it was possible to create the Armies which overthrew the Germans and proved invincible in every theatre of War.' They added, however, that '[o]ne cannot but feel that the spirit of the race, which alone made this possible, deserves that no effort should be spared to ameliorate the conditions which have brought about such deplorable effects upon its health and physique'.[39] But in a different sense, the history of degeneration was only just beginning: according to George Steiner, 'we are certainly since Nietzsche and Spengler, "terminalists". Our view of history, says Lévi-Strauss in a deep pun, is not an anthropology, but an "entropology"'.[40] Steiner himself has argued that language perhaps degenerated irredeemably in the light of the literally unspeakable Holocaust: here lies the death even of tragedy.[41] For Steiner, as in a different intellectual context for Mosse, it is Nazism, the Second World War and 'the Final Solution' which constitute the unique and incontrovertible points of reference for the discussion of barbarism in all Western culture pre-1939 and post-1945. For others writing in and beyond 1914, the First World War represents the decisive passage into darkness, the fundamental bleak image of modern culture and memory. Thomas Hardy thus wrote in a preface to his *Late Lyrics* in 1922 that '[w]e seem threatened with a new Dark Age', a catastrophe which can be traced perhaps to 'the barbarizing of taste in the younger minds by the dark madness of the late war, the unabashed cultivation of selfishness in all classes, the plethoric growth of knowledge simultaneously with the stunting of wisdom'.[42]

Certainly the belief in society's remorseless decline and fall is still

---

[39] *Report upon the Physical Examination of Men of Military Age*, p. 23; cf. Soloway, 'Counting degenerates', (per.), p. 159.
[40] Steiner, *Difficulty*, p. 186.　　[41] Steiner, *Tragedy*.　　[42] Hardy, *Lyrics*, p. xiv.

manifest today, as Patrick Brantlinger has shown in his rich compendium *Bread and Circuses* (1983). He demonstrates that from the classics onwards (Horace: 'our fathers, viler than our grandfathers, begot us who are even viler; we shall bring forth a progeny more degenerate still'[43]), each age has believed itself the witness of unprecedented pathology and has repressed the memory of previous utterances. 'Growing efficacy involves growing degeneration of the life instincts', writes the author of *The Decadence of the Modern World* (1978), as though oblivious of the pit-falls of nine-teenth-century degenerationism: 'Every progressive impulse must sooner or later become fatigued'.[44]

The effect of Brantlinger's demonstration that the lament for contempo-rary decadence has a long history, or to take another example from a recent book, that each decade believes itself uniquely plagued by hooligans,[45] is somewhat paradoxical: on the one hand it alerts us to the relativity of such absolute claims and discloses their place in a much longer series of com-mentaries. On the other, it too easily suppresses historical difference by petrifying discourses into apparently unchanging, age-old mythologies – hooligans, bread and circuses, degeneration. My insistence here is that when studied closely within historical limits, important and revealing differences do emerge in the meaning of seemingly homogenous and timeless concepts.

But let us pursue a little further the possible argument that there is no specific later-nineteenth-century language of degeneration; thus, it might be insisted, the notion, or at least the question, of things getting worse, degenerating culturally, racially and universally, punctuates Western phil-osophy, politics and religion from, say, Plato to Rousseau to Hegel. Thus in *The Republic* we find the statement that

since decay is the lot of everything that has come into being, even this constitution will not abide for ever, but will be dissolved. And its dissolution will be as follows: To all living things, not only to plants that grow in the earth, but also to animals that live upon its surface, come times of fertility or barrenness of soul and body ... Now those whom you have trained to be leaders of the city, in spite of their wisdom will not be able by calculation and perception to manage the production of offspring in your race so that it shall either be good or not be at all, but it will escape them, and they will some time or other beget children wrongly.[46]

[43] *Odes*, III, vi, 46–8, translated in Brantlinger, *Bread and Circuses*, p. 69; cf. Horace, *Odes*, p. 194.
[44] Sinai, *Decadence*, p. 5; cf. 'Our modern world is not only in disarray and crisis but is also in deterioration and decay ... Every civilization has a history: a beginning, an interlude of growth and a time of contraction and decline ... All things in history move toward both fulfillment and dissolution, toward the fuller embodiment of their essential character and toward death.' (pp. 4–5)
[45] See Pearson, *Hooligan*.
[46] Plato, *Republic*, pp. 240–1, section 546.

Or take Rousseau in *The Discourse on the Origin of Inequality*: 'we are almost prompted to believe that we could write the history of human illness by following the history of civilised societies'.[47] The savage, it seemed, had wanted nothing ('[h]is imagination paints no pictures; his heart yearns for nothing', p. 90) whilst modern society lived in a frenzy and paroxysm of desire. Speaking from the age of enlightenment, Rousseau reasoned that reason itself was symptomatic of decline. He projected an original innocence (even whilst confessing its actual one-time existence to be doubtful), and insisted that civilisation had produced a certain degeneration: 'Men are wicked ... Yet man is naturally good ... What then can have corrupted him to this point, if not the changes that have come about in his constitution, the progress he has made, and the knowledge he has acquired?' (p. 147). As we are told at the beginning of *Emile*, 'all is good in leaving the hands of the Author of things; everything degenerates in the hands of man';[48] or, more specifically, in speaking of how clothes distort and constrict women's bodies: 'It seems to me that this abuse, which is carried to an incredible degree of folly in England, must sooner or later lead to the production of a degenerate race' (p. 330).

Even Hegel was to declare in the *Lectures on the Philosophy of World History* that: 'A nation makes internal advances; it develops further and is ultimately destroyed. The appropriate categories here are those of cultural development, over-refinement, and degeneration; the latter can be either the product or the cause of the nation's downfall.'[49] The nation, in short, has an aim and a terminus, a point of historical exhaustion:

When the spirit of the nation has fulfilled its function, its agility and interest flag; the nation lives on the borderline between manhood and old age, and enjoys the fruits of its efforts ... The natural death of the national spirit may take the form of political stagnation, or of what we call habit. The clock is wound up and runs automatically ... Thus both nations and individuals die a natural death. (p. 59)

Hegel then has a notion of degeneration and social death, but it is important to note at the same time, that this is quickly subsumed within a dominant philosophical commitment to progress. One nation may degenerate and expire, he acknowledges, and indeed some parts of the globe are in a permanent and immutable state of stagnation and lifelessness – Africa in particular (pp. 173–90) – but there is always another state to carry the torch of progress and history forwards. The death of one nation will indeed serve the life of another higher state: 'It then serves as material for a higher principle' (p. 60). Or again still more explicitly: 'This progress is evident even when the national spirit destroys itself by the negativity of its thought,

---

[47] Rousseau, *Discourse*, p. 85. [48] Rousseau, *Emile*, p. 1.
[49] Hegel, *Lectures*, p. 56.

because its knowledge, its thinking apprehension of being, is the source and matrix from which a new form – and indeed a higher form, whose principle both conserves and transfigures it – emerges' (p. 61). World civilisation is not really threatened by degeneration and death. It is rather that for Hegel there are inevitable losers and deaths in an ineluctable historical march of progress.

The notion of decline, if held at a sufficient level of generality, can evidently be identified at numerous points in a history of political discourse. Held at that level, one could even say that theories of progress always seem to involve the implication of potential inversions, recalcitrant forces, subversive 'others', necessarily to be excluded from the polity. Hence there may appear to be a continual discursive tension between the construction of political identities and the designation of the pathological and insidious outsider. So how can one justify the historical periodisation of this seemingly ubiquitous idea: degeneration? One might remark at once, as a kind of preliminary point, that the second half of the nineteenth century is characterised by an enormous output of medical and natural scientific writings on social evolution, degeneration, morbidity and perversion: from Morel's *Treatise* through Lombroso's *Criminal Man*, Maudsley's *Body and Will*, Lankester's *Degeneration*, Krafft-Ebing's *Psychopathia Sexualis*, Nordau's *Degeneration*, and so on. Behind each of those texts, one discovers an avalanche of similar books, pamphlets, and articles.[50] But more importantly one can trace a shift not only in the quantity of discussion but in its very nature. Degeneration moves from its place as occasional sub-current of wider philosophies and political or economic theories, or homilies about the horrors of the French and the Industrial Revolutions, to become the centre of a scientific and medical investigation. This can be understood in both a sociological sense (the name of the authors of the key works on degeneration are very often qualified with titles as doctors, anthropologists and zoologists) and in a discursive sense: the texts appeal to the authority of natural scientific truth and, increasingly, to various forms of evolutionary naturalist theory. The potential degeneration of European society was thus not discussed as though it constituted primarily a religious, philosophical or ethical problem, but as an empirically demonstrable medical, biological or physical anthropological fact.

[50] For example, Hirsch, *Genie und Entartung*, 1894; Arndt, *Biologische Studien. II. Artung und Entartung*, 1895; Dallemagne, *Dégénérés et déséquilibrés*, 1895; Robin, *Dégénérescence de l'espèce humaine*, 1896; Möbius, *Ueber Entartung*, 1900; Berthet, *Les Dégénérés dans les écoles primaires*, 1906; Charpentier, *Dégénérescence mentale et hysterie*, 1906; Danel, *La Notion de dégénérescence, particulièrement dans l'étude du mouvement littéraire et artistique contemporain*, 1907; Brumke, *Ueber Nervöse Entartung*, 1912; Thulie, *La Lutte contre la dégénérescence et la criminalité*, 1912; and so on.

Crucially, degeneration in the second half of the nineteenth century served not only to characterise other races (for instance in the view that other races had degenerated from the ideal physique of the white races), but also to pose a vision of internal dangers and crises within Europe. Crime, suicide, alcoholism and prostitution were understood as 'social pathologies' endangering the European races, constituting a degenerative process within them.

Evolutionary theory and racial anthropology were imbricated with an imperialistic insistence on the racial superiority of the world's colonisers over the colonised, but they also reflected back on European society in deeply unsettling ways. Indeed social questions involving crime, moral decadence and racial pollution began to intersect more and more insistently around the middle of the century. Between the 1820s and the 1840s a massive new literature had emerged charting the phenomenon of crime in the cities: a plethora of sensational stories fetishised, romanticised and reviled the criminal mysteries of a Paris, a Naples, a London. Dangerous classes and dangerous races multiplied in literature.

In *The Holy Family* in 1844, Marx and Engels noted this powerful preoccupation with crime in European society, or as they put it with 'the mystery of degeneracy in civilisation'. Not only in novels like those of Eugene Sue, but also '[f]or Parisians in general and even for the Paris police the hide-outs of criminals are such a "mystery" that at this very moment broad light streets are being laid out in the Cité to give the police access to them'.[51] Marx and Engels cite this new concern with mystery, the mystery of degeneration, as one instance of a broader idealistic inversion of material reality which marked Hegelianism. Ideas and mysteries were cast as the imaginary subjects, whilst the material world was simply a predicate of those subjects.

This point is worth making here because Marx and Engels' critique is another way into understanding the specificity of the medico-psychiatric discourse of degeneration in the second half of the nineteenth century. Degeneration was increasingly seen by medical and other writers not as the social condition of the poor, but as a self-reproducing force; not the effect but the cause of crime, destitution and disease. The putative biological force of degeneration produced degeneracy in society. Such a theory could be said to have involved a deep confusion of subject and predicate analogous to the confusion which Marx had discerned, via Feuerbach, in Hegel. In their critique of idealism, Marx and Engels make just this point:

In the speculative way of speaking, this operation is called comprehending the substance as the subject, as an inner process, as an Absolute Person and that comprehension constitutes the essential character of Hegel's method ... After thus

---

[51] Marx and Engels, *Holy Family*, pp. 77–8.

far dissolving real relations, e.g. right and civilization, in the category of mysteries and thereby making 'mystery' a substance, [the idealist] ... transforms 'mystery' into self-existing subject incarnating itself in real situations and persons so that the manifestations of its life are countesses, marquises, grisettes, porters, notaries and charlatans, love intrigues, balls, wooden doors, etc. Having produced the category 'mystery' out of the real world, he produces the real world of that category.[52]

Marx and Engels go on to politicise the very idea of progress against which 'mysteries' of crime and retrogression are posed. The idea of progress in short, they suggest, has a political history: it is important to consider what constitutes progress, what is excluded from it, what is deemed recalcitrant, backward, primitive to it; and it is crucial to note when theories of progress disavow the fact that they are articulated from a position, on behalf of certain classes and interests:

The position is the same with 'progress'. In spite of 'progress's' pretentions, continual retrogressions and circular movements are to be observed. Not suspecting that the category 'Progress' is completely empty and abstract, Absolute Criticism is so profound as to recognise 'Progress' as being absolute and to explain retrogression by supposing a 'personal adversary' of progress, the mass. (pp. 112–13)

By contrast, communist and socialist writers, they claimed, 'proceeded from the observation that ... all progress of the spirit has so far been progress against the mass of mankind, driving it to an ever more dehumanized predicament' (p. 113). However much Marx and Engels may have in their turn produced an idealised, naturalised version of progress, the point here is that one could apply the critique of idealism to the discourse of degeneration which emerges powerfully in the later nineteenth century. Degeneration slides over from a description of disease or degradation as such, to become a kind of self-reproducing pathological process – a causal agent in the blood, the body and the race – which engendered a cycle of historical and social decline perhaps finally beyond social determination.

In methodological terms, my insistence is that intellectual history cannot be written without attention to the discourse, specific culture, implicit historiography, position of address, in and through which ideas are organised and delimited. I show that even in the case of what appears as a crude and undifferentiated 'socio-biological' ideology, there were in fact always differences. Polemics against biological reductionism for instance often cite a figure like Lombroso without regard to the Italian context of his work. He becomes simply the pseudo-scientist *par excellence*, an indiscriminate metaphor for positivism in general. Alternatively, he and his

[52] *Holy Family*, p. 82.

associates are sometimes adduced, in somewhat antiquarian fashion, mere 'curiosities'.

Certainly to glance at the table of contents in many nineteenth-century socio-biological texts is to confront a now strange and fantastic agenda of 'subjects'. An extreme example is provided in a work entitled *Evolution by Atrophy in Biology and Sociology*, translated from the French in 1899, which ranges across such issues as the decadence of financial institutions, crayfish, plants, leaves, the budgets of Belgium, Germany, France and England, the development of landed property, rudimentary organs in human beings, plants, worms, nations, molluscs, dinosaurs, cities, the decline of empires from Rome to China.[53]

Or consider the American Eugene Talbot's *Degeneracy. Its Signs, Causes and Results* (1898) which under the general title 'degeneracy' has such sub-headings as 'ethical', 'intellectual', 'sensory', 'spinal', 'nutritive' and 'local reversionary'.[54] These co-reside with sections on 'degeneracy in the negro', 'giantism', 'feet degeneracy', 'sexual degeneracy' and 'juvenile obesity' (*passim*). Talbot's work contains macabre pictures of the de-formed foetus, criminals and bodily anomalies. Photography authenti-cated the writing; the descriptions explained the images. Thus the juvenile criminals we are shown, are coded for us as 'puny, sickly, scrofulous, often deformed with peculiar, unnaturally developed heads, sluggish, stupid, liable to fits, mean in figure and defective in vital energy, while at the same time they are irritable, violent, and too often quite incorrigible' (pp. 18–19). The essence of crime, Talbot insisted, was to be found in 'parasitology':

The essential factor of crime is its parasitic nature. Parasites, in a general way, may be divided into those which live on their host, without any tendency to injure his well-being (like the dermodex in the skin follicules); those which live more or less at his expense, but do not tend to destroy him; and finally, those which are destructive of the well-being of man and lack proper recognition of individual rights which constitutes the essential foundation of society. (p. 318)

When Talbot came back to these issues in 1921, the more spectacular assumptions listed above had disappeared and the terms of the discussion appear recognisable to us as early forensic science. Nevertheless the text is still fundamentally concerned to classify the physiognomy of the criminal and the law-abiding, and to ground social observations in irrefutably objective images (Talbot had by now introduced photographs from the world of molecular biology to reinforce the argument[55]).

Perhaps the best-known instance of bizarre 'social diagnosis' of this type

---

[53] Demoor *et al.*, *Evolution by Atrophy*. [54] Talbot, *Degeneracy*, pp. 37–8.
[55] See Talbot, *Developmental Pathology*.

is Max Simon Nordau's *Degeneration* translated into English in 1895 from the German (*Entartung*, 1892). The writer who had in fact changed his name from Südfield to the more Germanic Nordau, was born in a Jewish family in Budapest in 1849. He studied medicine, before travelling widely, eventually settling in Paris in 1880 where he acted as a correspondent for the German-language Budapest paper, *Pester Lloyd*.[56] The young Freud called upon him there with a letter of introduction whilst studying with Charcot at the Salpêtrière, but apparently was not favourably impressed.[57] In a series of books, but above all in *Degeneration*, Nordau argued that madness, suicide, crime and pathological literature symptomatised modern times – 'We stand now in the midst of a severe mental epidemic; of a sort of black death of degeneration and hysteria'.[58] Having borrowed various contemporary terms and ideas from the works of Morel, Lombroso, Maudsley, Taine, Charcot and others, Nordau argued that modern society was witnessing a terrible crisis born out of the growing division between the human body and social conditions. In the nineteenth century, he lamented, civilised humanity grew 'fatigued and exhausted, and this fatigue and exhaustion showed themselves in the first generation, under the form of acquired hysteria; in the second, as hereditary hysteria'.[59] He offered a detailed physiological explanation of that fatigue, involving descriptions of brain cells, nerves and decomposing tissues (pp. 46–9). He confided later that '[v]ery probably the cell of the degenerate is formed a little differently from that of sane men, the particles of the protoplasm are otherwise and less regularly disposed' (p. 253). Perhaps in the very long run, he speculated, the fatigued nineteenth-century body would catch up with social evolution:

The end of the twentieth century, therefore, will probably see a generation to whom it will not be injurious to read a dozen square yards of newspapers daily, to be constantly called to the telephone, to be thinking simultaneously of the five continents of the world, to live half their time in a railway carriage or in a flying machine ... It will know how to find its ease in the midst of a city inhabited by millions ... (p. 54)

Nordau was obsessed by the relation between fin-de-siècle culture and hysteria. He found massive obfuscation and disorders of speech in famous writers and painters. Society was besieged by '"impressionists", "stipplers", or "mosaists", "pappilloteurs" "quiverers" or "roaring colourists"', all of whose styles became 'at once intelligible to us if we keep in

[56] See Avineri, *Modern Zionism*, p. 101.
[57] Freud, we are told, met Nordau in Paris in 1886, but found him 'vain and stupid and did not cultivate his acquaintance'; see Jones, *Freud*, I, p. 205.
[58] *Degeneration*, p. 537; cf. Nordau, *Lies*, p. 1: The 'world of civilization', he declared, 'is an immense hospital ward'.
[59] Nordau, *Degeneration*, p. 40.

view the researches of the Charcot school into the visual derangements in degeneration and hysteria' (p. 27). Nordau was appalled by the blurring of the line between science and fiction – his favourite target was Zola. The imaginative writer carries off

unfinished scientific hypotheses, complete[s] them by means of his own fantastic conceits and teach[es]: 'Do you see? this man ... has become what he is because his parents have had such and such attributes, because he has lived here or there ...' [The novelist thereby does] what is not his office ... he gives us false science ... (pp. 487–8)

Even contemporary ghost stories, he objected, now 'come on in scientific disguise, as hypnotism, telepathy, somnambulism' (pp. 13–14). For Nordau, naturalism was only one facet of a cultural disease which had been disseminated by the Enlightenment and Rousseau in particular:

We discover the very first traces [of the disease] in the literature of the latter part of the last century ... While the upper classes were following an uninterrupted round of corrupt gaieties ... whilst the self-sufficient bourgeoisie saw nothing beyond the length of their noses ... [all] of a sudden Jean Jacques Rousseau lifted his voice in a ringing appeal for deliverance from his surroundings ... [60]

Whilst Nordau's survey of the other European countries led him at one point to the conclusion that contemporary France could 'congratulate herself upon the best condition of political health of any European country' (p. 5), this reflected the seriousness of the crisis he perceived in England, Germany and Italy, rather than any real cause for complacency. Indeed more typically, in and beyond the Paris which he had made his home, Nordau saw disorder:

On every street corner in the large cities, excited orators are preaching the gospel of Communism and violence; the masses are preparing to get possession of the government and drive the ruling bourgeoisie out of the snug offices and sinecures which they have enjoyed since 1789 ... (p. 5)

Nordau's work was sometimes celebrated, but also frequently denounced as charlatanism. It was nonetheless charlatanism deemed significant enough to merit refutation: as in, for instance, the anonymous *Regeneration: a Reply* (1895), and Shaw's *The Sanity of Art* (1908).[61] Often, moreover, it was not the validity of degeneration as a diagnostic category which was questioned, but only Nordau's imprudent generalisations and his 'hysterical' style of address. Indeed accusations of degeneracy began to fly back upon him. Nordau 'has haunted the hospitals and

[60] *Lies*, pp. 6–7.
[61] Note that *Degeneration* was rapidly translated from German into many languages including English, French, Spanish, Italian and Russian.

asylums, and made for himself a little world of his own, peopled by the ghastly figures of the diseased, the dying and the degenerate', declared *The Bookman*.[62] Nordau 'has been soaked up to his neck in Darwinism', said the *Saturday Review*, he 'assumes the grand air with his readers, poses as a "scientist" with the best of them, but he has evidently read his biology and psychology out of popular manuals, and carelessly'.[63] The crisis Nordau had described was real, but passing rather than permanent, argued Janet Hogarth in the *Fortnightly Review*: 'In a generation more, the degenerate may be a mere sporadic survival, little likely to persist amid a race endowed with sound minds and healthy nerves'.[64] But this was no reason not to enjoy Nordau's lively style: 'Meanwhile let us be grateful to Dr Nordau for his display of graphomania. It is not every higher degenerate whose passion for writing has made him so entertaining a critic. Or if there is really more method in his madness let moralists be left to find it out' (p. 592).

Criminologists and psychiatrists, including Lombroso himself, to whom Nordau had dedicated *Degeneration*,[65] would perhaps have liked to distance themselves from the scientific philistinism and positivist 'mania' of Nordau. We do not know how much his strange 'case' truly shocked the scientists upon whom Nordau had drawn. It may have contributed something to that broader unease with the notion of natural science as the key to all mythologies which began to inflect late-nineteenth-century culture, as evidenced in the later spiritualist work of such hitherto staunch naturalists as Lombroso himself. Even so brief an example will suggest the crucial refraction which took place between literary and scientific languages. Indeed the present study examines certain novels, notably those of Emile Zola, which pose profoundly the themes, and what one might call the problematic, of degeneration within naturalist writing.

But one must guard against a literary critical account which conjures degeneration as a kind of exotic and innocuous 'by-way' of the nineteenth century, however irresistible it appears to turn the degenerationist writers into pathological objects themselves. The issue remains politically and culturally important. Here I seek to reconstitute the complexity of the ideas at the time, and to show how they were part of the inheritance of both Left and Right. Indeed even in the case of Nordau, politics were complex. He was after all not only a polemicist against decadent literature, but also a leading figure in the Zionist movement.[66]

62 Peck, 'Degeneration and regeneration', (per.), p. 404.
63 *Saturday Review*, *Nordau's Paradoxes*, p. 89.
64 Hogarth, 'Literary degenerates', (per.), p. 592.
65 Note Lombroso's *Le Crime: causes et remèdes* (1899) was in turn dedicated to Nordau.
66 See Avineri, *Modern Zionism*, ch. 10. On the turn of the century racial theories of various other Zionists see Mosse, *Crisis*, pp. 124–5.

Moreover, for all his denunciation of the depraved tastes of modern mass society, Nordau preached primarily against the upper classes and the urban intelligentsia; he placed his faith in the workers, the peasantry and portions of the bourgeoisie. These 'healthy' parts of the population, 'vast masses of the people', will 'rapidly and easily adapt themselves to the conditions which new inventions have created in humanity'.[67] Nordau has in this respect something in common with Sorel, another of Cesare Lombroso's admirers in the 1890s.[68] Humanity resembled a vast torrent of lava, Nordau declared. He promised that '[t]he outer crust [of humanity] . . . cracks into cold, vitrified scoria but under this dead shell the mass flows, rapidly and evenly, in living incandescence' (p. 540).

'TOWARD THE FINAL SOLUTION'?

However sensitive one may be to the specificities of discursive context, it is perhaps now impossible to read nineteenth-century texts on racial degeneration without an implicit teleology. Thus one easily refers to Nazism as the apotheosis of such earlier socio-biological ideas. George Mosse's history of European racism is indeed entitled *Toward the Final Solution* (1979) and declares: 'any book concerned with the European experience of race must start with the end and not with the beginning: 6 million Jews killed by the heirs of European civilisation'.[69] When Mosse discusses Gobineau in France, Lombroso in Italy, Galton and Pearson in England, Nazism is always close at hand.[70]

To read nineteenth-century German writings on social evolution, the decline of races, the twilight of civilisations, is to recall at once that subsequent Nazi history, that terrible dream of racial regeneration through eugenicism, sanitisation of culture, exhibition and excoriation of 'degenerate' arts,[71] and elimination of 'inferior' peoples. Hans Frank, veteran Nazi, chief jurist of the movement, and subsequently Minister of Justice under the Third Reich, declared in a speech in 1938:

---

[67] *Degeneration*, p. 541.
[68] See the conclusion to part I below.
[69] Mosse, *Final Solution*, p. xi. Cf. 'The Nazi implementation of racial policy was essentially the climax of a long development which we have analysed from its source in the eighteenth century.' (p. 231)
[70] *Final Solution*, pp. 56–7, 75. Note how the discussion of Morel and Lombroso (pp. 82–6) is removed from any specifically French or Italian context.
[71] An exhibition of 'degenerate art' was held in Munich in 1937. It proved enormously popular. More than two million people attended the exhibition which sought to link Africa, primitivism, expressionism, insanity, Judaism, bolshevism and anarchism. In Munich at the same time was to be found an exhibition entitled the 'House of German art', which demonstrated the official view of 'good' healthy painting. See Schoenberner (ed.), *Artists*, pp. 61–2, and Whitford, 'Triumph', pp. 252–9.

National Socialism regards degeneracy as an immensely important source of criminal activity … in an individual, degeneracy signifies exclusion from the normal
'genus' of the decent nation. This state of being degenerate or egenerate, this
different or alien quality, tends to be rooted in miscegenation between a decent
representative of his race and an individual of inferior racial stock. To us National
Socialists, criminal biology, or the theory of congenital criminality, connotes a link
between racial decadence and criminal manifestations.[72]

We are told by a recent historian that 'the appeal to science [was] the most
important'[73] of the various modes of legitimating Nazi territorial expansion. Various studies have sought to trace links between earlier science and
Nazi ideology, for instance the implication of the later-nineteenth-century
German scientist and populariser of evolutionary theory, Ernst Haeckel,
in the subsequent ideas of the Third Reich:

Biology in Germany, which might have been expected to stand in the way of the
mystically false ideas of the Nazis, came rather to their support and much of the
basis of that support is directly traceable to the influence of Haeckel himself.[74]

Haeckel is usually remembered today, if at all, for his particular formulation of a 'biogenetic law' which was axiomatic in the work of many
nineteenth-century thinkers and which fascinated Freud in the 1920s and
1930s. It contended that the history of the development of the individual
passed through (or when aberrant failed to pass through) the stages of
development of the race or species as a whole – 'ontogeny recapitulates
phylogeny'.[75] From such a notion, it was possible to think of the individual
as in quite a literal sense the summation and standard bearer of the history
of the race.

Haeckel used 'the doctrine of descent' to repudiate socialism. Attempts
by Marxists to share in the prestige of Darwinism by finding for their
politics an evolutionary rationale, led to loud protest from Haeckel and his
followers. It was exactly the naturalness of *difference and hierarchy*, they
argued, which biology demonstrated. Haeckel's biology was connected in

---

[72] Hans Frank, *Nationalsozialistische Strafrechtspolitik*, Munich 1938, p. 32, quoted in
Bleuel, *Strength*, p. 209. On German eugenics in the inter-war years and relations with the
Eugenics Society in London, see Jones, *Social Darwinism*, p. 167; cf. Graham, 'Science and
values', (per.), pp. 1,135–44; Mosse, *Final Solution*, pp. 226–7. Note that only certain
aspects of Darwinism were appropriated in Nazi ideology, see Mosse, *Crisis*, p. 103. On the
continuing attempt from the period of German unification until the 1940s to define a
German citizen against the stereotype of a rootless, degenerate Jew, see *Crisis*, pp. 99–103;
cf. Bleuel, *Strength*, ch. 7, 'Degeneracy'. On Germany, cf. Genil Perrin, on the idea of
dégénérescence in German psychiatry (e.g. Griesinger, Schule and Krafft-Ebing); Nye,
Crime, pp. 335–6; Gilman, *Difference*, esp. chs. 9 and 10; for a bibliography of German
historical work on eugenics and degeneration see Bock, 'Racism and sexism', (per.) and
Noakes, 'Nazism and Eugenics'.
[73] Smith, *Ideological Origins*, p. 144.
[74] Gasman, *Scientific Origins*, p. xxii.
[75] See the definition given in Haeckel, *Evolution*, I, pp. 2–3; cf. Gould, *Ontogeny*.

intricate ways to his enchantment with pan-Germanism and the Bismarck-ian state[76] and to his dread of biological deterioration and national decline.

In 1878, responding to the public charge of Rudolf Virchow, the radical liberal scientist, that Haeckelian monism led to socialism and was therefore a dangerous doctrine, Haeckel had angrily responded: 'I ask myself in surprise, "what in the world has the doctrine of descent to do with socialism?"'[77] As far as Haeckel was concerned: 'the two theories are about as compatible as fire and water'. Whilst socialism, he wrote 'demands equal rights, equal duties, equal possessions, equal enjoyments for every citizen alike', the doctrine of evolution proves 'in exact opposition to this, that the realization of the demand is a pure impossibility, and that in the consti-tutionally organized communities of men, as of the lower animals, neither rights nor duties, neither possessions nor enjoyments have been equal for all the members alike nor ever can be'.[78]

The nineteenth century is often constituted in the historiography of Nazism as the murky point of departure for subsequent atrocities of speech and action. There is indeed a large secondary literature tracing the in-tellectual 'roots' or 'origins' of Nazism back through nineteenth-century 'scientific' sources on race and then into German Romanticism: geneal-ogies have even been suggested from Luther to Hitler.[79] This very notion of a quasi-natural genealogy or network of 'roots' may risk reproducing something of the organicist assumptions supposedly under investigation.[80] Too often such readings have condensed and simplified the political reso-nances of earlier texts, fitting everything into a tidy chronology or some-times a simple 'family tree' of ideas, directly presaging the death camps.

But in fact to understand the earlier history of social Darwinism in Germany, it would be necessary, amongst other things, to analyse the ways in which Darwin was employed and transposed in a nineteenth-century German liberal struggle against religion, and more particularly Catholi-cism. In this respect, the specifically degenerationist version of Darwinism advanced in the late-nineteenth century by the zoologist Anton Dohrn was taken by Haeckel to represent an unwelcome reintroduction of religion into evolutionary theory. If such a theory as Dohrn's were true, Haeckel observed,

---

[76] See Gasman, *Scientific Origins*, p. 18.

[77] Gasman, *Scientific Origins*, p. 111. For Virchow's organicist representation of the state, see Virchow, *Cellular Pathology*, p. 130: 'What is an organism? A society of living cells, a tiny well-ordered state; with all the accessories – high officials, underlings, servants and masters.' See also Weindling, 'Cell State'.

[78] Gasman, *Scientific Origins*, p. 112.

[79] See McGovern, *From Luther to Hitler: The History of Fascist-Nazi Political Philosophy*, 1941; Butler, *The Roots of National Socialism*, 1968; Glaser, *The Cultural Roots of National Socialism*, 1978; Lindemann, 'Intellectual Roots of Nazism', (diss.).

[80] For an interesting critique of such historiography, see Blackbourn and Elie, *Peculiarities*.

and all animals were really degenerate descendants of an originally perfect humanity, man would assuredly be the true centre and goal of all terrestrial life; his anthropocentric position and his immortality would be saved. Unfortunately, this trustful theory is in such flagrant contradiction of all known facts of paleontology and embryology that it is in fact no longer worth serious scientific consideration.[81]

To follow the nuances of the German debate and the complex transformation from a liberal individualist to a statist Darwinism is beyond my scope here, but suffice to say that many questions are begged by that approach which straightforwardly prosecutes various nineteenth-century authors – Nietzsche and Wagner figure prominently – on the charge of intellectually prefiguring, fostering and sanctioning a subsequent totalitarian history. One of the problems with this perspective indeed is that a chilling genealogy could also be constructed for England and France. Much of the lineage traced out in, say, Raymond Williams' *Culture and Society* (1958), could no doubt be made available for a genealogy of English fascism. Racist, anti-semitic, anti-democratic or misogynistic passages can be found not least in, say, Carlyle, Arnold and Ruskin. But to pose the 'hypothetical' case of a genealogy of English fascism against the 'real' case of German Nazism is to begin to see the difficulties and problems produced by any such an approach to history, the risk of finding in the end a kind of transhistorical gallery of Nazi premonitions. Such is the strategy of Karl Popper for whom both Plato and Hegel are prototypes of National Socialism.[82] On the other hand the insistence on the historical specificity of discourses should not become a blind and parochial refusal to draw comparisons and make connections. What is needed is a reading strategy which does not collapse history in an anachronistic and reductionist way, but which nevertheless seeks to remain sensitive to shifts and affiliations across time and place. Maybe it would be impossible, even if it were deemed theoretically desirable, to avoid teleology altogether in the reading of nineteenth-century degenerationism. Nevertheless the central emphasis here is not on the question of the 'legacy' of earlier social-scientific ideas. The aim is not to provide in any sense an 'apologia' for or exoneration of this intellectual past, but to reconstruct some of the political and cultural contradictions at issue in nineteenth-century scenarios of degeneration, and moreover to refuse the comforting mythology which (often by reading backwards from the 1930s and the War) allies them exclusively with the intellectual world of the far Right.

[81] Haeckel, *Evolution*, II, pp. 219–20.
[82] See Popper, *Open Society*, I, p. 81; cf. Plato was 'a totalitarian party-politician' (I, p. 169); 'I believe that Plato's political programme far from being morally superior to totalitarianism, is fundamentally identical with it.' (I, p. 87) Hegel was 'scandalous', full of 'sinister consequences', a 'tragi-comedy of German idealism' which led to such 'hideous crimes' (II, pp. 32, 87).

My choice of material is highly selective. This can be defended in the conventional way with regard to the virtually limitless number of writings from the nineteenth and early twentieth century which have a relation to this theme even within the countries under discussion. Furthermore there is a nineteenth-century literature on degeneration in, amongst other places, Russia, North and South America, Spain and Scandinavia with which I cannot deal here. But perhaps the omission of a close investigation of German and Austrian material on degeneration may seem particularly surprising, even if, fortuitously, a highly detailed study of health, race and politics in Germany is in fact shortly to be published.[83] The selection of Italy, France and England for analysis in the present study, whilst in part influenced by practical constraints of my existing knowledge and interests, also followed from a sense that the idea of racial degeneration in Germany is, at least in one respect, relatively familiar from the secondary literature on Nazism. It should also be noted that important work is available on various questions and fields, from representations of blackness in Germany to fin-de-siècle Viennese culture, attitudes to art, the Avant-Garde and sexuality, all of which touches at points on contemporary conceptions of degeneration.[84]

Perhaps one is less startled by now to discover the existence of such a discourse in German and Austrian nineteenth-century intellectual and scientific history than in other countries just because of the vast historiography of Nazism and its 'origins'. This can have an unwarrantedly reassuring, or even anaesthetising effect on our perception of the rest of Europe. For whilst this recognition of Hitler as the 'single most important figure in the history of European racism'[85] has an obvious and overwhelming reason, it may become a mere stock assumption in our reading and interpretation of earlier material. Not only is the reader inclined to transpose from nineteenth to twentieth century, but also to displace other European countries on to Germany. Earlier examples can be taken from France or England which seem to have incipient fascist connotations. It will be part of the aim in the account below to situate such examples historically, to suggest the contemporary fears to which they spoke, but Charles Féré's *Dégénérescence and Criminality*, for instance, written in 1888, is at once disturbing and repellent, if for no other reason, than that it seems to evoke the image and the rhetoric of later totalitarianism, subsequent genocide perpetrated by the Nazis. For Féré, criminality

---

[83] Paul Weindling, *Health, Race and German Politics between National Unification and Nazism, 1870–1945*, Cambridge (forthcoming).

[84] In addition to the various works cited in the immediately preceding pages, cf. Poliakov, *Aryan Myth*; Schorske, *Fin-de-siècle Vienna*; Gilman, *Blackness*; Timms, *Karl Kraus*; Timms and Collier (eds.), *Visions*.

[85] Mosse, *Final Solution*, p. 204.

represented a failure of 'adaptation' and thus social waste matter to be liquidated: 'The impotent, the mad, criminals or decadents of every form, must be considered as the waste-matter of adaptation, the invalids of civilization ... general utility cannot accommodate the survival of the unproductive'.[86] But such a view was already part of a large chorus at the time of its expression, which in its turn drew upon earlier nineteenth-century critiques of the economically unproductive and parasitic, for instance in Saint-Simon and Fourier. Féré expressed deep concern about the viability of the Third Republic. The appeal to the metaphor of the organism, and the description of the degenerates who threatened it were part of a widely shared language in the period. Féré suggested that civilisation had undermined the very productivity on which its sexual and economic future depended through its interference in the process of natural selection and elimination:

Without 'changing human nature', as J.-J. Rousseau demanded of the legislator, it is impossible to [accept] [social] solidarity without reservation in a society where a certain number of members are unproductive and destructive ['dans une société où un certain nombre de membres sont improductifs ou destructeurs'] ... incapable of rendering anything, above all when these individuals run the greatest risk of procreating offspring even more degenerate than themselves. Society is an organism; like all organisms, it is threatened by death each time one of its organs ceases to function. (p. 106)

Society was an organism threatened by death. For Féré, as for many others, degeneration appeared to represent a terrible and inverted process of accumulation in the racial economy, a bizarre mirroring of the laws of capital. Pathology was being 'saved up' in the national stock: 'Heredity needs to be accumulated, capitalised in some way, before finding expression in a morbid entity to which one can give a name.'[87]

When Edwin Ray Lankester, the well-respected English Darwinian zoologist and author of *Degeneration. A Chapter in Darwinism* (1880), re-wrote his major article on zoology for the new edition of the *Encyclopaedia Britannica* in 1910–1911, he thought it appropriate to pass from the issue of evolutionary degradation to the question of eugenics (the potential science of racial improvement through rational breeding, proposed by Darwin's cousin Francis Galton[88]). It is to science, not to political ideologies, he declared, that 'we have to look for the protection of our race', 'even the English branch of it – from relapse and degeneration'. He referred specifically to the problem of the city and its increasing population: 'That increase, it has been shown, is due to the early marriage and excessive

86 Féré, *Dégénérescence*, pp. 103–4.   87 'L'Hérédité', (per.), p. 438.
88 See part III below.

reproduction of the reckless and hopeless, the poorest, least capable, least desirable members of the community'.[89] The existence of a problem, the reproduction of the feckless, hopeless and undesirable, seemed to Lankester undeniable. The terms of a solution, a final solution, were rather more controversial and obscure: this was, as he ruefully confessed, an 'exceedingly difficult and delicate' matter. (p. 1,039)

[89] Lankester, 'Zoology', p. 1,039.

PART I

France

◁ ═══ ▷

2

Dégénérescence and revolution

DEGENERATION WITHIN

It would be possible to argue that degeneration must primarily be understood as one intellectual current within a far-wider language of nineteenth-century racist imperialism. Admittedly, sectors of the population of the imperial metropolis were eventually bracketed off with the races of the empire but, so this argument might proceed, the real 'hegemonic task' lay in the ideological construction of 'inferiority', 'savagery', 'atavism', 'moral pathology', in the 'far-flung' countries which came increasingly under Western political control. At moments of particular ideological crisis over the terms of government and mastery in the Empire, for instance in England after the Indian Mutiny in 1857 or during the Governor Eyre controversy between 1865 and 1868, the notion of physical, mental and technological backwardness was used to justify the formidable use of military force in the suppression of rebellions just as elsewhere it was used to condone the philanthropic paternalism of the missionary.[1]

Work by Fabian and Said, two examples briefly discussed below, emphasises nineteenth-century European projections of inferiority and degeneracy on to the non-European world. My main concern here, however, will be with the 'internal' crises, the 'domestic' worlds at issue in the language of degeneration which have received far less scrutiny in the recent critical historiography of racism and the human sciences.

In *Time and the Other. How Anthropology Makes its Object* (1983), Fabian points out that colonised peoples became the object of a new discourse which facilitated and legitimised European domination. Anthropology's very assumption of a Western observing subject and a non-Western object projected back into a 'primitive' past, furnishes not only a telling and damning indictment of its ideological complicity in imperialism, so the argument goes, but also provides a key to the very structure and limits of the discipline. The spatial distancing and elevation of the Western anthropologist from the 'material' was further enhanced by the alienating dimension of nineteenth-century evolutionary time. This account is clearly

---

[1] See Semmel, *Governor Eyre Controversy*. Cf. Bolt, *Victorian Attitudes*, p. 77.

in some respects a helpful way of demystifying the notion of the advanced and the primitive, but in other ways it mystifies in its own turn:

Anthropology ... is a science of other men in another Time. It is a discourse whose referent has been removed from the present of the speaking/writing subject. This 'petrified relation' is a scandal. Anthropology's Other is, ultimately, other people who are our contemporaries ... Among the historical conditions under which our discipline emerged and which affected its growth and differentiation were the rise of capitalism and its colonialist-imperialist expansion into the very societies which became the target of our inquiries. For this to occur, the expansive, aggressive and oppressive societies which we collectively and inaccurately call the West needed Space to occupy. More profoundly and problematically, they required Time to accumulate the schemes of a one-way history: progress, development, modernity (and their negative mirror images: stagnation, underdevelopment, tradition).[2]

Although striking a note of caution at one point ('the expansive ... societies which we collectively and inaccurately call the West') Fabian is convinced that all particular ethnography is 'in the end about the relation-ship between the West and the Rest' (p. 28). Stagnation and underdevelop-ment are imputed by the West to its colonised object, not to itself. This argument in effect flattens out historical differences, contradictions, shifts, within Europe or the West; it abstracts them into singular categories and thus takes, as it were, certain nineteenth-century ideologies at their word, accepting the arrogant coherence they may have projected as indeed their unproblematic quality, their true characterisation. The point I want to make here is that the 'aggression' of evolutionary discourse may have had as much to do with perceived 'terrors', 'primitiveness' and fragmentation 'at home' as in the colonies.

Edward Said's rich and compelling work *Orientalism* (1978) tends at points to this same abstraction of categories. The West's self-projection in a variety of nineteenth-century literary texts is bequeathed on some oc-casions to Said's historical account of 'Western consciousness'. Said writes: 'the imaginative examination of things Oriental was based more or less exclusively upon a *sovereign Western consciousness* out of whose un-challenged centrality an Oriental World emerged, first according to general ideas about who or what was an Oriental, then according to a detailed logic governed not simply by an empirical reality but by a battery of desires, repressions, investments, and projections'.[3] The quotation ends with the sense that the coherence of the West was indeed an ideology (a matter of desires, repressions, investments, and projections), but it appears to sug-gest initially that there was a sovereign consciousness, a Western ego, which was not only master of the other, but 'master in its own house'; in

---

[2] Fabian, *Time*, pp. 143, 144.   [3] Said, *Orientalism*, p. 8, emphasis added.

short that at the level of discourse, the desired repression was achieved. In fact it is not clear that Said does take that view. At one point he comments that:

Along with all other peoples variously designated as backward, degenerate, uncivilized, and retarded, the Orientals were viewed in a framework constructed out of biological determinism and moral-political admonishment. The Oriental was linked thus to elements in Western society (delinquents, the insane, women, the poor) having in common an identity best described as lamentably alien. Orientals were rarely seen or looked at; they were seen through, analysed not as citizens, or even people, but as problems to be solved or confined or – as the colonial powers openly coveted their territory – taken over. (p. 207)

Yet he does little to develop the implications of that putative world of internal degeneration ('delinquents, the insane, women, the poor', who were inalienably part of the imperial society) for orientalism. The point is made and then generally abandoned. Evolutionary anthropology functioned not only to differentiate the colonised overseas from the imperial race, but also to scrutinise portions of the population at home: the 'other' was outside and inside. Imperialism, no doubt, was the discourse which sought to bind the myriad realities of the colonial 'power' into a discursive unity. Social Darwinism and other social evolutionary theories in the later-nineteenth century underpinned the supremacist rhetoric, but the spectre of internal degeneration continually haunted it.

If we look at the development of the word *dégénérescence*, we will see that it evolved not only in relation to a colonial 'other'. Morel's *Treatise*, for instance, was concerned not only with degeneration in distant civilisations and races, but also in France. The object of the racial anthropology which emerged in the period was not only Africa or the Orient, but also the 'primitive' areas and groups within the home country. One can usefully recall here a remark by Mary Douglas in *Purity and Danger* (1966):

Four kinds of social pollution seem worth distinguishing. The first is danger pressing on external boundaries; the second, danger from transgressing the internal lines of the system; the third, danger in the margins of the lines. The fourth is danger from internal contradictions, when some of the basic postulates are denied by other basic postulates, so that at points the system seems to be at war with itself.[4]

Dégénérescence evoked all of these dangers in Morel's work, but above all danger from internal transgressions rather than inter-racial 'pollution'. Moreover, as we will see, the effect of this conception did both reflect and engender 'internal contradictions' in the ideologies of progress.

The new possibilities of, and ensuing vogue for, travel amongst the upper echelons of French provincial towns had reinforced a recognition of

[4] Douglas, *Purity*, p. 122.

how socially and anthropologically alien were the human faces in the hinterlands of the country, how internally contradictory was the population of France. The French historian Maurice Agulhon points out that:

Between 1830 and 1840, long journeys through the French provinces ceased to be a rarity ... [and] became a form of cultivated leisure.[5]

Travel afforded not only romantic delight, the charming contemplation of pastoral France, but also the panic-stricken perception of social division.[6]

Even under the Third Republic, France was far from 'one nation' culturally or linguistically. Eugen Weber's *Peasants into Frenchmen* (1976) shows the extraordinary 'modernising' effort which was made to unify France and her rural populations. This was a traumatic and lengthy process of cultural, educational, political and economic self-colonisation which should not be forgotten in the discussion of the motives and anxieties of imperialism and the expansion of empires. The vexed question of converting 'peasants into citizens' also dominated the thinking of Piedmontese government officials and intellectuals in the decades after Italian unification. Lombroso's theory of atavism and indeed his whole criminological project owed a great deal to the 'problematic' of Italy's fragmentation. But as my discussion below suggests, there were also significantly different connotations in French and Italian conceptions of crime, regression and degeneration.

The medical concern with hereditary degeneration in France coalesced with fears about a fundamental disorder of national history. Moreover *dégénérescence* was subsumed within the historiography of the Revolution during the second half of the nineteenth century; it underpinned a critique of the social order and *laissez-faire* political economy; it came to bear in the language of social defence against crime, anarchy, madness and revolt. A history of revolutionary change and counter-change was more or less explicitly addressed by the new racial theories of the 1850s and beyond. The question of biological reproduction was placed at the very centre of historical process by Morel and his colleagues. Concern at the unhappy repetition of revolution was invested in the image of disorderly reproduction. In the aftermath of the Franco-Prussian War and the Paris Commune, *dégénérescence* helped 'explain' the 'morbid involution' of 1789.

Morel argued that the intellectual inferiority of other races had to be distinguished from the much more serious and immutable problem of degeneration *within* 'civilisation':

---

[5] Agulhon, *Republican Experiment*, p. 10.
[6] Cf. Zeldin, *Intellect*, ch. 1, 'The national identity', which begins with this anecdote: 'In 1864, an inspector of education, touring in the mountains of the Lozère, asked the children at a village school: "In what country is the Lozère situated?" Not a single pupil knew the answer. "Are you English or Russian?" he demanded. They could not say.'

Between the intellectual state of the wildest Bosjeman and that of the most civilised
European there is less difference than between the intellectual state of the same
European and that of the degenerate being. The first, in fact, is susceptible of a
radical modification, and his descendants can revert to a more perfect type. The
second is susceptible only of a relative amelioration, and hereditary influences will
fatally weigh upon his posterity. He will remain all his life what he is in reality – a
specimen of degeneration in the human species, an example of a morbid deviation
from the normal type of man.[7]

Morel's *Treatise* involved the apprehension (in both senses) of recurrent
disorder. The 'degenerate being', unlike the primitive, was 'susceptible
only of a relative amelioration and hereditary influences will fatally weigh
upon his posterity' (p. 221). It was not by chance that the theory of
degeneration emerged in these terms at a moment when French history
appeared most vividly (and not only to Marx), to repeat itself, the first time
as tragedy, the second time as farce.

In Ribot's *Heredity* (1875), one finds the following discussion:

In the east, the harem, with its life of absolute ignorance and complete indolence,
has, through physical and moral heredity, led to the rapid decay of various nations.
'We have no harem in France,' says a naturalist, 'but there are other causes, quite
different in their origin, which tend ultimately to lower the race. In our day,
paternal affection, with the assistance of medical science, more certain, and possessed of more resources, makes more and more certain the future of children, by
saving the lives of countless weak, deformed, or otherwise ill-constituted creatures
that would surely have died in a savage race, or in our own a century ago... The
descendants go on degenerating, and the result for the community is debasement,
and finally, the disappearance of certain groups'.[8]

The East is not seen here as confirming the West in its glory, strength,
virility, power (the dominant thesis in Said's *Orientalism*); but as a parallel
instance in the course towards degeneracy. The appeal to superiority over
other races, which was formidably reasserted in the final decades of the
nineteenth century in France, as in the other European nations, was
projected over perceptions of social division at home. Boulangism, syndicalism, anarchism, the Decadent movement, socialism, feminism, the
Dreyfus affair were continually predicated by opponents within a language
of degeneration and social pathology.[9] Moreover the pathologising definitions offered by hostile social commentators, contributed to the self-
definition of certain movements, for instance anarchism and literary
Decadence. 'Society disintegrates under the corrosive action of a delin-
quescent civilization', weighed down by 'refinement of appetites, of sen-

[7] 'Analysis', (per.), p. 221.
[8] *Heredity*, p. 304. Ribot (1839–1916) was a philosopher and psychologist. He founded the
Revue philosophique de la France et de l'étranger.
[9] See Nye, *Crime*.

ons, of taste, of luxury, of pleasures; neurosis, hysteria, hypnotism, rphinomania, scientific skulduggery, extreme schopenhaureism', *Décadent* declared in 1886.[10] A cult of decadence flourished in the late-nineteenth century. But the scientific social pathologist intensified the reviled literary identity of the decadent through an insistent conjuring of pathology, endless proclamation, definition and castigation of morbidity.

The discursive construction of subject and other in the human sciences cannot be posed only in terms of the contrast, West/East, White/Black. Social evolution and degeneration formed two sides of a later-nineteenth-century ideology, turning between an ideal fiction of unity and a dread of cultural, national, racial disintegration. *Dégénérescence* had its resonances in the apocalyptic visions of socialism, conservatism, liberalism. But the term did not simply constitute some rhetorical 'instrument' on behalf of certain professional or political interests. It was not only an expedient discursive device to be wielded, say, in a long struggle by the medical profession in general, and the psychiatric profession in particular, to gain power in the courts and in the framing of law.[11] It was not just manufactured strategically in order to fabricate a conception of crisis. Nor did it exclusively serve a long-standing positivist ideal, born from Saint-Simon and Comte, of a scientific 'coup' upon the reactionary and incompetent state. Indeed against the grain of Comtean optimism, *dégénérescence* confronted the possibility that crisis was not cathartic but terminal. Perhaps pathology had infiltrated women, the proletariat at large (in whom Comte had placed so many hopes for the future[12]), even the bourgeois professional.[13] It should be noted, however, that the scientist was usually conspicuously absent from such a list (at least when the list was compiled by scientists rather than novelists), placed outside the reach of morbidity. It was an important omission. Ribot declared in 1875 that 'the person, the *ego*, the thinking subject, assumed as a perfect unity, is but a theoretic conception. It is an ideal which the individual approaches as he rises in the scale of being, but to which he never attains.'[14] Despite such perceptions, doctors from Morel to Lombroso to Maudsley, did write from the seemingly unruffled position of the perfectly unified thinking subject. Degeneration, with its putatively vitiating and fragmenting effect on the will of the

[10] *Le Décadent*, 1 (10 April 1886), p. 1.
[11] An emphasis to be found in Nye, *Crime*; Dowbiggin, 'Degeneration and Hereditarianism'; Goldstein, *Console*.
[12] See Leroy, *Histoire*, III, ch. 12; Therborn, *Science, Class and Society*, p. 190.
[13] As the psychiatrist Magnan warned: 'un héréditaire peut être un savant: un magistrat distingué, un politicien, un administrateur habile, et présenter au point de vue moral des "défectuosités profondes"' ('Remarks', (per.), p. 99).
[14] Ribot, *Heredity*, p. 236.

sufferer, was at once universalised as the potential fate of all and, parad
cally, particularised as the condition of the other.

In medico-psychiatric investigations, alcoholism, sexual perversic
crime, insanity, declining birth rates, syphilis, prostitution, anarchism
suicide rates, economic performance, and so on, become the intertwined
signifiers of cultural crisis. I seek to suggest discursive continuities and to
map some of the terms, limits and shifts of a shared language of degeneration. If this approach suggests a certain eclecticism in the presentation of
material, cutting across different 'disciplines' (psychiatry, criminology,
biology, the novel), I argue that the parameters of such fields of investigation as were drawn in the nineteenth century, should not simply be
inherited in our analysis. Indeed the aim here is exactly to demonstrate the
contiguity and convergence of models of degeneration across distinct
forms of social commentary.

One weakness of the Foucauldian power/knowledge model which
informs much recent discussion of the nineteenth-century human sciences,
from anthropology to criminology to medical-psychiatry, is that by focussing on the presumed strategic effects of certain shifts in the perception
of say, crime, madness, race and sexuality, it often underplays the internal
textual struggle, the work of representation needed to achieve the illusion
of unity, of singular power and mastery. One needs to address simultaneously the 'force' of a felt crisis of powerlessness in certain texts and
ideologies, the complex transformation of social anxiety and political fear
into seemingly self-possessed imperious and 'imperialist' discourse. Thus
consider this anecdote and its possible interpretation.

In the 1880s, the psychiatrist Benjamin Ball told a story to his students in
Paris. During the July Monarchy, an official of Louis-Philippe had been
charged with the negotiation of a treaty with Morocco delimiting the
boundary between that nation and Algeria. The line of demarcation was
not precisely drawn all the way through the interior because the French
official accepted the word of the Moroccans that the remote boundaries
could be left undecided since the territory concerned was virtually unin-
habited. Unfortunately, the French had thus allowed themselves to be
tricked by the cunning 'natives'. This provided a useful lesson to psychiatrists, declared Ball: 'just as we know today that on the allegedly uninhab-
ited [North African] territory there exists a population of some six
hundred thousand', so too 'in that region also believed deserted and
situated on the frontier between reason and madness . . . are housed not six
hundred thousand, but several million inhabitants'.[15]

The story suggests the triumphalism of a psychiatry which identified

[15] Ball, 'Les Frontières', (per.), p. 1.

itself with an empire,[16] asserting its place in the corridors of power, colonising and defining the territory of the insane. But it also hints the anxiety of a profession which believed that the drift in the numbers of the mad was only upwards. The discourse of degeneration may have served the interests of psychiatry, in so far as it claimed medical expertise essential in the field of criminality and indeed in the very framing of laws, but it was never simply 'instrumental'; it articulated fears beyond the merely strategic, fears of inundation, the subject overwhelmed at every level of mind and body by internal disorder and external attack.

MOREL

This section examines the intellectual career of Morel in the context of mid-nineteenth-century France, before considering the place of hereditarian theory and *dégénérescence* in other French writing, principally of Buchez, Taine and, in a later chapter, Zola. My aim is to describe Morel's formulation of degeneration and to suggest why it was produced, and to what senses of crisis it spoke, in the 1850s and more powerfully still beyond 1870–71.

Bénédict Augustin Morel was born in Vienna in 1809. By the time of his death in 1873, he had lived through two French empires, two republics, two kingdoms, two invasions and three revolutions.[17] Little is known of Morel's parents other than that they were French (his father furnished supplies to Napoleon's army hence their residence in Vienna in 1809) and that their infant was abandoned into the hands of a priest in Luxembourg during the tumultuous period of the Napoleonic retreat.

Abbé Dupont, and his servant Marianne became virtual adoptive parents of the child. At the age of twelve, Morel was placed in the seminary of St-Dié in France, where he remained throughout his adolescence and where he became a follower of Lammenais' progressivist strand of Catholicism with its stress on the need for active and devout intervention in the present social world. As a result he came into conflict with the conservative authorities at the seminary and was expelled – in his own eyes a martyr to the cause of progress and liberty. This was the era of the 1830 Revolution and, in true Balzacian fashion, the impoverished young man drifted to Paris, where he had a living of sorts as a freelance journalist. He managed to find a position as assistant and tutor to a rich Franco-American family with

---

[16] Cf. Goldstein, *Console*, p. 333: 'the psychiatrist Benjamin Ball [summoned] ... an episode from French colonial history to justify the professional imperialism of the psychiatrists'.

[17] For bibliographical information I draw particularly on Constant, 'Introduction', (diss.), and Martin, 'La Dégénérescence', (diss.); see also Lasègue, 'Morel', (per.); Motet, 'Eloge', (per.); Genil-Perrin, *Histoire*; Friedlander, 'Morel', (diss.); Drusch, 'Entre deux discours', (diss.); Borie, *Mythologies*; Dowbiggin, 'Degeneration and Hereditarianism'.

whom, apparently, he lived for four years. During that time Morel learned English and was drawn to the study of medicine. Despite material hardship (shared with his friend, Claude Bernard[18]), he qualified as a medical doctor in 1839. In those years of medical study, he met other doctors and intellectuals such as Cerise, Buchez and Roux Lavergne with whom he looked forward to the triumph of progress in both church and state.

After a brief and unhappy experience as a general practitioner (in which, like so many other young doctors in the period, he waited in vain for clients to arrive at his shabby rooms[19]), he was able to enter the field of hospital psychiatry thanks to an introduction (effected by his friend Bernard) to J. P. Falret. Morel went to study at the Salpêtrière, becoming Falret's secretary and translator; he had learnt German as a child, and was thus able to aid his superior, who wished to become conversant with the work of the German school of medical-psychiatry.

Morel undertook a series of investigative journeys to other European countries for some of the time at least accompanying the patient of a doctor Ferrus.[20] He sent back a series of seven letters during the 1840s which were published after his return to Paris in the recently founded *Annales médico-psychologiques*.[21] These letters described the state of psychiatry and the incidence of insanity abroad, displaying a detailed knowledge of foreign theorists, practitioners, and asylums. He was interested in the topic of cretinism and was deeply impressed by the work of the influential Dr Guggenbühl in Switzerland.[22]

Cretinism was indeed a major medical puzzle; in the 1830s and 1840s it was the subject of various official investigations and novelistic representations. During the 1840s, for instance, Charles Albert, King of Sardinia had established a commission for its study.[23] Many explanations of cretinism were competing for attention in the period. The role of iodine deficiency was yet to be discovered and refined. Low ground, it seemed, and the poisons it unleashed, had a role to play in the disease.

Thus, for instance, William Farr, Victorian Britain's first great medical statistician,[24] campaigned against the dangers of cretinism on low land in this period. Farr's interest in cretinism went back a long way; in his student days, he had measured the heads of cretins whilst visiting the Swiss valleys.[25] By the late-1840s, he was arguing that marshy ground often pro-

---

[18] See Genil-Perrin *Histoire*, pp. 44–5.
[19] On the wider question of medical unemployment and underemployment in the 1830s and 1840s, see Goldstein, *Console*, pp. 147–51.
[20] See Constant 1970, 'Introduction', (diss.), pp. 17–18.
[21] See Morel, 'Pathologie mentale' (1845–47), (per.).
[22] See Morel, 'Pathologie mentale' (1846), (per.), pp. 163–80, 363–87.
[23] See Friedlander, 'Morel', (diss.), p. 38.
[24] See Eyler, *Victorian Social Medicine*.
[25] *Victorian Social Medicine*, pp. 154–5.

duced terrible deformations in the body. The historical record showed, he insisted, that people bred on such land failed to create social institutions and were prey to invasion and conquest on account of their racial weakness.[26]

The problem of cretinism was compelling and shocking. The reader of Balzac's *The Country Doctor* (1833) will surely remember the representation of the cretin. The cavalry officer in the novel:

felt a thrill of surprise and horror at the sight of a human face which could never have been lighted up with thought ... in short, it was the wholly animal face of an old dying crétin... At the sight of deep, circular folds of skin, on the forehead, the sodden, fish-like eyes, and the head, with its short, coarse, scantily-growing hair ... who would not have experienced ... an instinctive feeling of repulsion for a being that had neither the physical beauty of an animal nor the mental endowments of a man, who was possessed of neither instinct nor reason, and who had never heard nor spoken any kind of articulate speech?[27]

Balzac's 'enlightened', rationalist country doctor is moved by a veritable sense of mission to eradicate cretinism from a countryside hitherto ruled by the 'superstition' of priests and peasants:

All the favourable conditions for spreading the hideous disease are there; the air is stagnant, the hamlet lies in the valley bottom, close beside a torrent supplied with water by the melted snows, and the sunlight only falls on the mountain-top, so that the valley itself gets no good of the sun. Marriages among these unfortunate creatures are not forbidden by law, and in this district they are protected by superstitious notions... So crétinism was in a fair way to spread all over the valley from this spot. Was it not doing the country a great service to put a stop to this mental and physical contagion? But imperatively as the salutary changes were required, they might cost the life of any man who endeavoured to bring them about. (p. 26)

Balzac was not the only novelist to explore the topic of cretinism, nor Morel the only foreigner to be excited by the work of Guggenbühl. When Dickens, in collaboration with W. H. Wills, was surveying advances in the treatment of idiocy for a piece in *Household Words* in 1853,[28] he discussed reports of a new method employed by Dr Guggenbühl in Switzerland. The putative changes in the creatures who reside at his clinic in the mountains are shown to be spectacular. One child began treatment as a 'stunted withered skeleton, covered with a livid wrinkled, cold skin', but 'advanced rapidly towards a perfect development ... the skin became elastic ... the wrinkles of the face vanished, the old-woman expression disappeared, and the pleasing traces of youth became apparent' (p. 315).

---

[26] *Victorian Social Medicine*, p. 156.   [27] Balzac, *The Country Doctor*, pp. 22–3.
[28] Dickens, 'Idiots', (per.).

Morel was highly impressed by the hygienic regime in the clinic, but he was also much taken by the Swiss doctor's acknowledgement that there existed two quite distinct 'species' of clinical cases: complete and incomplete cretinism. The complete category was made up of 'those individuals in whom all that constitutes human nature from the point of view of perception, feeling, love, will, speech, action and caring for one's own life is altogether destroyed, to the point where man finds himself below the brute'.[29] Although committed to the social amelioration of the condition of the cretin, this conception suggested a fixed and incurable category of individual which lay beyond the reach of environmental or medical cure. Despite the very etymology of the word (Cretin, from Christian), it was exactly the common humanity of these 'creatures' which was decisively called into question.

Morel's writing on cretinism in the 1850s, with its stress on hygiene and incurability came to the attention of the Archbishop of Chambéry in Savoy, who also studied the disease.[30] They began an exchange of open letters in the *Annales médico-psychologiques*, published subsequently as a book.[31] The Archbishop had argued, not without some reason, that the prime cause of the disease lay in the mineralogical constitution of the soil and reproached Morel for advocating the prophylactic efficacy of segregation and hygiene instead.[32] Morel disagreed and continued to develop his own account. The theory of *dégénérescence* which became the key term in his work lay enmeshed in this subtle shift of emphasis around the problem of cretinism. The cretin was transposed into a mere exemplification of a wider idea of *dégénérescence*.

Morel stressed the social implications of the incurability of certain types of cretin and emphasised their constitutional pre-disposition to the disease:

I do not believe in the curability of cretinism when the illness is confirmed. All the pedagogic procedures, and best hygienic influences are in vain in the case of the complete cretin. He will remain what he is: a monstrous anomaly, a typical representation of the state of *dégénérescence*, which nothing could prevent . . . (p. v)

For the true cretin, in short, it was too late for a cure. In this representation, the cretin's body became the degenerate's body. The individual continued to be seen as prey to a vitiating environment, but, in some cases, body and mind were both hopeless, quite beyond reformation. The doctor, Morel declared, had to do what was possible, and trace the rigorous demarcation between the modifiable and the unmodifiable being ('l'être modifiable de celui qui ne l'est pas') (p. v). Cretinism in the *Treatise* which Morel

[29] Morel, 'Pathologie mentale' (1846), (per.), p. 364.   [30] See Billiet, *Observations*.
[31] Morel and Billiet, *Influences*.   [32] Morel and Billiet, *Influences*.

published in 1857, became the exemplification of a broader racial and historical degeneration in societies. The cretin, for all his or her pathos and helplessness, was subsumed by Morel in a much wider and more menacing picture: the uncontrolled reproduction of degenerates. The cretin was an instance, and an emblem, of racial degeneration. The notion of degeneration became more elastic and expansive, whilst the prognosis of the degenerate became more rigid.[33]

Thus Morel advocated the efficacy of establishing 'retreats' in the mountains for the worst cases of cretinism and other hopeless conditions, as a means of safeguarding society against the harmful moral and physical effects of social and sexual intercourse. The apparent paradox of these candid opinions is that they came from a 'progressive' psychiatric figure – Morel was a staunch advocate of non-restraint and other advanced therapeutic ideas.

Cretinism was conceived by Morel through the dominant hereditarian optic of the mid nineteenth century. In the wake of 1848, heredity had hardened into a key term in many aspects of medicine and anthropology. This shift was complex and, certainly, had been taking place for several decades, but 1848 was an important moment in heredity's petrification as the perceived central problem of nationality, madness and crime.[34] In Prosper Lucas' encyclopaedic *Treatise on Natural Heredity*, the two volumes published respectively in 1847 and 1850, we are told that history itself is only meaningfully construed through the science of heredity. The events from 1848 to 1850 seemed to confirm the stress on inheritance and historical recurrence which Lucas had already set out in volume one in 1847:

From whatever point of view one approaches it ... heredity presents immense problems. In the social sphere, it evokes first [the question of] ... property. In the political sphere ... the *principle* and *succession* of sovereignty. In the civil sphere ... the *principle* and *succession* of ownership in art, literature, science and industry ... in the natural order, [heredity is] ... a *law*, a *force*, and a *fact*; one of the great marvels of existence ... [35]

[33] 'Degeneration can be congenital or acquired, complete or incomplete, susceptible of improvement or incurable; and these important distinctions will furnish further materials of classification. The extreme limit of degeneration exists when the individual is not only incapable of propagating his kind in normal conditions, but shows himself completely impotent, whether in consequence of the non-development of the genital organs, or from the absence of all prolific power. Cretinism arrived at this extreme point, affords us a striking example of this summary of all the degenerations. The cretin is a pre-eminently degenerate being...' Morel, 'Analysis', 10 June 1857, (per.), p. 268.

[34] Cf. Borie, *Mythologies*, pp. 12–13, 70; Alexander, 'Administration', (diss.), pp. 61–2, 171; Coleman, *Death* (on Villermé's shift towards pessimism); Harris, 'Murders', (diss.), pp. 86–7; Nye, *Crime*, p. 62.

[35] Lucas, *Traité*, I, pp. 5–6.

In Lucas' account the stress fell on the reproduction of constant inherited features over generations. Morel's *Treatise*, however, was concerned rather with the dynamic patterns which underpinned a chain of changing pathologies across generations. In other words, it was an inquiry into the self-generating differentiation of an original 'degeneration' as it played itself out across the history of families. But the elements of fatalism which this suggests must be placed alongside other connotations. These hereditarian theories were articulated in a social medicine committed in other respects to amelioration, cure, the mastery of disease. My intention here is not to 'settle' that contradiction, but to stress indeed as a central argument that the language of degeneration was continually over-determined both in its motives and its resonances.

When Morel returned to France in 1845, after suffering a fever in Venice, he found himself once again in straitened circumstances.[36] By now in his mid-thirties, he was a regular contributor to the *Annales médico-psychologiques*, but he was still without a medical post. His professional situation, however, was to change in 1848. Whilst Morel stood on the side-lines, his friend Buchez participated in the Revolution and became indeed the president of the National Assembly.

In his obituary of Morel, Motet wrote:

these honest men who prepared a revolution without anticipating all its consequences, were the inspired apostles of progress rather than the ambitious seekers of power. One sees them rise, like Buchez, and then return without bitterness, and without regrets, to the silence of their obscure labours.

Morel was not drawn in by them to the political movement. He was preoccupied with the material difficulties of existence. The three years from 1845 to 1848 were particularly tormented ones for him.[37]

Through Buchez' patronage, Morel received a medical post at Maréville (Meurthe) in 1848, the year of the Revolution. Thus began his career as a provincial hospital doctor. Disputes over therapeutic methods, and personal rivalries with Renaudin, the new director at Maréville, led Morel to request and to gain a transfer to the asylum of Saint-Yon near Rouen in 1856,[38] where he was to stay until his death in 1873.

Morel was no isolated 'crank' or out-dated reactionary. He was, if not one of the famous Parisian 'authorities', at least a highly respected provincial expert in mental medicine, seen by his colleagues as a liberal, progressive and charitable figure. As Lasègue put it in an obituary, Morel had always kept his table and his house open to the sick, despite his own

---

[36] See Constant, 'Introduction', (diss.), p. 20.   [37] Motet, 'Eloge', (per.), p. 94.
[38] See Constant, 'Introduction', (diss.), p. 26.

illness, living in full and benign community with his patients.[39] Whilst often attending the meetings of the Medico-Psychological Society in Paris, regarded as an expert authority when medical opinion was requested by the courts, lauded once again by his colleagues in the late 1850s after the publication of the *Traité*, it was in fact Magnan, the new key theorist of *dégénérescence* in the decades after Morel's death in 1873, who was to enjoy real fame in the capital. It was only from the 1870s onwards that *dégénérescence* was taken to be of undisputed importance in clinical psychiatry.[40] It took national defeat by Prussia and the Paris Commune to seal the importance of this word in historiography, social diagnosis, cultural critique.[41]

THE EMPIRE OF PATHOLOGIES

What conception of *dégénérescence* was produced in Morel's famous *Treatise* of 1857? The term was applied to the patterns of heredity in societies, and specifically to deviations from the 'normal type' of humanity.[42] It did not signify the reproduction of a constant anomaly from one body to another (which was the emphasis in Prosper Lucas' *Treatise*, 1847–1850); it was concerned rather with an infinite network of diseases and disorders, and the patterns of return and transformation between them.[43] Morel pulled together a bewildering array of physical conditions, moral and social habits; from hernias, goitres, pointed ears, absence of secondary teeth, stunted growth, cranial deviations, deaf and dumbness, blindness, albinism, club-feet, elephantitis, scrophula, tuberculosis, rickets and sterility to the effects of toxins like alcohol, tobacco and opium; he explored disturbances of the intellectual faculties and the noxious tendencies of certain forms of romanticism which resulted in languorous desires, effeteness, reveries, impotence, suicidal tendencies, inertia, melancholy and apathy. For Morel, the human being was a unified ensemble, composed of matter and of spirit. Physical degeneration could not but lead to eventual intellectual and moral collapse and vice versa. *Dégénérescence* was the name for a process of pathological change from one condition to another in society and in the body. A vast array of disorders were, as Morel's colleague, Moreau (de Tours) put it, part of the 'empire of the law of inheritance',[44] merely 'different branches of the same trunk'.[45] Madness here could

---

[39] Lasègue, 'Morel', (per.), p. 590.
[40] See Dowbiggin, 'Degeneration and Hereditarianism'; Martin, 'La Dégénérescence', (diss.).
[41] See Lidsky, *Les Ecrivains*.
[42] See Morel, *Traité des dégénérescences*, p. 5.   [43] *Traité des dégénérescences*, p. 335.
[44] Moreau (de Tours), *Psychologie*, p. 104.   [45] *Psychologie*, p. 99.

appear partially developed, as for instance 'moral insanity', but it was always part of a deeper and all-encompassing biological process. Morel's work with its stress on the inter-relations of mental diseases was part of an important wider challenge to Esquirol's notion of 'monomania', with its suggestion of the isolated *idée fixe*, a single, pathological preoccupation in an otherwise sound mind.[46] Morel's work was far removed from a dominant Lockean conception in the eighteenth century which had primarily defined madness in terms of intellectual disorder or 'mistaken reasoning'. Madness for Morel and many of his colleagues could not necessarily be seen or heard, but it lurked in the body, incubated by the parents and visited upon the children. It had no precise borders, but it involved a progressively intensifying tyranny of the body over the spirit or soul. Freedom of the will was increasingly lost to the body.

Dégénérescence had a hidden narrative development – a genesis, a law of progress, and a denouement. Complete idiocy, sterility and death were the end points in a slow accumulation of morbidity across generations.[47] This notion of the degenerate's eventual sterility, much contested elsewhere (for instance in late Victorian and Edwardian eugenic arguments about the degenerate metropolitan working class), at once reflected and intensified powerful French fears about the decline of the birth rate. Thus in 1895, Dr Legrain would echo a very widely shared view when he saw in alcoholism and other social pathologies, 'the slow but fatal brutalisation of the individual; intellectual and physical sterilisation of the race with its social consequences: the lowering of the intellectual level and depopulation, indubitable causes of the decline of civilised nations'.[48]

Whilst seen to stem from acquired diseases (drawn from poverty, immoral habits, unhealthy work and so on), *dégénérescence* tended to imply an inherent physical process, an immanent narrative within the body and across bodies, beyond social determination, or even the possibility of normal perception. It could just as well be concealed as revealed by the exterior of the body, and thus whilst Morel acknowledged its importance, phrenology was of limited use.

We have said enough to show that the typical character of the head in degenerate beings will not be the sole element of our classification... The distinctions do not rest only upon external differences, but upon internal differences also...[49]

Indeed throughout the second half of the nineteenth century, the question of the visibility of degeneration was contested. An anthropology whose most famous exponent was Broca sought to find the contours of

[46] See Goldstein, *Console*, p. 190, and generally ch. 5.
[47] Morel, *Traité des dégénérescences*, p. 344.
[48] Legrain, *Heredité et alcoolisme*, p. 59. [49] *Traité des dégénérescences*, pp. 70–1.

racial difference and social degeneracy in the shape and weight of the skull.[50] If the skull could be 'scientifically' analysed, it was hoped by late-nineteenth-century racial anthropologists, perhaps phrenology might be resuscitated once again to reveal, amongst other things, the patterns of moral pathology.

The dream of finding the 'map' of the criminal had long been one of the promises of phrenology. The *Zoist*, a journal dedicated to mesmerism and phrenology in early-Victorian England, had confidently seen vice displayed in the form of the skull. Thus it could write of a murderer's cranium: 'the whole coronal surface – the seat of the high moral feelings, sloped off strikingly at the sides, so that the organs of the sense of *justice, veneration* and *benevolence* were very *narrow* and *defective*'.[51] Or as the author of a popular manual entitled *Physiognomy Illustrated* could enthusiastically write in 1872, once all the features had been fully documented, no criminal would dare to walk the streets for his countenance would be 'a sign-board denoting the rottenness within'.[52]

Morel's conception of degeneration was far more complex than such a popular taxonomy of images, or such a dream of finding 'the signboard' of criminality. Whilst he earmarked the surface features of degeneracy (bodily stigmata), he also evoked a mysterious and hidden world of pathology. Even when Magnan had re-located the concept in ever starker evolutionist terms in the 1880s, it never lost its mystique and mystery, the sense of its fundamental invisibility. The tension between the image of the degenerate and the unseen essence of degeneration rejoined a tension inherent in earlier discourses on 'the dangerous classes' of the city. Perceived as visibly different, anomalous and racially 'alien', the problem was simultaneously their apparent invisibility in the flux of the great city.[53]

Although it suggested, potentially, a process which could exceed all boundaries of class, region and time, *dégénérescence* was deployed as though an instrument of social differentiation, a means of specifying 'neutrally' the 'dangerous classes' of France:

beside this civilized society, there are [other varieties] ... which possess neither intelligence, responsibility nor moral sentiment ... whose spirit finds no enlightenment nor consolation in religion. Some of these varieties have been rightly designated as the *dangerous classes*.[54]

---

[50] See Schiller, *Paul Broca*; Gould, *Mismeasure*.   [51] *The Zoist*, 3 (1846), 130.
[52] Simms, *Physiognomy*, p. 37.
[53] See Chevalier, *Labouring Classes*; Frégier, *Des Classes dangereuses*; for a classic account of the mid-nineteenth-century writer and the paradoxes of visibility and invisibility in the city crowd, see Benjamin, *Baudelaire*.
[54] Morel, *Traité des dégénérescences*, p. 461, n. 1.

The nineteenth-century representation of the dangerous classes which has its best-known study in the work of Louis Chevalier,[55] has figured heavily in recent attempts to explain Morel's conception of degeneration. But in this work Morel is often not so much explained, as explained away; the *Treatise* is seen simply as a reflection of material reality. Morel's text, it has been argued elsewhere, must be understood in a wider context of social anxiety about the city at a time of sustained urban immigration and demographic flux. The number of vagabonds apparently rose throughout the years of the July monarchy in both the countryside and in the towns.[56] According to the official statistics of 1842 there were four million beggars out of a total population of thirty four million, and a further four million people were classed as very poor.[57]

The first half of the century witnessed the growth of an urban proletariat but also of an unemployed 'floating' population within the cities. The numbers in Paris are said to have doubled during the first half of the nineteenth century.[58] The vast influx could only intensify the massive squalor, overcrowding, misery and disease of city life, whilst doing nothing to alleviate the horrors on the land. Thus Morel's work is seen to reflect that crisis and to offer on behalf of his profession, the 'solution' of a benevolent social medicine.

The era of the July monarchy was the era of *laissez-faire* ideology and, in opposition, of the rise of socialism and social Catholicism as movements committed to the systematic intervention of the state for the improvement of social conditions. It is against this reality and this set of competing ideologies, it has been suggested, that Morel proselytised on behalf of a medical profession committed to the prevention of the social conditions of degeneration and aloof from political squabble:

we do not accuse ... we describe the action of degenerative causes, and we seek to understand how the morbid varieties of the species are formed.[59]

The social effects of the mass movement of populations from the time of the Napoleonic Wars to the mid nineteenth century were represented in innumerable novels. To a bourgeoisie frightened not without reason about their property and self-interest, the Paris population seemed to contain immutably alien races, peoples constitutionally incapable of settling, a tribe of vagabonds and nomads.[60] When Thiers declared in a speech on 24 May 1850 that '[i]t is the mob, not the people that we wish to exclude: it is the heterogeneous mob ... a mob of persons so mobile that they can

---

[55] Chevalier, *Labouring Classes*.   [56] Martin, 'La Dégénérescence', (diss.), I, p. 110.
[57] Martin, 'La Dégénérescence', (diss.), I, p. 110.
[58] Martin, 'La Dégénérescence', (diss.), I, p. 112.   [59] *Traité des dégénérescences*, p. 644.
[60] See Chevalier, *Labouring Classes*.

nowhere be pinned down and have not succeeded in establishing any regular home for their family',[61] the mob signified not simply a riotous congregation, but a potentially distinguishable category of beings. On the other hand, the problem of the mob's definition, delineation and isolation within the general 'social physiology' remained. There was in short a spectre haunting the ruling classes, as Morel put it, 'a permanent danger for European societies' whose only solution could be the total '*moralisation of the masses*'.[62] But that spectre cannot be understood with reference to a *simple* material reality, as though there are straightforward concrete causes and discursive effects.

The theory of *dégénérescence*, I suggest, needs to be understood as an ideological production, a complex process of conceptualising a felt crisis of history. It emerged at just the moment when liberal progressivism was so powerfully in trouble. After 1848 and the foundation of the Second Empire, there was a deep sense of confusion about the patterns of historical change and repetition. *Dégénérescence* exemplified the radical contradiction of faiths in that period. It is irreducible to one message, motive, or 'interest group'.

The terror at stake in the *Treatise* cannot be simplified into mere conscious expediency. The fact that the professional interests of psychiatry were in jeopardy in this period should not lead one to assume that psychiatry's pronouncements were reducible to the mere defence of the institution. Nevertheless Morel certainly was preoccupied by the seemingly remorseless rise in the numbers of the insane and the apparent inability of mental medicine to cure its patients.

The incessant progression in Europe, not only of insanity, but of all the abnormal states which have a special relation with the existence of physical and moral evil in humanity, was ... a fact which struck my attention.[63]

Mental medicine, he argued, should not concern itself with curing the incurable, but with changing the social conditions which produced *dégénérescence*:

Ignorance ... of the distinctive character of these morbid varieties introduces a deplorable confusion in treatment. Where moral therapeutics should exert its influence, reigns the repressive force of the law; and from another angle, hopes, which must be cruelly deceived in practice, direct all the activity of medicine towards the cure of unmodifiable beings ... (p. 487)

[61] Translated in Chevalier, *Labouring Classes*, p. 364. Cf. from the original speech: 'Ce sont ces hommes qui forment, non pas le fond, mais la partie dangereuse des grandes populations agglomérées; ce sont ces hommes qui méritent ce titre, ... le titre de multitude ... la vile multitude qui a perdu toutes les républiques.' Thiers, *Discours parlementaires*, IX, p. 40.
[62] *Traité des dégénérescences*, p. 437.
[63] *Traité des dégénérescences*, pp. vii–viii.

Various historians have recently argued that the theory of degeneration served as a convenient method of explaining away the widely perceived and criticised failure of psychiatry to 'cure' very many of its patients. Incurability in short was now affirmed as an unavoidable fact of nature.[64] The function of the asylum was re-defined not as a 'cure', but as humane segregation of the degenerate and the dangerous. It is then also suggested that psychiatry concealed its materialism beneath a cloak of idealism. The theory of degeneration was left rather vague, we are told, so that it might mesh with Catholic and classical jurisprudential principles of free will during the period of the Second Empire when the authorities were capable of virulent anti-materialism and polemics against free will could be censured or even censored.[65]

In the anti-clerical climate which increasingly characterised the Third Republic, psychiatry apparently reverted to a powerful scepticism. Religious 'ecstasy' became the stuff of psychiatric diagnosis and explanation within medicine's recently 're-colonised' domain of hysteria and hypnotism.[66] In an age when (in England) even the efficacy of prayer was statistically tested,[67] some French psychiatrists transported the lives of the saints to the world of psycho-pathology.[68] In short, we are told that psychiatry became the tool of anti-clericalism. The work of Charcot linked in with, if it did not directly 'reflect', a regime hostile to church power.[69] In each epoch, then, it can be argued, psychiatry served its own interests and gained power in the law courts. By refusing the drastic determinism of a Lombroso in Italy, French psychiatry basked resplendently in the world of Belle Epoque Paris. There was no exact Italian, German or English equivalent of the cultural *élan* of French psychiatry in this period. The furious debates between the school of Charcot and Bernheim, the university Chairs in psychiatry, the massive publicity for the profession emanating from certain celebrated trials,[70] marks the relatively successful 'career strategy' of a profession despite all the hostility and set-backs which had met it.

To imagine that such an account, however, could adequately explain the language of nineteenth-century psychiatry is in a sense to forget the discursive world of psychoanalysis which followed it. Language, motives,

[64] See Martin, 'La Dégénérescence', (diss.), I, p. 22.
[65] See Dowbiggin, 'Degeneration and Hereditarianism'.
[66] See Goldstein, *Console*, ch. 9, on Charcot and anti-clericalism in the Third Republic. Goldstein sees Charcot's discourse on hysteria as one of the most successful ventures in an 'expansionist movement' of the profession. On positivism and republican anti-clericalism, cf. Dansette, *Religious History*, I, pp. 310–13.
[67] On Galton's endeavours in this field see Forrest, *Galton*.
[68] See Goldstein, *Console*, ch. 9.
[69] See Dowbiggin, 'Degeneration and Hereditarianism'.
[70] See Harris, 'Murder under Hypnosis'.

interests, theories are never exhausted in the functional 'utility' perceived by contemporaries or subsequent historians. The language of degeneration, it can be said, served interests just as it articulated desires and fears. Interest, however, is far from a self-evident category. What interests are desired? What desires are constituted in, or repressed from, the definition of interest? Suffice to say for the moment that the 'professionalisation argument' does not by any means provide an adequate account of degeneration, precisely because it views language so reductively and strategically. This is again to return to the central argument: degeneration reveals contradictory politics and ideas, not the clarity of a single 'position'.

The first Revolution seemed to such varied commentators as de Bonald, de Maistre, Saint-Simon and Comte to have opened an enormous epistemological breach from the eighteenth century, a vast distance of knowledge and historical sophistication.[71] The 1848 Revolution was again perceived by contemporary intellectuals to constitute both an historical and historiographical rupture. The uniqueness of the present was no longer seen as the consciousness of Revolution in absolute (as in the aftermath of 1789–1815), but the experience of the pathological *reproduction* and transformation of revolution. This, I suggest, is a crucial discursive site of Morel's *dégénérescence*. 1848 was understood in relation to 1789 and 1830 but at the same time, it seemed to demonstrate the radical unpredictability of change, the irreducibility of new social phenomena to earlier models. Remember how Morel's *Treatise* proposed not the reproduction of a constant anomaly but the process of pathological differentiation across generations. The condition of the degenerate, as Dr Legrain was to put it in 1889, was indeed protean and polymorphous, constantly differing from its own past forms.[72]

In the wake of 1848 there was an extraordinary flurry of historical interpretation and re-orientation. Certainly to many contemporaries the vicissitudes of revolution seemed to call into question the very terms of liberal progressivism. Pessimism began to colonise liberalism in increasingly powerful and sustained ways. 'Pessimism,' wrote Charles de Remusat in 1860, 'has made great progress in recent times'.[73] Many Frenchmen,

---

[71] There is no space here to provide a fuller account of this contention. See Leroy, *Histoire des idées*, II; Manuel, *Prophets*.

[72] 'Le dégénéré apparaît alors comme une vaste synthèse, un conglomérat d'états morbides différentes, au milieu desquels il est obligé de se frayer une voie, en conservant très difficilement sont équilibre. Ses délires sont multiples, polymorphes, protéiformes.' Legrain, *Hérédité et alcoolisme*, p. 6.

[73] Remusat, 'Pessimisme', (per.), p. 729; cf. Swart, *Sense of Decadence*, p. 91.

he added, who thirty or forty years earlier had been full of hope and enthusiasm for the principles of the Revolution had now come to the conclusion that modern democracy was no more than 'turbulent decadence'.[74]

Ernest Renan, to take another example, whose *The Future of Science* (written in 1848 but not published until 1890) exemplified the utopian positivism prevalent under the July Monarchy, had grave misgivings about the direction of society during the period of the Second Empire.[75] Renan had viewed the French Revolution as the hallowed beginning of modern progress, indeed of social self-consciousness itself. Convinced of the inevitable tendency toward progress, he argued that 1789 was humanity's first attempt to direct its own destiny. It was, he said, the moment where humanity had grown up ('the moment corresponding to that where the child, led thus far by its spontaneous instincts … becomes a free and morally responsible person', p. 25). The Revolution was the supreme point of historical origin, the genesis of history itself: 'The true history of France begins in 89; everything which preceded it was the slow preparation of 89' (p. 25).

Beyond 1848, Renan's view of the Revolution became more apologetic and bitter-sweet: 'I have inherited from my mother', he declared in his *Souvenirs*, 'an invincible taste for the Revolution, which made me love it in spite of all the evil I have spoken of it'.[76] Renan developed his critical views of the genesis of modern France, tracing its evils back to the late Middle Ages when the ideals of freedom and honour introduced into France by the Germanic tribes had been destroyed by unscrupulous kings like Philip the Fair and Louis XI.

The course of political events in 1848, and then from 1848 to 1851 bewildered those liberals who had envisioned modern history as inexorable advance. Moreover, conservative denunciations of liberalism gained a new influence and power. The journalist Louis Veuillot used the power of the popular press in the battle against democracy and free thought. In his newspaper *L'Univers*, terms such as liberty, science and progress were characterized as pernicious and 'incendiary' ideas.[77]

Initially, however, the 1848 revolution had appeared to Catholics like Veuillot to be compatible with the interests of the church. As Dansette, the historian of Catholicism in France, observes:

---

[74] Remusat, 'Pessimisme', (per.), p. 729.
[75] Renan, *L'Avenir*; cf. the discussion in Swart, *Sense of Decadence*, p. 95.
[76] Quoted in Soltau, *French Political Thought*, p. 219 (no footnote given); cf. Lidsky, *Les Ecrivains*, pp. 12–14, on the widespread disillusionment with 1848, the growing artistic disaffection with 'the people' and the perception of their banality.
[77] See Swart, *Sense of Decadence*, p. 88.

In streets running with blood, workers searched for priests to give extreme unction to the dying. In the provinces, ceremonies of blessing trees of liberty would shortly symbolize the union between the Church and the newly born Republic.[78]

The number of electors was increased from 240,000 to nine million[79] which enabled the church to regain a great deal of political power by enfranchising sections of the peasantry and curbing the power of a hitherto frequently anti-clerical bourgeoisie. 'The flag of the Republic', declared Monsieur Donnet, Archbishop of Bordeaux, in the early months of 1848, 'will always be a flag of protection for religion.'[80] 'Who nowadays would dream of defending the monarchy?', asked Veuillot, 'immoral with Louis XIV, scandalous with Louis XV, despotic with Napoleon, stupid until 1830, and cunning if nothing worse until 1848.'[81]

But the course of the Revolution, and in particular the killing of the Archbishop of Paris,[82] moved the Church squarely together with the forces of reaction. 1848 also accelerated the 're-Christianisation' of substantial portions of the bourgeoisie faced by the spectre of communism.[83] This was evident in the passing of the Falloux Law (1850) which granted the Church freedom for secondary education and representation in the Council of the University.[84]

The alarm of liberal Catholicism found acute expression in Raubot's *The Decadence of France* (1850), where it was argued that the massive centralisation of French life and the domination of Paris had fostered communism and revolution. Paris was the heart and brain of the country, he said, but it was a brain menaced by madness, and a heart enfeebled by disease.[85] Having considered France under such headings as the army, navy, population, administration, agriculture, education system, wealth and crime rates, Raubot could only hope that divine aid would save the nation (p. 128).

In Gaume's massive study, *The Revolution* (1856), decline was attributed to the eclipse of Catholicism over the centuries. The causes of evil were inter-linked, Gaume argued, but could be summarily divided as follows: the French Revolution, Voltaireanism, Caesarism, Protestantism, Rationalism, the Renaissance.[86] The author insisted that he spoke objectively and came to his conclusions through the impartial judgement of

---

[78] Dansette, *Religious History*, I, p. 249; cf. Vidler, *Social Catholicism*, p. 33.
[79] Dansette, *Religious History*, I, p. 250.
[80] Quoted in Dansette, *Religious History*, I, p. 249.
[81] Quoted in Dansette, *Religious History*, I, pp. 249–50. On Veuillot, cf. Zeldin, *Intellect*, p. 1,026.
[82] See Agulhon, *Republican Experiment*, p. 61.
[83] See Hammen, 'Spectre', (per.). [84] See the *New Catholic Encyclopaedia*, VI, p. 17.
[85] Raubot, *De la Décadence*, p. 45. [86] Gaume, *La Révolution*, I, p. 9.

natural and historical facts. It is interesting that despite his hostility to science and liberalism, Gaume nevertheless based his authority not only on theology but also on his good faith as a *disinterested*, clinically-detached observer of national degeneration. Revolutions, which had repeated themselves one after another through the European cities, proved that, as he put it: 'We are the children of our fathers: we carry the weight of their heritage'; and thus the 'genealogical history of present evil is of a capital importance'.[87] The sub-title of his work was indeed 'the propagation of evil from the Renaissance to the present'. Certainly, he warned, nobody should imagine that the Revolution was dead. On the contrary, history since the Renaissance was one long revolution against the Church: thus until 1789 sovereignty had passed over to royalty; from 1789 it had passed into the hands of the bourgeoisie; and today it was moving into the hands of the people (p. 19).

The theory of *dégénérescence* was bound up with the problematic of the Revolution's repetition, the sad lineage of 1789, through its intoxication, criminality, imbecility and eventual self-extinction. Morel's treatise, with its procession of themes – alcoholism, cretinism, crime, pollution, insanity and sterility – spoke to, and displaced, deep concerns about the genealogy of history.[88] In the aftermath of 1848, the problems of history were displaced into the problem of inheritance. This offered a discursive asylum for disorders and the disorderly with one voice, even as the discourse glimpsed the potential disaster of civilisation. The next section examines the work of Philippe Buchez, Morel's friend and champion at the Medico-Psychological Society in Paris, and by inter-linking the evolution of Buchez's ideas with certain decisive moments in his career, suggests why the notion of *dégénérescence* appealed to this famous Saint-Simonian Catholic socialist after the 1848 Revolution.

BUCHEZ

Gentlemen: The question of the *dégénérescence* of the human species has been born. The word *dégénérescence* itself is new. Trévoux's dictionary in the 1771 edition, supposedly complete, does not mention it.[89]

---

[87] *La Révolution*, I, pp. 9–10.
[88] For a stimulating and provocative polemic from the Right on historiography and the symbolism of the repetition of the Revolution, see Furet, *French Revolution*. On nine-teenth-century conservative fears about the return of the Terror, horror at the colour red, etc. cf. Agulhon, *Republican Experiment*, pp. 98–9.
[89] Buchez, 'Rapport', (per.), p. 455.

With these awesome words, the Christian socialist, Philippe Buchez signalled the birth in 1857 of a new question in an address to the Medico-Psychological Society in Paris, of which he had been an influential member since its official foundation in 1852.[90] He was speaking in honour of his friend Morel's recently published treatise. The aim in the following discussion is to trace some key factors in Buchez's adoption of that thesis in his later work, beyond the 1848 revolution.

Buchez asked his colleagues at the Society to consider the polarities and anomalies of France's population, and the impossible social contradiction they engendered:

[Consider] a population like ours, placed in the most favourable circumstances; possessed of a powerful civilization; among the highest ranking nations in science, the arts and industry. Our task now, I maintain, is to find out how it can happen that within a population such as ours, races may form – not merely one, but several races – so miserable, inferior and bastardised that they may be classed as below the most inferior savage races, for their inferiority is sometimes beyond cure.[91]

Morel, he declared, was the first theorist to grasp the contradiction in a truly scientific manner. He had illuminated the phenomenon of urban crime, whose dark, mysterious and ever-expanding symbolism had haunted political language and popular novels for several decades.[92] Moreover he had contributed to the defence of society by proving that crime was a symptom of degeneracy; it was to be understood as an effect of a given biological and moral identity.

Dr Morel points out ... [that] it is from the midst of ... the degenerates that most of the bandits, incendiaries, hardcore criminals come ... and on a higher level, even from the well-to-do classes, incorrigible debauchers, false spirits, and people of evil instincts who are a scourge and a danger to society.[93]

Buchez acknowledged that Morel was not the first writer to consider degeneration. He attributed the modern 'authorship' of the term to the great eighteenth-century naturalist Buffon (p. 455). But for Buffon, we are told, it had meant 'simply physiological modifications which could not possibly be considered alterations of human nature' (p. 455). Morel's contribution was to show that degeneration *did* involve an alteration of human nature. Indeed the relationship of the degenerate to 'the family of mankind' was now a vexed question, since the process of morbid inheritance produced decisive transformations in morality, the body and reproduction:

[90] See Dowbiggin, 'Degeneration and Hereditarianism', p. 215.
[91] 'Rapport', (per.), p. 456.
[92] See the discussion above and Chevalier, *Labouring Classes*.
[93] Buchez, 'Rapport', (per.), p. 462.

nobody had [previously] affirmed that certain diseases, certain intoxications, certain habits in the parents had the power to create in the children a consecutive state, a special organic state, indefinitely transmissible right up to the point of the extinction of the race if nothing had been done to change it; in a word what Morel calls *dégénérescence*. (p. 456)

Buchez correctly emphasised the distance between a theory such as this and ideas on progress and degeneration developed by *philosophes* and physiocrats in the eighteenth century. In Buffon's *Natural History* (1749–88), the word degeneration described the bodily changes manifested in migrating populations who had abandoned their ideal environment. The body was inflected by the conditions of a new and more difficult milieu. Of course this view was 'Eurocentric'; it assumed the European as the human starting point, the base from which difference occurred, the standard against which change was calibrated. But, strikingly, Buffon assumed that race itself was pliant, a slate on which environment was written, erased, re-written. Moreover he insisted on the overarching unity of mankind. Whilst he admitted that the differences between humans of the North and the South might lead to the suspicion that the African and the Laplander belonged to different species, he went on to reject this argument, insisting that 'one man [ie. mankind] was originally created'.[94] This 'faith' was confirmed by the natural fact that 'the White, the Laplander and the Negro are capable of uniting, and of propagating the great undivided family of mankind' (p. 2). Biblical and naturalist truths were mutually confirming. Degeneration was a reversible process of bodily change – black would run back into white (the assumed standard colour), if blacks came back to Europe (the assumed point of departure).[95]

In Turgot's theory of progress in the same period, contemporary 'barbaric' societies were seen as vestiges of previous stages in the development of mankind. Such societies had been held back largely because of their isolation.[96] For Turgot, as for Buffon, different degrees of development did not preclude a model of human unity. Although Turgot recognised decadence and uneven development, he sought to demonstrate from the

---

[94] *Natural History*, IV, p. 2.
[95] 'The Asiatic, the European, and the Negro, produce equally with the American. Nothing can be a stronger proof that they belong to the same family, than the facility with which they unite to the common stock. The blood is different; but the germ is the same. The skin, the hair, the features, and the stature have varied, without any change in the internal structure. The type is general and common: and if, by any great revolution, man were forced to abandon those climates which he had invaded, and to return to his native country, he would, in the progress of time, resume his original features, his primitive stature and his natural colour. But the mixture of races would produce this effect much sooner.' (*Natural History*, IV, p. 3)
[96] See Manuel, *Prophets*, p. 34.

ethnographic record that some society in the world was always carrying the torch of progress forward. As Frank Manuel puts it in *The Prophets of Paris* (1964), Turgot believed that 'each people, nation, and tribe could be located in time on some rung of the ladder of progress' (p. 35).

Turgot was optimistic not only that progress was inevitable, but also that its acceleration was now guaranteed by the global diffusion of Enlightenment knowledge and by the continuing advance towards perfection within the theories of the Enlightenment itself.[97]

The belief that the dissemination of science across the globe constituted the key to progress was bequeathed by *philosophes* such as Turgot and Condorcet (who fell with the Revolution) to Saint-Simon, Fourier and Comte.[98] But where in Turgot and Condorcet society was likened, typically, to mathematical and mechanical models, Saint-Simon stressed the bodily analogy. In the work of Saint-Simon and his followers, a physiological model of society coalesced with, and in some respects displaced the social mathematics of the late-eighteenth century. Moreover Condorcet's belief in human ability to control progress in the future, was replaced in Saint-Simon by a vision of inevitable laws beyond human agency.[99] This was an exceedingly complex transformation which cannot be encompassed here, but what needs to be stressed is the emergence of an organic model which proposed the irreducible difference of each body, individual and society. Society was cast as a body which could grow and develop, but also suffer illness, crisis, perhaps even death. Fourier, for instance, was to stress the drastic aging of society since the French Revolution. In the last thirty years, he claimed in 1841, it had aged the equivalent of 300 ordinary years.[100]

The organic model contained all those latent symbolic possibilities, but in the later work of Buchez, the balance of emphasis shifts. He had been a keen adherent of Saint-Simon's social physiological model since the 1820s, but it was only in the 1850s that the theme of degeneration really impinged significantly upon his belief in progress and development. Where the Enlightenment had seen communication as the key to the dissemination of knowledge and progress, medical psychiatry beyond the mid nineteenth century laid an unprecedented stress upon the morbid lines of connection which linked present bodies with the past and the future, the dead with the living and the unborn, as though the dangerous classes had entered into the very physiology of France itself. The account below traces Buchez's accommodation of morbidity and degeneration within his theory of progress.

[97] See Manuel, *Prophets*, p. 41.   [98] Cf. Leroy, *Histoire des idées*, II, ch. 7.
[99] See Baker, *Condorcet*, pp. 371–82.   [100] See Fourier, 'Epilogue', p. 602.

Philippe Buchez was born in 1796.[101] His father, a firm republican apparently inspired by the ideas of Rousseau, held a post in the administration of the municipal tax bureau. Buchez's mother, a devoted Catholic, died in 1813.

In 1812 he began his studies in Paris which would lead in 1824 to his qualification as a medical doctor. The youthful Buchez followed courses by Lamarck, Cuvier and Geoffroy Saint-Hilaire in Paris. In this heady intellectual atmosphere, he lost his faith, the faith of his mother: 'I could not escape a teaching', he explained, 'which enveloped me entirely and which attacked me on all sides; I began by being ashamed of my beliefs, then I became, as my teachers, incredulous and finally a materialist.'[102]

In the uncongenial atmosphere of the Restoration, Buchez immersed himself in a world of political intrigue, plotting the downfall of the Bourbons. In the early 1820s, he was involved in founding the 'Charbonerie française' which aimed at the overthrow of the monarchy and the convocation of a national assembly.[103] After several arrests, Buchez had turned by the mid-1820s to the relative safety of writing, inspired by Saint-Simonian ideas, and indeed by the master's plea for the development of 'social physiology'.[104] Although he did not meet Saint-Simon, who died in 1825, he was introduced to members of the school by Prosper Enfantin. Buchez shared the commitment to the topic and the realisation of progress, but was soon drawn away from the Saint-Simonian school, repelled by the Pantheistic creeds which were developing. Indeed Buchez remained loyal to the Catholic Church, albeit in an eccentrically progressivist interpretation of what that really meant. He sought to recover a Christian tradition which would be in essential harmony with the revolutionary principles of 1789. As he put it in the huge documentary history of the Revolution which he co-edited between 1834 and 1838, 'the French Revolution is the last and most advanced consequence of modern civilisation', and modern civilisation 'has emerged entirely from the gospels'.[105] Buchez indeed deplored the fact that the church had not been true to its social mission on behalf of the oppressed; a deplorable spirit of Protestant individualism had overtaken Catholicism.[106] The task of scientific history, he argued in the *In-*

---

[101] Biographical information is drawn from the *Nouvelle Biographie générale* (1855), VII, pp. 698–9; Castella, *Buchez*; Cuvillier, *P. J. B. Buchez*; Petri, *Historical Thought*. See also Friedlander, 'Morel', (diss.); Dowbiggin, 'Degeneration and Hereditarianism'.

[102] Quoted in Petri, *Historical Thought*, p. 2.

[103] See Castella, *Buchez*, p. 19.

[104] See Ott's introduction to Buchez, *Traité de politique et de science sociale*, p. XXI.

[105] Buchez, *Histoire parlementaire*, I, p. 1. Cf. the similar view of his friends and medical colleagues Boulland, *Essai*, and Ott, who remarks (*Manuel*, II, p. 250): 'The French Revolution is only the conclusion of the progress accomplished in past centuries, the social fruit of Christian revelation.'

[106] See Petri, *Historical Thought*, p. 12.

troduction to Science (1842), was precisely to teach more than individual salvation, to harness the ephemera of particular events to an overarching interpretation and to show the place of each unit in the organic body. Everybody, present, past and future, was bound up in a larger social collectivity:

All men, all generations, all peoples, of whatever time, be it present, past or future, are united by the bonds of reciprocal dependence, as too by a community of function and responsibility; whence as a result ... they form a [single] society embracing every century.[107]

Scientific history and social physiology were counterposed by Buchez to all individualism. He advanced a theory of two inter-connecting physical-historical forces: 'la force circulaire', the law of organic repetition (example: the process of digestion); 'la force serielle': the law of development and of organic change (example: the development of the embryo[108]). Social advance could be grasped as a complex coalescence of these two forces, structured repetition and development. Buchez acknowledged that retrogression was a real force. But it was illustrated at this stage (i.e. before 1848) by the example of certain morbid tribes far away from France:

[they display] a scrophulous constitution which has become the condition of the race. They are as ugly as weak; as unintelligent as wretched. They are short-lived, apparently conserved only to present us with an example of the state of degradation into which the human species can fall, when it abandons the light of duty and succumbs to the unique temptations of its animal nature. (II, p. 360)

Although endorsing the ideal of the Fall, Buchez projected retrogression to distant tribes. Like Morel, he argued that the scientific analysis of reproduction, confirmed the idea of original sin. The physical degradation of Adam as a result of his disobedience 'is not completely beyond scientific explanation' (II, p. 361).

Robust parents, he insisted, produced robust children, whilst those suffering from nervous maladies passed them on to their offspring (II, p. 344). In modern society, the indiscriminate mix of parents obscured but did not cancel this law. But neither the notion of original sin, nor the hypothesis of retrogression, led Buchez to a pessimistic social, political or philosophical conclusion at this time. Society, he insisted, could not be reduced to the analogy of individual life or death or sinfulness:

In society there is, in reality, nothing corresponding to what one calls youth and decrepitude in the individual; generations do not succeed each other one by one; everything is mixed up, so that birth, death, adolescence, maturity, old age are

---

[107] *Introduction*, I, pp. 75–6.   [108] *Introduction*, II, pp. 37–40.

always present at the same time ... Society is ... a collective being, destined to live indefinitely, with an energy [ever undiminished]. (I, pp. 47–8)

But in the 1850s there is a significant shift of emphasis in Buchez's account. It is not surprising perhaps that the radiant vision of history suffered some problem in confrontation with his 'unsentimental education' in 1848, the 'Year of Revolutions'. It was indeed a fateful year for Buchez; after the toppling of the July Monarchy, his Catholic and republican credentials, enhanced by his medical work at the barricades, combined to effect his election to the Legislative Assembly and almost immediately afterwards to its presidency.[109]

Buchez was caught off guard by the growing crisis about the direction of events on the streets and the deep dissatisfaction felt with the bourgeois compromise over which he was presiding. His own sense of the degeneration of the Revolution was brought home to him unforgettably by the events of 15 May when a group of demonstrators, led by Barbès, Huber, Blanqui and Blanc, burst into the Chamber and demanded radical measures from the Assembly, above all material support for the struggle in Poland.[110] In Tocqueville's words the crowd broke into the Assembly

carrying various emblems of the Terror ... Buchez, the President, whom some regard as a rascal and others a saint, but who on that day was undoubtedly a great fool, rang his bell as hard as he could in an attempt to obtain silence, as if in present circumstances, the silence of the multitude was not more to be feared than its shouts.[111]

Tocqueville went on to describe his horror at the consequences of Buchez's indecision:

It was at that moment that I saw a man go up onto the rostrum, and although I have never seen him again, the memory of him has filled me with disgust and horror ever since. He had sunken withered cheeks, white lips and a sickly malign, dirty look like a pallid, mouldy corpse ... I was told that this was Blanqui.[112]

Buchez was equally appalled by these scenes. When the black flag and the phrygian cap were exhibited, he shouted to Huber: 'In the name of heaven ... These are scenes from the Bicêtre'.[113] The Bicêtre was a Parisian asylum.

[109] See Dansette, *Religious History*, I, p. 251; cf. Castella, *Buchez*, p. 31.
[110] See Agulhon, *Republican Experiment*, pp. 51–2.
[111] *Recollections*, pp. 117–18.
[112] *Recollections*, p. 118; cf. the description of the conflict in the Assembly in Cuvillier, *P. J. Buchez*, pp. 66–7; Agulhon, *Republican Experiment*, p. 52.
[113] Quoted in Castella, *Buchez*, p. 31; the story is perhaps apocryphal; in Williams, *Horror*, p. xii, we are told that Dr Ulysse Trélat cried out in the National Assembly on 15 May 1848, 'Blanqui, Barbès, Sarbier, Huber. All of them are mad. They belong in the Salpêtrière, not here.' Cf. Ott's description in his introduction to Buchez, *Traité de politique et de science sociale*, pp. l–li.

On 5 June, when his term of office expired, Buchez asked the Assembly to choose a new candidate since his health was insufficiently robust to continue in the task.[114] It appears that he had by this point in any case antagonised both the Right and the Left. Resignation was his least humiliating option. In the following months he took an active part in opposing the election of Louis Bonaparte, which in turn was to lead, upon the *coup* of 2 December 1851, briefly to his arrest.[115]

In the 1850s Buchez returned to medicine. He was involved in the formation of the Medico-Psychological Society and during the cholera epidemic of 1854 he went back to active medical practice.[116] In his writings of these years he continued to cherish hopes of social progress. Neither the Revolution nor the Gospels, he declared in a work on the formation of French nationality in 1859, could ever be permanently lost, even if there were harsh setbacks.[117] Buchez incorporated the concept of *dégénérescence* within his troubled political language in the 1850s:

Man can perfect his organism, enhancing its power in different ways, but he can also weaken and vitiate it. These results, good or bad, are passed on to [his] children. Both bad and good are organically inheritable; but God wished it to be in such a way that the bad led rapidly to *dégénérescence*, and, where too strongly implanted, the race quite quickly became sterile. (II, pp. 182–3)[118]

In the words of Dr Ott, the friend and colleague who introduced Buchez's posthumous volume of 1866: '[he] was moved by the downfall of the Republic but his hope and his faith in the future remained unshaken'.[119] But was that faith really unshaken? In Buchez's final work there was a new emphasis upon the idea of degeneration and betrayal – the morbid transfiguration of progress, the vertiginous revolution of the Revolution itself. He stressed that a group of 'exaggerators' had emerged after 1789 who dishonoured the Revolution and triumphed in 1793 (p. 500). This group 'was made up of semi-savage natures, uneducated outcasts, who understood nothing but brutality and coarseness' (p. 500).

The fanaticism of 1793, he argued, brought religion and revolution into conflict: it was then that 'Catholicism was insulted' and there were

---

114 See Castella, *Buchez*, pp. 31–2; Petri, *Historical Thought*, p. 18.
115 See Castella, *Buchez*, p. 32.
116 Castella, *Buchez*, p. 32.
117 Buchez, *Histoire de la formation*, II, p. 187.
118 'L'homme peut perfectionner son organisme, en accroître la puissance dans des directions diverses; mais il peut aussi l'amoindrir et le détériorer. Ces résultats, bons ou mauvais, sont transmissibles aux enfants. Le mal comme le bien sont organiquement héréditaires; mais Dieu a voulu que le mal conclût rapidement a dégénérescence, et que la race ou il s'est trop fortement implanté devînt assez promptement stérile.'
119 *Traité de politique et de science sociale*, p. lv.

'scandalous apostasies' (pp. 500–1). Where earlier he had castigated the Church for failing to respond to the Revolution, now he castigated the Revolution for betraying Catholicism.[120] Nostalgia and regret were worked up into a political theory, a theory of degeneration.

Buchez's account of revolution in the 1830s shared a great deal with Michelet; his account in the 1860s anticipated the pathologising imagery of Taine. In Taine, however, the subject of the next section, we see a further shift in the language of *dégénérescence* – its discursive appropriation after 1871 in a new avowedly naturalistic counter-revolutionary history. Moreover where Buchez had participated in the Second Republic, and charted in his writing the failure of that participation and its profound disappointment, Taine watched the Second Empire and the Third Republic, quintessentially detached, tracing from afar the history of degeneration, the degeneration of history.

TAINE

J'ai horreur de la foule' (Taine)[121]

My argument is that the credibility of the conception of degeneration owed a great deal to the broad crisis of liberal social optimism in the face of revolution. It constituted, in part, an attempt to conceptualise the morbid passage of history itself. From the 1870s to the 1890s, degeneration became the veritable common sense of innumerable scientific and cultural investigations. I explore the profoundly influential language of degeneration in two great projects: Taine's *Revolution* and, in a further chapter, Zola's Rougon-Macquart cycle of novels.

Taine had a special status in the later-nineteenth century as the modern historian and critic *par excellence*, who used science to look through the veil of a flawed and fatal idealism which had emanated disastrously from the Enlightenment. In the words of the Goncourts' *Journal*, he was 'the incarnation in flesh and bone of the modern critic'.[122] In certain quarters in England too, Taine was revered for his advanced sceptical mind (he was a great Anglophile and this of course enhanced his reputation there). In 1894, for instance, *The Gentleman's Magazine* published a comparison of Carlyle's and Taine's respective histories of the French Revolution.[123] Whilst Carlyle, we are told, had offered 'fervent emphasis' and 'passionate pictur-

---

[120] See Petri, *Historical Thought*, pp. 68–9, on Buchez's earlier ambivalence (certainly not simple hostility) towards the Terror of 1793 compared with his later outright repudiation.
[121] Quoted in Boutny, 'La Jeunesse', (per.), p. 263.
[122] Goncourt, *Journal*, II, p. 77.
[123] Wilson, 'Carlyle and Taine', (per.).

esqueness',[124] ill-informed by detailed evidence, Taine had now provided a fully 'scientific' analysis.

The difference between Carlyle and Taine could not be understood simply in terms of narrative content or political sympathy. They were divided, crucially, by style of address, by the terms of their authority, by the truth they claimed and proselytised. The subject in Taine's narrative spoke with the authority of medicine and 'science'; it was the authority of that voice which impressed such younger contemporaries as Durkheim, Le Bon, Janet, Tarde, Lombroso, Freud and Zola.[125] As one admirer put it in 1928, Taine

did not seek to write exactly the history of the Revolution; he gave himself the task of writing its psychology, or if you like its psycho-pathology... In that respect, his pages on the Revolution remain the most important edifice of social psychology in the whole of the last century.[126]

Taine's history, by contrast with Carlyle's, was imbricated with medico-psychiatric and evolutionary naturalist language. Thus the psychology of the revolutionaries was located in contemporary evolutionary terms, and even likened to degenerates and atavists. The historian was thus a kind of doctor of past pathologies – a Lombroso of the archives,[127] whose political opinions could be paraded as scientific fact by *The Gentleman's Magazine*:

[The revolutionary minority recruits amongst] the human cast-offs [*ce rebut humain*] who infest the capitals, amongst the epileptic and scrophulous rabble, heirs of a vicious blood, who ... bring *dégénérescence* into civilisation, imbecility, the distraction of an enfeebled temperament, retrograde instincts and an ill-constructed brain.[128]

The Revolution was the conscious project of a few individuals, Taine argued, but for the vast majority, it was nothing but a field of psycho-somatic stimuli. As *The Gentleman's Magazine* remarks, where 'Carlyle always assumes the deeds of revolution to have been the action of the

[124] 'Carlyle and Taine', (per.), p. 349. Cf. Taine's own view of Carlyle in *History of English Literature*: he writes always 'in riddles', 'employs figures at every step'; 'a stream of misty passion comes bubbling into his overflowing brain, and the torrent of images breaks forth and rolls on amidst every kind of mud and magnificence' (p. 648); '[Carlyle] confounds all styles, jumbles all forms, heaps together pagan allusions, Bible reminiscences, German abstractions, technical terms, poetry, slang, mathematics, physiology, archaic words, neologies. There is nothing he does not tread down and ravage' (p. 650).
[125] See *Revue blanche*, 13 (1897), pp. 263–95.
[126] Gibaudan, *Les Idées*, pp. 165–6.
[127] Taine and Lombroso were mutual admirers. Thus Lombroso wrote 'Taine has truly been my master, the one master I have had after Darwin.' *Revue blanche*, 13 (1897), p. 283. On Taine's view of Lombroso see the beginning of part II below.
[128] Wilson, 'Carlyle and Taine', (per.), p. 350, my translation.

totality of the French people ... Taine knows and shows that those gruesome excesses and infra-human crimes were the product only of the Jacobin minority'.[129] A minority planted the seeds of revolution, but the real if unconscious gestation took place in the crowd. I will suggest below that in Taine and more acutely still in the crowd theorists he inspired, the 'leader' and 'the crowd' became key terms. Moreover those terms were sexualised and pathologised in specific ways.

In the mid-1850s, Taine had attended courses in medicine and psychiatry in Paris which he would declare an invaluable preparation for his historical work.[130] He frequently expressed what he took to be the axiomatic connection between the historian of revolution and the morbid psychologist.[131] Taine's *Revolution* developed a commonplace of nineteenth-century medicine, the view that social revolt could gravely disturb the body and mind, and indeed set off an epidemic of insanity.[132]

In *Clinical Studies* in 1852, for instance, Morel had considered what was indeed a much canvassed debate on the influence of politics in the production of mental lesions.[133] It was a subject, he argued, demanding complex and impartial consideration. On one page he discounted any drastic direct effect on mental health: 'amongst the numerous insanity cases under our observation, the direct influence of political ideas has only been proved on a few occasions' (I, p. 254). Moreover he acknowledged that revolutions had revitalised the condition of many neuropaths; it was not unknown for

---

[129] 'Carlyle and Taine', (per.), p. 350.

[130] On Taine's interest in the Salpêtrière, and his view that madness had played a great part in the course of history, see Taine's letter to Edouard de Suckau (25 May 1855), Taine, *Life and Letters*, II, p. 83. ('It seems to me that madness has played a very great part in this world'; 'My physiological studies are teaching me history...'). It should be noted that a detailed consideration of Taine's significant body of early work on intelligence and individual psychology is not offered here; this caveat, however, does not invalidate the general points made above and below.

[131] Taine described his account of French history as analogous to a medical consultation in which the patient was France and the illness comparable to syphilis. (Letter to Ernest Havet, 24 March 1878), Taine, *Life and Letters*, III, p. 191. ('I could compare this evil to an attack of syphilis badly doctored. The universal suffrage of 1848, an evil sore, was due to this and in 1870–1 two fingers of the patient – Alsace and Lorraine – fell from him... My book, if I have the health and strength to finish it, will be a conference of physicians.')

[132] Pariset, head doctor at the Bicêtre in 1822 argued that great and rapid social change had increased the rate of madness. In France, a revolution followed by wars had damaged the minds of the people; see Alexander, 'Administration', (diss.), p. 297; for other examples of this view see pp. 297ff. Cf. Baron Haussman's fears about insanity and revolution during the Second Empire. Haussman noted that 'a set of circumstances arrives throwing the mass of common people into the current of passion, and the whole nation will seem seized by vertigo and madness. Sometimes the fury of a violent minority, intimidating peaceful people abashed and dazed by terror, is enough to shake and overturn the scaffolding so prudently contrived. No longer is this simply disorder, it is a revolution!' Haussman, *Mémoires*, I, pp. 171–2.

[133] Morel, *Etudes cliniques*, I, p. 254.

such great events to 'imprint' themselves on the sickly organisation of the insane, fostering a new 'vigour' (I, p. 254). But on the next page, however, Morel was careful to add the view that whilst political upheavals could in some circumstances lead to improvement ('crises favorables', I, p. 256), their appearance all too often led to terror and misery, fears of the future and potentially fatal hereditary modifications in future generations (I, p. 256). After 1870–1, the second gloomy view predominated. If we look at Morel's last contributions to the *Annales médico-psychologiques*, and indeed at numerous other articles in the *Annales* during the 1870s, we can see an intense new concern with the hereditary consequences of social upheaval.[134] In an article in 1875, for instance, another doctor considered at length the damage caused to French society by recent history, and came to this conclusion:

The terrible events which overcame France in 1870 and 1871 have had, amongst other disastrous effects, those of determining a great number of cases of mental alienation. The grave episodes of the war, the political crises which preceded them ... the diversity of opinions ... the territorial invasion, and the devastation which followed it ... migration, fatigue, privation ... epidemic maladies ... disappointed ambition ... came down, blow after blow, on a nervous and impressionable people, who formerly regarded themselves as the leaders of the world, and all these events happened with a vertiginous rapidity ... shaking [many minds] and sinking a good few ...[135]

The link between criminality and revolt, alcoholism and social anarchy came to the fore of the agenda. Moreover these themes were linked up to the vexed question of racial memory. The subterranean memories of the individual and of the race, it was now argued, had to form part of historical understanding. The slate of history could not be wiped clean, the past could be repressed but never lost.

It appeared that 1870–1 manifested the effect of a previous inheritance, a 'deep and sombre lake' of degeneration. In war and civil war, France faced merely the crisis of its inherited discontents. The overburdened racial-historical memory of the nation had accumulated to a point which could only bring disorder or dissolution. In *Heredity* (1875), the philosopher and psychologist Theodule Ribot wrote:

[134] Cf. Lunier, 'Influences', (per.), p. 174, 'the emotions and the reversals of every kind which accompanied the invasion and the insurrection of 18 March 1871, had to lead to an explosion [in the number of] cases of madness'; and Morel, 'Du Délire panophobique', (per.), p. 345. '... it will be clear to everybody that the events of war in these terrible years (1870–1871) have increased exceptionally the number of victims of [terrifying delusions]' ('impressions terrifiantes').

[135] Hospital, 'Souvenirs', (per.), p. 11. On the hereditary alcoholism of the Communards, see also Ribot, *Heredity*, p. 87; Féré, 'L'Hérédité morbide', (per.), p. 40, on how social disorders and insurrections unleashed criminal instincts and the insanity of the degenerate; also see Boucherau and Magnan, 'Statistique', (per.).

The phenomena of memory, considered in their *ultima ratio*, are explained by the law of the indestructibility of force, of the conservation of energy, which is one of the most important laws of the universe. Nothing is lost; nothing that exists can ever cease to be. In physics, this is admitted readily enough; the principle is well-established, and confirmed by so many facts that doubt is impossible. In morals, the case is different: we are commonly so accustomed to regard all occurrences as the results of chance, and as subject to no laws, that many at least implicitly admit the annihilation of that which once was a state of consciousness to be possible. Yet annihilation is as inadmissable in the moral as in the physical world; and but little reflection is needed to see that in all orders of phenomena it is alike impossible for something to become nothing, as for nothing to become something.[136]

In this vision nothing could be lost – hence the recurrent memory and realisation of revolution, each worse than the one before. Conservation was, as it were, the first 'thermodynamic' law of memory and history:

We daily experience thousands of perceptions, but none of these, however vague and insignificant, can perish utterly. After thirty years some effort – some chance occurrence, some malady – may bring them back; it may even be without recognition. Every experience we have had lies dormant within us: the human soul is like a deep and sombre lake, of which light reveals only the surface; beneath, there lies a whole world of animals and plants, which a storm or an earthquake may suddenly bring to light before the astonished consciousness (p. 48).

Taine can certainly be read in relation to such medico-psychiatric and psychological commentary. Like the *Annales médico-psychologiques*, Taine's *Revolution* continually delineated pathology within a portion of the population. Yet Taine also portrayed its sheer valency, a force overflowing the boundaries, infecting the whole race, bringing indeed a veritable democracy of the pathological.

During the Revolution, Taine showed, even the normally quiescent subject was overcome by the visual and linguistic experience of revolution, thrown back in psychological terms to the evolutionary past. Something of Darwin's ape and Lombroso's criminal atavist informed this representation of revolution:

His anger is exasperated by peril and resistance. He catches the fever from contact with those who are fevered ... Add to this the clamours, the drunkenness, the spectacle of destruction, the nervous tremor of the body strained beyond its powers of endurance, and we can comprehend how, from the peasant, the labourer, and the bourgeois, pacified and tamed by an old civilisation, we see all of a sudden spring forth the barbarian, and still worse, the primitive animal, the grinning, sanguinary, wanton baboon, who chuckles while he slays, and gambols over the ruin he has accomplished.[137]

---

[136] Ribot, *Heredity*, p. 46.
[137] Taine, *Les Origines*, I, p. 70. The translation is from Taine, *The Revolution*, I, pp. 52–3.

But the vision of the simian individual, in all its grotesque clarity, is counterposed to a conception of history as invisible racial degeneration. Taine's language moved continuously between the representation of the psychopathology of individuals and society. The individual body and society stood as dead metaphors of one other as though their figurative relation could be naturalised and dissolved in the literal idea of the nation's *dégénérescence*. We see this not only in Taine's overall project to trace the history of the Revolution as a history of degeneration, but in numerous phrases throughout his writing. Thus, for instance, he wrote in a letter of 'the morbid germ which entered the blood of a diseased society [and] caused fever, delirium and revolutionary convulsions',[138] or again '[c]entralization and universal suffrage ... have impaired [France's] constitution to the causing of both apoplexy and anaemia'.[139]

For Taine, the French Revolution bequeathed a process of degeneration which reached its apotheosis in the Franco-Prussian War and the Paris Commune.[140] In his view there was no possibility of a mass society freely or democratically choosing anything – their choice was mediated by a racial history which stretched behind and beyond them. The theory of degeneration at one level focussed, defined and marginalised certain groups (cretins, criminals, the insane and so on) but it also envisioned the return of those pathological 'others' upon society.

The aim here has been to suggest the contradictory resonances of degeneration in certain naturalist writings. It is a mistake to perceive it as simply an idea which could be deployed rhetorically in a given argument. Degeneration needs to be grasped as part of a productive process of language, always in excess of the theory or concept into which it was petrified. In French medical-psychiatry, degeneration was seen to crystallise a problem of reproduction, a problem which, it seemed, could no longer be entrusted to the self-regulation of the family. It was a matter which demanded with ever greater urgency the intervention of a social

---

[138] Taine, *Life and Letters*, III, p. 228 (letter to G. Monod, 6 July 1881).

[139] *Life and Letters*, III, p. 230 (letter to G. Saint René Taillandier, 20 July 1881). Cf. 'Each in this community is like the cell of an organised body: the fundamental requirement of all the little fragmentary lives, whether they know it or not, is the conservation of the great total life in which they are comprised as musical notes in a concert' (Taine, *The Revolution*, II, ii, p, 141).

[140] Writing to Madame Taine in 1871, Taine declared of France: 'I can only consider her either criminal or insane' (26 March 1871), *Life and Letters*, III, p. 30. Or again from Oxford in May: '... I have just heard of all the horrors going on in Paris – the burning of the Louvre, the Tuileries, the *Hotel de Ville*. The miscreants! The savage wolves! And with petroleum! ... The savages who wantonly destroy such masterpieces are beyond the pale of humanity!' (25 May, 1871), *Life and Letters*, III, p. 49. Note that according to Lidsky (*Les Ecrivains*, p. 11), all well-known writers with the exception of Vallès, Rimbaud, Verlaine, Villier, L'Isle Adam and Victor Hugo (who adopted a 'neutral' position at least during the events) were against the Commune and often wrote with extraordinary virulence.

medicine, a ministering doctor to restore the sanctity of the family, symbolic locus of society's fundamental order, and concomitantly of its potential destabilisation, adulteration and danger. The family was the crucial fortification, but simultaneously the most precarious institution, in a world perceived to have been threatened, dislocated and subverted by revolutions, commercial speculations, political reactions: in short by endless change and uncertainty.[141]

The medico-psychiatric theory of degeneration was a symptom of and a putative solution to a massive uncertainty in the terms of social representation. Promising to bring to light the forces of disorder, it continually lost track of them amidst the wider racial crisis it disclosed. Degenerationist texts thus came back again and again to the problem of the degenerate in an attempt to identify the locus of disorder. Taking cretins and other dangerous elements out of social circulation was now deemed crucial, since it was impossible to envisage inhibiting that wider circulation, flux, exchange, perceived as the very condition of modernity.

In a rising chorus through the late-nineteenth century, doctors, politicians and journalists demanded that the dangerous, the fallen, the habitual criminal, the prostitute and the anarchist be removed from social circulation.[142] But as the developing science of crowds demonstrated, modernity was sometimes cast as the origin of pathology. The language of degeneration in the second half of the nineteenth century was caught in something of a double bind. It signified that morbidity was confined *within* a restricted number of bodies, even as it suggested that the 'social organism' bred the very disorders which threatened it. The modern world, as seen through the eyes of a Taine, a Zola or a Gustave Le Bon was bound up in an ambiguous biological and cultural regression, involving, amongst other things, the threat of mass politics, anarchism, the vexed question of the enfranchisement of women, and of the crowd's potential eruption and regression at the behest of morbid, excitable leaders. Degeneration kept returning as an urgent issue and a deep contradiction in the contemporary novel, above all in Zola's Rougon-Macquart project tracing the morbid destiny of a family across the years of the Second Empire.

---

[141] Cf. Donzelot, *Policing*, p. 173: 'In the middle of the century, the dictionaries of hygiene inserted a few positive considerations regarding non-artificial means of contraception. Starting in 1857, that is, after the publication of Morel's [*Treatise*], they grew rich in imperious advice regarding indications and contraindications for matrimony. Eugenism was not far in the future. For the doctors, it was a matter of treating sexuality as the business of the state, thus transcending the arbitrariness of families, morality, and the Church.'

[142] See Nye, *Crime*, ch. 6.

3

◁ ══════════════════════════════════════ ▷

Zola's prognosis

THE QUESTION OF HEREDITY

Ah! That question of Heredity; what a subject of endless meditation it supplied him with! (Zola, *Dr Pascal*)

A science which could master disorder and provide a master narrative of disorder: this, it is often said, was a naive dream of Zola's naturalism. The discussion below will question the adequacy of that conception, but certainly in the eyes of many scientific 'experts' at the time, medicine had to be defined and guarded against an art which was obsessed with, but unqualified for, the representation of degeneration and pathological sexuality. Science in general, it appeared, was threatened by fictions which were themselves prurient and degenerate. The 'obscenity' of a Zola or an Ibsen was in part the refusal to respect the 'proper' spheres and borders of art. Science, it was insisted, had to be jealously defended against the encroachment of naturalist authors and the laconic proclamations of self-styled 'decadents'.

An important aspect of the scandal of a late-nineteenth century novel like *Against Nature* (*A Rebours*, 1884) by Joris-Karl Huysmans, was the pleasure taken in the narrative of decomposition, the disintegration of bodies and families. Here, it seemed, was nothing less than the novel's love affair with degeneration. The central character of the story, Duc Jean Des Esseintes is born into an aristocratic family which has been slowly degenerating for at least two centuries, dissipating its strength, impoverishing its stock, caught up in a vicious circle of maladies. By the time of the narrative's present (the late-nineteenth century), the family has only one survivor. Des Esseintes is the final degenerate of the 'ancient house'.[1] Anaemic and highly strung, his childhood had been overshadowed by sickness, his maturity by chlorosis, general enfeeblement, effete tastes, depravity and insanity. He enjoys a life of sheer dissipation, obsessed by a desire to preside over the supremely refined debauch. Yet finally Des Esseintes seeks medical advice about his gathering fatigue and lethargy. The doctors tell him to lead a quiet life, but 'soon his brain took fire again', and he begins

[1] Huysmans, *Against Nature*, p. 17.

74

to imagine, and then indulge in, 'unnatural love affairs and perverse pleasures'. His decline continues and 'impotence [is] not far off' (p. 23).

Des Esseintes proceeds to give an extraordinary funeral banquet in honour of his lost virility. (Remember how sterility and extinction were the end points in Morel's chronology of the course of *dégénérescence*.) The food, the dining room, even the garden are shrouded in varying shades of black:

While a hidden orchestra played funeral marches, [the guests dined off] ... black-bordered plates [and] ... enjoyed turtle soup, Russian rye bread, ripe olives from Turkey, caviare, mullet botargo, black puddings from Frankfurt, game served in sauces the colour of liquorice and boot-polish, truffle jellies, chocolate creams, plum-puddings, nectarines, pears in grape-juice syrup, mulberries and black-heart cherries. (p. 27)

The sheer excess of detail allies the text with the saga of decadence it chronicles. It is at one level a fantastic pastiche of the naturalism in which Huysmans had been caught up. Zola indeed reproached Huysmans, one-time member of his Medan group, for 'leading the school astray' with this 'terrible blow to Naturalism' (see Baldick's introduction, p. 10). Des Esseintes, with '[a]ll the leavan of insanity that a brain over-stimulated by neurosis can contain ... fermenting within him' (p. 117) is given free play over the narrative. He creates an exquisitely artificial haven, and gorges on a thousand material and aesthetic delights. Just as *A Rebours* became the treasured textual inheritance of Wilde's Dorian Gray, so Des Esseintes finds his parentage in Poe and Baudelaire:

[With Baudelaire] he had finally reached those districts of the soul where the monstrous vegetations of the sick mind flourish. There, near the breeding-ground of intellectual aberrations and diseases of the mind – the mystical tetanus, the burning fever of lust, the typhoids and yellow fevers of crime – he had found, hatching in the dismal forcing-house of ennui, the frightening climacteric of thoughts and emotions. (pp. 146–7)

The text comes in the end to acknowledge its own pathological situation. In the midst of a degenerate literature, its own style mirrors the morbid features it diagnoses:

a literature attacked by organic diseases, weakened by intellectual senility, exhausted by syntactical excesses, sensitive only to the curious whims that excite the sick, and yet eager to express itself completely in its last hours, determined to make up for all the pleasures it had missed, afflicted on its death-bed with a desire to leave behind the subtlest memories of suffering had been embodied in Mallarmé in the most consummate and exquisite fashion. (p. 199)

If there was agreement on anything in the Medico-Psychological Society in the later-nineteenth century, it was that degeneration was no laughing matter. Moreover, such novelistic excess constituted in the moral sphere a dangerous corollary to the pathologies at work in the physical sphere.[2]

No novelist professed so close a relation with modern medicine, nor aroused so much indignation, as Huysmans' former mentor, Emile Zola. Indeed the twenty-volume Rougon-Macquart cycle of novels had set out to trace the decline of France during the period of the Second Empire, following the history of a single degenerate family across successive generations.

In theory, Zola portrayed his own language as a diagnostic tool, his method as truly experimental.[3] Zola's novels divided the doctors on the issue of medical inaccuracy. Martineau, for instance in a thesis entitled *The Scientific Novel of Émile Zola* (1907), was highly critical of its pretensions to 'science' and spoke of the writer's 'incredible fatuity':[4]

Zola's descriptions are strangers to his theories, the living parts of his work have nothing to do with either the naturalist system or the medical ideas he announced at the beginning. Nothing is less scientific than the scientific novel.[5]

In the earlier view of the *Annales médico-psychologiques*, Zola's writing was also shown to be less unimpeachably scientific than he had hoped. In a discussion recorded in 1897, Dr Toulouse commented on the special study he had made of Zola.[6] Rejecting Lombroso's contention that the novelist

---

[2] As Nordau put it, Huysmans displays 'the classical type of the hysterical mind without originality, who is the predestined victim of every suggestion . . . he swerved from naturalism, by an abrupt change of disposition, which is no less genuinely hysterical, overwhelmed this tendency and Zola himself with the most violent abuse, and began to ape the Diabolists, particularly Baudelaire. A red thread unites both of his otherwise abruptly contrasted methods, viz., his lubricity. That has remained the same. He is, as a languishing "Decadent", quite as vulgarly obscene as when he was a bestial "Naturalist"' (*Degeneration*, p. 302). Such 'decadence', he argued, was simply the morbid apotheosis of naturalism: 'The vanguard of civilisation holds its nose at the pit of undiluted naturalism, and can only be brought to bend over it with sympathy and curiosity when, by cunning engineering, a drain from the boudoir and the sacristy has been turned into it' (*Degeneration*, p. 13).

[3] See Zola, *Experimental Novel*.

[4] Martineau, *Le Roman scientifique*, p. 37; cf. Kellner, *Retrospective*, pp. 4–11, for other critical nineteenth-century medical reviews of the Rougon-Macquart project. Note however that other figures discussed in the present volume admired Zola's 'scientific' representations. Thus De Sanctis (1972: vol. XIV, 452), for instance, noted that Zola was a great 'painter of corruption', but at the same time a symptom of an age obsessed by pathology. Lombroso admired Zola's accurate representation of anarchism in *Germinal* (Lombroso, *Gli anarchici*, p. 49). Sighele, who met Zola in Rome in 1894 (see Ternois, *Zola*, p. 114), praised Zola's wonderful anticipations of scientific discourses on crime, women, crowds, anarchism etc. (see for instance Sighele, *La donna nova*, pp. 37–9; *Letteratura tragica*, p. 8; cf. Ferri, *Arringhe e discorsi*, pp. 301–13).

[5] Martineau, *Le Roman scientifique*, p. 261.

[6] See Toulouse, 'Recent research', (per.). Note too that the *Annales médico-psychologiques* and Dr Toulouse were not in any simple sense hostile to Zola. They endeavoured instead 'dispassionately' to chart his genius and pathology.

was epileptic, Toulouse deemed Zola , in fact, only 'a neuropath who has long suffered from nervous complaints' (p. 119).[7] In Toulouse's full report of his anthropometric, craniometric and genealogical investigation, there was a bizarre preface where the novelist spoke of his own brain as encased in glass and fearlessly offered it as a public exhibit.[8] This confidence in his

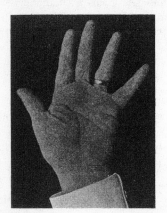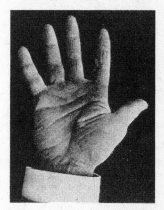

1 and 2   The medico-psychological investigation of Zola, from Toulouse, *Emile Zola. Enquête médico-psychologique sur la supériorité intellectuelle*

[7] Cf. Zola's own much earlier self-diagnosis, as recorded in the Goncourts' *Journal* (3 June 1872): 'Zola came to lunch and said: "look at the ways my fingers tremble!" And he told me of an incipient heart disease, of a possible bladder ailment, of a threat of rheumatism in the joints. Never have men of letters seemed more stillborn than in our day, and yet never have they worked harder or more incessantly. Sickly and neurotic as he is, Zola works every day from nine until half past twelve and from three until eight.' Baldick, *Pages*, p. 199.

[8] Toulouse, *Emile Zola*, p. vi. 'Mon cerveau est comme dans un crâne de verre, je l'ai donné à tous et je ne crains pas que tous viennent y lire.')

own transparency was hardly justified by the formidably dense statistics which followed. The inquiry had been, in the view of the American criminologist MacDonald, 'the most thorough [yet] made of an individual in society',[9] and covered Zola's ancestry, childhood and adult medical history. It revealed the strange intestinal pains which plagued him from the age of twenty to forty, the cystitis which afflicted him from forty-five to fifty, the cardiac problems which he suffered from the age of thirty-five – the same time that 'morbid ideas made their appearance'.[10] There were sections on his mental evolution, numerous charts, diagrams and measurements; there were illustrations of the shape of Zola's hand, finger prints, circulatory organs, respiration, digestive apparatus, muscular system, nervous system, sensation and perception, memory, attention and reaction time, ideas, emotivity, sentiments, morbidity, will and writing.[11] Toulouse also canvassed the opinions of other experts, the result of which is summed up by MacDonald:

Magnan classes him among those degenerates who though possessing brilliant faculties, have more or less mental defects ... Toulouse says he has never seen an obsessed or impulsive person who was so well balanced. Yet Zola is a neuropath, that is a man whose nervous system is painful. Heredity seems to have caused this tendency, and constant intellectual work to have affected the health of his nervous tissues. Now, it is a question whether this neuropathical condition is not an excitation that has given rise to the intellectual ability of Zola. Whether a diseased nervous system is a *necessary* cause of great talent or genius is another question; yet pathological facts have been such constant concomitants of great talent and genius that the relation seems to be more than a temporal one and suggests the idea of cause and effect.[12]

Zola's fascination with science stemmed, it seemed to Toulouse, from his hereditary condition. Toulouse's diagnosis was mild-mannered, however, when compared with Nordau's vitriolic diatribe against Zola and the Medan Group: 'Does he think that his novels are serious documents from which science can borrow facts? What childish folly! Science can have nothing to do with fiction.'[13] But it was as much Zola's hesitation as his appropriations which threatened 'science'. At points in Zola's novels, the explanatory certitude of the social pathologist was undermined. As the next section seeks to show, a kind of hesitation can be felt sometimes, cutting against the grain of the medical positivism simultaneously espoused, unsettling the scientific assurance of the accusing subject.

[9] MacDonald, *Study*, p. 467.   [10] MacDonald, *Study*, p. 469.
[11] See Toulouse, *Emile Zola, passim*.   [12] MacDonald, *Study*, p. 484.
[13] *Degeneration*, p. 489; cf. ch. 6, 'Zola and his school'.

FROM DOCTOR TO PATIENT

The cry from the heart of the positivist age runs thus: if one could only believe scientifically in immortality. (Barthes)[14]

The title *Dr Pascal*, the final work in Zola's twenty-volume Rougon-Macquart cycle, connotes at once medicine and religious philosophy, something of the conjuncture of faiths which informed the author's own famous transposition of medical credentials to the novel:

It will often be but necessary for me to replace the word 'doctor' by the word 'novelist' to make my meaning clear and to give it the rigidity of a scientific truth.[15]

Pascal's role as doctor and experimentalist appears to free him from his family name, Rougon. Asked to explain his own place on the huge family tree he has compiled, Pascal claims a kind of neutrality.[16]

His studied refusal to recognise his surname, the force of his family's past in his own identity, leads to a dangerous delusion. Pascal's dispassionate inquiry rules out introspection as unscientific. He views his own family as a mere historical document, as though it has nothing to do with him. The belief that the title 'Doctor' can displace the surname, freeing the subject from the psycho-pathological inheritance of the family, leads Pascal back into a deluded positivist imaginary outside desire and division, where language simply resolves all needs and demands. Enthralled by the physical sciences, he is shown to be unconscious of his own subjectivity, the conflicts and splits which constitute his very identity.

Pascal spent years collecting, collating, analysing the history and the degeneration of the – his – family. But it is a knowledge he is forced to conceal, above all from a mother determined to destroy his research and thereby to exonerate the name of the family:

---

[14] 'Poe's "Valdemar"', p. 140.
[15] Zola, *Experimental Novel*, p. 101.
[16] 'Me? Oh! what is the use of speaking of me? I don't belong to the family. You can see what is written there. "Pascal born in 1813. Innateness. A combination in which the physical and moral characteristics of the parents are so blended that nothing of them appears manifest in the offspring."' 'These words came from him like a cry of relief ... "Yes", he added, "folks make no mistake about it. Have you ever heard the townspeople call me Pascal Rougon? No they have never called me otherwise than mere Dr Pascal."' (*Dr Pascal*, pp. 130–1)

No! no such thing as a family would be possible should people begin dissecting and analysing this and that – the nerves of one, and the muscles of another. It would disgust one with life. (p. 18)

He hides all his documents in an enormous locked cupboard.[17] In her quest to wrest away the manuscripts, those blue-prints, as it were, of Zola's novels, Madame Rougon is supported by her son's woman servant and by Clotilde, his niece. There is indeed a conspiracy to wrest away the scientific secrets of the novel. Pascal doggedly proceeded, however, faithful to the hereditarian paradigm of his 'science':

He had started from the two principles of invention and imitation: heredity or reproduction on the basis of similarity; innateness or reproduction on the basis of diversity ... He had gone by degrees from the gemmules and pan-genesis of Darwin to the peri-genesis of Haeckel, taking Galton's stirps on the way. (pp. 35–6)

Pascal discovers that heredity does not involve a transmission of identical features from generation to generation (the dominant thesis of Prosper Lucas[18]), but a complex chain of differences in the real world. The theory of resemblance was

upset by living facts. Heredity, instead of being resemblance, was but an effort toward resemblance, counteracted by circumstances and surroundings. (p. 37)

Dr Pascal, whose subtle researches on dead ancestors have blinded him to his own implication in the 'tragedy' of the family he documents, only comes to know the existence of his sexual identity when he is caught up in a scandalous love-affair with his niece, Clotilde. Only then does his dispassionate pursuit of science collapse. Clotilde, we are told, is almost his daughter: a child 'whom his brother had confided to him, whom he had reared paternally and who had now become a temptress' (p. 167). The explosion of their reciprocal desire draws him away from a science which

[17] Cf. Zola who, when advised that two of his letters were being put up for auction, professed himself unmoved and quite disinclined to prevent the sale despite his earlier view that Flaubert's niece should be discouraged from publishing her dead uncle's letters. In his own case, he said, 'I have no secrets, the keys are in the cupboard locks; my letters can be published one day, they won't belie any of my friendships nor any of my assertions.' Quoted by Hemmings, 'Review', (per.), p. 396.

[18] Lucas, *Traité philosophique et physiologique*.

has involved the negation of all passion. (One might recall, of course, Zola's own 'paternal' passion for a young woman late in his life.[19] Or indeed, take the hint of the protagonist's name, and remember Comte's passion for Clotilde de Vaux.[20])

A rush of blood was making his temples beat ... His vision of regal youth had taken shape ... Then he was afraid lest he might catch her in his arms and kiss her wildly, madly ... (p. 166)

Early in the novel, Pascal's beliefs are differentiated from Clotilde's. Whilst he is religiously faithful to his science, she worships 'the Unknowable' and reproaches him for sowing seeds of doubt. To her wish for certainties, he replies:

'You are impatient,' ... 'if ten centuries be necessary, one must wait for them ... we have reached that turning-point, the end of the century, wearied, enervated by the frightful mass of knowledge that the century has stirred and sifted. And now the everlasting need of lies, the everlasting need of illusions, is again tormenting humanity and leading it backward to the lulling charm of the Unknown.' (pp. 89–93)

Dr Pascal represents the crisis of Zola's naturalism. It constitutes in a sense 'that turning point' for the novelist, at 'the end of the century, wearied, enervated by the frightful mass of knowledge'. The novel dramatises a late-nineteenth-century intersection of positivism, mysticism, naturalism and Catholicism. The confrontation of these faiths culminates in the troubled representation of sexuality and indeed the unsettling of any claim to a fully 'dispassionate' position. The novel, it could be said, subverts the Zola, naturalist novelist *par excellence*, who in *The Experimental Novel* (1880) had embraced Claude Bernard's dream of pure

---

[19] Zola's liaison with a young laundress, Jeanne Rozerot began in 1888. *Dr Pascal* was dedicated to her.

[20] Comte had married Caroline Masson and later called this tie the 'only capital error of my whole life'. They separated four times altogether, first in 1826 and finally in 1842, after which their relations became ever more acrimonious. His relationship with Clotilde de Vaux lasted only a year. She died in 1846 at the age of thirty. Having begun by offering her 'the affection of an older brother', Comte was soon complaining of insomnia resulting from thinking about her. He became ill and depressed, lamented the baseness of men, suffered a nervous breakdown similar to that which precipitated his earlier suicide attempt. He signed his letter 'your devoted husband', whilst she replied to 'her tender father'. See Wright, *Religion*, p. 13.

empiricism.[21] The position of detached genealogist is analysed in the novel, disclosed as an alienation of the self (albeit plenitude is soon recuperated by the final sentimental portrayal of Clotilde as the embodiment of a regeneratory motherhood and the intermittent image of France as a world with 'plenty of life in her yet', p. 101). Pascal is shown to be nothing but the final twist in the history of 'the degenerate family' he charts. The novel itself then, continually twists around, at once questioning and endorsing hereditary determinism. Pascal's *hubris*, after all, is exposed by heredity itself – *dégénérescence* brings him down. The doctor is not wrong to chart the lineage of degeneration, only wrong to place himself beyond its reach.

Despite the obscurity of heredity ('so dim, so vast and fathomless, like all the sciences which are yet immature, lisping but their first words, and over which imagination still reigns supreme', p. 38), and the sordid genealogical history he uncovers so close to home, Pascal had been initially heartened by his investigations, convinced that medicine could find the means of regenerating an ailing humanity:

a long study that he had made of the supposed hereditary character of phthisis had lately revived within him his failing faith in the healing art, and at the same time, imbued him with the wild but noble hope of regenerating humanity. ... [after investigations in alchemy] [a] vast hope opened out before him ... he fancied that he had discovered the universal panacea, the elixir of life, which was to stamp out human debility. (pp. 38–40)

Dr Pascal ends 'optimistically', concluding the Rougon-Macquart cycle with a happy ending – the vision of motherhood beyond Pascal's death. But the terms of that optimism involved calling into question a scientific discourse on degeneration which had by now projected the social narrative into very bleak representations.

Just as Pascal denies his own hereditary condition, so the novel projects its image of Clotilde and her baby beyond its own morbid genealogy,

---

[21] On Bernard's own dreams of a neutral science of politics based on his own experimental methods, see Olmsted and Olmsted, *Claude Bernard*, p. 170. In Bernard's notebook (*Pensées*, 1865–9) there are various comments on politics and history which are very close to Zola's conceptions as discussed here. Thus Bernard wrote:

Even politics should become experimental some day, but it would have to be an observational science first, and it is not even that yet. Even when it grasps the laws of political and historical phenomena, it will not be able to control them.

It will be able to attain this end only by *physical* procedures, by controlling diet, hygiene; it will render individuals moral. (*Claude Bernard*, p. 170)

Or again:

The civilisation of a nation is a movement toward death. The upper classes do not go down again. There must always be primitive or barbarous men who become civilised and rise. If this renewal does not take place, society dies like an organism deprived of cellular renewal. (*Claude Bernard*, p. 171)

beyond the degeneration which Zola's cycle has shown to be all-pervasive. Through this rhetorical delimitation, degeneration can be conceptualised as finally cathartic. But in the interim of the novel, between its beginning (images of the diligent scientist, Enlightenment, Civilisation), and ending (Clotilde, Motherhood, Nature, Regeneration) passion explodes. Pascal's desire is fraught with dangers, inevitably caught up in the bad blood of the family.

His death in one sense marks the end of degeneration. But origins and endings are uncanny in Zola – as though, despite his passion for scientific exactitude, the periodisation of pathology given in contemporary mental medicine will not do. In Zola, the unease about the limits of *dégénérescence* is also an unease about the limits of the national crisis: can the decline of France be confined to any dates or held within any historical limits: 1789, 1793, 1830, 1848, 1851, 1871 . . . ? Members of each generation of the family are born before a series of key dates: Tante Dide in 1768 – before 1789, Madame Rougon in 1792 – before 1793, Pascal in 1812 – before the end of the First Empire, Clotilde in 1847 – before 1848.[22] Yet the decadence of the family and France exceeds those births and years.

The sickly Maurice is overwhelmed by these issues in *The Debacle* (*Le Débâcle*, 1892), the novel which charts the Franco-Prussian War and the Commune:

The degeneration of his race, which explained how France, virtuous with the grandfathers, could be beaten in the time of their grandsons, weighed down on his heart like a hereditary disease growing steadily worse and leading to inevitable destruction when the hour came. (p. 322)

Maurice is overtaken by madness and joins the Communards. Yet his companion Jean remains a 'wise peasant', rooted to the land, property and France. The image of the healthy peasant is salvaged here in *The Debacle* from the morass of corruption, misery and degeneration with which Zola had earlier surrounded rural life in *The Earth* (*La Terre*, 1887):

And there the two of them stood facing each other for several seconds, one worked up by the fit of madness that was infecting the whole of Paris, a malady of long standing with its roots in the evil ferment of the previous reign, the other strong in his common sense and ignorance, still healthy from having grown up far-away from all this, in the land of hard work and thrift. (p. 470)

It was the healthy part of France, the reasonable, solid, peasant part, the part which had stayed closest to the land, that was putting an end to the silly, crazy part which had been spoilt by the Empire, unhinged by dreams and debauches. And France

[22] See Granet, *Le Temps trouvé*, p. 29.

had to cut into her own flesh and tear out her vitals hardly knowing what she was doing. But the blood-bath was necessary, and it had to be French blood, the unspeakable holocaust, the living sacrifice in the purifying fire. Now she had climbed the hill of Calvary to the most horrible of agonies, the nation was being crucified, atoning for her sins and about to be born again. (p. 504)

In *La Bête humaine* (1890) Jacques is also haunted by the question of the source of his own malady. He speculates ever more anxiously and helplessly on the distant ancestral crime which still constrains his will. It seems ever clearer to him that the origin of his depravity is bound up with some long-lost feminine crime:

Did it come from the remote past, some malady with which women had infected his race ... passed down from male to male since the first betrayal in the depths of some cave?[23]

The train which forms the continuing motif of the novel, focusses that obsession with communication, circulation, destination. The railway is implicitly linked to Zola's narrative project, the body and the lineage of heredity.[24]

This narrative is freighted with crimes, a train of interlocking transgressions, moving towards the final image of the novel: a driverless locomotive that 'roared on and on' (p. 336), bearing drunken soldiers to the disasters of the Franco-Prussian War to be charted in *The Debacle*.

France is trapped by a destiny of defeat; the individuals are fixated by the inheritance of their own bodies and the imprisoning fascination of others:

Still without letting go of [Severine], [Roubard] looked closely into her face, he seemed to be fascinated and held there as if he were trying to trace in the blood of her tiny blue veins everything she had admitted. (p. 39)

In the end, however, it is Jacques, not Roubard, who murders Severine. The novel charts his hopeless attempt to flee from the hereditary curse which hangs over him.

At certain times he could clearly feel this hereditary taint ... [There were] sudden attacks of instability in his being, like cracks or holes through which his personality seemed to leak away. (p. 66)

Jacques becomes a kind of automaton, a prisoner of his own inherited madness, driven by the instincts of his body:

---

[23] *La Bête humaine*, p. 67.

[24] '[The train] like a huge body, a gigantic creature lying across the land, with its head in Paris and joints all along the line, limbs spreading out in branch lines, feet and hands at Le Havre and other terminal towns. On and on it went, soulless and triumphant, on to the future with a mathematical straightness and deliberate ignorance of the rest of human life on either side, unseen but always tenaciously alive – eternal passion and eternal crime.' (p. 58)

At such times he lost all control of himself and just obeyed his muscles, the wild beast inside him. . . . He was coming to think that he was paying for others, fathers, grandfathers who had drunk, generations of drunkards, that he had their blood, tainted with a slow poison and a bestiality that dragged him back to the woman-devouring savages in the forests. (p. 66)

Jacques is enslaved and depersonalised by the criminal pre-history he carries in his body ('[h]is body moved along, but his personality was not there', p. 239), in conflict between 'civilisation' and bestial, misogynistic discontents:

But now the sight of this white breast seized his whole attention with a sudden, inexorable fascination and with a revulsion he still consciously realised, he felt an imperious need rising in him to get the knife from the table and come back and plunge it to the hilt into this woman-flesh. (p. 237)

In the novel, Zola frequently deploys the physiognomic registers most famously associated with the Italian criminal anthropologist, Cesare Lombroso.[25] Thus the face, body, gait, can be read off like a language, to reveal atavistic nature. Floré for instance, who eventually derails the train, causing a major disaster, has 'big greenish eyes and low forehead' (p. 50); Roubard has a 'rather flat head', 'thick neck', 'eyebrows [which] met across his forehead' (p. 22). The simian features of crime write themselves on Jacques' face at the moment of murder. His 'lower jaw was thrust so far forward like that of a ravening beast, that it quite disfigured him' (p. 328). The novel has a varied cast of murderers: the passionate, jealous killer, the cold calculating poisoner, the psychopath, the woman maddened by desire, and each of them has certain physiognomic tropes. But the physical index of crime is neither infallible nor adequate. This is signified by the innocent Cabuche, with his 'powerful shoulders', 'low brow', 'huge fists', looking in short 'every inch the murderer' (pp. 123, 355).

In the Rougon-Macquart cycle, degeneration functions within and beyond the body, within and beyond the limits of a given chronology or a taxonomy of the visible. Degeneration's time and space is decipherable and ever obscure: at once the mysterious price and the antinomy of civilisation, of evolution and desire. In *Nana* (1880) degeneration becomes sexual fascination itself, continually held up as an image, but ever in excess of what can be seen. The body of Nana fails to reproduce the species, but engenders a prolific train of defeated male victims. She is portrayed as at once the castrator, *femme fatale* and harbinger of anarchy, rejoining thereby a continuing constellation of the novels and, as I will suggest below, of

[25] See below, part II.

contemporary political theories of crowds too. In that constellation, images of depraved women, political unrest, biological degeneration and the threat of levelling or homogenisation, continually run into one another:

[It] was the story of a girl descended from four or five generations of drunkards, her blood tainted by an accumulated inheritance of poverty and drink, which in her case had taken the form of a nervous derangement of the sexual instinct. She had grown up in the slums, in the gutters of Paris; and now, tall and beautiful, and as well made as a plant nurtured on a dungheap, she was avenging the paupers and outcasts of whom she was the product. With her the rottenness that was allowed to ferment among the lower classes was rising to the surface and rotting the aristocracy. She had become a force of nature, a ferment of destruction, unwittingly corrupting and disorganizing Paris between her snow-white thighs.[26]

Here the materiality of degeneration gives way to a deeper mystery of destruction: Nana's potent effect is more than the sum of her features; she symbolises the very depravity of the metropolis with its contradictory images of fixity and movement, its perpetual flux of shifting crowds.

At the beginning of *L'Assommoir* (1877), Nana's mother, Gervaise, gazes at the city crowd through a window,

dizzily watching the stream pouring through between the two squat tollbooths of the octroi, an endless stream of men, horses and carts . . . an endless procession of men going to work . . . and the throng flowed on into Paris to be continually soaked up.[27]

Gervaise and Coupeau are gradually soaked up and consumed by the city. They sink lower and lower through the metropolis, like water through a sponge. The decline is signalled by Coupeau's actual fall from a city roof: 'His body came down in a sagging curve, turned over twice and flopped into the middle of the road with the thud of a bundle of washing dropped from a great height' (p. 126). The fall is charted physically and morally across a succession of stages in which their bodies and minds are ever more pliant:

But with the joy of living he developed the joy of doing nothing, letting his body go slack and his muscles degenerate into a delicious inactivity, as if idleness, steadily gaining ground, were taking advantage of his convalescence and permeating his whole body with a tingling numbness. (p. 132)

And the smacking kiss they gave each other full on the mouth amidst the filth of her trade was a sort of first step downwards in their slow descent into squalor. (p. 152)

---

[26] *Nana*, p. 221.   [27] *L'Assommoir*, p. 24.

Coupeau ends up in the Bicêtre hospital, scrutinised by a psychiatrist, a figure like the great Parisian psychiatrist and clinical theorist of *dégénérescence*, Valentin Magnan. As Coupeau degenerates ever further towards delirium and death, the dispassionate psychiatrist asks Gervaise, 'in the hectoring manner of a police inspector': 'Did this man's father drink?' 'Did the mother drink?' 'And you drink too?' (p. 413)

From a psychiatric point of view these were certainly apposite questions: Morel for instance was quoted as saying, 'I receive insane patients daily at [the hospital], in whom I can trace back the origin of their malady to nothing else but the habitual intoxication of their parents'.[28] Alcoholism was seen to lie deep amidst the roots of *dégénérescence*.

But in the description of Coupeau's decomposition, the psychiatric theory gives way to insistent literary echoes and visual images. At the end of this Zola novel, we are offered the spectacle of the individual's degeneration towards extinction. We are shown a kind of theatre of the disintegrating material being. Like Rameau's nephew in Diderot, Coupeau's dying limbs perform a fantastic orchestral mime, frantically playing all the parts. The body is revealed as a performer which, in the wings of death itself, desires its speaking part. As though recalling Poe's Monsieur Valdemar, Coupeau seems suspended in an interminable interim of dying, subject to the ceaseless chatter of his limbs, struggling to utter the impossible performative 'I am dead':[29]

Well, the job was complete now, the tremor had run down from the arms and up from the legs, and the trunk itself was now joining in the fun! ... Giggles were running round the ribs, and the tummy was gasping as if it were bursting with laughter. Everything was joining in the dance, and no mistake! The muscles took up their positions opposite their partners, the skin vibrated like a drum, even the hairs waltzed and bowed to each other ... The dance seemed to be going on right down deep in his flesh, the very bones must be jerking about. From some remote source tremors and waves were flowing along under the skin like a river. When [Gervaise] pressed a little harder she could sense, as it were, cries of pain coming from the very marrow of his bones. (p. 420)

CROWD REGRESSION: FROM ZOLA TO BE LE BON

The women would yell and the men's teeth would be bared like the jaws of wolves ready to bite.[30]

---

[28] Quoted in *British and Foreign Medico-Chirurgical Review* (1860), p. 288.
[29] See the discussion of performatives and Poe's story in Barthes, 'Poe's "Valdemar"'.
[30] Zola, *Germinal*, p. 335.

There is a great social current which is carrying humanity to its doom, with the formula of equality which does not exist in nature, but the current is there and we cannot escape it.[31]

Biology, politics, history continuously intersected one another in later-nineteenth-century naturalist writing. Thus the very title of Zola's *Germinal* cross-referenced the issue of reproduction and the Revolutionary calendar, bringing those two images to bear upon a violent social conflict in later-nineteenth-century France, at least hinting the question of whether democracy and equality might somehow be 'against nature'. The mob of miners who rampaged through the villages and countryside of the novel evoked for contemporary readers the real violence of the times (such as the crowd murder at Decazeville[32]), but also echoed the imagery of former revolutionary excesses. Moreover these connotations of past and present were linked implicitly to current evolutionary ideas, the Spencerian notion, for instance, of evolution as the passage from the homogeneous to the heterogeneous structure,[33] and, conversely, to a vision of degeneration or dissolution as the organic return to the undifferentiated state. In political terms, regression could be epitomised in Zola's novel by the image of castration as the return to the sexually and socially undifferentiated state. In a famous climactic scene of the novel, a mob of frenzied women from the striking village hunt down and castrate a man identified with the bosses:

'Doctor him like a tomcat!' ... The horrible trophy was greeted with shrill imprecations. ... They spat on it, thrusting forward their jaws, repeating in a furious outburst of contempt: 'He can't do it now!! He can't do it now! It isn't even a man they've got left to shove in the ground'. (pp. 351–2)

The strike had driven the community to desperation and unleashed primitive instincts: 'All the old Flemish blood was there, thick and placid, taking months to warm up, but then working itself up to unspeakable cruelties . . . until the beast in them was sated with atrocities' (p. 341). The crowd threatened the return of the primitive, but also the revolutionary past:

Yes, one night the people would break loose and hurtle like this along the roads, dripping with bourgeois blood, waving severed heads and scattering gold from rifled safes. (p. 335)

---

[31] Bernard, *Pensées*, quoted in Olmsted and Olmsted, *Claude Bernard*, p. 171.

[32] On the murder of Watrin by 2,000 miners in January 1886 at Decazeville which preoccupied such crowd theorists as Le Bon, Tarde, Sighele and Fournial (several sources claimed the women castrated him), see Barrows, *Distorting Mirrors*, pp. 20–1.

[33] See Peel, *Herbert Spencer*.

The image of castration is particularly significant; the strikers seek to sever the productivity of the bosses and the women extend that to severing the reproductive capacity of a particularly hated oppressor. Whilst in fact 'female castration' constituted a real potential medical response to the putative hysteria and insanity of women,[34] male castration was cast here as the genuine menace, the very image of national sterility, extinction and chaos.

If we are to understand this scene in Zola historically, it is not enough simply to allude to the writer's personal fantasy. Indeed we need briefly to turn from the novel, and situate the scene within a broader late-nineteenth-century iconography, thus to show a wider investment of political meaning in the image of castration. Women, shown to be a crucial agent of degeneration either (in various eugenic views) by bringing new pathological cases into the world or (in neo-Malthusian literature) by failing to reproduce in sufficient quantity healthy children for the nation, were also seen as peculiarly violent and atavistic in gatherings.

In a piece on the sexual iconography of 1848,[35] Neil Hertz has drawn attention to various of Freud's observations on castration, which can perhaps usefully be cited here too. Thus in a piece on 'Fetishism' in 1927, Freud considered castration and the terror he imagined the little boy felt when he first discovered his mother had no penis, because 'if a woman had been castrated, then his own possession of a penis was in danger; and against that there rose in rebellion the portion of his narcissism which Nature has, as a precaution, attached to the particular organ'. Freud then adds: 'In later life grown men may experience similar panic when the cry goes up that Throne and Altar are in danger . . .'[36] The loss of stability and identity at the political level potentially intersected with a deep-seated infantile panic about castration. One may question the universality of Freud's formulation here and again when he writes in 'Medusa's Head', '[t]o decapitate = to castrate. The terror of Medusa is thus a terror of castration that is linked to the sight of something.'[37] But certainly in our period, when the nation appeared so chronically endangered, there was a kind of figurative 'cathexis' between such political and sexual terms which is quite evident in contemporary representation.[38] Sexual conduct and the

---

[34] See Nordau, *De la Castration de la femme*, 1882; cf. Alexander, 'Administration', (diss.), p. 175.

[35] Hertz, *End of the Line*, ch. 9.

[36] Freud, *Fetishism*, p. 153.

[37] Freud, *Medusa's Head*, p. 273.

[38] In the conclusion to *Marianne into Battle* (1981) Agulhon asks what it would mean to investigate the 'linguistic gender' of France as it had been deployed in nineteenth-century political discourse. He comes at the end, in short, to a question which his account of

consequences of human reproduction, after all, were seen to be critical political issues, since they involved the potential bio-social degradation of France. The aim here is succinctly to contextualise that nexus of images and its relation to the historiography of the Revolution in some late-nine-teenth-century writing on crowds.

Gustave Le Bon, a notorious misogynist, medical doctor, anthropologist, populiser of science[39] (best-known today perhaps via the references in Freud's *Group Psychology*) lauded Taine, but acknowledged his failure to abstract historical facts into a wider social science.[40] Taine, he wrote, had thus been unable to reach the deepest level implicit in his study of revolution – the crowd in itself. Le Bon dabbled in a wide world of contemporary science, psychiatry and anthropology; he attended Charcot's lectures on hysteria and was a keen contributor to the Parisian Society of Anthropology and its journal.[41] Le Bon also ventured into the field of craniometry where he found men's brains bigger than women's and 'civilised' brains bigger than those of 'savages'.[42] From Charcot's hysterics, Broca's skulls and a variety of other contemporary scientific projects, Le Bon began to speculate on the image and the essence, the evolutionary anthropology and the innate psychology, of the crowd. In various of his popular works, the crowd became the centre of a putatively scientific attention. It was endowed with a psychology, depicted as an ominous force unsettling the stability of the individual by connecting each member with a crowd of primitive ancestors. The crowd embodied the vicissitudes of racial history,

revolutionary iconography has hitherto scrupulously avoided. What sexual connotations were provoked, he asks, in the very gender of 'une Republique' or 'un Royaume'? He abandons such questions immediately upon asking them, as though in the end their pursuit would be nothing short of embarrassing: 'The sex of a Nation! . . . One can imagine how far up the garden path of socio-psycho-analytical meditation one could be led if one pursued that track. We must admit that we would put no great faith in such a venture, believing that to apply categories of individual psychology to collective concepts could lead one to make the mistake of taking metaphors for realities. To remain on the level of generally accepted facts, we would simply point out that the nineteenth century was marked by an extreme inequality between the sexes, that women were much despised and that, in a period which we might today call 'phallocratic', the fact that the Republic was personified as Marianne was a considerable handicap for it.' (p. 185) The last sentences are perhaps anodyne, but more damagingly Agulhon has polarised 'individual psychology' and 'collective concepts' in such a way as to by-pass the question of a language which conceptualises both. Is it not possible indeed that the garden path of 'socio-psycho-analytical meditation' may prove a royal road to the further analysis of political discourses past and present? Such meditation carries risks of essentialism (and hence the continual need for historical specification), but the material in the present discussion cannot be understood unless one proceeds on a number of levels and with sensitivity to psychoanalytic insights.

[39] On Le Bon, see Nye, *Origins*; Barrows, *Distorting Mirrors*.
[40] See McClelland, 'Aspects', (diss.), p. 213.
[41] See Nye, *Origins*, pp. 30–3.
[42] See Nye, *Origins*, pp. 30–3.

expressing no less than 'the unconscious aspirations and needs of the race'.[43]

Where Taine had offered a 'psychopathology of history', Le Bon developed a sociological and psychological conception of the crowd as the place of inevitable regression. The expressed aim was to instruct politicians in the defence of the social order against mass democracy, syndicalism and anarchism under the Third Republic.[44] Hence the sub-title of Le Bon's *Political Psychology* was *Social Defence*.

It was essential, argued Le Bon, to recognise the given conditions of modern society. Romantic denunciations of modernity were futile. France was today – whatever the paradox – a crowd civilisation. Le Bon always rejected ruling-class fatalism in the face of this undoubted degeneration:

The future is indeed within us and is woven by ourselves. Not being fixed, like the Past, it can be transformed by our own efforts.[45]

Whilst the laws of the crowd were pre-determined (crowds were never the authors of their own actions), an elite could manoeuvre society to its conscious political design, thereby shaping the future. An analogy was made to the relationship of the hypnotist and the woman subject.[46]

This strategy of government entailed recognition of certain first principles; crowds, like magnetised subjects, instinctively sought leaders. Yet usually the crowd's leader had 'himself been hypnotised by the idea, whose apostle he has since become'.[47] The crowd was atavistic in its behaviour – a throw back to the evolutionary past of the individuals who composed it. The leader was usually a degenerate, recruited from 'the ranks of those morbidly nervous, excitable, half-deranged persons who are bordering on madness'.[48]

Le Bon insisted that the very act of gathering in a group constituted a moral and evolutionary decline. Revolutions in general, and the French Revolution in particular, exemplified that descent. Le Bon warned of the danger of historical repetition, the 'repetition compulsion' of revolution.

[43] Le Bon, *The Crowd*, p. 200. Cf. Borie, *Mythologies*, p. 180, on the move from the language of heredity to the language of the racial unconscious. Note Le Bon's early work on inheritance and reproduction, Le Bon, *Physiologie*. My argument is that the discourse of crowd science was in fact inextricably enmeshed in a nineteenth-century language of, and set of assumptions about, inheritance, pathology, reproduction, degeneration and evolution.
[44] See Nye, *Origins*; Barrows, *Distorting Mirrors*.
[45] Le Bon, *World Unbalanced*, p. 12.
[46] Le Bon, *The Crowd*, p. 118.
[47] *The Crowd*, p. 118.
[48] *The Crowd*, p. 119.

'If the Commune of 1871 had endured', he declared ominously, it would have 'repeated the Terror'.[49] All revolutions were 'a return' to barbarism (p. 652); socialism was 'a regression' to the past. (p. 653)

The crowd was not just an aggregate of people in a geographical space; it was also the point of connection between present and past – between the individual and a vast array of ancestors. The crowd inverted the law of evolution and moved from present to past. Instead of individual development, it tended towards homogeneity: 'personal characteristics vanish in the crowd'.[50]

Nevertheless Le Bon also argued that the crowd's psychology was characteristically feminine: like 'women it goes at once to extremes'.[51] This perception of the crowd as feminine (in accordance with its linguistic gender, 'la foule') constituted a significant part of the image. Within the tradition of French positivism and within the late-nineteenth-century context of an emerging women's movement, it inverted the earlier Comtean faith in the proletariat and women as sources of future progress.[52] From the late nineteenth century, French alarmist debates about the decline of the birth rate interacted with fears about the rise of feminism. The notion of a 'grève des ventres', a womb-strike by women protesting against their subordination to the species function (and the putative national duty) of reproduction, was picked up in the neo-Malthusian literature as a symbol of the current demographic crisis of underpopulation and of the social decadence which accompanied and fostered it.[53] Le Bon conflated the crowd and women; he developed an argument to be found throughout nineteenth-century medicine regarding women's psychological and physiological sensitivity to civil strife.[54] Social disorder exacerbated the constitutional and emotional differences of the sexes, pointing up the weakness, hysteria and dangerousness of women.

Women were seen by Le Bon and Tarde, the other best-known French crowd theorist of the late-nineteenth century, as not only the passive victims, but also the active agents of revolutionary disorder. From the image of the *tricoteuses* of the 1790s, to the *petroleuses* of 1871, women were cast as the quintessential embodiment of political anarchy:

---

49 'Psychologie', (per.), p. 652.
50 Le Bon, *Psychology*, p. 103.
51 *Crowd*, p. 35.
52 On Comte's belief that proletarians and women were the allies of positivism, see Therborn, *Science*, p. 190; cf. Leroy, *Histoire des idées*, III, ch. xii. But on Comte's fear of premature revolution see III, p. 237. Comte insisted that intellectual differences between the sexes were fundamental and inalienable (III, p. 243).
53 See Ronsin, *La Grève*.
54 See Alexander, 'Administration', (diss.), ch. 4, 'The psychiatric conception of a woman's nature and role'.

by its routine caprice, ... its credulity, its excitability, its rapid leaps from fury to tenderness, from exasperation to bursts of laughter, the crowd is woman, even when it is composed, as almost always happens, of masculine elements.[55]

Revolution, in its desperate bid for equality, in fact dramatised for these social scientists, the inalienable fact of difference, between classes, sexes and individuals. The emancipation of women, argued Le Bon, would run against this differential descent of the sexes upon which civilisation was based.[56] It would amount inevitably to social regression. 'Democracy' in any form indeed tended to pull civilisation towards the primitive 'homogeneity' from which, like an organism, it had slowly differentiated itself.[57]

Although the discussion in part II traces differences between French and Italian theories of degeneration, nevertheless for the Italian social scientists, the emancipation of women seemed equally imprudent. Many of Lombroso's supporters emphasised the fact that women were always at a more backward point of intellectual development than men.[58] According to one disciple, Scipio Sighele, women committed less crime than men, but when they did, they were 'more cruel, brutal and depraved than men'.[59] Women were innately extreme creatures ('either angels or demons'[60]) and by their very nature rushed to the vanguard of disorder. As Lombroso put it

in revolutions, women become terribly infuriated, if they manage to stir themselves at all. In 1789, women always took the side of revolt, and the most ferocious revolt at that ... In 1799, the women of Naples, inflamed by an epidemic of passion, descended even to cannabalism; they traded and ate the flesh of the republicans as had the women of Palermo in the insurrection of 1866.[61]

On the one hand the crowd was referred to female psychology, on the other hand, it was likened to a neuter or neutering force. The function of a science of the crowd was precisely to deflect that force, to neutralise the dangers it posed to the individual and society.

The image of revolution, the crowd and threatening, castrating sexuality converged in the imagery of these texts. The crowd in society, like the woman in reproduction, 'held unknowingly in its hands the fate of the world'.[62] Sighele wondered whether in modern society, there was not in fact a 'neuter form' of human being, caught between the masculine and the feminine, 'amphibians of the human world'. The 'modern', 'independent'

---

[55] Tarde, *L'Opinion*, p. 195.   [56] See Barrows, *Distorting Mirrors*, ch. 2.
[57] Herbert Spencer viewed women's relation to men as analogous to savages' relation to civilisation. On Le Bon's debt to Spencer see Barrows, *Distorting Mirrors*.
[58] See Gallini, *La sonnambula*, p. 284.
[59] Sighele, *La donna nova*, p. 17.
[60] *La donna nova*, p. 19; cf. Gallini, *La sonnambula*, p. 305.
[61] Lombroso, *La donna delinquente*, p. 59.   [62] Sighele, *L'intelligenza*, p. 3.

woman, he lamented, had 'horribly deteriorated' when compared with Christ's Magdalene.[63] The struggle for suffrage and civil rights were intrinsically absurd, he added.[64] Women were victims and agents of biological and historical degeneration. Sighele arrived at the overwhelming recognition that

> [the crowd's] role is awesome, immense, but passive. In relation to what is called civilisation, it has been like the fecund woman whose love sustains and rewards work ... Its anonymous glory has always been that of procreating, unknown to itself, the genius which then enrichens it ... but taking the other side of the coin, the crowd has been neither wife nor mother, but only woman, and most often its role has been that of crucifying saviours.[65]

Of course, the attribution of cruelty, intellectual inferiority and nervousness to women has a long and complex history, running back through European literature to classical mythology. And certainly the connection between the French Revolution and feminine depravity was not a late-nineteenth-century invention, nor an exclusively Continental idea. Burke in 1790 for instance had described the procession of captive royalty from Versailles to Paris 'amidst the horrid yells, and shrilling screams and frantic dances ... of the furies of hell, in the abused shape of the vilest of women'.[66] In much conservative English writing during the nineteenth century, France appeared to anticipate England's potential fate. In such imagery, France was often cast as sexually double – at once threatening to 'penetrate' and infiltrate beyond its borders, and yet perceived as quintessentially passive in the face of its own self-engendered despoliation.

In France itself medical and sociological discourses in the later part of the century placed the theme and the trauma of revolution in a schema of evolution and degeneration; the body was seen as the crucial point of intersection between history and biology. The rhythms of the body were related to the perceived recurrence of historical events. According to some commentators the 'periodicity' of the female body had a particular relation to social atavism, the relapse into 'blood letting' and anarchy; women were seen as peculiarly cruel and irrational during menstruation.[67] Part of the

---

[63] *La donna nova*, p. 173.   [64] *La donna nova*, p. 189.
[65] *L'intelligenza*, pp. 3–4.   [66] Burke, *Reflections*, p. 165.
[67] See for instance Lombroso and Ferrero, *Female Offender*, p. 222. On menstruation and madness see Morel, *Etudes cliniques*, I, pp. 236ff, 271–306; on the pathological circulation of various fluids (e.g. blood, sperm, saliva, urine) see I, pp. 428–47; cf. Lucas, *Traité philosophique et physiologique*, II, p. 916; on 'menstruation and puberty', see Le Bon, *Physiologie*; see also Barrows, *Distorting Mirrors*, 58.

   In England cf. the view of one commentator addressing the Anthropological Society in London in the late-1860s: 'It is not improbable that instances of feminine cruelty (which startle us as inconsistent with the normal gentleness of the sex) are attributable to mental excitement caused by this periodic illness' (Allen, 'Real differences', per., p. cxcix). Or

extraordinary obsession with hysteria in late-nineteenth-century French culture was certainly bound up with these perceptions of society as a racial body repeatedly troubled and convulsed by a pre-history it could never repress nor fully remember. Nordau again provides a stark quotation:

To this general cause of contemporary pathological phenomena, one may be added special to France. By the frightful loss of blood which the body of the French people suffered during the twenty years of the Napoleonic wars, by the violent moral upheavals to which they were subjected in the great Revolution and during the imperial epic, they found themselves exceedingly ill-prepared for the impact of the great discoveries of the century, and sustained by these a more violent shock than other nations more robust and more capable of resistance. Upon this nation, nervously strained and predestined to morbid derangement, there broke the awful catastrophe of 1870.[68]

Recent studies of late-nineteenth-century crowd psychology in France[69] have stressed the relation of Le Bon's and Tarde's work to the politics of mass democracy in the Third Republic. I have not endeavoured here to reiterate their detailed social-historical contextualisation of crowd theory in the face of Boulangism, the Dreyfus Affair, anarchist bombings and the emergence of revolutionary syndicalism, but have simply emphasised some discursive continuities in the sexual-political conception of degeneration from Zola to Le Bon.

From Morel in the 1850s to the crowd theorists of the end of the century, the degeneracy of 'the people' was conceived as nexus of past and present: at once embodying the corruptions of a certain modern society (industry, the city, toxins, noise, speed and so on) and representing a mere front-line concealing an infinite multitude of ancestors. Moreover just as every human subject was composed of an incalculable union of cells, so the crowd was an amalgamation of units into one 'organism'. The reproduction of the body across time and the revolution of the people at a given moment were bound up in an infinitely complex ensemble which, so it seemed, demanded the formation of new kinds of investigation.

The move from a Morel to a Le Bon marks an important shift of emphasis from the degenerate individual or family to the crowd, or rather to crowd civilisation. Yet in both representations, history was conceived as

---

cf. Havelock Ellis, *Man and Woman*, ch. 11, 'The functional periodicity of women': 'While a man may be said, at all events relatively, to live on a plane, a woman always lives on the upward or downward slope of a curve.' (p. 284) And again 'on the psychic side, even in good health [women display]... greater impressionability, greater suggestibility and more or less diminished self control' (p. 290); 'whenever a woman commits a deed of criminal violence it is extremely probable that she is at her monthly period' (p. 292); cf. Showalter, 'Victorian Women', pp. 322–3.

[68] *Degeneration*, p. 42.
[69] Nye, *Origins*; Barrows, *Distorting Mirrors*.

a morbid racial movement from revolution to revolution and body to body. Morel's *dégénérescence* ended in the condition of sterility; the representation of the crowd theorists characteristically ended in the image of castration, cannibalism, mutilation, homogeneity. Sexual and political anxieties were brought together in such writing, only to be displaced and disavowed by the 'disinterested' narrator. There is no better illustration of the simultaneous conflation and negation of those anxieties at stake in so much nineteenth-century naturalism than this entry in the Goncourts' *Journal* on Bastille Day, July 14 1883:

I dreamt last night that I was at a party, in white tie. At that party, I saw a woman come in, and recognised her as an actress in a boulevard theatre, but without being able to put a name to her face. She was draped in a scarf, and I noticed only that she was completely naked when she hopped onto the table, where two or three girls were having tea. Then she started to dance, and while she was dancing took steps that showed her private parts armed with the most terrible jaws one could imagine, opening and closing, exposing a set of teeth. The spectacle had no erotic effect on me, except to fill me with an atrocious jealousy, and to give me a ferocious desire to possess myself of her teeth – just as I am beginning to lose all my good ones. *Where the devil could such an outlandish dream come from? It's got nothing to do with the taking of the Bastille!*[70]

[70] *Journal*, pp. 45–6, emphasis added; cf. Gay, *Bourgeois Experience*, pp. 198–9.

4

The wake of *dégénérescence*

The early 1870s had brought a flood of works in France whose very titles evoked the sense of political impotence and national catastrophe: *La Fin du monde latin, 1871! Les Premières Phases d'une décadence, Des Causes de la décadence française, La Chute de la France, République ou décadence?, La France dégénérée*.[1] The defeat of the Second Empire had not even involved a coalition of European powers, as had been the case in 1815. War in 1870 had been followed by the Commune. To writers like Taine and Le Bon in the last quarter of the century, that demise was only comprehensible through the optic of racial-historical degeneration. Durkheim, a very different writer, was also captivated by the medical analogy of sickness and health, and indeed by scientific models in general. As Stephen Lukes tells us, he was attracted 'far more than any of his interpreters have realized by the language of "collective forces" and "social currents" and in general, the analogy of thermodynamics and electricity'.[2] Durkheim perceived 1870, year of defeat, as the moment of inception of a sociology[3] in which certain pathologies of 'hypercivilisation' were opened up to investigation.

Durkheim used new categories of heredity, pathology and nervousness such as neurasthenia[4] to explain social phenomena, and above all the vexed question of the forces and limits of social solidarity.[5] It was felt to be an urgent task in the troubled socio-political world of the Third Republic. Durkheim, like Taine, rejected the idea of the abstract individual to be found in classical economics, and insisted that people were to be studied in relation to the 'collective conscience' generated in society.[6] Yet the society

---

[1] See Swart, *Sense of Decadence*, p. 124. [2] *Durkheim*, p. 35.
[3] *Durkheim*, p. 396.
[4] On neurasthenia, see Ellenberger, *Discovery*, p. 243; Nye, 'Medical Model', p. 58.
[5] See Nye, *Crime*, pp. 152–4; Hirst, *Durkheim, Bernard and Epistemology*, ch. 4; cf. Durkheim's declaration in *Suicide* that 'it is not because a society possesses more or less neuropaths or alcoholics, that it has more or less suicides ... *dégénérescence* in its different forms constitutes an eminently suitable psychological terrain for the causes which make a man decide to kill himself ... Admittedly, in identical circumstances the degenerate kills himself more easily than the healthy subject' (*Le Suicide*, p. 53).'
[6] See Lukes, *Durkheim*, pp. 4–5.

itself was abstracted in his work into normal and malignant realms, which indeed could only be distinguished through a science of social pathology.[7]

Durkheim's critique of individualism, which can only be briefly mentioned here, may be seen as one late, important variant of a wider set of organicist discourses with a very complex nineteenth-century history.[8] A crucial earlier point of development can be traced in the counter-revolutionary reaction (notably in the work of de Bonald and de Maistre[9]), but such language was also taken up in a plurality of interlocking socio-political theories across the first half of the century – Saint-Simonianism, social Catholicism, socialism and positivism.[10] Morel's conception of degeneration in the 1850s engaged with those discourses. But it also provided a new medical model with which to oppose individualism. By the 1870s and 1880s, *dégénérescence* informed a multitude of arguments and social representations. Robert Nye has shown the extraordinary pervasiveness of the medical model of national decline in political debates and social movements in the Third Republic.[11] Campaigns against syphilis and prostitution in an epoch increasingly haunted by its supposed relatively declining birth rate owed much to the anxieties about the degeneration of motherhood, family life and reproduction.[12] From Jaurès to Maurras, political discourse was obsessed by the question of national defeat and the ensuing chaos; the issue of alcoholism, habitual crime, and depravity were cast through the image of a social organism whose capacity for regeneration was in question.[13] National defeat, degeneration and social pathology appeared to be caught up in an endless reciprocal exchange. Thus it was said that of every one hundred male participants in the 18 March insurrection in 1871, twenty-five were recidivists and twenty-five of every hundred women were prostitutes.[14] Dreyfusards and anti-Dreyfusards of the 1890s interpreted the crisis in terms of France's putative trajectory towards either degeneration or regeneration.[15] They saw the patterns either of an advance or decline towards republicanism. Maurras, one of the new leaders of the Right was convinced that he witnessed France's decadence and racial debasement.[16] The threat was cast as both internal (notably the corrosive

---

[7] *Durkheim*, p. 28.   [8] See Leroy, *Histoire des idées*, ii.
[9] Leroy, *Histoire des idées*, II, ch. 3; cf. Swart, *Sense of Decadence*, p. 50.
[10] See Leroy, *Histoire des idées*, ii, ch. 7; cf. Manuel, *Prophets*.
[11] Nye, *Crime*.
[12] See Nye, *Crime*, pp. 160–1; cf. Winter and Teitelbaum, *Fear*.
[13] See Nye, *Crime*, pp. 155–7.   [14] See Nye, *Crime*, p. 74.
[15] See Nye, *Crime*, pp. 297–9; cf. Soltau, *French Political Thought*, p. 367.
[16] See Curtis, *Three Against*, ch. 6.

effect of the Jews) and external (the continual menace of foreign corruption). Barrès and Sorel, for all their differences, shared a conviction that France was suffering from 'lack of energy' and bloodlessness.[17] For Barrès this could only be grasped and counteracted through homage to the dreadful world of the dead, through the ancestors who transmitted 'the accumulated heritage of their souls'.[18] Society should recognise 'the law of eternal decomposition'.[19] The dead were the soil, and therefore to be hallowed. Each act which 'denies our earth and our dead means a lie which sterilizes us'.[20] Barrès described himself as 'an advocate of the dead', a connoisseur of cemeteries in Venice, Toledo, Sparta, Persia, and above all Lorraine.[21]

Across the whole political spectrum, abstract individualism was interrogated. The very theory and rationale of punishment was reconceived in these decades in the influential work of Renouvier as the rights of an organism to protect itself from attack.[22] The language oscillated between a physical determinism (which Renouvier officially denounced) and a voluntarist social contract, albeit increasingly hedged in by biological precautions.[23]

The 1870s and 1880s saw *dégénérescence* elaborated into a complex nosological system in the clinic and disseminated as the very currency of social and political debate.[24] Valentin Magnan, the psychiatrist of Zola's *L'Assommoir*, enjoyed a highly successful Parisian career which in itself bore witness to the double impact of the discourse – its increasing specification and sophistication within psychiatry[25] and its social generalisation as a supposedly wide-spread phenomenon of the age. Magnan aimed to use evolutionary theory to free *dégénérescence* from the Catholicism which still pervaded it in Morel.[26] Magnan's version of *dégénérescence* had a powerful impact, speaking to the hopes and fears of Parisian culture in the wake of France's military defeat and social turmoil. His teaching at the St-Anne Hospital was acclaimed and his interventions at the Medico-Psychological Society given great attention. Up until his death in 1916 he was still admired by students and devotees.[27]

Psychiatry came to an unprecedented cultural prominence in late-nine-teenth-century Paris as was exemplified most famously in the celebrated

[17] Curtis, *Three Against*, ch. 6.   [18] Barrès, *Amori*, p. 278.
[19] Barrès, *Amori*, p. 279.   [20] Barrès, *Amori*, p. 278.
[21] Curtis, *Three Against*, p. 113.
[22] See Nye, *Crime*, p. 69.   [23] *Crime*, p. 69.
[24] Harris, 'Murders and madness', (diss.), p. 95; Dowbiggin, 'Degeneration and Hereditarianism'; Martin, 'La Dégénérescence', (diss.) II, pp. 266–8.
[25] See Borie, *Mythologies*, p. 154.
[26] See ch. 2 above.   [27] See Drusch, 'Entre deux discours', (diss.).

Tuesday lectures of Charcot at the Salpêtrière and in his grand banquets for politicians, artists, scientists and princes.[28] Certain hysterics, according to Charcot, were caught up in complex networks of pathological inheritance, Zolaesque narratives of morbid transformation.[29]

Hereditarianism here should not be understood as excluding environmentalism. French culture had long remained wedded to a Lamarckian paradigm which assumed the reproduction of acquired characteristics.[30] For complex reasons (which have been the subject of much recent scholarship[31]), French culture and science were notoriously slow in accepting Darwin's theory of selection, or even in acknowledging the importance of his work. As I shall show later in the discussion of Lombroso, French and Italian criminologists parted company over the question of environmental determination. A crude version of Darwinism was used by Lombroso to insist that many criminals were immutable atavists;[32] the dominant strain in French thought insisted in often explicitly Lamarckian terms, on the continuing interaction of heredity and milieu and hence the impossibility and immorality of complete fatalism.[33] But even here the issue is more complex; first, Darwin himself and many of his followers were Lamarckian at least in certain of their assumptions,[34] notwithstanding the crucially non-Lamarckian key assumption of 'natural selection'. Nor were the issues of environmentalism and heredity definitely settled by Weismann's theory of the germ plasm.[35] Even Mendelism was to be the scene of conflict, dispute, varying possible socio-biological theories.[36] Second, French theories of heredity often produced confusingly contradictory

[28] On Charcot see for instance Ellenberger, *Discovery*; Sulloway, *Freud, Biologist*; Didi-Huberman, *Invention*; Goldstein, *Console*.
[29] 'Quioqu'il en soit dans sa famille, il n'y a pas à signaler d'autres cas semblables, au sien, il n'y a donc pas lieu de relever ici le caractère d'hérédité similaire, mais on peut, par contre, invoquer l'hérédité de transformation. Son père était atteint de gravelle, représentant ainsi l'infusion arthritique si fréquente dans les familles nerveuses, mais voici qui est plus topique. Une grand' tante maternelle a été aliénée, il a une soeur qui est hystérique et sa mére, quoiqu'elle n'ait pas eu de maladie bien personnifiée, etait extrêmement irritable et sujette à souffrir de douleurs neuralgiques très intenses siégeant à la tete.' (Charcot, *Leçons du Mardi*, p. 416)
[30] See Conry, *L'Introduction*, and L. L. Clark, *Social Darwinism*. Note Darwin complained in February 1863 that his work had 'produced no effect whatever in France' (quoted in Clark, *Social Darwinism*, p. 10). Only in 1878, after six times rejecting him, did the French Academy of Sciences elect him a corresponding member of its botany section (but not its zoology section) (see *Social Darwinism*, p. 11).
[31] See Conry, *L'Introduction*; L. L. Clark, *Social Darwinism*; Corsi and Weindling, 'Reception'.
[32] See part II below.
[33] See Nye, *Crime* and part II below.
[34] On Darwin's theory of pan-genesis and its Lamarckian connotations, see George, *Darwin*.
[35] See Szreter, 'Decline', (diss.); Nye, 'Medical Model', p. 58; *Crime*, p. 164; Harris, 'Murders and Madness', (diss.), p. 96.
[36] See Schneider, 'Toward the improvement', (per.).

connotations in relation to the environment. Thus in Morel, the environment was continually adduced as a key factor in degeneration, but nevertheless a sense comes through in the *Treatise* of the decisive immutability of the degenerate family tree, its remorseless journey towards extinction. In short to trace out differences in the later-nineteenth century in terms of a radical bi-polarity of Darwinism and Lamarckianism raises as many questions as it resolves. By the 1870s Darwinism's impact was certainly being registered in French psychiatry and other human sciences. Its eventual assimilation in one way reinforced the fatalistic aspect of the conception of *dégénérescence*. But Lamarckianism still underpinned the language of eugenic projects in the early-twentieth century. A French Eugenics Society was founded shortly after the first international congress had been held in London in July 1912. Despite Weismann's theory of the indestructibility of the germ plasm and the rediscovery of Mendelism, most eugenists strongly believed that 'superior' and 'inferior' acquired characteristics could be passed on directly.

Nevertheless by the 1890s, the critique of *dégénérescence* was gathering pace. Many doctors and psychiatrists from both France and abroad, including the young Freud, treated the model with a new caution and scepticism, whilst terms like neurasthenia and hysteria were attributed with many of its reasonances. The word was slowly losing its specificity and its mystique, its point of difference from heredity in general, in serious medicine and psychiatry.[37] That critique was exemplified in the second edition of the Paris medical psychiatrist Benjamin Ball's *Leçons sur les maladies mentales* in 1890. Ball acknowledged the 'seductive' appeal of the theory of *dégénérescence*; but under critical analysis, he argued, it in fact dissolved into a 'series of hypotheses without proof and of assertions without authority'.[38] He was careful to avoid making the false connections which, in his view, bedevilled the work of many of his colleagues. Thus, for instance, to establish a link between the city and madness was not to say that the city produced madness – since perhaps a disproportionate number of the mad were drawn to the city (p. 375). The number of the mad, he noted, was always dependent on the vagaries of the method of counting (p. 372). Nevertheless despite such qualifications, he agreed that civilisation probably had increased madness and that this was usually transmitted hereditarily. But Morel's specific version of *dégénérescence*, he maintained, was no longer credible; nor was the work of Magnan and his followers capable of superseding the fundamentally jumbled theory on which it

---

[37] See Martin, 'La Dégénérescence', (diss.) II, p. 277. On a similar process of critique and dissolution of the word 'degeneration' in Italy, see Nicasi, 'Il germe della follia', p. 318.
[38] Ball, *Leçons*, p. 998.

depended. Ball spoke of the 'abuse of language' and the deep and systematic confusion of the general with the particular (pp. 370, 993–7). What had occurred was 'a veritable usurpation of the rights of the clinic for the benefit of a preconceived idea' (p. 997). Ball offered this ironic refutation of Magnan's infinitely flexible diagnoses of *dégénérescence*:

... every degenerate can present each feature one after another; today a dipsomaniac, tomorrow a pyromaniac. Hazard, that anti-scientific divinity, seems to preside over the course of this curious malady. (p. 995)

That ridicule perhaps anticipated a wider 'evaporation' of certain forms of pessimistic language in French culture. Koenraad Swart in *The Sense of Decadence* (1964), a compendium of the idea of decadence in nineteenth-century France, describes the gradual dissolution of gloomy themes in the ten years preceding the outbreak of World War I. He notes the revived nationalism which followed the Tangiers crisis in 1905 and the Agadir incident of 1911. By 1912 and 1913, the rebirth of French nationalism had become the topic of the day; '[m]ilitary and patriotic themes suddenly became fashionable in novels, plays, and songs'.[39]

In 1912 Henri Bergson declared that he was impressed by the numerous manifestations of French moral regeneration.[40] In a similarly optimistic vein, the Abbé Ernest Dimnet wrote a book in the last weeks preceding the outbreak of war, which blamed France's former misfortunes on the 'baneful philosophy' and the 'lawless literature' which had originated in the Second Empire and had then found its fullest expression in the works of a naturalistic novelist like Zola and 'a decadent poet' like Mallarmé. He held the nihilistic mentality responsible for the defeat of 1870 and for the persistent weakness of France after the war, when the spirit of materialism and scientism had been elevated to government policy. From 1876 to 1905 France had rapidly declined under a political system which disclosed no consistent principle other than anti-clericalism. Against this gloomy background the author portrayed the miraculous revival of the nation since 1905.[41]

Dégénérescence had emerged in and identified itself with, an intellectual world of positivism and scientism which was now under attack. Yet even in the early twentieth century critique of evolutionary positivism mounted by, for example, Henri Bergson, we see some strange debts to degenerationism. In the early stages of his intellectual career, Bergson had been a follower of Herbert Spencer, the great Victorian evolutionary philosopher. He admired him for his constant effort to stay close to empirical material

---

[39] Swart, *Sense of Decadence*, pp. 193–4.
[40] *Sense of Decadence*, p. 202.   [41] *Sense of Decadence*, p. 202.

and for his imaginative attempt to make evolution the principle of philosophical thinking. But he soon felt disappointed in Spencer for his inability to grasp the specificity and the irreducibility of life forces.[42] Bergson's critique of 'adaptation' centred precisely on this notion of an inherent life force, which, he argued, certainly had to adapt in order to survive, but which was always radically in excess of the mere history of its adaptations:

It is quite evident that a species would disappear, should it fail to bend to the conditions of existence which are imposed on it. But it is one thing to recognise the outer circumstances are forces evolution must reckon with, another to claim that they are the directing causes of evolution ... The truth is that adaptation explains the sinuosities of the movement of evolution, but not its general directions, still less the movement itself.[43]

Metaphysics, he argued, sought to enter into this inherent life force, to pass beyond the relative process of adaptation and differentiation. This led him to the seemingly startling proposition that metaphysics, not evolutionary materialism, was *'the science which claims to dispense with symbols'*.[44] Rationalism, he wrote, like empiricism 'remains equally powerless to reach the inner self ... it considers psychical states as so many fragments detached from an ego that binds them together' (p. 28). Bergson's truly 'intuitive philosophy' would be a distillation of metaphysics and positive science (it 'would put more science into metaphysics and more metaphysics into science', p. 63). This vision of an irreducible life force was used to refute an evolutionary determinism which saw every choice as nothing but the triumph of the strongest mental force over the weakest in an ineluctable 'struggle'.[45] Evolution, he argued, could not be conceived as the passage through time of a predictable process. Interestingly, however, and very much to our purpose here since it shows one further turn in the language of degeneration, its appropriation in the process of a critique on evolutionism, Bergson used the model of evolutionary regression to refute a deterministic progressivism. The human species, he argued, 'represents the culminating point of the evolution of the vertebrates'; on the other hand, 'a group of species that has appeared late may be a group of degenerates; but, for that, some special cause of retrogression must have intervened'.[46] Or, as he wrote earlier on in the same volume:

We have supposed, for the sake of simplicity, that each species received the impulsion in order to pass it on to others, and that in every direction in which life evolves, the propagation is in a straight line. But, as a matter of fact, there are species which are arrested; there are some that retrogress ... Thence results an increasing disorder. No doubt there is progress, if progress means a continual advance in the

---

[42] See Kolakowski, *Bergson*, p. 13.   [43] Bergson, *Creative Evolution*, p. 107.
[44] Bergson, *Introduction to Metaphysics*, p. 8.   [45] See Kolakowski, *Bergson*, pp. 19–20.
[46] *Creative Evolution*, p. 141.

general direction determined by a first impulsion; but this progress is accomplished only on the two or three great lines of evolution on which forms ever more and more complex, ever more and more high [sic] appear; between these lines run a crowd of minor paths in which, on the contrary, deviations, arrests, and set-backs are multiplied. (pp. 109–10)

The point is not to insist that Bergson's language was really identical to Morel's or Magnan's; but to suggest that the very critique of scientism and evolutionism here was caught up partially in the same assumptions.[47] An organic theory of degeneration refracted in myriad ways through late-nineteenth-century culture. As Curtis has observed, political nomenclature in general was subject to continually shifting nuances in this period: 'Terminology undergoes a constant change of meaning. To trace the word *progressiste* from 1885 to 1906 is to witness a political somersault from a left-wing group to a conservative group supporting clericalism'.[48] To trace the word *dégénérescence* from the 1850s to the 1890s, one might add, is to witness a somersault from the language and the crisis of social Catholicism, liberalism and socialism under the Second Empire, to the idioms of republican anti-clericalism, positivism, naturalism and explicitly counter-revolutionary polemic after 1870–1871; but it is also to witness the remarkable tenacity of the model as such. Perhaps it is not so strange then that in the 1890s, Georges Sorel, the 'revolutionary', should share with Taine, the counter-revolutionary, a profound admiration for Cesare Lombroso, the criminal anthropologist who had written out – and written off – the distinctive persona of the atavist.

Sorel moved spectacularly across the political spectrum. As Zeldin puts it, he was one of the 'precursors of the floating voter': 'Marxism, syndicalism, royalism, fascism, bolshevism, excited him one after the other'.[49] His thought has of course been claimed by both Left and Right,[50] often in a fruitless attempt to singularise what was always 'the methodological, scientific, epistemological and ethical pluralism that pervades his work' (p. 15). How else indeed, other than in terms of a very curious political trajectory,

---

[47] Cf. Hughes, *Consciousness*, p. 118, on Bergson's late work: 'To put it uncharitably, it was a kind of majestic biological fantasy ... it equated intuition with the animal world and postulated an all-pervading vital impulse, an *élan vital* that came "gushing out unceasingly ... from an immense reservoir of life"'. One might compare in this sense the evolutionism of the Oxford ethical school in Britain, see Freeden, *New Liberalism*; Collini, *Liberalism*. Cf. Ritchie's acknowledgement that 'Degeneration enters in as well as progress' (*Darwinism and Politics*, p. 16). He pleaded for cooperation: ... 'if we are still reminded that only through struggle can mankind attain any good thing, let us remember that there is a struggle from which we can never altogether escape – the struggle *against* nature, including the blind forces of human passion' (p. 100). 'May we not hope that by degrees this mutual conflict will be turned into mutual help?' (p. 101)

[48] Curtis, *Three Against*, p. 5.

[49] Zeldin's foreword to Jennings, *Georges Sorel*, p. vii.　　　[50] *Georges Sorel*, p. 1.

could we understand Sorel's eulogies to Lombroso, so soon before he was to develop, via Bergson, a critique of the mechanistic and deterministic aspects of Marxism and to endorse the radical freedom of the will, the uniqueness of the individual? We need to answer this question not only in relation to Sorel's 'personal eclecticism', but also in relation to the deep ambiguities in the language of degeneration from Morel to Lombroso.

In the 1890s Sorel was still committed to the notion that Marxism was ultimately and directly 'scientific' (p. 42). He criticised the French theory of *dégénérescence* for its vagueness and its parochialism; indeed, he argued, despite the vituperative attacks it had suffered, Lombroso's Italian work on atavism improved on the French concept.[51] Moreover it confirmed Sorel's own belief in the inferiority of women and blacks.[52] Science, he said, in a piece quoting Magnan, Nordau, Lombroso and Zola, showed that women were closer to children, less evolved and frequently the victims of other intellectual infirmities. (p. 466) Lombroso had proved how remarkably few women displayed the signs (stigmata) of degeneration. But this was precisely because they lagged behind; they were less involved in the flux of evolutionary process and hence bore fewer of the potential telling signs of degeneration. (p. 466) Women were more likely to be victims of the 'law of inertia'. If this evolutionary backwardness was natural to women, then prostitution, he thought, could be called their most natural unnaturalness. The prostitute's nature was 'erotic', hence a transgression of natural femininity. But prostitution was also emblematic of women – their most typical choice of depravity. Prostitution, wrote Sorel, was indeed the essence of female crime, because it marked the peculiar nature of women's primitivism. Where a savage man might have become a bandit, the savage woman would become a prostitute who should rightly be excluded from society (p. 467).

This series of articles in the French *Scientific Review*, is astonishing from a writer now associated with the critique of scientism, and the denunciation of bourgeois illusions of progress and the justification of violence.[53] In the 1890s Sorel accepted the Lombrosian link between the rebel and the criminal.[54] Crowds, he wrote, always have a large criminal element at times of revolution. Moreover successful revolutions naturally repeated themselves through time, just as criminal crowds naturally grew larger in volume. 'Terror' played the largest role in the acts of the crowd, and the

---

[51] Sorel, 'La Crime politique', (per.), pp. 208–9. But note the deployment of the word *dégénérescence* in Sorel, *Réflexions*, p. 109: '*dégénérescence* of the capitalist economy' ('dégénérescence de l'economie capitaliste'; 'cette dégénérescence . . .'); in the same work he could write that there was no real scientific way of predicting the future (p. 176).

[52] See Sorel, 'La Crime politique', (per.), p. 466; cf. Jennings, *George Sorel*, p. 40.

[53] See Sorel, *Illusions*; cf. Jennings, *Georges Sorel*, p. 126; Kolakowski, *Bergson*, p. 101.

[54] See Sorel, 'La Crime politique', (per.), p. 564.

individual was reduced to a frightened beast.[55] In the crowd, Sorel contended in the same passage, women were particularly ferocious.

Sorel defended Lombroso from a critique which (as we shall see below) was being levelled at him from delegates at the International Congresses of Criminal Anthropology. Sorel sympathised with Lombroso's dilemma – caught between legal classicists who accused him of over-emphasising, and determinists who charged him with underestimating, heredity (p. 208). The Italian, he insisted, had inaugurated a science through which 'the true criminal' could be distinguished from the sick and the abnormal (p. 209). Here lay the means of isolating those delinquents who were capable of regeneration through a regime of work, from the hopeless cases (p. 209).

Amidst the twists and turns of the vast literature on degeneration, one aim in the present discussion has been to show how one comes back repeatedly to what appears to be an inherent structure of contradiction, two different trajectories in the conception of degeneration. On the one hand, the 'experts' desired to isolate a social threat – to reveal, transport, castrate and segregate 'noxious elements'. On the other hand, it seemed that degeneration lay everywhere, demanding massive campaigns of public hygiene, the closer investigation of whole populations. The shared problematic of degeneration across the period could perhaps be summarised as follows: was degeneration separable from the history of progress (to be coded as 'regression', 'atavism' or 'primitivism'), or did it reveal that the city, progress, civilisation and modernity were paradoxically, the very agents of decline? These key questions and contradictions were at issue in French, Italian and English texts. They cut across the various figures explored here in some detail. But this is not to argue for a static model, a rigid structure informing every debate. Rather it is to see recurrent and *shared* discursive tensions, continually inflected, specified, re-formulated in *different* social and political contexts: shared in so far as Europe by the later-nineteenth century had a common political, scientific and literary culture: different insofar as England, France and Italy were always radically distinct societies – the loci of separable histories and historiographies.

[55] ('[O]n peut déjà dire que la terreur joue le plus grand rôle dans ces actes. Dans la foule, l'homme a peur; il a le vertige, d'autant plus facilement qu'il est d'un tempérament plus faible; il perd la direction de sa volonté; il resemble à un félin; il déchire sa victime, comme le fait une bête affolée par la peur', 'La Crime politique', p. 564.)

5

Lombroso's criminal science

ATAVISM AND ANARCHY

You have shown us lubricious and ferocious orangutans with human faces; certainly, being such they can act no other way; if they rape, steal, and kill, it is invariably on account of their nature and their past. The more reason for us to destroy them as soon as one is sure that they are and will remain orangutans. On this account I have no objection to the death penalty if society finds profit in it.[1]

This passage was contained in a letter addressed by Taine to the Italian criminal anthropologist, Cesare Lombroso in 1887 and subsequently published in the preface to the 1895 French edition of *Criminal Man*.

Taine's support was no doubt welcome; two years earlier at the International Congress of Criminal Anthropology, Lombroso had come under sustained criticism from the French delegates, because of his fatalistic view of the delinquent.[2] The adoption of the Italian approach to crime, argued Lacassagne, one of the leaders of the French group, would mean for jurists and legislators 'to do nothing but cross their arms, or construct prisons in which to gather these misshapen creatures'.[3]

Part II investigates the terms of Lombroso's fatalism. It compares the 'positivist' school of criminal science with 'classical' theories of punishment and draws out certain differences between Italian and French positivist language. Focussing on the conception of degeneration and atavism in a newly founded 'criminal anthropology', it suggests the terms of Lombroso's master-narrative of crime, disorder and anarchy, his relentless search for unification.

To say that Lombroso's theories of crime, like all others, were inextricably connected with the particular political world in which they emerged, is by now perhaps to express a critical commonplace. The designation of the criminal is, of course, bound up, in complex ways, with the opposing but reciprocal process of defining the good citizen, or the good subject, in specific societies, in particular periods. In Joseph Conrad's *The Secret Agent* (1907), Karl Yundt, one of the anarchists, made the point

---

[1] Lombroso, *L'Homme criminel*, I, pp. ii–iii. [2] See the discussion below, pp. 139ff.
[3] *Actes* (First Congress), 1885, p. 165.

when he ventured the following damning view of Lombroso and the new 'science' of criminology which had developed in the later-nineteenth century:

'Lombroso is an ass.'
Comrade Ossipon met the shock of this blasphemy by an awful, vacant stare. And the other, his extinguished eyes without gleams blackening the deep shadows under the great, bony forehead, mumbled ... 'Did you ever see such an idiot? For him the criminal is the prisoner. Simple, is it not? What about those who shut him up there – forced him in there? Exactly. Forced him in there. And what is crime? Does he know that, this imbecile who has made his way in this world of gorged fools by looking at the ears and teeth of a lot of poor, luckless devils? Teeth and ears mark the criminal? Do they? And what about the law that marks him still better – the pretty branding instrument invented by the overfed to protect themselves against the hungry? Red-hot applications on their vile skins – hey? Can't you smell and hear from here the thick hide of the people burn and sizzle? That's how criminals are made for your Lombrosos to write their silly stuff about.'[4]

But, although the point is often accepted in principle, the precise terms and implications of Lombroso's ideology in the period have rarely been analysed in subsequent critique, at least outside Italy.[5] How do we understand the relation between Italian society and the discourse which Lombroso produced? The importance of criminal anthropology extends way beyond the particular culture of post-unification Italy; but we cannot simply by-pass that context, if we are to understand this work historically and politically. It is only in relation to the perceived crises of 'the Peninsula' that we can begin to analyse the ideas of this 'imbecile who has made his way in a world of gorged fools'.

Whilst Lombroso enjoys at present a certain notoriety, there exists very little serious social historical analysis in English of his highly influential theories of crime. In the existing secondary literature on deviance and the history of criminology, almost no attention is given to the Italian context of Lombroso's work. He is either 'the pioneer of modern criminology', to be revered for his insights despite the failings of his methodology (the initial view of Radzinowicz for instance[6]), or alternatively a crank who wrote 'silly stuff' about criminals with malformed heads. Either way he is quickly despatched. He serves as a curious footnote to late-nineteenth-century literary studies – there are the famous references to him in, for instance, Conrad, Tolstoy and Bram Stoker,[7] and he was an important inspiration for Max Nordau who dedicated *Degeneration* to Lombroso. Recent pol-

---

[4] *The Secret Agent*, p. 47.
[5] For some recent Italian perspectives see, for instance, Bonuzzi, 'Economia politica', (per.); Bernart and Tricarico, 'Per una rilettura', (per.); Villa, 'Scienza medica'; *Il deviante*.
[6] See for instance Radzinowicz, 'Lombroso', (per.)
[7] *The Secret Agent*, ch. 3; *Resurrection*, pp. 402–3; *Dracula*, p. 342.

emics against scientific reductionism in such books as Taylor *et al.*'s *The New Criminology*, Gould's *The Mismeasure of Man* and Rose *et al.*'s *Not in our Genes*, invoke him as a crude and extreme exponent of biological determinism – the pseudo-scientist *par excellence*, a kind of metaphor for an aberrant tradition. Lombroso is of course the sinister measurer of skulls: sinister, but then again sometimes invested with a certain antiquarian charm – something out of the world of Madame Tussaud's.

Lombroso's theories, however, were not simply eccentric nor aberrant. In the specific historical context in which they were first articulated, they did indeed 'make sense', they spoke powerfully to a particular crisis, and provided a new language of social representation. Positivist criminology had important ramifications within post-unification Italian politics generally – and even, too, within late-nineteenth-century socialism. Moreover, there are significant connections to be made between Lombroso's school, and various fascist projects and debates of the 1920s and 1930s.

A progressive critique of Lombroso's positivist criminology and its language of degeneration must engage with the historical world in which the discipline emerged. I will try to show the coherence and credibility of Lombroso's work on social evolution, atavism, degeneration in later-nineteenth-century Italy; the ways in which his research responded to, and was constrained by, the discursive concerns and political pressures of that time and place.

Cesare Lombroso was born in Verona in 1835, the son of Zefora Levi and Aronne Lombroso. Initially well-to-do, his family's wealth slowly dwindled, due apparently to Aronne's poor management of money. The family had lived in North Italy for many generations, within the sizeable Jewish community to be found across both Lombardy and the Veneto. One of Zefora's cousins David Levi, was a Mazzinian activist, and as such was a source of inspiration and fascination for the young Cesare.[8]

At the age of fifteen, whilst still at school, Cesare's interest in Italian history was revealed in two precocious journal articles on the Roman Republic and on early agriculture,[9] the first of the enormous output of publications to follow. As a student, however, Lombroso studied medicine at Pavia, beginning work there in 1852. After two years he moved to Padua, then to Vienna and finally back to Pavia.[10] He was drawn to French and

---

[8] For biographical information see Antonini, *I precursori*; Lombroso Fererro, *Cesare Lombroso*; Wolfgang, 'Cesare Lombroso'; Bulferetti, *Lombroso*; Colombo, *La scienza infelice*; Levra (ed.), *La Scienza*; Villa, *Il deviante*. For a detailed biography of Lombroso's writings, see Paola and Gina Lombroso, *Cesare Lombroso*, pp. 215–30.

[9] Lombroso, 'Saggio sullo studio', (per.), and 'Schizzi', (per.).

[10] See Villa, *Il deviante*, p. 105.

Italian positivism, German materialism and English evolutionism, and away from prevailing philosophical doctrines of free will then current in certain Italian academic circles. Lombroso was soon clear about his intellectual hostility to the still-dominant classical theory of crime and punishment developed a hundred years earlier in Pavia by Cesare Beccaria. Whatever its secular credentials in principle, classical theory dove-tailed in practice with a religious notion of free will and responsibility for sin. It may well be that for the Jewish Lombroso, the anti-Catholic strain of Italian positivism held a particular and immediate attraction.[11] Lombroso's racial background was perhaps a factor in the hostility with which church, aristocracy and certain sections of the Torinese bourgeoisie greeted his work, but there were other palpable political and ideological reasons for this mutual suspicion as well.

It has been shown elsewhere how Darwinism encompassed and quickly overran the relatively weak tradition of physical science in 1860s Italy; it was rapidly applied to wider historical and political fields.[12] Certainly, by the 1860s and 1870s, Lombroso, amongst others, was not slow to see the implications of physical anthropology and evolution for contemporary Italian society. His conception of evolution was not Darwinian as such (although he did read Darwin[13]), but a conflation of contemporary biological and anthropological ideas from many authors, such as Moleschott (whose *The Circulation of Life* Lombroso translated from German into Italian[14]), Morel, Haeckel, Broca and Spencer.[15] But in a sense any quest for a 'pure' Darwinian affiliation in this period is an historical anachronism. Darwin himself, after all, was, for much of the time, 'Lamarckian', not to mention an admirer of Haeckel, Spencer and Galton.[16] On the

---

[11] See Lombroso's research on anti-semitism, *L'antisemitismo*.

[12] See Landucci, 'Darwinismo', pp. 110–14; Pancaldi, 'Darwinismo ed evoluzionismo', especially pp. 155, 176, 203; Giacobini and Panattoni (eds.), *Il Darwinismo*. The first translation of *The Origin of Species* appeared in 1864 by Canestrini and Salimbeni. The wider debate about the issue of the human place in evolution became more dramatically charged with a much publicised lecture by Filippo De Filippi in Turin in 1864. In 1863, Huxley's *Man's Place in Nature* and Lyell's *The Antiquity of Man* had appeared and both were soon circulating in France and Italy. Huxley's book was translated into Italian in 1869 (see Pancaldi, 'Darwinismo ed evoluzionismo', pp. 155, 175–6); for a comparison of Darwinism's reception in Italy, France and Germany, see Corsi and Weindling, 'Darwinism'; cf. Paul, 'Religion and Darwinism', which contrasts the power Catholicism was able to wield in Spain against Darwinism with its relative impotence in Italy. Neither was the Italian Church able to draw so readily upon the repertoire of Lamarckian rebuttals of Darwinism which characterised the debate in France (pp. 408–9).

[13] See Bulferetti, *Lombroso*, p. 172.

[14] *La circulazione della vita*, translated by Lombroso, was published in Italy in 1869; see Cosmacini, 'Problemi', pp. 820–4.

[15] See Bulferetti, *Lombroso*, p. 172; Minuz, 'Gli intellettuali', p. 230.

[16] See below, part III.

other hand, as I shall discuss below, there were differences between Italian and French criminology which owed something to the distinction between a French Lamarckian tradition (with its stress on use-inheritance and hence environmental agency) and an Italian strand of Darwinism (stressing racial struggle, selection, elimination, regression).

In 1858 Lombroso received his medical degree at Pavia. Between 1859 and 1865, he was a volunteer doctor in the new national army and in 1862, served in the military campaign against brigandage in Calabria.[17] Like Morel some years earlier, Lombroso was interested in cretinism and pellagra which for two centuries or more had been endemic in certain parts of Italy.[18] Like Morel, Lombroso was committed to the extension of a social medicine; his early work uncertainly counterposed environmental and hereditarian explanations. Later of course he became committed to the reconstruction of an old tradition of phrenology and its application to those 'dangerously diseased' and 'degenerate' groups of the population. F. J. Gall and J. C. Spurzheim had much earlier developed phrenology from the idea that the brain was the 'organ of the mind', containing the different temperaments and emotions within defined areas whose shape lay imprinted in the form of the skull.[19] Lombroso harnessed phrenology, or rather what was now being refined into 'craniometry', to a specifically evolutionary theory of racial development. He charted the physical differences in brain and body between groups of the Italian population which he had already split-off and designated according to their social 'savagery'.

But, as we will see, the designation of savagery was hardly an uncommon response to the peasantry in this period. It was a virtual reflex of the governing castes of the North when they ventured into the rural hinterlands and especially into the South and the Islands. Indeed Lombroso's early publications on the Italian situation are striking rather for their emphasis on environmental determination and for the radical, social remedies they proposed for poverty. The primary cure for social disorder, the young doctor insisted, would be the breaking-up of large estates and the redistribution of property to the peasantry.[20] The state, he argued, should appropriate the land, since the nobility and clergy had shown themselves unfit to develop agriculture. Mere repression of the endemic unrest, Lombroso continued, would never bring long-term order; the real issues in the South were drainage, irrigation, schooling, diet, the price of medicines for

---

[17] See Bulferetti, *Lombroso*, p. 91.   [18] See Lombroso, 'Ricerche', (per.).
[19] See Young, *Mind, Brain and Adaptation*.
[20] See his writings on the South in the 1860s and 1870s, re-published in Lombroso, *In Calabria*. See especially pp. 148–51.

the poor, pollution, hygiene, the efficient construction and administration of hospitals and prisons.[21]

In 1862 he conducted anthropometrical researches on three thousand soldiers in order to investigate the ethnic diversity of the Italian people.[22] His early work, as I have indicated, stressed environmental conditions, but also the racial variation of the population. As time went on, it was as though the image of the material body in its history across generations, and the patterns of its ethnic differentiation across the society, became an obsession, gradually displacing all other considerations from the centre of Lombroso's vision. With the aid of statistics (that 'avalanche of numbers'[23] generated by the new nation), wax-works, drawings and photographs,[24] Lombroso sought to 'freeze' the processes of evolution in the body. He endeavoured to isolate the features of inherited backwardness, the burden of atavism (atavist, from the Latin *atavus*, ancestor) which plagued the state. That tension, already explored in part one, between the invisible biological danger and a science which construed the visual signs of pathology is again at issue in the Italian work, although with a rather different balance.

Northern Italians sometimes said that Calabria evoked Africa. Indeed the 'Dark Continent' was said to begin respectively at Bologna, Florence, Rome, or Naples, depending on the birth place of the speaker.[25] The South was cast as a form of other world, racially different, a space to be explored, penetrated, contained, colonised.[26] As one of Lombroso's followers, Alfredo Niceforo would later write in a work entitled *Northern Italians and Southern Italians* (1901):

Not all the parts which compose [Italy's] multiple and differentiated organism have progressed equally in the course of civilisation; some have remained behind, due to inept government or as the sad result of other factors and are unable to advance except at great effort, whilst the others have progressed dynamically. The Mezzogiorno and the Islands find themselves in the sad condition of still having the sentiments and customs, the substance if not the form – of past centuries. They

---

[21] *In Calabria*, pp. 161–3. Note that Croce despite his general hostility to Lombroso's work paid tribute to his research on pellagra which had contributed to a general medical campaign to reduce mortality rates; see Farolfi, 'Antropometria', p. 1,181.

[22] See Wolfgang, 'Cesare Lombroso', p. 175.

[23] I borrow the phrase from Hacking, 'Taming of chance', (per.).

[24] There is a huge collection of Lombroso memorabilia in the Museum of Criminal Anthropology in Turin. See Colombo, *La scienza infelice*, and Levra, *La scienza*.

[25] See Bosworth, *Italy*, p. 5.

[26] See Salvadori, *Il mito del buongoverno*; Farolfi, 'Antropometria', p. 1,204; Asor Rosa, 'La cultura', pp. 909–25 ('s'affacia il Meridione'). On the projects for producing a unified language (Manzoni, Ascoli, Carducci etc.) see Asor Rosa, 'La cultura', pp. 900–9.

are less evolved, and less civilised than the . . . [society] to be found in Northern Italy.[27]

For the intellectuals and politicans of the post-unification period in Italy, there remained a running contradiction between the achievement of nationhood, and the social realities of division and fragmentation, the myriad cultures and sub-cultures, separate languages, customs, economies, worlds in which Italy was constituted and threatened. Here lay the efficacy of Lombroso's social evolutionary model; it brought all those contradictory social processes together into an apparent discursive unity. If Lombroso's writings were dense with confusions, contradictions, evasions, they nevertheless claimed to have advanced an instrumental and scientific methodology. Crime, hysteria, superstition, parasitism, insanity, atavism, prostitution, crowds, peasantry and brigands became the circulating figures of disorder in a language which sought altogether to stave off metaphor. But these figures were never of course unmediated 'objects'. The naivety, but also the force, of this positivism lay in its attempt to deny the presence of metaphor, to imagine that by caging its shadowy images within rigid, visible taxonomies, subversion could be staved off from civil and political society. Presences designated as subversive were thus ritually conjured in order to be objectified and denounced: exorcised in language and exorcised from power.

In Asor Rosa's encyclopaedic account of 'culture' in the Einaudi history of Italy,[28] there are numerous examples of the nationalist lament for the irrationalist belief and local allegiances of the population in the period after unification. In certain commentaries, the lack of unity in the present was counterposed to the communes of the Middle Ages, when, so it was believed, society really was organic. De Sanctis, for example, in a lecture in 1872 entitled 'Science and life' declared:

The man of the Middle Ages, so very sturdy [*robustissimo*] in his feelings and imagination, in the fullness of his liberty and in the ardour of his passions, found at every step, limits which he accepted willingly, because they were not imposed with violence from outside, but were the product of his own conscience.[29]

---

[27] Niceforo, *Italiani*, pp. 3–4. In 1861 Farini stated on arrival in the kingdom of Naples as governor after its liberation by Garibaldi: 'This is not Italy! This is Africa: the bedouins are the flower of civic virtue besides these [ignorant peasants]', see Allum, *Italy – Republic without Government*, p. 8. Cf. Niceforo, *L'Italia barbara*, pp. 35, 47–53, where we are told that the brigandage of the South and of Sardinia were typical of a more primitive race, and that the infusion of Arab blood into feudal Sicily was responsible for the Mafia. Related arguments can be found in, for instance, Alongi, *La Mafia*; Niceforo, *Richerche*; *La mala vita*; Lombroso, *Delitti*; Russo and Serao, *La Camorra*; Paola Lombroso and Carrara, *Nella penombra*; Nicotri, *Rivoluzioni*; cf. Salvadori, *Il mito del buongoverno*.

[28] Asor Rosa, 'La cultura'.

[29] De Sanctis, 'La scienza e la vita', p. 322.

The Middle Ages were conceived as an epoch in which the institution of the family was strong and there was no problem about social place or roots or belief; commune civilisation was thus counterposed to a modern individualistic world; De Sanctis again:

Man lived as though rooted to his soil, to his forebears, to his house, church, class and Commune [*suo Commune*]. He was enclosed in powerful organisms [*potenti organismi*] which recalled him to the duties he had to fulfil, rather than rights to be claimed. (p. 323)

This social-organic conception of the desirable society was shared by the positivists of the North (although not in its medievalist form) and the neo-Hegelians of Naples (amongst whom De Sanctis was a central figure[30]). The comprehension of 'Italy' (in both a spatial and intellectual sense) was the common problematic of both sides. They parted company, however, over the role of modern science. In De Sanctis' view, science was irremediably symptomatic of modern liberalism and egoism. It was a charge which positivists like Lombroso took very seriously and which they were at pains to rebut. Where the neo-Hegelians searched for the 'spirit' of Italy, the Lombrosians would search for its body.

The neo-Hegelian critique of materialism had castigated science because it failed to 'cure' the social symptoms it diagnosed. In the same lecture at Naples, De Sanctis began by asking incredulously whether science was really a force of regeneration:

What can it do? ... Is to know really to be able? Is science itself life, the whole of life? Can it arrest the course of corruption and dissolution, renew the blood, harden the metal? I hear it said: nations rise through science. Can science really perform this miracle?[31]

Science indeed was deemed a catalyst of decline:

Science is the product of the mature age, it does not have the force to re-make the course of time ... Science grows at the expense of life. The more you give to thought, the more you take away from action. (p. 318)

Lombroso's work insisted that science was not a symptom of degeneration, but a means of regeneration. If he denied the validity of grand metaphysical ideas, he was nonetheless profoundly idealistic in his desire to serve the nation through the scrupulous impartiality of his social theory. Lombroso's language sought to purge itself of extravagant metaphor, to produce a pure medium of description. He counterposed the artistic expressions, handwriting, fiction, of the delinquent and the law-abiding, the

---

[30] See Asor Rosa, 'La cultura', p. 866.   [31] De Sanctis, 'La scienza e la vita', p. 317.

insane and the sane. Hundreds of examples of 'delinquent' art and writing were eventually gathered in Lombroso's Museum.[32] The history of language had deeply interested the young Lombroso. The naturalistic philology of Paolo Marzolo (1811–68), with its attempt to produce a natural history of the human being via the study of the evolution of language was particularly dear to him, as the name of his daughter, Paola Marzolo Lombroso, suggests.[33] But whilst he sought to find in language and writing an historical relation to current pathology and atavism, he imagined that his own discourse could be instrumental, freed from the partiality and subjectivity of its own past. The 'stigmata' of contemporary art and literature were meticulously listed. Thus in the fine arts, he detected,

exaggerated minuteness of detail, the abuse of symbols, inscriptions, or accessories, a preference for some one particular colour, an unrestrained passion for mere novelty [which] may approach the morbid symptoms of mattoidism.[34]

Whilst in literature and science, he discovered,

a tendency to puns and plays upon words, an excessive fondness of systems, a tendency to speak for one's self, and substitute epigram for logic, an extreme predilection for the rhythm and assonances of verse in prose writing even an exaggerated degree of originality may be considered as morbid phenomena. (pp. 359–60)[35]

If the social pathologist's language was to be transparently functional, the degenerate's language as well as much contemporary culture was merely self-revelatory, disclosing nothing but its own aberrant history. Tattooing was understood as literally the trace of a 'primitive' language on the body of the 'lower orders';[36] and the criminal's words and pictures were no less than an autobiography of warped inheritance, atavism and pathology.

[32] See Colombo, *La scienza infelice*, and Levra (ed.), *La scienza*.

[33] The young Lombroso was highly intrigued by the work of Marzolo, a medical doctor, who worked on language and contributed towards the end of his life to Cattaneo's journal *Politecnico*. Marzolo sought to reconstruct the evolution of language, bringing to light the sedimented traces of its past; see Villa, 'Scienza', pp. 1,152–3.

[34] Lombroso, *Man of Genius*, p. 359.

[35] An extraordinary range of writers were brought under scrutiny; for instance Nerval, Dostoyevsky, Hoffman, De Musset, Poe, Baudelaire, Flaubert, the Goncourts, Zola and even on occasion Darwin himself. See Gould, *Mismeasure*, p. 132; Lombroso, *Delitti*, part IV, ch. 3, 'Il delinquente ed il pazzo nel dramma e nel romanzo moderno'; Ferriani, *Delinquenti*; Mandalari, *La degenerazione*, Sighele, *La delinquenza settaria*, pp. 28–9; *L'intelligenza*; *Letteratura tragica*; *Letteratura e sociologia*; Ferri, *Arringhe e discorsi*, pp. 301–13. On Darwin as the perfect neuropath, see Lombroso, *Man of Genius*, pp. 356–7; Colp, *To be an Invalid*.

[36] See Gould, *Mismeasure*, p. 133.

Lombroso's discourse sought to comprehend Italy. But even after Italy achieved political expression, there remained the overwhelming difficulties of creating loyal political subjects and moving from regional elites to a national governing class; above all, there remained the task of realising a peasantry committed in any way to the fact and the idea of the national state. According to optimistic estimates around the period of unification, eight out of one thousand Italians spoke the national language and seventy-five percent of the population were illiterate.[37] The ruling classes were even cut off linguistically from the majority of the people. In the view of De Meis, another of the neo-Hegelians, the sovereign was of paramount importance in fashioning some kind of unity out of this fragmented cultural situation;[38] Italy was desperately in need of ideal symbolism and supervision. As he wrote in 1868:

When ... one admits into the Body Politic, not only men of the third category – the semi-uncultured [*i semi-incolti*] – but even those of the fourth, the very lowest rank, illiterate and uncouth ... then there is born the absolute need for a form of liberal, progressive and *enlightened despotism* which impedes the passions from unleashing themselves ... (pp. 58–9)

De Meis insisted that Italy could only be a democratic country when the people were fused together and civilised. For the present, one had to recognise the divisions and infinite intermediate gradations between 'ancient people' and 'modern people'. The classification was worked out in considerable detail:

no intelligence is possible between the semi-philosophic middle class and the semi-animal lowest class. But the opposition is less precise between the upper middle class (we specify, gentlemen, the semi-cultured, members of the liberal professions, so called scientists ...), and the lower middle class (we specify again: city artisans, above all industrial artisans, the noble, whether he be rich or penniless, uncultured or given to laziness, the ignorant and idle proprietor, and all the obtuse and stupid minds in general). (pp. 53–4)

In this account, the criterion for social classification turned on each individual's level of 'culture'. Nobles, for instance, could not be grouped together according to birth alone, for their place depended on education, manners, sensibility. The polarity of cultured and uncultured, however, ran over into an evolutionary opposition between higher and lower. A sense of animality was evoked especially when the peasantry were under discussion.

A major study in English, comparable to Weber's *Peasants into Frenchmen* (1976) remains to be written about the ideological process of creating

[37] See Salomone, *Italian Democracy*, p. viii; Asor Rosa, 'La cultura', pp. 839–40.
[38] De Meis, *Il sovranno*.

Italians. But certainly many of Weber's arguments could be directly transposed to the Peninsula. The book analyses the bourgeois perception of the
French peasantry in the context of the internal 'colonization' of France.
Through a veritable 'civilising' mission, under the Third Republic, the state
worked to forge the nation. Weber points out that this was a 'work in
progress', an active process of constituting national identity. He describes
the contemporary sense of linguistic and cultural disunity of and within the
regions, the myriad social divisions and contradictions which appeared to
constitute France, but also to call it into question.[39] In d'Azeglio's words
the Risorgimento had 'made Italy', but it had not 'made Italians'.[40] The
ruling classes could not but remark over and over again the enormity of the
problem, the incredible 'backwardness' of a large fraction of the population. As Cavour was to declare:

My task is more laborious and troublesome now than in the past. To constitute
Italy, to merge together the diverse elements which compose it, to bring the North
and the South into harmony, offers as many difficulties as the war with Austria and
the struggle with Rome.[41]

In the 1890s, Lombroso could only reiterate the same sad problem when
he confronted the issue of anarchism:

One would have to be blind ten times over if, comparing ourselves to Norway,
Switzerland, Belgium, we do not realise that, set against our ridiculous wish to
excel, we are the second most backward, if not the most backward amongst the
peoples of Europe with regard to morality, wealth, education, industrial activity,
agriculture, [and] justice ... We hold, instead, the first place when it comes to
uncultivated, malarial land, endemic illness ... crime and the weight of taxes.[42]

The chimera of national unity was the implicit concern of much of
Lombroso's research. Criminality was part of the problematic of 'making
Italy'. Each area appeared distinct, but also distinctly self-divided – as
Lombroso ruefully admitted: 'Even in evil, Italy is not bound together'.[43]
Reviewing twenty years of Italian legal statistics, Lombroso was convinced
that the surest conclusions of all concerned the enduring reality of regional
divisions fostered through dialects, the press, physiognomy, manners, race
and above all criminality (p. xviii). His work sought to settle the definition

---

[39] Weber, *Peasants into Frenchmen*, especially ch. 7, 'France, one and indivisible'.
[40] Clark, *Modern Italy*, p. 2.
[41] Quoted in Artom, 'Il Conte de Cavour', (per.), p. 145.
[42] Lombroso, *Gli anarchici*, 135; for similar comments by Pasquale Villari, one of the leaders
of the Italian positivist movement, see Asor Rosa, 'La cultura', p. 899.
[43] 'L'Italia, adunque, non è fusa nemmeno nel male', Lombroso's preface to Fornasari di
Verce, *La criminalità*, p. xx. Cf. the preface to Lombroso, *Sull' incremento*, which noted
the rising tide of crime which threatened to submerge civilisation. Lombroso added that his
work was inspired not by love of any sect or party, but of the country at large.

of the political subject, by fixing more clearly and inexorably those who were beyond the pale of polity and society. He endeavoured not only to turn 'peasants into Italians', but also to separate out those who were incapable of such a conversion. He saw his contribution as part of that double 'work in progress'.

Lombroso's career advanced through various hospital and university appointments. Between 1863 and 1872, he was responsible for the welfare of mental patients at hospitals in Pavia, Pesaro and Reggio Emilia. By 1876 he held a post in legal medicine and public hygiene at Turin university where he was later made professor of psychiatry in 1896 and of criminal anthropology in 1906.[44] In 1880 with Ferri and Garofalo, he founded a journal, the *Archivio di psichiatria, antropologia criminale e scienza penale*, which became an influential mouthpiece of the positivist movement. Lombroso in short was firmly installed amongst the scientific, positivistic Northern intelligentsia,[45] internationally renowned through his own publications, those of his followers, his journal and the international congresses of criminal anthropology which took place in various European capitals from 1885 until the First World War. Although Lombroso was venerated at the congresses as the great pioneer of a scientific criminology, there was intensifying criticism from foreign delegates of his grossly inconsistent methodology and extreme biological fatalism. Acrimonious debates ensued, the Italians even boycotted the third congress in Brussels,[46] but Lombroso's fame or notoriety was guaranteed, for he stood at the centre of the controversy.

Lombroso was not immune to this sustained foreign critique. He began to inflect his singular doctrine of atavism – reversion to more primitive stages of evolution – with the more complex French theory of degeneration stressing environmental corruption and the passage of pathologies across generations of the family (see above, part I). And in part this shift from the notion of atavism to degeneration reflected a growing sense of disenchantment with the whole direction of 'Italy' – the perception of an ever wider gap between the ideals of the Risorgimento and the squalid realities of political power and factionalism in the new state. 'Atavism', it could be argued, localised the problem of crime to certain distinct and immutable creatures. But Italy's problems appeared, even to the Lombrosian group, to be less and less localised. With the expansion of the cities and the social

---

[44] Wolfgang, 'Cesare Lombroso', p. 171.
[45] A list of the leading Italian positivist intellectuals compiled by Asor Rosa ('La cultura', p. 879) shows the overwhelming majority based in the North.
[46] See the letter of protest in the preface to the *Actes* (Third Congress), 1893.

problems this generated, degeneration appeared to go way beyond the issue of rural brigandage, provincialism and superstition.[47]

Nevertheless there were significant differences of emphasis between Italian and French criminal sciences up until the First World War. One should not exaggerate Lombroso's flexibility; new theories did not, on the whole, divert the course of Lombroso's work. On the contrary they were simply subsumed within subsequent editions of the same books. Thus French research on degeneration was incorporated in later editions of *Criminal Man*,[48] but the central thesis remained intact. Indeed by the 1890s, certain hitherto staunch followers like Enrico Ferri began to distance themselves somewhat from Lombroso's still inflexible devotion to 'atavism'. As Arthur Griffiths put it in a report to the Home Office after attending the Geneva Congress in 1896, Lombroso was unyielding in the face of considerable dissent from his position. Nobody could doubt his fidelity to his own discoveries:

Perhaps the most remarkable, and not the least interesting feature of the Congress was the tenacity with which Dr Lombroso held to his views. It is impossible to be brought into personal relations with this distinguished savant without being impressed by his sincerity, and the depth of his convictions ... Once in the course of the Congress, when very hardly pressed by certain hostile remarks, he cried, 'What do I care whether others are with me or against me? I believe in the type. It is my type; I discovered it; I believe in it and I always shall.'[49]

The theory of atavism was not only a matter of fervent belief, but also part of a broader conception of politics and society. Although far less politically militant than some of his collaborators like Enrico Ferri and Scipio Sighele, Lombroso's early work on pellagra, as I have already suggested, was hostile to the interests of the aristocracy with its huge land-holdings and political parochialism. Lombroso opposed traditional tariff policies which had penalised consumers, tenant farmers and agricultural labourers in the interests of powerful land-owners. The aristocracy, like the criminal population, he argued in early writings on the south of Italy, was anathema to the interests of a modern rationalist state.[50]

The connection between upper and lower-class forms of parasitism was developed in stark terms towards the end of the century by Scipio Sighele, the major Lombrosian theorist of the crowd. The upper classes exhibited signs of paralysis and atrophy: the lower classes signs of incomplete evolution, and thus simian brutality.[51] Writing in the face of Italian colonial adventurism, Sighele dreamed of a Greater Italy, the glory of empire, and a

---

[47] See Bulferetti, *Lombroso*, p. 69.   [48] See Villa, 'Scienza', p. 1,163.
[49] Griffiths, *Report*, pp. 12–13.   [50] See *In Calabria, passim*.
[51] Sighele, *La delinquenza settaria*, p. 24.

future when government transcended the petty politics and factionalism of parliament and successfully mastered the crowd.[52]

Lombroso, it should be noted, however, did not endorse the idea of an Italian empire. He was at one time a member of the Socialist Party and was selected as a municipal councillor in Turin.[53] These facts must be stressed; for Lombroso is today viewed as a political reactionary, progenitor of a resurgent socio-biology with conservative implications. We need to distinguish sharply the terms of Lombroso's politics, thus to recover the intersection between positivism and a section of 'the Left' in the late-nineteenth century. He was typically perceived at the time as a progressive figure, bringing evolutionary biology and physical anthropology to bear upon Italy's 'backwardness'.

Lombroso had recounted the moment of his key discovery about the criminal in a now legendary paragraph of self-celebration. On a gloomy morning in the winter of 1870, he had been trying in vain to discover anatomical differences between criminals and the insane. He examined the skull of the famous brigand Vilella and suddenly he had a flash of insight, a revelation redolent of the awe of nineteenth-century naturalism. In the brigand's skull he saw the traces of a past which should have been shed from modern Italy:

This was not merely an idea, but a revelation. At the sight of that skull, I seemed to see all of a sudden, lighted up as a vast plain under a flaming sky, the problem of the nature of the criminal – an atavistic being who reproduces in his person the ferocious instincts of primitive humanity and the inferior animals. Thus were explained anatomically the enormous jaws, high cheek bones, prominent superciliary arches, solitary lines in the palms, extreme size of the orbits, handle-shaped ears found in criminals, savages and apes, insensibility to pain, extremely acute sight, tattooing, excessive idleness, love of orgies, and the irresponsible craving of evil for its own sake, the desire not only to extinguish life in the victim, but to mutilate the corpse, tear its flesh and drink its blood.[54]

The criminal's phrenology and physiognomy revealed the presence of an ancestral past. Criminality for Lombroso was not 'unnatural' sin, nor an

---

[52] On Sighele's politics see Landolfi, *Scipio Sighele*, and Mucchi, *L'abbraccio*. On analogies made between Ancient Rome and the new expansionist Italy, see Mola, *L'imperialismo italiano*, pp. 129, 141–6. Sighele was a law pupil of Ferri's and became a champion of Italian nationalism and expansion; he was expelled from Austrian territory and received by Victor Emmanuel III on his return. He was elected president of a nationalist association in Florence in 1910; see Garbari, 'Il pensiero politico', (per.), pp. 398–9, and Garbari, *L'età giolittiana*, p. 48. On Sighele's hostility to the parliamentary system and bourgeois liberalism, see Garbari, 'Il pensiero politico', (per.) and Sighele, *La donna nova* and *Letteratura e sociologia*. However other of Lombroso's followers held quite different views. On Ferri's intense opposition to Italian colonial adventurism and war see, for instance, Ferri, *La marina militare*; *Il militarismo*, *La piu grande guerra*.

[53] See Levra (ed.), *La scienza e la colpa*.

[54] Lombroso, *Criminal Man*, pp. xiv–xv.

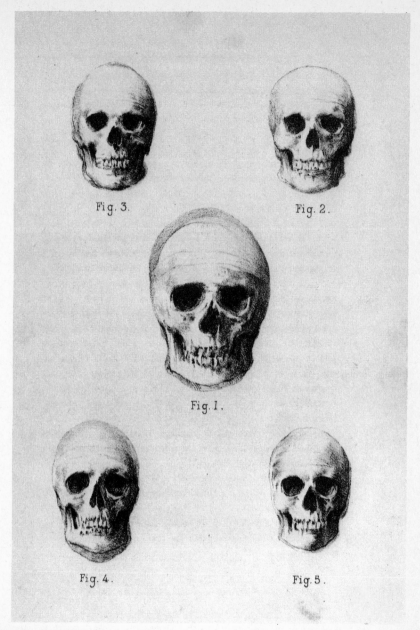

3 Lombroso's 'Criminal skulls', from *L'uomo delinquente*. These images were apparently produced with the aid of Galton's composite photography method (see plates 9 and 10). Eighteen skulls were combined to order to expose the essential cranial features of the delinquent.

4   Lombroso's 'Faces of criminality', from *L'uomo delinquente*

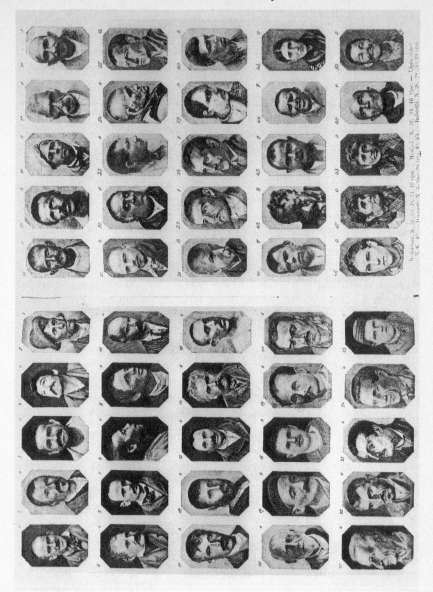

5　Lombroso's 'Faces of criminality', from *L'uomo delinquente*

act of free will, but the sign of a primitive form of nature within an advanced society. Following through this idea that crime existed throughout the world of nature, Lombroso managed to detect crime amongst certain anomalous children, insects, monkeys, even plants.[55] But if the criminal was 'natural', this did not imply, as for Durkheim, the need for a certain fatalism and the contention that crime was in some degree inevitable. Lombroso saw crime as bio-historical anachronism – the ontogenic development of the criminal was arrested. The anomalous individual thus languished behind phylogeny – the stage of evolution of the race as a whole.

For Lombroso criminality was 'natural' but unacceptable; natural in its relation to heredity (certain creatures fell behind in the course of evolution), unacceptable in its social consequences. The criminal class was in short an obsolete freight carried by the state. Unified Italy, he argued, would have to streamline evolution, eliminate the unproductive. The point of the positivist study of the criminal was to produce a science of social defence against atavism and anarchy. It was deemed pointless to pontificate on the moral responsibility of atavistic individuals, but crucial to separate them out from the rest of society. Hence in Italy and abroad, it could be used to endorse a plethora of policies calling for capital punishment, castration, segregation, state management of reproduction and radical distinctions in sentencing between 'born criminals' and other delinquents.[56]

Lombroso's science of crime was bound up with an anthropological, evolutionary conception of 'backwardness' and the primitive. Yet whilst there was a hierarchy of races, this was not a simple polarity of black as against white; or, rather, in the context of Italy certain problems remained even once white superiority had been assumed. In *The White Man and the Coloured Man* (1871), he had confirmed that:

Only we White people [*Noi soli Bianchi*] have reached the most perfect symmetry of bodily form ... Only we [have bestowed] ... the human right to life, respect for old age, women, and the weak ... Only we have created true nationalism ... [and] freedom of thought.[57]

The white races represented the triumph of the human species, its hitherto most perfect advancement. But then inside the triumphant whiteness, there remained a certain blackness. The danger was not simply external – the 'Dark Continent' of Africa just beyond Sicily – indeed the problem was that it could not be held to an outside. It could not even be

---

[55] See Gould, *Mismeasure*, pp. 125, 127.
[56] See Radzinowicz and Hood, *English Criminal Law*, part 1, ch. 1.
[57] *L'uomo bianco*, pp. 222–3.

6 Lombroso's 'Faces of criminality', from *Archivo di psichiatria, antropologia criminale e scienza penale*

held to the South of Italy. Each region had its cultural, economic, and political forces threatening the state. Enemies were without and within, dispersed everywhere. Lombroso's criminal anthropology sought to help contain the threat: to comprehend it scientifically and hence exclude it politically. He desired to unify the dangers, to hold them within a single conceptual model, in order to hold them outside the state, outside the fragile coherence of 'Italy'.

It did indeed appear to social commentators that crime was not so much endemic in, as natural to, the South. Riot had long been a part of a history which had known many invaders. Social disorder did not cease with victory in the national struggle; on the contrary it increased. The confrontation between the forces of the state on the one side and a riotous peasantry on the other, amounted to civil war. Exposure to the peasantry came as a rude shock to many of the leaders in the struggle for unification.[58]

Where post-unification 'Italy' signified anything at all to the bulk of the southern peasantry, it was above all likely to be such tangible and negative phenomena as new taxes, conscription and Piedmontese interference in traditional social practices. The new invasion by the Italian state constituted, not least, an onslaught upon 'brigandage', which was sometimes nothing else than the name given by the new government to any violent local opposition to the laws of Italy.[59] Yet violence and protest, however designated, persisted and even intensified throughout the first decades of Italy's existence.

Preventive detention was one amongst various practices frequently employed in later-nineteenth-century Italy to suppress social disorder. Lombroso and his followers sought to legitimate and improve the state's capacity to anticipate delinquency by revealing the true criminal in advance of any particular action and thus to extend the possibility of preventive detention.

Governments had a rapid turn-over. By 1892 there had been twenty-

---

[58] In a discussion of the peasantry and the Sicilian campaign, Mack Smith has traced the process through which even Garibaldi's forces would end up policing and suppressing the peasantry, most famously at Bronte, horrified by the 'savagery' and 'backwardness' they witnessed. If both the peasantry and the intellectual urban middle classes had a vested interest in *starting* a Sicilian revolution, and thus facilitating Garibaldi's victory, the outcomes they desired were quite antithetical: 'the triumph of either meant ruin to the other; for a successful political revolution would give the proprietors even more power over their tenants and labourers, while on the other hand social revolution spelt a *jacquerie*. From this fact grew quickly a wide diversity of aim' (Mack Smith, *Italy*, p. 197). Ippolito Nievo, one of Garibaldi's officers, noted that they had received the help of various brigand gangs who sought to fight not only the Bourbons but also the landowners and thus 'we are now forced to act as police against the very men who were our allies until yesterday' (p. 199). Cf. Nicotri, *Rivoluzioni*, p. 126, where there is a discussion of Bixio and the 'necessary' repression of the hypnotised and hysterical crowd at Bronte.

[59] See Blok, *Mafia*, pp. 98–102. For a broader investigation into the vexed question of defining banditry, see Hobsbawm, *Bandits*.

eight governments in the thirty-two years of the United Kingdom of Italy's existence.[60] The army occupied a crucial role in the internal defence of Italy against the urban and rural strikes, demonstrations, anarchism, riots and brigandage which persistently confronted the state in different parts of the country. The anomalies of Italy's police system to this day stem in part from the particular instability which surrounded Italy's foundation. The *carabinieri* was indeed a regular military police force, trained and organised by the Ministry of War. Usually there would be a division in each province, and in rural areas, they were often the only significant police presence. Many patriotic writers represented them as the fearless and heroic force of order, battling against a backward, hostile, crime-ridden country.

There were myriad threats to the liberal unity of the state from Catholicism to anarchism, from socialism to brigandage. But the threats were also displaced into the realm of imaginary oppositions – a whole anthropology of the normal, the pathological, the atavistic, as in Lombroso's mythologies.

In the face of the perceived banality and paradox of parliamentary politics which for thirty years had shown itself at once stagnant in its cynical *trasformismo* and chronically unstable (incessant reshuffles of government were needed to achieve it), many intellectuals were drawn into the 'third force' of socialism which was institutionally established as a party in 1892.[61] Indeed socialism opened unprecedented political and ideological gaps within the ranks of the Northern bourgeoisie.

To the important criminological positivist Enrico Ferri, whom, borrowing Huxley's tag, one might term Lombroso's 'bulldog' at least until the 1890s, socialism appeared as an essentially statist scientific creed, beyond the irrational squabble of existing politics, in harmony with the doctrine of evolution. It was in this manner that Ferri produced his famous trinity of

---

[60] I take this and the following general points from Clark, *Modern Italy*.

[61] See Asor Rosa, 'La cultura'. That sense of disillusionment can be felt in Lombroso's work in the 1890s. Thus in the preface to a book on Calabria in 1897, Lombroso observed that much of the book had been written in the 1860s, when it was still possible to wear the uniform of the Italian army without blushing (Lombroso, *In Calabria*, p. v). The Italian revolution, he observes, was full of promise, but sterile in practice (p. viii). Reviewing the levels of crime in Calabria between 1862 and 1897, Lombroso found only stasis or worse. All one could say, he noted, was that the only difference unification had made was to add new modern crimes (those pertaining to 'civilization') to the barbaric crimes of the past (p. 98). On the general question of the intellectual disillusionment with late-nineteenth century Italy see Asor Rosa, 'La cultura', ch. 1. Garibaldi for instance wrote in October 1880, when Stefano Canzio was imprisoned for a political crime: 'I used to dream of another Italy'; cf. Carducci, who wrote in 1886 that the sublime days of the struggle for unification had been replaced by an infinitely trivial milieu (pp. 824, 831). For an account of D'Annunzio's diatribes against the sordid world of parliamentary politics see pp. 832–3. On the general question of Italian intellectual disillusionment, see Bellamy, *Modern Italian Social Theory*.

Darwin, Spencer and Marx.[62] Other of Lombroso's supporters such as Sighele rejected socialism, formulated anti-parliamentary polemics and contributed proposals for government by an 'elite'. Ferri and Garofalo (a Neapolitan magistrate who represented the other key figure in the Lombrosian 'triumvirate') disputed precisely this issue of the scientific credentials of socialism.[63]

It was, however, anarchism (fostered by the Russian exile Bakunin) rather than the socialism of Marx which had generated most anxiety amongst the ruling classes in the 1860s and 1870s.[64] Between 1865 and 1867 Bakunin lived in Naples, which was to become the first major centre of anarchism in the country.

Bakunin was confident of the revolutionary potential of the Italian peasantry and student classes.[65] Italians were indeed quickly to become leaders in the anti-authoritarian wings of the International. Furthermore in 1874 a band of anarchists attempted a 'coup' in Italy; they marched from a base at Imola to seize Bologna. Other attempts ensued which were always defeated. A certain aura of pathos and farce has attached itself to these incidents and passed into Italian folk-lore. One must however remember Garibaldi's earlier successful victories with what had appeared on the face of it an equally derisory 'army'. Certainly the anarchist campaigns were seen at the time as seriously threatening. Nevertheless they did fail disastrously and anarchist strategy was changed to 'propaganda by the deed'. In November 1878 an anarchist, Giovanni Passanante, tried to stab the King at Naples. Cairoli, the Prime Minister, threw himself in the way. What he gained in acclaim for bravery, he more than lost in criticism at this supreme example of government incompetence. The outcry about the inadequacy of 'social defence' contributed to the fall of his government.[66]

The anti-anarchist drive of 1878–9 succeeded in containing the threat to the state, forcing many revolutionaries abroad, into hiding or prison. This helped to consolidate the appeal of organised socialism. Nevertheless anarchism remained, sometimes in reality, sometimes in governmental minds, near the heart of agitations through the 1880s. Italian anarchists were to play a substantial role in international terrorism through the 1890s, notably in the assassinations of the President of France in 1894, of the

---

[62] Ferri, *Socialism and Positive Science*. Ferri described revolution as the final stage of evolution (the critical moment of its achievement), not by any means the same thing as 'tumultuous and violent revolt' (p. 122). Ferri advocated 'scientific socialism' and rejected 'old methods of revolutionary romanticism' (p. 124). Socialism, he argued, said only that '*[m]en are unequal, but they are all men*' (p. 9).

[63] See Ferri, *Discordie*. On Garofalo, see Allen, 'Garofalo'.

[64] See Clark, *Modern Italy*.

[65] See Clark, *Modern Italy*.   [66] Clark, *Modern Italy*, p. 75.

Prime Minister of Spain in 1897, of the Empress of Austria in 1898, and of King Humbert himself in 1900.[67]

Lombroso argued that anarchists like other criminals suffered from hereditary bodily anomalies.[68] Their influence could be understood as a form of epidemic disease. Disease provided multifarious resonances in the discourses on crime. Thus hereditary maladies and epidemics, disfiguring conditions and secret tumours could all be adduced as illustration at different points of the argument on the inherited and environmental causes of delinquency. At the time of unification, medical facilities were extremely under-developed in much of the country;[69] yet within the social evolutionary terms of the scientific intelligentsia, the body was the crucial site of the national condition. Racial fitness was deemed critical in the international 'struggle for survival'. Within Italian culture of the late-nineteenth-century period, one encounters a similar cult of sport and the healthy body to that in Germany, France and England.[70]

When one speaks of Lombroso's positivism, this does not suggest that he was directly a Comtist (even the textual availability of Comte's works, or for that matter Spencer's, to seminal Italian positivists like Ardigò has recently been called into question[71]), but that he shared the confidence in natural science as the great key to social advance and social explanation, and viewed knowledge as itself an evolution from religion to metaphysics to 'positive' science.[72] Such positivism traced the simultaneous progress of knowledge and society in the nineteenth century. Unlike some of the Comteans, however, Lombroso saw positivism not as representing the eclipse or transcendence of nationalism and its politics, but rather its fulfilment, its final confirmation. Asor Rosa has deftly shown how key figures in Italian positivism like Ardigò and Trezza, used an organic

---

[67] See Clark, *Modern Italy*, 75; cf. Joll, *Anarchists*, p. 118.

[68] Lombroso, *Gli anarchici, passim*; cf. the discussion of anarchism in the *Actes* (Fourth Congress) (1897), pp. 111–19.

[69] See De Peri, 'Il medico e il folle'.

[70] On ideas of regeneration, nationalism and imperialism see Landucci, 'Darwinismo', p. 115; on science and the 'hygiene' of the population see Babini *et al.*, *Tra sapere e potere*; cf. Preti, *I miti dell' impero*. Between 1886 and 1888 in France, Pierre de Coubertin reacted to the crisis of degeneration by advocating the introduction of the gymnastic and athletic exercises he had admired in England and the United States. In 1888 a national league for physical education was founded in France. In 1895, Coubertin set up an International Olympic Committee, a prelude to the first Olympic Games held in Athens in 1896. See Weber, 'Coubertin', (per.).

[71] Asor Rosa suggests that many of the internationally renowned figures with a bearing on the positivist movement, (such as Spencer, Darwin, Comte, Strauss, Renan, Taine and Mill) were known only at second hand by some of the Italian intellectuals who endorsed them ('La cultura', p. 882). Ardigò apparently had not read Spencer when he wrote on psychology in 1870 because there was no copy in Mantua and he could not afford to order one.

[72] See Charlton, *Positivist Thought*; cf. Grupp (ed.), *Positive School*, pp. 150–1, which discusses how Ferri saw the history of criminology as analogous to Comte's three stages (pre-classical superstition, classical abstraction, positivist science).

concept of the state in order to reject the relevance of 'abstract' radical ideals to the Italian context. Whilst appearing to endorse internationalism and democracy (although not 'the religion of humanity') as worthy ideas, they in fact produced elsewhere an *apologia* for the *status quo* or at best gradual reformism.[73] They insisted that since history 'evolved' naturally in each country, it could not be overthrown by revolution or any other 'artificial' departure.

Italian and French positivist theories of crime are often discussed as though they were identical; but there were critical differences arising from the respective contexts of their elaboration. It was thus important that in Italy, unlike in France during the Second Empire, the church was identified as hostile to the new state. Italy's unification had involved not only the defeat of Austria, but also a secular victory over the Catholic Church. The Italian positivist criminologists in their critique of free will were confronting not only classical jurisprudence but also Catholicism by calling into question the very utility of terms like sin or evil.

In France in the 1850s and 1860s however, the state was increasingly identified with the power of the church. Frank determinism and the denial of free will were at odds with both the church and the ethos of government. Recent secondary work, already described in part one, has stressed how materialist medicine nuanced its arguments in such a way as to evade, or at least cloud the question of free will.[74] Although, of course, there was to be a powerful relation between 'science' and anti-clericalism in the decades which followed under the Third Republic, it was significant that B. A. Morel who had first elaborated the theory of hereditary degeneration in the 1850s professed himself to be a devout Catholic.

If we are to understand the different 'structures of feeling' between criminal science in France and Italy we need to look also at the question of the symbolism around the repetition of revolution, which, I have argued, was powerfully invested in Morel's *dégénérescence*. In French medico-psychiatric representations after 1848, it was suggested that the 'experience' of political and social disorder had infiltrated the human system at large and been reproduced; political and physiological 'unrest' had coalesced. Bourgeois protest in 1789 had undergone metamorphosis and culminated in Terror; the Revolution of 1830 had its counterpart and its legacy in the 'anarchy' of 1848. Beyond 1871, a further twist could be seen in the pattern of revolutionary inheritance. For Taine, France, like a convulsed body unable to escape the maladies of its past, had collapsed in military defeat and the struggle of the Paris Commune.

In Morel's elaborated theory, the degenerate family did not simply

---

[73] 'La cultura', p. 894.   [74] See Dowbiggin, 'Degeneration and Hereditarianism'.

reproduce one morbid condition across the generations but rather showed a fantastic capacity for morbid transmutation, successive bodies manifesting respectively the ravages of alcoholism, hysteria, insanity, idiocy and cretinism. From Morel and Taine, to Zola and Le Bon, crime was cast up in an infinite entanglement with the 'lapsarian moment' of the Revolution. For these writers in France it was as though degeneration might be a tragic irreversible fact of the body and revolution a given condition of the race. In one sense, the French revolution had overthrown 'Heredity', (the monarchy, the aristocracy, the religious concept of original sin), but ironically in the nineteenth-century society which emerged beyond it, hereditary *dégénérescence* appeared to have become incorporated (literally embodied) as an indeterminate potentiality of the French race. In part one it was indicated that even such writers as, say, Jaurès, Durkheim and Sorel were partially caught up in these discursive assumptions.

By contrast with that side of Morel's and Magnan's discourse which stressed degeneration's infinite potential for dissemination, Lombroso stressed the recalcitrance of certain specific anti-social lineages. It was as though in Italy, despite all the problems, the genealogy and physiognomy of crime could be drawn and separated from the benign prospects of national history in a culture still living in the faint glow of Risorgimento ideals, whilst in French medico-psychiatric theory, crime, society and national defeat were more persistently seen to be profoundly fused and confused. Certainly Lombroso, like Morel, saw criminality as deeply

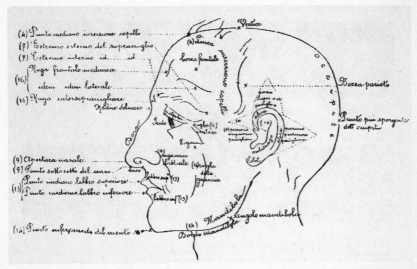

7 In search of a scientific physiognomy of the criminal, from Ottolenghi, *Trattato di polizia scientifica*. This diagram illustrates the multitude of features which had to be assembled by the Lombrosian forensic investigator.

8   In search of a scientific physiognomy of the criminal, from Ottolenghi, *Trattato di polizia scientifica*. A taxonomy of ear types.

threatening to a progressive society, but he was sure that this ran against the grain of evolution and contemporary history – Lombroso was not prey to Morel's ambivalent Catholicism. In many French theories of degeneration, we find 'past' and 'present' to be less simplistically counterposed, as though 'morbid' history weighed more heavily and reached further. If there was a spectre haunting the Society of Medical Psychology in Paris in the 1870s and 1880s, it was the very infinitude of degeneration, as though society was no longer distinguishable into labouring and dangerous classes, but had been circumscribed by pathology. In this image, disorder circled the degenerate body and the noxious milieu without beginning or end. In Taine and Zola, *dégénérescence* defied the nosology leading towards sterility as outlined by Morel, implicitly hinting instead (despite ritual disavowals) that it could know no historical extinction.

Of course this dichotomy between France and Italy is simplistic. First, because there was no small number of writers in France (most famously Taine but also, as was shown earlier, Sorel[75]), who had considerable sympathy for Lombroso. Second, there was a powerful and influential French anthropological tradition, whose most famous representative was Broca, which was concerned in part, like Lombroso, to trace in the anomalies of skulls a table of racial differences, just as there was to be an important forensic endeavour to isolate the mark of the criminal from ear and nose types to fingerprints.[76] Third, French degenerationism was always internally contradictory. On the one hand, the concept of degeneration was formulated in mental medicine from the 1850s as an identity quite alien to (indeed, the imaginary spectre of) the French middle class. It was conceived as a fixed identity of all those unfortunate or dangerous classes who threatened social order. On the other hand, what Morel and those who followed him insisted was that degeneration was not a fixed identity, but a ubiquitous process. In this second scenario, degeneration was envisaged not as 'insemination' amongst degenerates leading reassuringly to extinction, but an uncontained 'dissemination', scattering forth pathologies. It was as though disorder had become uncontainable, spread all over the place, vitiating all classes. Fourth, the theories of the Lombrosian crowd theorists, notably Scipio Sighele, introduced a kind of sociology of atavism in which the division normal/pathological became more and more difficult to sustain. This work, which had its real moment in the 1890s,[77] reflected a broader shift in Italian political commentary away from the problems of 'primitivism' in rural areas, to the disorders of an emergent 'mass society'

[75] See ch. 4 above.　　[76] See Schiller, *Paul Broca*; Bertillon, *La Photographie Juridicaire*.
[77] See for example Sighele, *Il delitto politico*; *La folla delinquente*; *La delinquenza settaria*; 'Le Crime collectif'; Rossi, *L'animo della folla*; Vasto, 'Il contaggio', (per.); cf. Mucchi, *L'abbraccio della folla*.

in the expanding cities.[78] We can trace a new investment in the notion of cultural degeneration, just as the specifically psychiatric credibility of *dégénérescence* and the criminological validity of atavism were waning.

In Lombroso's work on 'criminal man', however, the first scenario (that of degeneration as 'the other') was more easily sustainable. Thus whilst Lombroso had carried on providing phrenological and physiognomic stigmata to demarcate the image of the criminal, French theoreticians internalised degeneration, speculating on the 'invisible lesions' of the nervous system, an obscure and secret world of morbidity. For the Catholic Morel in the 1850s, France was a fallen world to be regenerated through a positivist pantheon of medicine and science; for Taine and Zola in the 1870s and 1880s, hereditary degeneration had reached almost everywhere.

Although we have traced a significant but problematic national division between French and Italian positivist theories of crime in the late-nineteenth century, nevertheless the new criminological school across the two countries, had a sense of collective identity defined against the abstraction of the so-called 'classical' school. If classical discourse found its partial expression in the Napoleonic Penal Code, it had perhaps its most famous Enlightenment theorisations in the work first of Beccaria in Italy, then of Bentham in England. There were differences between their positions, but what was shared was a critical insistence that the criminal should be treated as a rational subject, able to calculate. As Bentham put it: 'Men calculate, some with less exactness, indeed, some with more: but all men calculate.'[79]

Beccaria's *Crime and Punishments* (1764) displayed the direct influence of the French Enlightenment. He rejected the supposedly *ad hoc* basis of previous sentencing: its putative eclecticism, inequality, and barbarity. Punishment, he demanded, should no longer depend upon the vagaries and vicissitudes of judges, nor the social status of the offender; instead it should be an entity in a set code. Crime was to have a fixed exchange rate in punishment. Every infraction would receive a given punishment just in excess of the benefits of the crime.[80]

For classical theory, each being was a person, a subject of law, subject to law. This ideal placed the onus on proving the terms for exclusion from the polity. Such an argument of course underpinned early-nineteenth-century

---

[78] See for instance Lombroso and Ferrero, *Female Offender*, p. vi. Despite all the expenditure, they noted, the statistics continued to get worse and pathology spread its range ever further; cf. Bulferetti, *Lombroso*, p. 69.

[79] Bentham, *Principles of Morals and Legislation*, pp. 173–4.

[80] Beccaria, *Dei delitti*, p. 45. Cf. Monachesi, 'Cesare Beccaria'; Venturi, 'Beccaria and Legal Reform'.

radicalism in its insistence that all were legal subjects and rightfully political subjects unless proved otherwise, and not the converse. Thus for
Bentham, for whom Beccaria was a kind of guiding beacon of rationalism
to be set against the traditionalist Blackstone, universal suffrage (or at least
suffrage for all men, although he eventually advocated suffrage for women
also[81]), was desirable on the grounds that everyone should be a free subject,
pursuing independent self-interest. In Bentham's words:

If, in the instance of any *one* individual of the whole body of the people, it be *right*
that the faculty of contributing to the choice of a representative . . . be possessed and
exercised, – how can it be otherwise than right, in the instance of any one *other* such
person?[82]

Bentham had to prove to his own satisfaction that certain categories of
person could not be considered 'self-interested'. Thus he would have
excluded idiots and infants because they were clearly not 'capable of
exercising [the suffrage] to the advantage either of others or of themselves'
(III, p. 452).[83] But these were the exceptions which proved the rule.

Clearly the continuities between classical and positivist schools are as
striking as the differences. Both were insistently rationalist; both saw
themselves as pitted against superstition, the forces of the past, the weight
of precedent. Moreover one finds overlaps in their respective projects – for
instance the shared desire to 'illuminate' the criminal. Bentham's 'Panopti-
con' indeed epitomised the dream of making the criminal into a perfect and
literal spectacle: each prisoner exposed at all times as a silhouette to the eyes
of the guard, and moreover made available as the edifying object of public
visits.[84] Positivist criminology sought the drastic extension of that visibility
– the criminal made visible outside the prison too, revealed in the contours
of a distinctive physiognomy, even in advance of a crime.

Whilst it appears that the move from classicism to positivism was also a
shift from the discourse of jurisprudence to that of medicine, even here it is
easy to over-simplify. After all Bentham saw his utilitarianism as a social
medicine, or a chemistry, confronting the quackery and alchemy of traditional law. In his critique of Blackstone, he declared his wish:

To purge the science of the poison introduced into it by [Blackstone] and those who
write as he does, I know but of one remedy; and that is by *Definition*, perpetual and
regular definition, the grand prescription of those great physicians of the mind,
Helvetius and before him Locke.[85]

[81] See Harrison, *Bentham*, p. 213. [82] Bentham, *Works*, III, p. 452.
[83] Cf. Harrison, *Bentham*, pp. 211–12. [84] See Foucault, *Discipline*, esp. pp. 195–228.
[85] *A Comment on the Commentaries*, in *Collected Works*, p. 346.

Or again:

medicine, commonly so-called, the medicine of the body ... has for its basis the
observations of the axioms of pathology, commonly so-called. Morals is the
medicine of the soul. The science of legislation ought to have for its basis the axioms
of pathology.[86]

Suffice to say here that the Lombrosians acknowledged the scientific
strivings of Beccaria and Bentham, describing classical penology as the first
moment in an epistemological evolution toward positivism.[87] It began
the process of critique of pre-Enlightenment irrationalism. But classical
penology was deemed naive in that it sought to attribute reason not only
to itself, but also to its object. It sought to bring the criminal within its
pale. Certainly the positivist critique of classical penology did not
seek to reintroduce irrationalism or subjectivism in its own method
or practice. Quite the contrary. It sought to preside before the law, as
arbiter of the rational and the irrational, the judge of the limits of each
sphere.

French and Italian positivist criminology stood in a complex relationship to the Enlightenment – at once its extension and its obverse; for in a
sense, what could have been more encyclopaedic than the quest to chart
every manifestation, every structure of the pathological? Moreover the
criterion of social defence became the mainstay of positivist theory; social
defence displaced individual reform or deterrence through punishment as a
rationale, and thus criminal dangerousness became a critical factor in
sentencing; this was nothing if not predicated on the doctrine of utility.
Nineteenth-century positivism held 'eighteenth-century theory' (the
charges were often levelled in such vague and global terms) ideologically
responsible for the excesses of the Revolution, partly for recklessly providing the masses with 'inflammatory' slogans and ideas, partly for its own
conceptual failure to recognise the innate differences between individuals.
The empirical fact of difference, so it was argued, made nonsense of
catchwords like 'Equality'.

The purpose of Italian criminal anthropology can be found then, in the
attempt to construct an ordered language for the containment of disorder

---

[86] Bentham's manuscripts at University College, London (32.6), quoted in Harrison, *Bentham*, p. 141.
[87] See for instance Ferri, *Enrico Pessina*, pp. 5–7, where Ferri noted his admiration for
Beccaria and declared that from Beccaria to Carrara and Pessina, the classical school led in
its turn naturally to the more advanced stage of positivism; cf. Ferri's discussion of Beccaria
in Ferri, *Arringhe e discorsi*, pp. 205–7; cf. Ferri's analogy between the history of criminology and Comte's epistemological stages, Grupp (ed.), *Positive School*, pp. 150–1. He
contended that 'when Cesare Beccaria opened the great historic cycle of the classic school
of criminology, he was assaulted by the critics of his time with the same indictments which
were brought against us a century later' (p. 51).

and, through that language, to formulate the definition of a political subject by elaborating ever more closely the criteria for political exclusion. Rationality was taken to be a rare distinction, not a universal 'birth right'. The rationale for retaining Italy's very narrow franchise[88] in the period after unification did not rest only on some imputed evolutionary immaturity of the 'masses' although it included that argument. It was not simply a question of waiting until the population had achieved the standards of civilisation, as in those liberal paternalist rationales for the British empire, which saw the task as contingent, a vigil, whilst the colonised children of the species evolved the capacity for self-government. On the contrary, as Lombroso's atavists reproduced, they fell back ever further, back through the time of the species.

UNDER ATTACK

Certain of the issues discussed above can be analysed in detail in the proceedings of the International Congresses of Criminal Anthropology held between 1885 and World War I. We find, for instance, delegates frequently defining criminological positivism as the logical consequence of a scientific critique of classical theory. The first Congress was indeed held in Rome at the same time as the more classically orientated International Penitentiary Congress.[89] This highlighted the differences between the two approaches; each sought to gain the attention of the politicians. The particularly urgent concern for Lombroso and his followers, was the imminent framing of an Italian penal code, which they hoped to influence – a largely vain ambition as it turned out.[90]

---

[88] In 1861, only 1.9% of the population are said to have had the vote; see Asor Rosa, 'La cultura', p. 841, and Salomone, *Italian Democracy*, p. viii. In 1882, the suffrage was extended. It retained a literary test, but reduced the minimum voting age from 25 to 21 and lowered the property qualification. The electorate was said to have increased from 600,000 to 2 million, i.e. from 2% to 7% of the population; see Seton Watson, *Italy from Liberalism to Fascism*, pp. 50–1. On Lombroso's opposition to universal suffrage in 1897, see Mack Smith, *Italy*, p. 209.

[89] On the rivalry between the two Congresses, see the *Actes* (First Congress of Criminal Anthropology) 1885, p. xii.

[90] The Zanardelli code reflected the anti-clerical drive of nineteenth-century liberalism and the classical penology of the Beccarian tradition. It allowed strikes (although this right was soon curtailed), restrained the clergy from interfering in politics and avoided consecutive sentencing for multiple offences. It allowed however, as strict classicism did not, for individual differences amongst offenders. Thus it permitted extenuating circumstances and conditions of impaired responsibility; see Spirito, *Storia*, pp. 232–6; Wise, *Italian Penal Code*, p. xxv. As Wise writes (p. xxi), 'In short, the Zanardelli Code, like the neo-classical school whose principles it reflected, took the atomistic individual of classical criminology and endowed him up to a point (but only up to a point) with both a past and a future.' In Ferri's view the Zanardelli Code was less progressive than the 1859 code it replaced; see Ferri, *Difese penali*, I, pp. 27–8.

The topics discussed ranged across many of the themes already mentioned above – born criminals, prostitutes, violent crowds. The first Congress was dominated numerically by Italians but there was a sizeable French contingent as well.[91] The French group did not necessarily deny that atavism constituted one form of degeneration, but they insisted on viewing criminality as involving a constant movement between organic and environmental factors, which they thought was absent from Lombroso's argument. Heredity and milieu were bound up in a reciprocal exchange. To speak of the 'born criminal' (the phrase coined by Ferri) seemed to make the task of reform hopeless; the relation between criminal and society was two-way. For Lacassagne, one of the leaders of the French group, the Italian School attributed to the criminal 'a kind of indelible stain, an original sin' (p. 166), deplorable in its therapeutic nihilism. Lacassagne attacked the vague and unproved use of words like 'atavism' or 'Darwinism', and urged caution. He rejected any absolute fatalism. In Lacassagne's famous Pasteurian formulation of the ceaseless movement between organism and environment:

The social milieu is the cultural broth of criminality; the microbe is the criminal, an element that gains significance only at the moment it finds the broth that makes it ferment. (p. 166)[92]

Metaphors from Pasteurian bacteriology lent themselves easily to the rhetoric of anti-hereditarian determinists. Of course they could be appropriated in contrary arguments too. To pose the dialectic between criminal and society, organism and environment, still begged the question of the origin of the 'microbe' which then found the 'broth'. Moreover, it did not lead inexorably to any particular political or legislative conclusion. Certainly it could be used to stress the need for environmental reform. But it did not preclude the train of argument which called for the elimination of the noxious human particles in society as a means of improving the milieu. Such eugenic proposals certainly had their adherents in France. For Lacassagne, however, the microbe metaphor was used here to suggest the fluidity of the relation between crime and society. He sought to move against the fixed terms of Lombrosian theory, with its given natures, its born criminals, its stigmata, its 'immobilising fatalism'.

In his opening address to the Congress, Lombroso sought to reassure his critics, not only the French delegates, but those Italian jurists who imagined that his new medical view was somehow 'soft' on criminals because it questioned the classical basis for punishment. In fact, Lombroso's

[91] See the list of participants at the front of the *Actes* (First Congress), 1885, i.
[92] 'Le milieu social est le bouillon de culture de la criminalité; le microbe c' est le criminel, un élément qui n'a d'importance que le jour où il trouve le bouillon qui le fait fermenter.'

remarks could only have confirmed the view of the French that he was too single-minded. Nevertheless, he concentrated on the apparent charge that his work engendered an alarming social compassion. On the contrary, Lombroso insisted, it was his own science above all others which aimed at

the elimination of criminals, penalties in perpetuity in a large number of cases ... [It] is we who wish to replace hypotheses by the results of comparative observations of honest people and criminals ... (p. 50)

Lombroso and his followers wanted science to play a critical role in the construction of the nation. At the outset we are presented with a series of diagrams, tables and charts concerning the organic anomalies to be found in the criminal. At the end of the volume recording the Congress, a series of maps shows the frequency and distribution of various crimes in Italy. It was as though the opening of the congress proceedings (like the genesis of Lombrosianism) focussed the outline of the criminal body and by the conclusion that body had been transposed into a map of the nation. There were even maps to show the distribution and chronology of revolutions (designated as progressive or regressive) in world history. The maps serve perhaps as a short-hand illustration of how Lombroso's *oeuvre* endeavoured to link the body, the nation and history. Criminal anthropology constituted at once a political geography, a conjectural history of civilisation, an evolutionary account of organisms and races.

'Political crime' was a major area of contention between delegates. Lombroso contributed the results of his joint researches on this subject with Laschi. Both pointed out the frequency and facility with which 'criminals placed themselves at the head of the masses'. Political crime, we are told, was important, because it interlocked the biological and the sociological – the atavism of the criminal and the moral suggestibility of the masses. Thus:

born criminals and habitual criminals are not only dangerous in themselves, but also because they can easily propagate an epidemic of imitation amongst the masses ... (p. 38)

Indeed nowhere was science deemed more important than in this domain, this meeting point between criminals and 'people'. The state, he noted, had to curb not only alcoholism, but also the intoxicating spread of mad ideas and actions amongst the masses, which had been starkly exemplified in the Paris Commune. The whole Lombrosian project, after all, assumed the possibility of separating the criminal from the people. Laschi went so far as to advocate the incarceration of the 'politically mad' and the 'criminally mad' in anticipation of social disorder (pp. 387–8). The report produced heated disagreement. One delegate, M. Lioy argued that many radical leaders had fought for progress against despotic governments; they had been quite the opposite of atavistic or immoral. Instead of seeking degeneracy amongst revolutionaries, he suggested that Laschi and Lombroso should have looked for it amongst oppressive rulers (p. 389). The topic had clearly generated an unseemly excitement amongst the delegates. One Italian diplomatically proposed that the Congress should move on to another topic, but Enrico Ferri returned to the argument in order to clarify the Italian position.

It was methodologically possible, and socially essential, he declared, to distinguish idealistic revolutionaries from pathological rebels. Thus the good struggle for the independence of the Italian nation could be distinguished from the regressive outbreaks (peasant riots, anarchist attacks and so on), which had occurred in unified Italy.[93] Ferri and Laschi insisted on their own patriotism – nothing degenerate in that – and argued for the dichotomy of patriotic struggle and anti-patriotic insurrection. Moreover they insisted that the actual body of the degenerate rebel was quite distinct from that of the idealistic revolutionary. Lombroso, in a rare moment of relativism, acknowledged how in another time and place their own congress might have been considered delinquent or subversive (p. 391).

The persistent differences between Italian and French theories of crime and a growing international disenchantment with Lombroso was also evident at subsequent meetings. This was put in forthright terms by the first contributor to the fourth Congress, who began his address by saying:

Despite the objections of M. Lombroso and his followers, one can declare today that the theses of the Italian school of criminal anthropology regarding the criminal type and the born criminal ... the fusion of the born criminal with the atavist and the epileptic, no longer bears credence. Numerous authors, above all in Germany and France, have demonstrated the fallacies.[94]

---

[93] Cf. Zimmern, 'Lombroso's new theory', (per.), pp. 203, 211, which differentiated revolutionaries from rebels ('embryos doomed to a certain death'): 'The impetuous character of revolts is still further shown by the fact that youths are constantly found as their instigators and furtherers, while in revolutions appear men of mature age'; cf. Lombroso, *Crime*, p. 434: 'those who start great scientific and political revolutions are almost always young, endowed with genius or with a singular altruism, and have a fine physiognomy; ... But if from the martyrs of a great social and religious idea we pass to rebels, regicides and "presidenticides", such as Fieschi and Guiteau, to the promoters of 1793 ... and to the anarchists, we see that all, or nearly all, are of a criminal type. These are rebels'; cf. Angioliella, *Delitti*; Gaspare, *Passanante*; Penta, *Degenerazioni*; Bianchi *et al.*, *Mondo criminale italiano*; Sernicoli, *Gli attentati*; Zocioli, *L'anarchia*.

[94] *Actes* (Fourth Congress), 1897, Opening Paper, p. 1.

One of the major papers was given by Dr J. Dallemagne on '*Dégéné-rescence* and criminality' (pp. 94–110). He stressed the movement away from Lombroso's theories and their replacement by a more sophisticated internalised notion of degeneration which had emerged by building on the work of Morel. Morel's researches were the corner-stone of modern theory, he said, because they examined the processes of racial decay from the perspective of biology and heredity. At issue for Morel and his follow-ers had been:

the reality of the progressive disappearance of a stock, a race, a species, through successive hereditary degradations ... (p. 95).

But French theory, we are told by Dallemagne, had also developed since the time of Morel; the weakness of his founding work lay in its mystical understanding of degeneration, an occult fatalism which always brought with it the hint of 'ancient Destiny' (p. 95). Dallemagne rejected Lombro-so's obsession with tabulating the superficially monstrous, (his 'teratology' as Dallemagne put it) and argued that the future of criminal science lay in the calibration of the body's relative capacity for resistance against the degenerative processes at work in the environment. Dallemagne later praised Ferri for his opposition to the Durkheimian contention that a certain amount of morbidity was normal (p. 224). But, paradoxically, he argued, Ferri was equally fatalistic in insisting that for certain individuals ('born criminals') crime was indeed the normal, even inevitable condition. Instead, Dallemagne argued, the individual was the point of nexus between a stock and a particular environment, and had a given capacity of resistance to degeneration which precluded fatalism. In place of a teratology (Lombroso), or a metaphysics of degeneration (Morel), criminology was proposed as a physics of the body's psycho-physical forces and resistances.

In Italy as in France, positivism in general was under sustained attack by the last decade of the nineteenth century.[95] Leading positivist figures like Pasquale Villari, were themselves growing increasingly uneasy about the adequacy of any exclusively 'scientific' theory of history. Villari asked in 1891 whether the human being could really be understood as the simple effect of its nature and history. Could science really explain art?[96] Villari came to the conclusion that there were certain ineffable qualities of 'taste', 'inspiration' and 'genius' which were, in the end, an irresolvable mystery.[97]

---

[95] See Asor Rosa, 'La cultura', p. 1,012.   [96] 'La cultura', p. 1,012.
[97] 'La cultura', p. 1,012.

Lombroso's criminological theory was a casualty of the mounting critique of nineteenth-century positivism in general. The sense of political renewal generated under Giolitti from 1903 to 1913 was coterminous with the growing philosophical dominance of neo-idealists like Giovanni Gentile and Benedetto Croce. If Lombroso's work was overtaken by such critiques and by other forms of determinism, the discourse it fostered and sustained was nevertheless responsible for many reforms and new initiatives in and beyond Italy.[98]

Through a Dr Vervaeck, for instance, a laboratory of criminal anthropology was established in the old prison of Minimes in Belgium in 1907.[99] By 1922 there was a network of laboratories in all the country's main prisons. The very idea of 'a laboratory' of crime, I suggest, rather than just any specific congruity in findings, is what allies such initiatives with the discursive world of Lombroso. Again it must be stressed that the language of degeneration, atavism and regression refracted way beyond any specific political programme. Lombroso's work must be understood within, and as a major contribution to, a late-nineteenth-century European-wide concern with the mind and body of the individual criminal. Refined versions of the Lombrosian project still persisted in Italy in the 1920s and 1930s. Pende and Di Tullio, for instance, carried on exploring the 'delinquent constitution' in its 'morpho-physiological' particularity during the fascist period.[100] In 1924 a laboratory of 'criminal biology' was founded in the prison of Staubing in Bavaria under the control of a Dr Viernstein. By the end of the 1920s it was only one of a number in which criminological eugenic research projects were explored.[101] Such laboratories were also founded in, amongst other places, Cuba, Argentina, Portugal, Poland and North America. The Penitentiary Congress held in London in 1925 voted in favour of the necessity of similar services in Britain (the question of Lombroso and England will be explored later). Lombroso's work was one major instance in a positivist emphasis on the criminal, rather than crime, which still persists to the present day. Moreover Lombrosian theory was repeatedly the subject of discussion and critique, be it from neo-classical theorists or from dissenting positivists, and significantly inflected the theories which criticised it, not least by predetermining the agenda for debate. Lombroso and his followers were often accredited with status as expert witnesses called upon by the courts where circumstantial evidence

[98] Cf. Nye, *Crime*, p. 101, which suggests that the extremism of Italian positivist science after 1870 reduced its influence elsewhere.

[99] See Radzinowicz, 'L'antropologia criminale', (per.), pp. 4–5.

[100] See Villa, 'Scienza medica', p. 1,176.

[101] See Cantor, 'Recent tendencies', (per.); Monachesi, 'Trends', (per.); Wise, *Italian Penal Code*, p. xxviii; Altavilla, *et al.*, *Enrico Ferri*, pp. 18–22. On the development of Italian eugenics under fascism, see Pogliano, 'Scienza e stirpe', (per.).

pointed to two equally likely culprits.[102] It would be the task of a further research project to look in detail at the dissemination of, and resistance to, Lombrosian theory in the courts, and indeed would need to be part of broader comparison of the relative importance of medicine and psychiatry in legal practice in different countries.

Robert Nye has suggested that by comparison with French psychiatry, the Italians were notoriously inflexible in their determinism and hence strictly limited in their impact on legal practice and legislation.[103] The point however can easily be overstated. Whilst it is true that the School failed to influence the penal code of 1889 in Italy, they were to come much closer to success in the 1920s. Enrico Ferri was invited to produce a new criminal code for Italy and was forestalled only by the advent of fascism.[104]

The relation between Ferri's criminological work and his bizarre political career also highlights my argument. Positivist theories of crime in late-nineteenth-century Italy with their strange conflation of evolutionary models, phrenology, physiognomy, folklore, and literary anecdotes, their vulnerable hypnotised crowds, cruel or hysterical women and outlandish brigands, may appear now as merely absurd. But the idea of the born criminal, the atavist and the degenerate had a definite coherence and credibility at the time. According to Mack Smith, Ferri, 'a political mountebank: handsome, eloquent and vain', 'was to change his mind many times before he ultimately flirted with fascism'.[105] But to Leon Radzinowicz, at one time Ferri's pupil in Rome, he was 'one of the greatest professors of criminal law in the twentieth century'.[106]

---

[102] Lombroso surveys his own contribution in *Crime: Its Causes and Remedies* (1911, pp. 436–7). When for instance he was asked to assess which of two stepsons was most likely to have killed a woman, Lombroso declared one of them to be, 'in fact the most perfect type of the born criminal: enormous jaws, frontal sinuses and zygomata, thin upper lip, huge incisors, unusually large head (1620cc.) tactile obtuseness ... with sensorial manicinism. He was convicted.' In another case, Lombroso argued less successfully for the conviction of a 'certain Fazio', accused of robbing and murdering a rich farmer. One witness had testified that she had seen him sleeping near the murdered man; the next morning he hid as the police approached. No other evidence of his guilt was offered:

Upon examination I found that this man had outstanding ears, great maxillaries and cheek bones, lemurine appendix, division of the frontal bone, premature wrinkles, sinister look, nose twisted to the right – in short a physiognomy approaching the criminal type; pupils very slightly mobile ... a large picture of a woman tattooed upon his breast, with the words, 'Remembrance of Celine Laura' (his wife), and on his arm the picture of a girl. He had an epileptic aunt and an insane cousin, and investigation showed that he was a gambler and an idler. In every way then biology furnished in this case indications which joined with the other evidence, would have been enough to convict him in a country less tender towards criminals. Notwithstanding this he was acquitted.' Cf. the discussion in Gould, *Mismeasure*, pp. 138–9.

[103] Nye, *Crime*, p. 102.
[104] See Wise, *Italian Penal Code*, p. xix; Radzinowicz, 'Ideology and crime', (per.), p. 1,056.
[105] Mack Smith, *Italy*, p. 191.
[106] Radzinowicz, 'Lombroso', (per.), p. 106.

Ferri was taught at school by Ardigò.[107] He was said to be a quick-witted pupil at both school and university.[108] Indeed he returned as professor in the law faculty at Bologna, three years after receiving his degree. He is remembered today largely as a capricious and charismatic socialist politican, the man who in 1903 captured the editorship of *Avanti* from Bissolati and became a leading figure in the party in the period of the 1904 congress.

In May 1886, he had been elected to the national parliament where he remained through eleven re-elections until 1924. He declared later that he had been 'a Marxist without knowing it'.[109] In 1890 he succeeded Francesco Carrara as professor of law at the university of Pisa, a succession which was indeed symbolic of the growing influence of criminological positivism: Carrara the most eminent neo-classicist succeeded by Ferri, the most eminent legal positivist.

Carrara was indeed the major mouthpiece of that Beccarian tradition outlined earlier. He was concerned to draw out 'the just measure of pain' according to a logical sliding scale of punishments, continually in excess of the benefits of the crime. The crucial first task, he wrote, was to work out abstractly a system of penal rules. The focus in short was on the code of punishments not the individual constitution of the criminal.[110]

Ferri lost the professorship he had taken over from Carrara, however, when he was drawn into the newly organised Italian socialist labour party in 1893. A famous socialist orator, Ferri lectured indefatigably from a large repertoire of speeches on scientific, economic, historical, and sociological subjects. He addressed audiences in Europe, and in South America where he gave some eighty lectures to enormous acclaim. In 1892 he had founded a legal journal, *La scuola positiva*, which sought to rival the classically inspired journal *Rivista penale*. Ferri founded a school for applied criminal law and procedure in Rome, which was to draw a circle of students from both Italy and abroad.[111]

After World War I, Ferri was invited by the then Minister of Justice, Ludovico Mortara, an old school friend from Mantua, to take the presidency of a commission which would prepare a new criminal code for Italy to replace the Zanardelli code of 1889.[112] The commission was to have a membership drawn from various schools of thinking. Once it became clear, however, that the overall ideological orientation was to be positivist, there were various resignations, and Ferri was able to deliver a refined version of his long espoused theory. The resulting document was presented

---

[107] See Ferri, 'Ricordi liceali', p. 249. [108] See Sellin, 'Enrico Ferri'.
[109] *Difese penali*, I, p. 8. [110] See Carrara, *Programma*, II, pp. 81, 84, 87–8.
[111] See Sellin, 'Enrico Ferri', pp. 291–2. [112] See Wise, *Italian Penal Code*, p. xxviii.

in 1921 but forestalled by the entry into power of the fascists who demanded a new code, unmoved by Ferri's attempts to resuscitate his document.[113]

Nevertheless Ferri made his support for Mussolini apparent in various articles[114] and was invited to be a member of the commission under Rocco, whose code was indeed adopted in 1930. Rocco's code represented the triumph of a penological eclecticism which amalgamated elements of classicism and positivism. It marked the rise of a so-called 'Third School', which sought to avoid the metaphysical philosophy of the classical approach, and the biological or sociological determinism of the positivists. The 'technico-juridical' school, as it has also been termed, made a new appeal to clarity of language in the framing of law. It sought to establish a 'pure' field of rights and penalties. Heavily utilitarian in scope (crime was defined as that which destroys or diminishes a 'good', or which sacrifices a human 'interest'[115]), it sought to produce new rigorous definitions of such terms as 'motive' and 'will' via a kind of jurisprudential logical positivism. Nevertheless in the new code, personal history and past criminal record are declared relevant to sentencing, representing an important shift in attention from the classical codes of fixed punishment to individualised 'treatment'. The detailed history of the relations between fascism, degenerationism and the discourses of crime is beyond my scope here. Suffice to say for the moment that Ferri was not unhappy with the 1930 code. As he put it in a footnote in the fifth edition of his *Criminal Sociology*:

While in the fourth edition [1900] I alluded hopefully to socialist trends – to which I have given my fervent enthusiasm . . . now in the fifth edition [1929] I have to note with regard to Italy that with the declining influence of the Socialist Party after the war, because it neither knew how to make a revolution nor wanted to assume the responsibility of power, the task of the social prevention of criminality was assumed and has begun to be realised by the Fascist Government which both in the 'Rocco Project for a [new] Penal Code' and in many special laws has accepted and is putting into effect some of the principles and the most characteristic practical proposals of the positive school.[116]

It would be highly misleading, however, to see Ferri's social evolutionary politics, criminological positivism and eventual fascism as representing the only position in, and outcome of nineteenth-century Italian socialism. It is true that Turati (1857–1932) one of the founders of the

---

113 See Sellin, 'Enrico Ferri'; Altavilla *et al.*, *Enrico Ferri*.
114 See Ferri, *Mussolini* and *Il fascismo*. Ferri exonerated Mussolini from all rumoured crimes (including the murder of Matteotti) and noted how positivism had previously gained few concessions from years of liberal government but was achieving a great deal under fascism.
115 See Spirito, *Storia*.   116 Ferri, *Sociologia criminale*, I, pp. 11–12, n.2.

Socialist Party, and editor of *Critica sociale*[117] had considerable sympathy with positivism in general and Lombrosianism in particular.[118] Positivism was after all seen as an ally in so far as it contributed to undermining a religious world view. But in *Crime and the Social Question* (*Il delitto*, 1883) he carefully delimited the area of his agreement. He praised the positive school for calling into question the 'responsibility' of the criminal, for insisting on focussing attention on the delinquent as a specific material being and for stressing the individual circumstances attending any crime in the real world. But he insisted that both the analysis and the solutions could not but turn on questions of poverty and injustice – how often do you see the rich in prison, he asked?[119] Furthermore, he affirmed that 'bourgeois society is the first delinquent' (p. 149). Lombroso's determinism had a worrying tendency to call into question not only the responsibility of the criminal, but also of the bourgeoisie. Turati did not dispute the existence of biological anomalies in criminals, nor the alarming increase in crime, but he located the causes in environmental hardships:

Instead of thinking of directly changing the organisation of individuals, it is easier and more fruitful to change the organisation of society. (p. 171)

In a vicious society, like the present one, he went on, there were inevitably vicious consequences. Thus 'remove the causes and you remove the effects' (p. 171). Socialism's ideal was the production of a society in which 'crime will be neither necessary nor useful' (p. 171).

Labriola, on the other hand, had little time for the Lombrosian group. As he put it to Engels in a famously forthright dismissal, much of the intelligentsia 'knows only the positivists, who are, in my view, representatives of the cretinous generation of the bourgeois type'.[120] Ferri crops up occasionally in the *Letters* (pp. 14, 123–4, 210), and is always dispatched with utter contempt as a charlatan.

Lombroso's death in 1909 prompted commentaries and reappraisals of positivist criminology from friends and foes. His body was hardly cold before Giovanni Gentile had launched a new attack on the positive school.[121] If Lombroso was to be acknowledged for his welcome emphasis on 'practical matters', argued Gentile, he was absolutely to be deplored for his vulgar materialism and above all for his negation of spirit, free will and God (p. 268).

A Catholic-medical critique of Lombroso was also mounted in this

[117] See Asor Rosa, 'La cultura', pp. 1,021–2; cf. Minuz, 'Gli intellettuali'.
[118] See Minuz, 'Gli intellettuali', p. 231.
[119] *Il delitto*, pp. 173–80.
[120] Letter, 30 March 1891, *Lettere a Engels*, p. 14.
[121] Gentile, 'Lombroso e la scuola italiana', (per.).

period. In a book in 1911, for instance, Dr Gemelli lamented that the church had failed to produce a modern discourse on crime. Lombroso, he warned, teaches 'us Catholics' that we must participate in current political debate, in order to criticise 'anti-Christian' positions' and provide a viable alternative theory.[122] Gemelli mocked the naivety of Lombroso's materialist methodology (that 'immense poem' as he put it, p. ix) and the crowning irony of his final conversion to spiritualism; the medium, Eusapia Paladino, had spectacularly 'hood-winked him' (p. 13).

In his last years Lombroso had indeed become fascinated with the question of life after death, and the possibility of making contact with the deceased. His final publications revealed an intense interest in spiritualism.[123] Where his work had hitherto concerned evolution, ancestry, regression back to beginnings, it now concerned scientifically ambiguous forces – hypnotism, hysteria, the future beyond the grave, the possibility of a materialist theory of spirits. Lombroso was an inveterate dabbler in those contemporary grey areas between 'orthodox' medicine and fringe practice, 'science' and 'superstition', clinic and theatre.

Hysteria and hypnotism had come to prominence in Northern Italian medical culture partly as a result of the massive cultural impact of the controversies in France between the schools of Charcot and Bernheim; but also because of the theatrical exploitation of hypnosis, which seemed to many to threaten the prestige of medical inquiries in this delicate field. Hypnotism was a vexed matter and the medical 'credentials' of the hypnotist provoked deep concern in a domain only recently re-appropriated by official medicine.[124] A major controversy took place over the performances of a certain Donato, the stage name of a Belgian, D'Hont, an ex-naval officer who from 1875 toured Europe and gave popular performances. As Morselli put it in 1886:

Since the end of April 1886, the city of Turin has been rife with rumours of the strange phenomena of 'fascination' at the Scribe theatre provoked by the well-known magnetiser Donato in young people unknown to him. Even though they were all healthy, they voluntarily submitted themselves [to him] before a huge audience, who were amazed by these magnetic manoeuvres.[125]

A debate raged back and forth between and amongst doctors, politicians and newspapers as to whether these performances were faked, whether they should be banned and whether Donato should be deported.[126] Dr

---

[122] *Cesare Lombroso*, p. 175.
[123] See *Ricerche* and the account in English in *After Death*.
[124] See Gallini, *La sonnambula meravigliosa*.
[125] Morselli, *Il magnetismo animale*, 1.
[126] See Gallini, *La sonnambula meravigliosa*, esp. pp. 188–95. On France, Donato and the perceived dangers of theatrical performances of hypnotism, cf. Harris, 'Murders', (diss.), pp. 207–17.

Morselli argued that nobody – not even the doctor – had the right to a 'monopoly', and hence stage hypnotism should be permitted.[127] Others were deeply concerned by the multiple sexual and criminal repercussions which might follow from the seduction and corruption of the acquiescent female at the hands of the skilful hypnotist.[128] One commentator cited Lombroso's anecdote about a rich gentleman, an amateur and corrupt hypnotist, who, merely from scientific 'curiosity', used to put two subjects of different sexes (the women often virgins) to sleep and then brought about their sexual liaison through 'suggestion'.[129] The question of the theatrical vulgarisation of hypnotism and the secret seduction of well-to-do women in the dubious consulting rooms of perverse amateurs ran over into much wider questions about the inherent 'suggestibility' of women and the masses at large. The language of hypnotism and hysteria entered into the new science of crowds which in these last decades of the nineteenth century was developing in both France and Italy. In November 1888, the Lombrosian Giuseppe Sergi gave a university course entitled 'epidemic psychoses'.[130] He argued that many religious transports and political convulsions were the effects of insanity. The power of leaders over the led was formidable, he argued, and was an urgent social and political concern. And indeed a huge Lombrosian literature erupted in these years to address the problem.[131]

In one way such work rejoined the evolutionary determinism of Lombroso's criminal anthropology; hence it explored the heredity and 'physiology' of the crowd, tracing the conditions of its atavism and regression. But the crowd constituted at once the apotheosis and the crisis of a science which had been from the beginning a project of social differentiation, obsessed by the distinct visual image of the criminal. How could the scientist grasp the physiognomy of the city's mass or chart the visible shift from the peaceful congregation into the violent mob? One could perhaps map changes in facial expression, and even find Darwin helpful in that field,[132] but Lombroso had always sought immutable contours, permanently telling lines, which precisely could not be wiped off the face at a stroke.

Faced by sustained and increasingly aggressive critique from delegates at criminological conferences, from neo-idealist philosophers, the church and legal profession, Lombroso started to delve beyond the visible, or even the material. He began to interrogate the terms of his science and to enter

---

[127] Gallini, *La sonnambula meravigliosa*, pp. 223–4.
[128] *La sonnambula meravigliosa*, p. 231.
[129] *La sonnambula meravigliosa*, pp. 230–1.
[130] *La sonnambula meravigliosa*, p. 302.
[131] *La sonnambula meravigliosa*, pp. 302–3; cf. Mucchi, *L'abbraccio della folla*.
[132] See Darwin, *Expression of Emotions*.

fields which he had been accused of previously ignoring. Lombroso turned his attention to the dead, much to the alarm, he tells us, of his more cautious colleagues.[133] They warned him that he risked ruining a scientific career and becoming ridiculous. Lombroso insisted however that his 'love of truth' forced him to proceed. He had always been sceptical about spiritualism, he explained, and indeed had always refused even to watch such experiments. Yet finally, in 1891, he agreed to observe a medium at work.[134] He saw a table rise high in to the air in broad daylight. Where else should this be but in a hotel in Naples, the Italian city most closely identified with idealist opposition to positivism? Two days later in the presence of other colleagues, he was to see the following scene:

in clear light, we saw a big curtain, which separated our room from a nearby alcove which was more than a metre away from the medium, carry itself suddenly towards me, surrounding and tightening around me. I could only free myself with some considerable difficulty.[135]

Lombroso was at a loss to explain what had happened. He was sure there had been no simple trick. He speculated on the hypersensitivity of certain bodies, radioactive waves, a fourth dimension.[136] Spiritualism, he acknowledged, was a whole hidden ocean, as yet uncharted by the geography of conventional science.[137] But stranger things were still to come. Eusapia Paladino told Lombroso that she could do far more than move tables and awnings around; indeed if she wished, she could even bring his mother back from the dead:

immediately afterwards I saw (we were in the semi-darkness of a red light), a rather small figure, as my mother's had been, detach herself from the curtain. She wore a veil and circled the table, until I, almost beside myself with emotion, begged her to speak once again, and she said: 'Cesare my son' ['*Cesar fio mio*'].[138]

This was strange, he confessed, since her habit was to use the Venetian term 'mio fiol'. Nevertheless removing the veil from her face, she proceeded to kiss him. She 'reappeared' to him albeit less distinctly than on this first occasion, at eight subsequent sittings held between 1906 and 1907 in

[133] See Lombroso, *Ricerche*, p. viii; cf. the hostile views of both Morel in France and Maudsley in England towards spiritualism. See Morel, *Swedenborg*, p. 62; 'We have studied Swedenborg as one of the most powerful personifications in modern times of that human tendency to appeal to the supernatural for the explanation of phenomena.' Swedenborg was 'the victim of hallucinations' (p. 62). Cf. Maudsley's lecture on the sources of error in seeing and believing ('Common Sources of Error').
[134] Lombroso's introduction to Barzini, *Nel mondo dei misteri*, pp. 3–4.
[135] Barzini, *Nel mondo dei misteri*, p. 4.
[136] *Nel mondo dei misteri*, p. 26.
[137] *Nel mondo dei misteri*, p. 28; perhaps subliminal thoughts, Lombroso suggested vaguely, could persist after death.
[138] Lombroso, *Ricerche*, p. 66.

Milan and Turin. But even as it seems that Lombroso was really embarking on a quite different kind of discourse, unlike any of his previous investigations, he brusquely moved on to give other examples, as though the case of his own mother could be but one further piece of objective evidence to weigh up in the balance.

The scene is indeed tantalisingly undeveloped, and yet an uncannily apposite ending to Lombroso's whole *oeuvre*. His own family was indeed by now directly involved in the Lombroso 'industry', researching, publishing, furthering the topic of criminal anthropology. Despite Lombroso's negative views about the scientific capacities of women,[139] his two daughters became disciples, collaborators and eventually his hagiographers.[140] Lombroso's science had at one level assumed the investigator's own transcendence of personality, history, subjectivity, origins. The séance in Naples fleetingly disclosed the phantoms of a personal history which had systematically been written out of so much of his research. It was deemed extraneous in all those self-effacing projects which tracked the body and the genealogy of criminals, prostitutes and the insane. Yet, in the end, he was unable to alienate the theme of ancestry altogether; he was haunted by voices and apparitions, the very silhouette of his mother. It is clear from his description that he was touched and disturbed by her words and caresses. He did not altogether abandon the possibility of a materialist theory of spiritualism. But between the fantastic conjuring of Eusapia Paladino and the gentle return of Zefora Lombroso, he laid to rest the ghosts of positive science.

[139] See Lombroso, 'Physical insensibility', (per.), and the chapter on Lombroso and the representation of prostitution in Gilman, *Difference and Pathology*.
[140] See P. and G. Lombroso, *Cesare Lombroso*; P. Lombroso and Carrara, *Nella penombra*; G. Lombroso, *Soul of Woman*.

PART III

England

◁ ═══════════════════════════════════ ═ ▷

6

Fictions of degeneration

'Suddenly it rained apes.'[1]

Much of the argument so far has depended upon little-known nineteenth-century material. But if we re-read some of the most familiar of all English-language fictions from the period we find degeneration a recurrent concern. What follows in this chapter is in part simply a demonstration of the existence of that preoccupation in literary texts; but the aim is also to take various examples where a certain interrogation of, or even resistance towards, degeneration is manifest.

'There are some trees, Watson', declared Sherlock Holmes,

'which grow to a certain height, and then suddenly develop some unsightly eccentricity. You will see it often in humans. I have a theory that the individual represents in his development the whole procession of his ancestors, and that such a sudden turn to good or evil stands for some strong influence which came into the line of his pedigree. The person becomes, as it were, the epitome of the history of his own family.'[2]

'It is surely rather fanciful' replied Watson (p. 494). Here was the voice of what is often taken to be the dominant English response to such 'theory', a pervasive 'Anglo-Saxon' scepticism towards the fanciful excesses of 'foreign' proposals. Holmes, however, does not give up his speculations. Close to the last adventure of the series, he muses: 'When one tries to rise above Nature one is liable to fall below it. The highest type of man may revert to the animal if he leaves the straight road of destiny' (p. 1,082) – a baneful conclusion to a story which has indeed shown the dangers of dabbling with science and its strange potions, echoing *Jekyll and Hyde* and Sherlock's own experiments in, or addiction to, cocaine. This tale, 'the adventures of the creeping man' (pp. 1070–83),[3] might be seen as a post-Darwinian counter-point to Poe's 'The Murders of the Rue Morgue'.

---

[1] Doyle, *Lost World*, p. 142.
[2] Doyle, *Sherlock Holmes*, p. 494. Note that Conan Doyle's own father, an epileptic and alcoholic, had lost his job as a civil servant and died when his son was eighteen. Arthur became a doctor, but by the late 1880s had abandoned medicine for a career of writing; see Edwards, *Quest*, pp. 11–12.
[3] The story was set in 1903 and first published in 1923.

Lowenstein, Holmes discovers, becomes ape-like after imbibing a 'wondrous strength-giving serum', drawn from the great black-faced monkey of the Himalayan slopes, and climbs all over the external walls of the house. At the end of the investigation, Holmes is very worried about the charlatans of science and the unknown dangers they may pose to human identity and society:

There is danger there – a very real danger to humanity. Consider Watson, that the material, the sensual, the worldly would all prolong their worthless lives. The spiritual would not avoid the call to something higher. It would be the survival of the least fit. What sort of cesspool may not our poor world become? (pp. 1,082–3)

To envisage the loss of 'our world' in this period was almost axiomatically to envisage a primitive 'lost world' or a degenerate 'after world' (as in Jefferies' *After London*, 1885), the vision caught up in the fantasies of evolution, paleontology and racial anthropology.[4] The loss of fixed hierarchies, places and temporal trajectories was thus marked in Conan Doyle's *The Lost World* (1912) by a space where dinosaurs, 'ape-men', native Indians ('little red fellows', p. 144) and adventurous white men (no women here: just the two squabbling professors, Challenger and Summerlee, the very English Lord John Roxton and the rugby-playing Irish narrator, Malone, all in the end the very best of friends) fight it out tooth and claw. Meanwhile, the ever-faithful 'negro Zambo' (p. 102) is shown to watch helplessly from a separate peak, unable to cross the divide towards his masters, but always unwilling to join the 'treachery' of the two Latin half-castes, or the self-interested retreat of the Indian luggage-bearers. The loss of bearings in time and place is immediately recuperated: degeneration is the antinomy of civilisation, the ape, the opposite of the white professor. The individual, Challenger tells us, echoing Holmes above, is a function of his genealogy: 'each separate *id* is a microcosm possessed of an historical architecture elaborated slowly through the series of generations' (p. 19). But Professor Challenger, to be blunt, is almost an animal, if a semi-sympathetic one: '[he] placed a soothing paw upon my shoulder' (p. 102). His extraordinary simian body is exposed more and more insistently through the pages of the story: 'At last we exposed that monstrous torso... it was all matted with black hair' (p. 102). 'Beside [Challenger] stood his master the king of the ape-men ... Only above the eye brows, where the sloping forehead and low, curved skull of the ape-man were in sharp contrast to the broad brow and magnificent cranium of the European, could one see any marked difference' (p. 124).

---

[4] On the widespread interest (including Conan Doyle's) in the 'missing link' of evolution in this period, see Millar, *Piltdown Man*; Weiner, *Piltdown Forgery*.

The intrepid party are soon overwhelmed by the fearsome apes of the Lost World. The whole dramatic representation of apes and men risks collapsing into hysteria, a fundamental confusion in which identities and genders are blurred: 'When the ape-man stood by Challenger and put his paw on his shoulder, the thing was complete. Summerlee was a bit hysterical, and he laughed till he cried. The ape-men laughed too . . . and they set to work to drag us off through the forest' (p. 143).

On the expedition's return to London, hysteria threatens to become farce. The affair provokes pandemonium amongst the public and the experts. Anticipating the incredulity of his audience, Challenger produces a primeval monster ('it was the devil of our childhood', p. 189) at the extraordinary scientific meeting, whereupon 'there was turmoil in the audience' and the prehistoric bird flies out the window. The narrative is caught in an ambiguous relationship to 'science', too close to the Victorian discourse of evolution and degeneration to interrogate it deeply, flitting between pastiche and a fundamental compliance, unable to see beyond the more superficial foibles of the scientist. It is unclear in the end quite who is the butt of the story's jokes:

[Challenger] 'The natives were Cucama Indians, an amiable, but degraded race, with mental powers hardly superior to the average Londoner'. (p. 31)

[Challenger to Malone] 'Round-headed', he muttered. 'Brachycephalic, grey-eyed, black-haired, with suggestion of the negroid. Celtic, I presume?' [Malone] 'I am an Irishman, sir.' [Challenger] 'Irish Irish?' [Malone] 'Yes, sir.' [Challenger] 'That, of course, explains it.' (p. 31)[5]

Conan Doyle was not alone in this scrutiny of the world of evolution and degeneration. H. G. Wells' *The Time Machine* (first serialised in 1894–5) had been after all an exemplary 'blue-print' of degenerationist concerns. Wells was at one stage a pupil of Thomas Huxley; he retained a deep interest in evolutionary theories and racial anthropology and an increasing apprehension about the future of British society.[6] The very

[5] Challenger was a kind of composite caricature, suggesting something of Huxley and also most obviously Lankester (discussed below), who, like Challenger, worked at the British Museum. Challenger we are told, had been an assistant keeper of comparative anthropology (p. 15). Cf. '"There is an excellent monograph by my gifted friend, Ray Lankester!" said he ... "The inscription beneath it runs: 'Probable appearance in life of the Jurassic Dinosaur Stegosaurus'"' (p. 35). Note also Challenger's cantankerous but ultimately 'correct' dispute with foreign experts: 'The English Professor had handled his subject in a very aggressive fashion, and had thoroughly annoyed his Continental colleagues' (p. 16).

[6] See Bergonzi (ed.), *H. G. Wells;* Kemp, *Wells and Culminating Ape;* Morton, *Vital Science,* pp. 100–14.

extinction of humanity, Wells warned in an article in *The Pall Mall Gazette* in 1894, could not be ruled out of consideration: 'No; man's complacent assumption of the future is too confident ... Even now, for all we can tell, the coming terror may be crouching for its spring and the fall of humanity be at hand. In the case of every other predominant animal the world has ever seen, we repeat, the hour of its complete ascendancy has been the beginning of its decline.'[7]

What Wells' time traveller discovers in the projected future of *The Time Machine* is a ruling class (the Eloi), which has become ever more beautiful, but 'indescribably frail', genderless, and mentally backward ('on the intellectual level of one of our five year old children'[8]). He encounters a world of 'ruinous splendour' (p. 29) and degeneration:

It seemed to me that I had happened upon humanity upon the wane. The ruddy sunset set me thinking of the sunset of mankind. (p. 31)

Ruin has apparently been brought about by excessive 'civilisation', or rather, too much interference in natural selection, a problem which had preoccupied Darwin and which deeply troubled many of his followers;[9]

For the first time I began to realize an odd consequence of the social effort in which we are at present engaged. And yet, come to think, it is a logical consequence enough. Strength is the outcome of need; security sets a premium on feebleness. The work of ameliorating the conditions of life – the true civilising process that makes life more and more secure – has gone steadily on to a climax. (p. 31)

Somewhere in the passage from Darwin's *The Origin of Species* (1859) through *The Descent of Man* (1871) to the end of the century, the dominant social implications of evolution, in the eyes of the evolutionists, alter markedly. It will be part of the function of the discussion in the next chapter to trace certain of these changes in connotation. *The Time Machine* gathers together some effects of that shift. But of course there are also continuities between this tale and earlier social criticism in the Victorian period. Wells projects the notion of 'two nations', stock image of the 1840s social novel, into a ghastly nemesis. The fictional crisis evokes specifically the fear of class separation in Victorian London. It predicts the working class descent into violent anarchy, the ruling class slide into the cloistered world of fantasy, decadence, neurosis.

[It] seemed as clear as daylight to me that the gradual widening of the present merely temporary and social difference between the Capitalist and the Labourer was the key to the whole position ... Even now, does not an East-end worker live in

---

[7] 'The extinction of man', (per.), p. 3.   [8] *Selected Short Stories*, p. 26.
[9] See the discussion in ch. 7 below.

such artificial conditions as practically to be cut off from the natural surface of the earth? (p. 47)[10]

If the urban poor in Wells, as more generally in the anthropological representation of 'outcast London' in the 1870s, 1880s and 1890s,[11] was depicted as the object of compassion, they were also the source of fear and loathing: 'there was an altogether new element in the sickening quality of the Morlocks – a something inhuman and malign' (p. 54). Thomas Carlyle had provided a powerful model for such brutalising description. Carlyle brutalised the Chartists in his description; he assumed their inarticulacy (their 'dumbness') and the impossibility of political dialogue. Wells, however, cannot simply return to Carlyle's castigation of ruling-class failure, for the question of moral responsibility for social division is now clouded by the intimation of the inexorability of natural process. The stark laws of evolution now intervened in the very terms of social theory:

Then I tried to preserve myself from the horror that was coming upon me, by regarding it as a rigorous punishment of human selfishness. Man had been content to live in ease and delight upon the labours of his fellow man, had taken Necessity as his watchword and excuse, and in the fullness of time Necessity had come home to him. I even tried a *Carlyle-like scorn* of this wretched aristocracy in decay. But this attitude of mind was impossible. However great their intellectual degradation, the Eloi had kept too much of their human form not to claim my sympathy, and to make me perforce a sharer in their degradation and their Fear. (p. 59, emphasis added)

The Time Machine is full of literary echoes: the social novel of the 1840s, Swift's Yahoos and Houyhnhnms, the Fall; but it recomposes its themes in relation to evolutionary and degenerationist theory:

The two species that had resulted from the evolution of man were sliding down towards, or had already arrived at, an altogether new relationship ... The Nemesis of the delicate ones was creeping on apace. Ages ago, thousands of generations ago, man had thrust his brother man out of the ease and the sunshine. And now that brother was coming back – changed! Already the Eloi had begun to learn one old lesson anew. They were becoming reacquainted with Fear. (pp. 54–5)

What sabotages the return to Carlylean terms is the perceived horror of scientific disclosure and intimation. At the end of the journey for the time

[10] Note the similarity between this fear and those of Henry Maudsley (discussed below). Thus for example, Maudsley criticised Galton's 'positive eugenics', aimed at encouraging reproduction amongst the fit, because he thought it did not deal sufficiently with curbing the unfit and 'the result might be two species of human beings; a result clean contrary to the philanthropic principles of a democratic age' (*Hereditary Variation*, p. 219).

[11] See Stedman Jones, *Outcast London*; Keating (ed.), *Unknown England*; Hulin and Coustillas (eds.), *Victorian Writers*. Amongst the primary literature, see, for instance, Greenwood, *Wilds of London*, *Low Life Deeps* and *Seven Curses*; London, *People of the Abyss*; Mearns, *Bitter Cry*.

traveller, beyond cultural degeneration and simian insubordination, lies the truth of physics. The traveller glimpses beyond all the fiddle with human destiny to the heat death of the sun predicted by the second law of thermodynamics:

[The] sun, red and very large, halted motionless upon the horizon, a vast dome glowing with a dull heat, and now and then suffering a momentary extinction ... All the sounds of man, the bleating of sheep, the cries of birds, the hum of insects, the stir that makes the background of our lives – all that was over. (pp. 75–8)

In the winter of 1898, Conrad complained of the intellectually numbing effect of living in a world whose sun was dying: 'The fate of a humanity condemned ultimately to perish from cold', he wrote to his friend Cunninghame Graham, 'is not worth troubling about. If you believe in improvement you must weep, for the attained perfection must end in cold, darkness and silence.'[12] But in *The Secret Agent* (1907), dedicated to H. G. Wells, the terms of the gloom multiply, fragment, lose any singularity or certainty. Thus the sinister Mr Vladimir mocks the former Ambassador's grim social perceptions (his deathbed words, 'Unhappy Europe! Thou shalt perish by the moral insanity of thy children!', p. 32), and 'prophetic and doleful dispatches [which] had been for years the joke of Foreign Offices' (p. 32). 'The sacrosanct fetish of today is science' (p. 34), we are told. Hence Comrade Ossipon fetishises the study of degeneration, appalled when his comrade utters the words 'Lombroso is an ass':

[Ossipon] nicknamed the Doctor, ex-medical student without a degree; afterwards wandering lecturer to working-men's associations upon the socialistic aspects of hygiene; author of a popular quasi-medical study (in the form of a cheap pamphlet seized promptly by the police) entitled *The Corroding Vices of the Middle Classes* ... (p. 46)

But if Lombroso is ridiculed, it is nevertheless no other than the Italian *savant* whose theory saves Ossipon from becoming the accomplice of Mrs Verloc:

He was scientific and he gazed scientifically at that woman, the sister of a degenerate, a degenerate herself – of a murdering type. He gazed at her, and invoked Lombroso, as an Italian peasant recommends himself to his favourite saint. He gazed scientifically. He gazed at her cheeks, at her nose, at her eyes, at her ears ... Bad! ... Fatal! ... Not a doubt remained ... a murdering type ... (p. 239)

The narrative had in a sense already conceded the hereditarian terms of reference in the very description of the murder: 'Into that plunging blow, delivered over the side of the couch, Mrs Verloc had put all the inheritance

12 Jean-Aubry, *Joseph Conrad*, I, p. 222.

of her immemorial and obscure descent, the simple ferocity of the age of caverns, and the unbalanced nervous fury of the age of bar-rooms' (p. 212).

'He was an extraordinary lad, that brother of yours ... A perfect type in a way' (p. 239), Ossipon observes of 'docile' degenerate Stevie, stooge of Verloc's plot. Stevie shambled along in his idiocy, 'a moral creature', unable to grasp that the function of the police was not to alleviate suffering:

'Police', he suggested, confidently
'The police aren't for that,' observed Mrs Verloc, cursorily, hurrying on her way.
Stevie's face lengthened considerably. He was thinking. The more intense his thinking, the slacker was the drop of his lower jaw. And it was with an aspect of hopeless vacancy that he gave up his intellectual enterprise. (p. 143)

The task of grasping the function of crime, punishment and policing recurs as a very problematic 'intellectual enterprise' through the book. The questions and answers are posed, recomposed and abandoned over and over. 'And what is crime?', asked Yundt in his tirade against the Italian criminologist (p. 47). For Chief Inspector Heat, criminals were 'his fellow-citizens gone wrong because of imperfect education' (p. 82). But the minds of the burglar and the police officer, we are told, are the same: 'Both recognise the same conventions, and have a working knowledge of each other's methods' (p. 82). Heat, one might say, is wedded to the classical theory of crime, unable to grasp 'degeneration', and altogether baffled by the phenomenon of anarchism: 'The mind of Chief Inspector Heat was inaccessible to ideas of revolt' (p. 82).

Conrad's fictions certainly registered, if in contradictory and elusive ways, the possible implications for human meaning of current biological and physical theories. Several books have recently appeared tracing the links between the works of Conrad and Darwin, the vast shared problem of reading nature, evolution, language, the human face, evil.[13] The signs linking evolution, progress and the West are radically disturbed by Conrad's protagonists. Figures like Kurtz, Lord Jim, Heyst, pose questions about development, urbanity and survival, interrogating evolutionary progressivism, blurring all clear divisions between the civilised, the savage, the degenerate, the unfit.[14]

'The way of the world', we are told in the enigmatically titled *Victory* (1915) is 'gorge and disgorge'. Degeneration is investigated, analysed, dislocated from any clear axis or trajectory in the novel; it circulates everywhere and is thus impossible to pose in a clear relation to evolution or progress – the 'noble' Heyst seeks in vain for a still, peaceful island where 'we can defy the fates', not the confused archipelagos of flux and struggle

---

[13] See, for instance, Hunter, *Conrad and Ethics of Darwinism*; O'Hanlon, *Conrad and Darwin*.
[14] See Tanner, 'Conrad and the last gentleman', (per.).

encountered by a Darwin or a Wallace. He is shown to be incapable of, perhaps unfit for, survival, when harassed by the evil triumvirate – Ricardo ('a jaguar', p. 288), Pedro ('an ape', p. 288), and Mr Jones (another 'gentleman', but no less than the spectre of death itself[15]).

Physiognomy is a crucial site of meaning and ambiguity in the novel. Mrs Schomberg has become visually impenetrable as a means of marital survival – 'the body is the unalterable mask of the soul' (p. 86); Schomberg, we are told, is 'no great judge of physiognomy' (p. 91); Ricardo is a jaguar, but on his face 'nothing could be read' (p. 14); 'I've had that schooling that you couldn't tell by my face if I meant to rip you up the next minute' (p. 119). The powerful reach of heredity in the determination of the individual and the race is an issue which Conrad 'inherits', partially interrogates, and sometimes appallingly rejoins and confirms in this fiction as in others: thus it is uncertain how we read the over-philosophical detachment of Heyst's father, the alcoholism of Lena's father, the enigmatic aetiology of Jones' insanity ('[y]ou don't want any more of our history do you?', he asks the hotel owner, p. 95), the 'Teutonic' evil of Schomberg or the 'Chinese' wall which Wang instinctively builds against his doomed master, Heyst.

A deep concern with the mysterious relation between the body and the determination of character can be followed through in a large number of contemporary novels which in other ways appear quite disparate. In Gissing's *The Nether World* (1889), physiognomy is once again determining: '[Joseph's] face was against him; the worn, sallow features, the eyes which so obviously made a struggle to look with frankness, the vicious lower lip, awoke suspicion and told tales of base experience such as leaves its stamp upon a man for ever' (p. 162). In *Demos* (1886) the body had been used even more pessimistically and conservatively to signify the inherent physical or rather physiological obstacles to social mobility. In place of Dickens' radical uncertainty, Gissing's narrative affirms a form of racial determinism: it is the differing 'quality' of blood and body which finally assures Richard Mutimer's degeneration and precludes his attempt to become a mine-owner. Richard's real affinity is with 'Demos', that 'tempest of savage faces'. Early in the novel he is shown to have a particular oratorical hold over the vulgar crowd, an ability to satisfy 'the raff of a city' with his intoxicating, radical diatribe against the wealthy. But in the end he is destroyed by the mob he has served. His biological 'essence', we are shown, is inextricably tied to his own racial-class heritage. Marriage to Adela is shown to be impossible, doomed by nature, or more particularly

---

[15] Jones 'looked remarkably like a corpse' (p. 102); cf. 'the spectral intensity of that glance' (p. 102).

by Richard's atavism and primitive egoism: 'The thin crust of refinement was shattered; the very man came to light, coarse, violent, whipped into fury by his passions, of which injured self-love was not the least' (p. 367).[16]

Gissing's work provides an interesting example of degeneration in the novel, which would merit an extended analysis; the aim here, however, is briefly to introduce a constellation of images and problems in fiction, which, as I will then show, have a far wider ramification in the language and politics of the later-Victorian period. There follow three final examples, popular novels by Wilde, Stevenson and Stoker, which represent once more a shared fascination with the science of crime and the physiognomy of degeneration. Where the work of doctors like Morel, Magnan, Lombroso and Maudsley sought in various ways to refine the taxonomic codes of insanity and criminality, a number of fictions of the later-nineteenth century characteristically probed the discrepancy between form, character and history, and implicitly interrogated the validity of any determinist methodology.

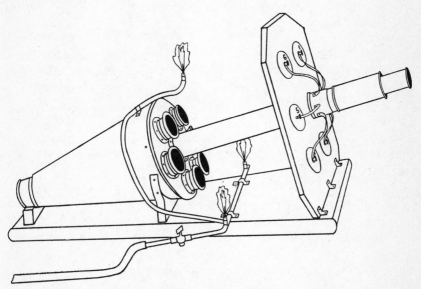

9   Galton's composite photography machine, from Pearson, *The Life, Letters and Labours of Francis Galton*

[16] Cf. the views of Henry Maudsley (discussed below): for instance Maudsley asked the reader to imagine a family suddenly thrown down from the aristocracy, physiologically unable to adapt: 'a secret unrest in the nature of the stock even after centuries might declare itself' (*Life in Mind and Conduct*, p. 338) and conversely 'the tradesman's spirit' can erupt into the spuriously 'noble' family which has sought to 'forget' its base ancestry. The 'commercial tincture' sometimes shows its 'crude nature' leading to 'startling reversion' (p. 339).

10   Criminal composites, from Pearson, *The Life, Letters and Labours of Francis Galton*

Francis Galton, Darwin's cousin, had sought to capture scientifically the very face of the subject's biological history. Indeed he invented a composite photography machine which would record the inherent physiognomic features of criminality and race.[17] Compare the protagonist in Wilde's *The Picture of Dorian Gray* (1890), who hides his true face, thereby disjoining vice from appearance. The disjunction of faces and essences is matched by the morbid schisms of London's geography. Dorian moves across 'this grey monstrous London',[18] flitting between 'polite' society and a grotesque East End underworld peopled by 'hideous' Jews (p. 57), 'half-castes', opium addicts, prostitutes and alcoholics – a vast gallery of 'monstrous marionettes' and 'squat, misshapen figure[s]' (pp. 205–8). Each criminal act however is written upon the portrait in Dorian's attic. His initial reaction is at once an extension and a macabre inversion of naturalist method. He looks upon his image with studied detachment, feeling an 'almost scientific interest ... Was there some subtle affinity between the chemical atoms, that shaped themselves into form and colour on the canvas, and the soul that was within him?' (p. 108) Briefly he takes up 'the Materialistic doctrines of the *Darwinismus* movement in Germany ... tracing the thoughts and passions of men to some pearly cell in the brain', and finding always 'the absolute dependence of the spirit on certain conditions, morbid or healthy, normal or diseased' (p. 148). This unhappy dabbling with science is part of Dorian's descent into degeneracy, not, as he imagines, a detached curiosity. Indeed his self-scrutiny is abandoned when he finds that despite all his efforts of will, he is the victim of excruciating reminiscences, a rebellious memory that 'like a horrible malady was eating his soul away' (p. 208).

The Strange Case of Dr Jekyll and Mr Hyde (1886), declared Wilde in 'The Decay of Lying', 'reads dangerously like an experiment out of *The Lancet*' (p. 912). In the story, Utterson, the lawyer, struggles to explain his strange presentiment of evil, this 'impression of deformity without any nameable malformation'.[19] Yet Utterson is overcome with a desire ('almost an inordinate curiosity', p. 38,) to see Hyde, the creature inscribed with 'Satan's signature' (p. 40). To Utterson, Hyde is inseparable from and yet irreconcilable with Jekyll: 'There *is* something more, if I could find a name for it. God bless me, the man seems hardly human!' (p. 40).

Dr Jekyll's occult medicine, like Dr Pascal's in Zola or Lowenstein's in Conan Doyle, offers no guarantee against the disintegrative discoveries which threaten his very identity. The riddle of atavism is only solved in Jekyll's final statement, delivered posthumously into the hands of his lawyer. We learn how an early recognition of the 'thorough and primitive

[17] See plates 9 and 10 above; see also Pearson, *Francis Galton*, II, p. 298; Sekula, 'Body and archive', (per.).
[18] *Dorian Gray*, p. 57.
[19] *Dr Jekyll and Mr Hyde*, p. 40.

duality of man' (p. 82) had led him to transgress the bounds of chemistry, to experiment with alchemy in a fabulous dream of separating good from evil. But even at the laboratory table he is soon lost in reverie, a rhapsodic intimation of 'the trembling immateriality, the mist-like transience, of this seemingly so solid body in which we walk attired' (p. 82).

Instead of the dream of transcending an animal history Jekyll discovers tragically that Hyde's 'ape-like spite' (p. 97) is overpowering. Ever larger quantities of the antidote are needed to suppress the fiend, for as the drug wears off, 'the animal within me' (p. 92) is once again 'licking the chops of memory' (p. 92). Sleep itself becomes the catalyst of Hyde's liberation. Jekyll awakes to find his hands 'corded' and hairy. (p. 88)

The inquiring doctor is reduced finally to a figure of pathos, the disconsolate prisoner of his own morbid condition. *Jekyll and Hyde* indeed rejoins and nuances a longer theme in the Victorian novel, in which the integrity of the physician's body and mind is cast into doubt: think of the excruciation of Lydgate in Eliot's *Middlemarch*, or of Jennings and Candy in Collins' *The Moonstone*; of Dr Watson, and his long convalescence from wounds received in the Raj, or of Sherlock Holmes himself, a different kind of 'detective' of the body, with his cocaine, mournful violin, nervous fits, ennui.

The modern reader cannot perhaps help but turn from this story to the world of Freud and psychoanalysis, to the 'id' in 'he' which Hyde spells out, but Jekyll disavows: 'He, I say – I cannot say, I' (p. 94).[20] For Stevenson, Hyde is never 'I'. Whilst Utterson, Enfield, Poole, Lanyon, the woman witness, Jekyll are all commentators, at least to some degree, Hyde is the one protagonist of the story who has no narrative of his own, but continually erupts in the body of the doctor. Of Hyde's future? 'God knows', writes Jekyll pathetically, 'I am careless; this is my true hour of death, and what is to follow concerns another than myself' (p. 97).

'My devil had been long caged', confesses Jekyll, 'he came out roaring' (p. 90). For Stevenson, one might say, the unconscious is hinted at occurring only at the level of the body and its discontents. Jekyll's tragic situation, we are told, 'cannot be mended by talking' (p. 44).[21] Utterson and Enfield at the beginning agree to silence: 'Let us make a bargain never to refer to this again' (p. 34), this terrible crime, the trampling of a little girl and its aftermath (women 'wild as harpies', p. 32, ready to kill Hyde): 'you start a question, and it's like starting a stone' (p. 33).

---

[20] Cf. Heath, 'Psychopathia sexualis', (per.), on which I draw here.
[21] Stevenson indeed declared himself unhappy with the sexual improprieties which came out in the story. He wrote in a letter that '*Jekyll* is a dreadful thing, I own; but the only thing I feel dreadful about is that damned old business of the war in the members. This time it came out; I hope it will stay in, in future'. Letter to J. A. Symonds (1886), Stevenson, *Works*, xxviii, p. 323; cf. Heath, 'Psychopathia sexualis', (per.), pp. 101–2.

Jekyll and Hyde: the story of a 'father's interest' (p. 89) and 'a son's indifference' (p. 89) involves a continual troubling of the 'family portraits'. Hyde destroys 'the portrait of [Jekyll's] father' (p. 96), challenging a certain version of the past and any stable, reassuring picture of ancestry. Hyde's own image is enough to destroy the composure of the lawyer Utterson:

as [Utterson] lay and tossed in the gross darkness of the night and the curtained room, Mr Enfield's tale went by before his mind in a scroll of lighted pictures. He would be aware of the great field of lamps of a nocturnal city; then of the figure of a man walking swiftly; then of a child running from the doctors; and then these met, and that human Juggernaut trod the child down and passed on regardless of her screams. (p. 37)

The narrative traverses, even as it is constrained by, the ambiguous divides between Victorian medicine and polite fiction, the tension of unspeakable sexual pathologies, where Dr Jekyll with his 'infinite sadness of mien' (p. 60) will know in the end only a certain romantic vision of 'abject terror and despair' (p. 61).

Jekyll and Hyde, it has been pointed out, appeared in the same year as Krafft-Ebing's *Psychopathia Sexualis*.[22] Bram Stoker's *Dracula*, on the other hand, was published in 1897, the year after the term 'psychoanalysis' is said to have been coined.[23] Nevertheless *Dracula* also inhabits a world of representation which now seems insistently and tantalisingly pre-Freudian, still caught up in the terms of Victorian degenerationism. The adjacent dates – signalling for Stoker as for Freud a critical, albeit relatively late, 'career launch' into fame – mask the enduring separation between their languages on regression, fantasy and demons, as between their respective interpretations of dreams. They were not at all, as one commentator has recently claimed, 'telling the same story'.[24]

Part of the novel's task was to represent, externalise and kill off a distinct constellation of contemporary fears. Corruption and degeneration, the reader discovers, are identifiable, foreign and superable; but the text also recognises a certain sense of failure – an element of horror is always left over, uncontained by the terms of the story as by the intrepid party who stalk the Count: an English aristocrat, a brave American hunter, two doctors, a lawyer and his devoted, dutiful (but endangered) wife. The ambiguities of representation in the novel are in part bound up with contradictions of connotation in the wider discourse of degeneration throughout this period: the process of pathological decay, it seemed, was at once precisely contained (there were certain identifiable degenerate

22 Heath, 'Psychopathia sexualis', (per.).
23 See Gay, *Freud*, p. 103.
24 Waller, *Living and Undead*, p. 66.

categories of being who eventually became sterile) and ubiquitous, affecting whole populations. The reassuring function of the novel – displacing perceived social and political dangers onto the horror story of a foreign Count finally staked through the heart – was undermined by the simultaneous suggestion of an invisible and remorseless morbid accumulation, poison passed from body to body, blood to blood.

The vampire is allowed no direct voice or expression, but nor is any other figure given full narrative mastery. The novel refuses to provide a synthesis, proceeding instead through a series of separate diaries, reports and letters. *Dracula* seeks to deal with a number of contemporary social debates, but reaches in the face of them a kind of paralysis, as though the narrative never quite comes to represent the danger it hints. There are points where the description seems frozen at the threshold between Victorian evolutionism and psychoanalysis:

I saw around us a ring of wolves, with white teeth and lolling red tongues, with long sinewy limbs and shaggy hair. They were a hundred times more terrible in the grim silence which held them than even when they howled. For myself, I felt a sort of paralysis of fear. It is only when a man feels himself face to face with such horrors that he can understand their true import.[25]

Although Professor Van Helsing is famed for his 'absolutely open mind' (p. 13) the novel chronically reverts to closed, cautionary tale, warning of the perils of a wandering consciousness or body, the potentially fatal risks of entering mysterious new places and knowledge: Trance/Trans/Transylvania. *Dracula* thirsts to cross a threshold into a new conception of subjectivity and science, say psychoanalytic, towards which simultaneously it seems to be remarkably resistant. We are shown how the doctors in the novel keep coming up against an impasse, rejecting any organic explanation of Lucy Westenra's illness, but reluctant to follow through to any alternative explanation: 'but as there must be a cause somewhere, I have come to the conclusion that it must be something mental'; 'I have made careful examination but there is no functional cause' (pp. 111, 114).

The novel, excruciatingly, says nothing of the sexual fantasies and fears it articulates so graphically as vampire attack and blood pollution. The text resists the 'temptation' to spell out any notion of sexuality, for which, indeed, it lacks a language: resistance, frustration, failure of insight are crucial 'themes' in Stoker's story, and it is as if the narrative itself took a certain delight in resistance, deafness to the very words on the page, despite its own admonition: '[Van Helsing to Seward] You do not let your eyes see nor your ears hear' (p. 191).

[25] Stoker, *Dracula*, p. 13.

Orthodox medicine itself is shown to be in much the same state as a sleep-walker, semi-consciously stumbling along well-worn routes, unable to cross conceptual frontiers and understand the condition of its patients: Dr Seward [of his patient Renfield] 'I do not follow his thought'; 'I wish I could get some clue to the cause'; 'I wish I could fathom his mind' (pp. 107, 116). Renfield constantly escapes the doctor's grasp: he slips all too easily out of his cell and any existing psychiatric schema. Seward never does get to the 'heart' of his 'mystery', never succeeded in becoming 'master of the facts of his hallucination' (p. 60), persisting too single-mindedly in his materialist research on the brain.

Only very slowly does he come to sense that his patient's condition is bound up with Dracula and some wider contemporary perversion of the evolutionary 'struggle for survival' which has blurred the question of 'fitness' and 'unfitness': 'My homicidal maniac is of a peculiar kind. I shall have to invent a new classification for him, and call him a zoophagous (life-eating) maniac; what he desires is to absorb as many lives as he can, and has laid himself out to achieve it in a cumulative way' (pp. 70–1). Seward's 'obtuse' reluctance to make any unconventional diagnosis about Lucy Westenra finally exasperates even his mentor, Van Helsing:

Do you mean to tell me, friend John, that you have no suspicion as to what poor Lucy died of; not after all the hints given, not only by events, but by me? (p. 191)

The subjects of hysteria and hypnotism, which for a long time in the nineteenth century had been pushed out to the fringes and beyond of orthodoxy and respectability, had lately been returned to the medical centre-stage, at least in Paris, and could no longer be dismissed as mere occult practice or superstition by the modern doctor:

[Van Helsing] I suppose now that you do not believe in corporeal transference. No? Nor in materialisation. No? Nor in astral bodies. No? Nor in the reading of thought. No? Nor in hypnotism? – [Seward] Yes . . . Charcot has proved that pretty well. (p. 191)

But the medical audience 'lured' from abroad by Charcot's famous Tuesday demonstrations at the Salpêtrière was frequently appalled to learn of the presence of another theatre of hysteria where quacks, charlatans and music-hall actors entertained large crowds. The individual could be seduced or induced to commit terrible crimes. Remember the discussion of Donato in the chapter above, who had caused sensation and scandal as he toured the European theatres. He risked, so it seemed to many respectable doctors and other responsible commentators, the moral overthrow of the all-too willing spectators and participants and provoked furious debate on the very legality of magnetism and hypnotism.[26] The 'hypnotic menace'

---

[26] See Gallini, *La sonnambula meravigliosa.*

becomes a matter of forensic investigation and grave public concern –
famous cases and trials underscore the possibility of subliminal manipulation, of innocent women induced to commit hideous crimes, even
'murder under hypnosis'.[27]

Whether Stoker, a man of the theatre who was later to express a particular interest in the question of imposture[28] (and Donato was unmasked on
stage for his tricks), knew of this directly we cannot be sure, but echoes of
the criminal trials, public performances and dubious private consultations
will have reached him. Certainly Dracula too is cast as a form of hypnotist
on the stage of Europe, part fake, part genius: '[Harker] I felt myself
struggling to awake some call of my instincts ... I was becoming
hypnotised';[29] '[Mina Murray] I was bewildered, and strangely enough,
I did not want to hinder him' (p. 287). The novel sets up a contest of
hypnotic powers: the good scientist and the evil vampire compete for the
loyalty of the wavering hysterical women, for whom there is only one step
from 'horrid flirt' (p. 58) to the 'nightmare' of a demonic possessed
sexuality:

She seemed like a nightmare of Lucy as she lay there; the pointed teeth, the
bloodstained voluptuous mouth – which it made one shudder to see – the whole
carnal and unspiritual appearance, seeming like a devilish mockery of Lucy's sweet
purity. (p. 214)

Everyone, it appears in the novel, is obliged to doubt not only their own
descent but their own health and mental order or else to fall into mere
self-delusion. Thus Mina Murray is forced to 'suppose I was hysterical' (p.
184). Lord Godalming 'grew quite hysterical' (p. 230) and even Van
Helsing, the seemingly secure centre of reason and wisdom – 'one of the
most advanced scientists of the day', 'both in theory and in practice' (p.
112) – enigmatically collapses at one point into a 'disturbed' and disturbing
condition. Seward records how in the face of Lucy's death, Van Helsing
became hysterical: 'he gave way to a regular fit of hysterics ... He laughed
till he cried and I had to draw the blinds lest anyone should see us and
misjudge' (p. 174).

Strange perturbations are frequently described, and not simply in relation to the external figure of Dracula, casting doubt on whether anyone
can be, as Lucy Westenra considers Seward, 'absolutely imperturbable' (p.
55). Indeed, thwarted in love, the doctor is forced to rely on drugs to put
him to sleep (p. 101). It is increasingly unclear what could constitute a
protection from degeneration and vice in the novel; whether for instance
'good breeding' means anything: for who could be better bred than Count
Dracula himself? Amidst the 'whirlpool of races' (p. 28) which made up

[27] See Harris, 'Murder'.   [28] See Stoker, *Famous Imposters*.   [29] *Dracula*, p. 44.

European history, the Count was descended from a noble line of 'survivors': 'for in our veins flows the blood of many brave races who fought as the lion fights, for lordship' (p. 28)

The novel is in one sense committed to the contradistinction of vice and virtue, purity and corruption, human and vampire; but it tacitly questions the possibility of such sharp separations, in this like so many medical-psychiatrists of the period convinced that no complete dividing line lay between sanity and insanity but rather a vast and shadowy borderland: '[Van Helsing] For it is not the least of its terrors that this evil thing is rooted deep in all good' (p. 241). Darwin too, it should be remembered, had already dealt his 'blow' to human 'narcissism' (as Freud was later to view it) by warning that there was no absolute evolutionary separation from the world of the animals, no escape from the stigma of that descent. Behind even the most imperiously 'contemptuous' human smile, one usually caught the glint of a set of once ferocious teeth:

He who rejects with scorn the belief that his own canines, and their occasional great development in other men, are due to our early progenitors having been provided with these formidable weapons, will probably reveal by sneering the line of his descent. For though he no longer intends, nor has the power, to use these teeth as weapons, he will unconsciously retract his 'snarling muscles' ... so as to expose them ready for action, like a dog prepared to fight.[30]

Stoker's text was paralysed at a threshold of uncertainty, at the turning point between a psychiatric positivism (which the novel derided), and the glimpsed possibility of a new exploration of the unconscious. The rejection of conventional science in the novel was conceived to involve not so much a leap into the future as a return to an earlier knowledge: Van Helsing stoically accepts and manipulates folklore, amalgamating it with the latest evidence from the laboratory and the clinic. He is forced repeatedly to point out the power of the irrational and the inexplicable, the fact that there were more wonders in heaven and earth than were dreamt of in nineteenth-century naturalist philosophy. Nevertheless he finally explains to the other protagonists that the fearful enigma of the vampire has to be approached not through a popular physiognomy but through the insights of a craniometry currently being developed in modern criminal anthropology:

The criminal always works at one crime – that is the true criminal who seems predestinate to crime, and who will of none other. This criminal has not full man-brain. He is clever and cunning and resourceful; but he be not of man-stature as to brain. He be of child-brain in much. Now this criminal of ours is predestinate to crime also; he too have child-brain ... The Count is a criminal and of criminal type. Nordau and Lombroso would so classify him, and *qua* criminal he is of imperfectly formed mind. (pp. 341–2)

[30] Darwin, *The Descent*, I, p. 127.

Stoker's novel refers to Max Nordau and Cesare Lombroso, to a whole realm of investigation into degeneration and atavism, which itself wavered between a taxonomy of visible stigmata and the horror of invisible maladies. There was an unresolved contradiction between the desired image of a specific, identifiable criminal type (marked out by ancestry) and the wider representation of a society in crisis, threatened by waves of degenerate blood and moral contagion. Like Lombroso and Morel, Jonathan Harker journeys from specific images of deformity (goitre in particular: 'Here and there we passed Cszeks and Slovaks, all in picturesque attire, but I noticed that goitre was painfully prevalent', p. 7), towards the citadel of full-blown degeneracy. From that early work on cretinism and goitre, a medicopsychiatric theory had emerged in which, as we saw earlier, the degenerate was cast as a kind of social vampire who preyed on the nation and desired, in Lombroso's words, 'not only to extinguish life in the victim, but to mutilate the corpse, tear its flesh and drink its blood'.[31]

The possible identification of the delinquent and the degenerate through physiognomy were, I have tried to suggest, part of the problematic of many late-nineteenth-century novels as of criminal anthropology itself in this period. Thus *Dracula*, full of aspiring physiognomists, seeking to probe demeanours, features and expressions, nevertheless seems to call such observations into question:

[Harker] 'Doctor, you don't know what it is to doubt everything, even yourself. No you don't; you couldn't with eyebrows like yours.' [Van Helsing] seemed pleased and laughed as he said: 'So! You are a physiognomist.' (p. 188)

Lucy points out to Mina that Seward 'tries to read your thoughts', and then asks '[d]o you ever try to read your own face? *I do*, and I can tell you it is not a bad study' (p. 55). Good and evil are sometimes written in the features, sometimes erased by them. Distance and perspective alter the nature of what is seen. Thus the 'women looked pretty, except when you got near them' (p. 3). Physiognomy is seen to be an enigmatic and potentially counter-productive study; the face is at once a camouflage and a symptom. Dracula after all can change his form at will, and even when in human shape his appearance seemed to mislead. Thus the Count's hands, for instance, seem initially to be 'rather white and fine', but on closer inspection, 'they were rather coarse – broad with squat fingers ... [and] hairs in the centre of the palm' (p. 18). 'The marked physiognomy' of his face is described in meticulous detail:

[31] Lombroso, *Criminal Man* (1911), p. xv.

high bridge of the thin nose and peculiarly arched nostrils; with lofty domed forehead, and hair growing scantily round the temples, but profusely elsewhere. His eyebrows were very massive, almost meeting over the nose, and with bushy hair that seemed to curl in its own profusion. The mouth, so far as I could see it under the heavy moustache, was fixed and rather cruel-looking, with peculiarly sharp white teeth; these protruded over the lips, whose remarkable ruddiness showed astonishing vitality in a man of his years. For the rest, his ears were pale and at the tops extremely pointed; the chin was broad and strong, and the cheeks firm though thin. The general effect was one of extraordinary pallor. (pp. 17–18)

Dracula picked up a wider debate on the physiognomy of the 'born criminal' and the nature of the recidivist (a figure who had increasingly dominated European debate on law and order in the last quarter of the century[32]); it might even be said to be *parasitic*, like its own villain, feeding off a social moral panic about the reproduction of degeneration, the poisoning of good bodies and races by bad blood, the vitiation of healthy procreation. The novel provided a metaphor for current political and sexual political discourses on morality and society, representing the price of selfish pursuits and criminal depravity. The family and the nation, it seemed to many, were beleaguered by syphilitics, alcoholics, cretins, the insane, the feebleminded, prostitutes and a preceived 'alien invasion' of Jews from the East who, in the view of many alarmists were 'feeding off' and 'poisoning' the blood of the Londoner.[33] Significantly, it is an unscrupulous Jew who aids and abets Dracula's flight from his hunters: 'We found Hildescheim in his office, a Hebrew of rather the Adelphi type, with a nose like a sheep, and a fez. His arguments were pointed with specie – we doing the punctuation – and with a little bargaining he told us what he knew.'[34]

The image of the parasite, as we will see in chapter seven below, informed late-nineteenth century eugenics and the biological theory of degeneration. For Edward Carpenter, for instance, primitive tribes were stronger than the civilised, because their society was 'not divided into classes which prey upon each other; nor is it consumed by parasites'.[35] In the view of Eugene Talbot: 'The essential factor of crime is its parasitic nature'.[36] The parasite, argued, Edwin Ray Lankester in his important 'revisionist' work *Degeneration, a Chapter in Darwinism* (1880) demonstrated the possibility of a successful evolutionary adaptation to the environment; that adaptation, however, really exemplified in his view

---

[32] See Nye, *Crime*; Radzinowicz and Hood, 'Habitual criminal', (per.); see also the discussion in the following chapter.
[33] See for example the testimony of Arnold White to the *Royal Commission on Alien Immigration* 1903, II, pp. 15–16, and the discussions below, pp. 215–16.
[34] Stoker, *Dracula*, p. 349.
[36] Carpenter, *Civilisation*, pp. 8–9.   [36] Talbot, *Degeneracy*, p. 318.

degeneration, the return from the heterogeneous to the homogeneous, the complex to the simple. Darwin it seemed to many had been too optimistic, had suggested, despite his relative caution in extrapolating from the biological to the political, that evolution and progress were tied together. He had thought too little about who and what might best survive in an arguably noxious and degenerate environment – late-nineteenth-century London for instance.[37]

Dracula descended on that London, thus descending in a sense into the much wider social debate of the 1880s and 1890s about the morbidity and degeneracy of the average inhabitant of the metropolis. The city dweller, it seemed, had become a monstrous physical travesty, but perhaps, despite Morel's assurance that degeneration led to sterility, in fact a reproductively successful creature. As the evil Count gloats, the bad blood he disseminates will spread even further, constantly finding new carriers: 'My revenge is just begun! I spread it over centuries, and time is on my side.'[38] Early in the novel, Dracula astonishes Harker by his perfect command of the English language and his familiarity with the lay-out of London. The Count explains that he has mastered this knowledge because he longed to 'go through the crowded streets of your mighty London, to be in the midst of the whirl and rush of humanity, to share its life, its change, its death' (p. 20). As he warns his guest/prisoner: 'you dwellers of the city cannot enter into the feelings of the hunter' (p. 18). When Harker finally realises what 'sharing' London's life and death actually means, he is utterly appalled by the vision of a future vampire-ridden city: 'perhaps for centuries to come, he might amongst its teeming millions, satiate his lust for blood, and create a new and ever-widening circle of semi-demons to batten on the helpless' (p. 51).

Stoker's novel, for all its mythological and folkloristic insistence, can be read in relation to a specific late-nineteenth-century discourse of degeneration. The novel in part explored and was in part imprisoned by its own situation: that powerful felt moment of crisis and interim ('this dreadful thrall of night and gloom and fear', p. 45), on the verge of the new century, in a kind of corridor between different forms of knowledge and understanding. The novel at once sensationalised the horrors of degeneration and charted reassuringly the process of their confinement and containment. The terrors and the contradictions of the representation were never quite removed; degeneration remained a problem in this text, as more widely in contemporary social and political description, despite the deeply consoling conservative representation of cheerful beer-swilling, cap-doffing London

---

[37] Cf. 'Degeneration amongst Londoners', *The Lancet*, 1 (February 1885), p. 265; cf. Stedman Jones, *Outcast London*, and ch. 7 below.
[38] Stoker, *Dracula*, p. 306.

labourers, Jonathan Harker's dramatic upward social mobility (he rises 'from clerk to master in a few years', p. 158), the fine, 'manly' comradeship of Dracula's hunters and Mina Harker's successful restoration as subservient, faithful wife and mother.

◁ ══ ▷

7

Crime, urban degeneration and national decadence

QUESTIONS OF CRIME

The following chapter surveys certain key conceptions of degeneration and atavism in Victorian and Edwardian social debate. The problem of periodisation is particularly difficult here. There is no real sense of a 'founding text' of degeneration or atavism in England, like Morel's *Treatise* (1857) or Lombroso's *Criminal Man* (1876); it is more difficult to coordinate the precise moments of a theorisation of degeneration which runs alongside, but also within, the terms of Darwinian evolution and its more obvious publication 'landmarks' – 1859 and 1871. In England, moreover, social theory itself was continually challenged not simply at the level of its content but its very right to existence. When Mill was advising the Saint-Simonian school on how to publicise their work this side of the Channel, he made the famous observation that to produce any effect in England it was necessary 'carefully to conceal the fact of your having any system or body of opinions, to instruct them on isolated points and to endeavour to form their habits of thought by your mode of treating simple and practical questions'.[1] English commentators could be notoriously complacent and insular in their perception of society, perhaps most especially in the 1850s and 1860s, apparently quite happy with piecemeal reforms and 'advances'. One medical journal, for instance, reviewing Morel's work on non-restraint, commented thus on his visit to England: 'We are indeed happy to reckon M. Morel among the converts to the modern system of treating the insane, and trust he may be a successful promoter of it in his own country',[2] as though the 'modern system' was exclusively England's benefaction to the Continent. The theorists of degeneration in late-Victorian England were also caught in a continual struggle not only to challenge the free will principles of law and the strength of the classical liberal tradition, but to get a governmental hearing for their theory at all.

Victorian society was of course troubled by social upheavals – powerfully so in the 1840s, the late 1860s and the 1880s, but it is nevertheless true

---

[1] Mill to D'Eichthal (9 February 1830), Mill, *Correspondance*, p. 127.
[2] *The British and Foreign Medico-Chirurgical Review*, 28 (July 1861), p. 184.

to say that there were no crises for the governing classes in the second half of the nineteenth century comparable in the enormity of their symbolic impact to 1848 in Europe, Italian unification and its massively troubled aftermath, or the Franco-Prussian War and the Paris Commune. Trouble in England could always be compared (either for purposes of diminution or inflation) with the convulsions abroad. Of course, there was Ireland,[3] but symbolically this was often to be held outside – an external enemy rather than an enemy within – thereby preserving the integrity of 'England' at least in ways which were discursively impossible in France or Italy. Alternatively, where commentators spoke in alarmist terms of the state of affairs in England, Ireland was cast as a kind of infectious malady, afflicting the hitherto healthy English body.[4] Almost as though theories of crime, madness and crowds might be catalysts of Continental 'anarchy', the belief in the relative poverty of 'social science' in Britain could appear to some commentators to be a safeguard against disruption: perhaps everything could carry on, it was hoped, discursively, socially, politically, as before. The idea of Britain's imperviousness to, and imperial disdain for, 'theory' was itself a kind of self-perpetuating and sometimes self-proving mythology. The whole theoretical edifice of Benthamism, to take an obvious example, was not only contested and resisted, but frequently discounted, marginalised or completely ignored by commentators seeking to insist on Britain's effective and admirable freedom from, rather than simply poverty of, theory. But neither the torpor of isolationism nor the will to amnesia successfully repressed disturbing visions and theories of degeneration, pollution or entropy. It was only necessary to mention the idea of heat loss

[3] On the anthropological drive to measure the evolution or degeneration of the Irish, see for instance, Curtis, *Apes and Angels*, p. 17, which discusses British anthropological research on ethnic differences between the Gaelic and the Saxon. In subsequent decades the supposed racial propensities of the Irish, in particular, their putative innate criminality, was used to explain Fenian activity. The English attributed increasingly bestial and simian features to the Irish stereotype (as for instance in political cartoons and caricature); cf. the laboratory, inspired by Francis Galton, which toured Ireland in the 1890s, recording the ethnic measurements of small groups isolated in the South; see Forrest, *Francis Galton*, p. 182. But cf. Matthew Arnold for a kind of ironic erosion of the liberal faith in the benevolence of the English working-class protestor: 'And then the difference between an Irish Fenian and an English rough is so immense ... [The Fenian] is so evidently desperate and dangerous, a man of a conquered race, a Papist, with centuries of ill-usage to inflame him against us ... But with the Hyde Park rioter how different! He is our own flesh and blood; he is a Protestant ... the question of questions for him is a wage question' (*Culture and Anarchy*, p. 63). Arnold sets up the conventional anthropological separation between the Irish and the English, but only to call into question precisely the anarchical drift of English social relationships in a mechanical *laissez-faire* age which had 'dissolved' the 'strong' feudal habits of subordination (p. 58).

[4] See for instance Salisbury's anonymous article 'Disintegration': 'Ireland is no doubt, the worst symptom of our malady. But we are not free from it here; it is beginning to infect us in this country also, though the stage is less advanced and the form is less acute' (Smith, *Salisbury on Politics*, p. 343).

and the ultimate death of the sun, to shatter the confidence of that most apparently ebullient of mid-Victorian evolutionary optimists and classical liberals, Herbert Spencer.[5]

Throughout the Victorian period there was deep concern about 'the criminal', a continuing sense from many quarters that delinquency was, if not a revolutionary threat, at least a nuisance, a puzzle and a social blight which undermined the national situation as a whole. As the *Saturday Review* wrote in 1862 during the 'garotting panic',[6] the whole society seemed positively to bear the rank smell of an inalienable criminality:

> It is clear that we have not yet found out what to do with our criminals. We neither reform them, nor hang them, nor keep them under lock and key, nor ship them off to the Antipodes. Our moral sewage is neither deodorised nor floated out to sea, but remains in the midst of us polluting and poisoning our air.[7]

Insanity and criminality were increasingly cast as symptoms of a wider social pathology. A specific bio-medical conception of degeneration was already to be seen in the 1850s and the 1860s. The 'condition of England question' was re-formulated in medical language in *The Lancet* and the *Journal of Mental Science* during those decades. If Britain's protection from change, corruption and pollution appeared to some to be guaranteed by its literal geographical separation – 'the island race' – what did Darwin and Wallace show if not the awesome world of natural metamorphosis to be found in islands? But despite increasing medical attention to the question of degeneration, commentators on crime and social pathology continually felt frustrated in their desire to alarm and galvanise 'a general public'. Thus when Havelock Ellis translated Lombroso's *Criminal Man* into English and wrote his own book on delinquency, he lamented the appalling English ignorance of Continental and even domestic developments in the science of crime.[8] Ellis had attended a couple of the Inter-

---

[5] Herbert Spencer found himself 'out of spirits for some days' when informed that the second law of thermodynamics implied that life would one day cease. He wrote pathetically to the physicist Tyndall in 1858: 'That which was new to me in your position enunciated last June, and again on Saturday, was that equilibration was death. Regarding, as I had done, equilibration as the ultimate and *highest* state of society, I had assumed it to be not only the ultimate but also the highest state of the universe. And your assertion that when equilibrium was reached life must cease, staggered me. Indeed, not seeing my way out of the conclusion, I remember being out of spirits for some days afterwards. I still feel unsettled about the matter, and should like some day to discuss it with you' (*Life and Letters*, p. 104). On the second law of thermodynamics, see Brush, *Temperature of History*.

[6] See Davis, 'London Garotting Panic'.

[7] *Saturday Review* (1862), p. 241.

[8] 'In Great Britain alone during the last fifteen years there is no scientific work in criminal anthropology to be recorded' (Ellis, *The Criminal*, p. 46). He cited amongst others the work of Broca, Morel, Lombroso, Krafft-Ebing, Tarde and Lacassagne. He also acknowledged the English contributions of Darwin and Maudsley (see pp. 32–43). Note that in 1894, Havelock Ellis met Lombroso at a medical conference in Rome, see Grosskurth, *Havelock Ellis*, p. 168.

national Congresses of Criminal Anthropology in Europe and was no doubt embarrassed to find his country so conspicuously absent from the list of delegates.[9] The sense that Lombroso had failed to make any significant impact on English social thought was shared by supporters and opponents alike, and often inherited in the accounts given by subsequent historians. The drive behind much nineteenth-century penal reform, after all, seemed geared to enshrining classical ideals of uniformity, indifference to the individuality of the offender.[10] In the words of a commentator in 1891 'the influence of Lombroso's books in Italy, France and Germany has been as immediate and decisive as that of "The Origin of Species". It is not to our honour that in England as yet he is so little known'.[11] Radzinowicz and Hood have recently reiterated the view that 'the English never fully accepted the idea that criminals were a separate species of mankind, and they regarded the worst of them as having some hope of redemption. And the notion of preventive social defence had to contend with deeply felt traditional liberal conceptions of justice.'[12]

The formation and struggles of the eugenics movement for national efficiency, population control, bio-metric investigation of aliens, criminals, the insane and the feeble-minded have received considerable recent scrutiny.[13] In the face of each such campaign we see formidable resistance in England, above all framed in the language of classical liberalism.[14]

The Eugenics Education Society, one can well argue, never really achieved its utopian ends although certain aspects of its language of crisis and its proposed remedies were widely accepted.[15] Moreover English mental hospitals, it seems, did not adopt the term 'degenerate' in any regular or systematic way. Psychiatry, Roger Smith concludes, in his book on medicine's attempt to gain a role in the courts,[16] was relatively ineffectual in that very aim throughout the Victorian period. Nor do we find exact

---

[9] At the second Congress there were participants from Italy, France, Germany, Argentina, Austria, Belgium, Brazil, Canada, Denmark, Spain, the United States, Holland, Mexico, Paraguay, Peru, Portugal, Romania, Russia, Serbia, Sweden and Switzerland. See the *Actes* (Second Congress), pp. 13–24. At the third Congress (1893), there were several British participants, including Havelock Ellis, who also attended the fifth Congress. At the fourth Congress (1897), there were a few more British participants, amongst them Morrison, Galton and Arthur Griffiths. Note indeed the discussion of Galton's methods for tracing finger-prints, *Actes* (Fourth Congress), pp. 35–8. The Congresses when taken as a whole suggest the relative poverty of British contributions and participation.

[10] See Garland, *Punishment and Welfare*.

[11] Zimmern, 'Lombroso's new theory', (per.), p. 202.

[12] Radzinowicz and Hood, 'Habitual criminal', (per.), p. 1,317.

[13] See for instance Searle, *Quest*, and *Eugenics and Politics*; Freeden, *New Liberalism*; Jones, *Social Darwinism*; Kevles, *In the Name of Eugenics*.

[14] See for instance Freeden, *New Liberalism*, p. 192.

[15] See the discussion in Searle, *Quest*, p. 60. The Mental Deficiencies Act (1913) represented a complex compromise with eugenic alarmism.

[16] See Smith, *Trial*, p. 32; cf. Clarke, 'Rejection', p. 30, on the failure of psychiatry to make significant social policy gains before 1914.

English equivalents of the 'degenerationist' novel of a Zola, or the history of a Taine. Lombroso was not a household name amongst the English bourgeoisie.

But, I suggest, the debate on these movements and ideas has sometimes become locked into a sterile (because simply bi-polar) argument about the 'success' of a degenerationist language of crime, insanity and race at the most direct levels (say in effecting wholesale changes in law and legal practice, or in gaining direct endorsement in government inquiries). The discussion below seeks to explore rather the structure of a simultaneous avowal and disavowal of degeneration in the late-nineteenth century, and to examine exactly what was rejected and what (wittingly or unwittingly) was accepted or simply assumed in the convergence of debate about races, criminals, cities and civilisations. The aim here is to follow through some of the themes explored earlier with regard to the language of degeneration: visibility and invisibility, the body and its reproduction as historical metaphor, conceptions of regression. I argue that it is the degenerate rather than degeneration which was most deeply opposed. The notion of society as an organism – living, reproducing, degenerating, dying – becomes an increasingly 'dead metaphor', in other words a metaphor used literally, in the social criticism of the late-Victorian period. It comes more and more powerfully to represent a putative source of knowledge about society rather than simply another rhetorical figure of it. The body itself was symbolised in new ways, its dramatised image standing as a figure of society, powerfully informing the critique of classical liberalism. There *was* sustained and growing pessimism in the 1870s and 1880s about the ramifications of evolution, the efficacy of liberalism, the life in and of the metropolis, the future of society in a perceived world of mass democracy and socialism. Degenerationist arguments emerged in response to social developments which, it was felt, made *laissez-faire* beliefs and biological rationales untenable; Herbert Spencer above all symptomatised what was now generally felt to be the unwarrantedly optimistic resonances of earlier Victorian evolutionary theory.

By the late-nineteenth century, there was certainly no shortage of English-language writings exploring degeneration. True, these were often perceived to be the works of cranks and faddists.[17] But the 'lunatic fringe' often brought into sharp relief, themes and ideas which, as I show below, had a wider circulation elsewhere. In the 1900s, the Home Office certainly took note of Lombroso's work, but was reluctant to accept, or at least to accept straightforwardly, any of his more controversial findings. When

---

[17] For some of the more extreme accounts of degeneration published in England and the United States, see for instance: Talbot, *Degeneracy*; White, *Efficiency*; Wilson, *Unfinished Man*.

they were directly challenged by 'outsiders' (sometimes from the United States) on the efficacy of the new scientific arguments, officials appeared dismissive. Thus, for instance, there was apparently little Home Office enthusiasm in response to the 'free advice' offered by an American follower of Lombroso, Dr MacDonald. In a letter to the Home Office, dated 21 July 1906, he noted President Roosevelt's support for a bill to establish a laboratory 'for the study of the criminal and defective classes' and suggested the English government would be wise to offer the same support.[18] The Home Office view, however, was that instead of MacDonald's laboratory of the criminal, '[a] far more important purpose is the collection of material for testing theories as to the physical progress of the race . . . for determining whether the population of England is degenerating or improving in physique'.[19] This already anticipates the point developed further on in my discussion: the opposition to the language of foreign criminology or psychiatry was often itself couched in similarly reductive bio-medical terms. The opinion of various medical inspectors was requested by the Home Office on the proposal for a laboratory. Several replied that such measurements as were canvassed by MacDonald were already being taken. Despite the apparent inertia of British officialdom, the intrepid American continued to correspond with the Home Office.[20]

The government was not simply impervious to such views. But the question of the criminal's anomalies was one thing, the individual's 'rights' under the law were another. There was a tradition of Victorian liberal hostility to calls for cumulative punishments of habitual offenders. In 1856, for instance, when Charles (later Lord) Wortley had asked Sir Horatio Waddington, the Permanent Under-Secretary of State at the Home Office, whether he approved of the life-long confinement of the recidivist, the latter was critical, calling it:

[A] very frightful punishment under any circumstances, inflicting civil death upon a man without the slightest hope; it seems to be the great objection to that sort of punishment, that it does not give the slightest hope to a man; it destroys every feeling which can render life in any respect desirable or even tolerable.[21]

---

18 Public Records Office, Kew: H.O. 45/10563.172511/2 (letter 21 July 1906).
19 H.O. 45/10563. 172511/1.
20 On 28 November 1912, he wrote to the Home Office, speaking enthusiastically once again about the benefits to be gained from the construction of laboratories. Under the subject 'scientific lesson from the attempted assassination of former President Roosevelt', he wrote: 'Millions of dollars are annually expended by Governments for the scientific investigation of the antecedents, peculiarities and behaviour of some little bacillus, causing the death of plants or animals, but little or nothing is given for a similar study of the larger human bacillus, which has caused Nations to suffer losses beyond human calculation' (H.O. 45/10563.172511/13 [letter 28 November 1912]).
21 Select Committee on Transportation 1856, *First Report*, p. 19, para. 186.

As Radzinowicz and Hood note, '[t]he very idea of arresting men and putting upon them the burden of proof that they lived honestly was, in the climate of the 1850s, quite unacceptable'.[22] One might add, perhaps, that in comparison with the Continent, it was also felt to be quite unnecessary, now that the troubled 1840s had given way to the 'benign' prospects of the 1850s.

By 1869, however, it was indeed a Liberal government which introduced the Habitual Criminals Bill. The notion of thus distinguishing the punishment of offenders on the basis of their past marked a major departure from the classical tradition of penology. The numerous critics of the bill argued that this change heralded a plethora of potential abuses of the rights of the individual, the penalising of the poor and the reversal of the whole basis of English justice (pp. 1,340–1). Because of all the compromises which were effected to achieve its passage, the resulting Act of 1869 was deemed ineffectual. In 1871, the Prevention of Crimes Act set out to remedy the deficiencies, providing tighter supervision of ex-convicts, introducing photography as a means of identification, and offering courts new discretionary powers in the punishment of 'habituals' (p. 1,343).

Home Office officials may have been unsympathetic to a Lombroso, but there was almost always a consensus that the problem of habitual crime was getting worse, even if overall crime rates appeared to be dropping in the last quarter of the nineteenth century because of an array of new alternative punishments and classifications like borstal; according to one recent estimate, the population of the convict prisons more than halved, from nearly 12,000 to less than 5,000, between 1871 and 1894 (p. 1,312). Indeed the putative decline in overall criminality, emphasised the recalcitrance of the 'recidivists'. More and more attention was paid to the social, biological, psychological 'case' of the multiple offender in England.

English concern about recidivism was matched and exceeded by developments on the Continent. The concern, suggests Robert Nye, was in fact widely shared in Europe in the 1870s and the biological terms kept sharpening.[23] By the 1880s in France, 'the most inveterate Republican supporters of transportation were willing to reach into the clinic for the language they used to describe recidivists and to make the abyss that separated the "accidental" from the "professional" criminal practically unbridgeable' (p. 76).

The view that the compulsive criminal could be differentiated anthropologically from other 'races of criminals' was not entirely new, of course, in the England of the 1870s. Henry Mayhew, amongst others, had earlier expressed the view that:

[22] See Radzinowicz and Hood, 'Habitual criminal', (per.), p. 322.   [23] *Crime*, p. 38.

My experience leads me to this melancholy result, that there is a large class, so to speak, who belong to a criminal race, living in particular districts of society; . . . these people have bred, until at last you have persons who come into the world as criminals, and go out as criminals, and they know nothing else.[24]

But he added that whilst a good number were 'incorrigible', nevertheless 'many of the habitual class may be reformed if rightly dealt with' (p. 154, para. 3,575). With the refusal of Australia's eastern colonies to accept more convicts at the end of the 1840s, the rapid growth of the English cities, the expansion and consolidation of the police force and the rise of evolutionary theory, the language of crime in general, and the nature of the 'hardened criminal' in particular, was recast.[25] By the 1880s and 1890s, a central concern amongst social investigators was the 'scientific classification' of the problem of recidivism and there was an increasingly wide-spread desire to use legislation to distinguish the recidivist from the first-time offender.[26]

The biological language became ever more inflated, and texts were continually produced lampooning the clumsiness and inadequacy of current legislation in the face of the intransigent nature of crime. Yet one must contrast this language with the 'prudent' words of government enquiries. Thus in the 1895 Departmental Committee on Prisons[27] chaired by Herbert Gladstone, we are told:

It may be true that some criminals are irreclaimable, just as some diseases are incurable and in such cases it is not unreasonable to acquiesce in the theory that criminality is a disease, and the result of physical imperfection. But criminal anthropology as a science is in embryo stage, and while scientific and more particularly medical observation and experience are of the most essential value in guiding opinion on the whole subject, it would be a loss of time to search for a perfect system, in learned but conflicting theories, when so much can be done by the recognition of the plain fact that the great majority of prisoners are ordinary men and women amenable, more or less to all those influences which affect persons outside. (p. 8)

The excesses of elaborate theories are counterposed in the Committee's emphasis on 'plain facts', but in a sense a great deal has already been

---

[24] Select Committee on Transportation 1856, *Second Report*, p. 151, para. 3,531.
[25] See Radzinowicz and Hood, 'Habitual criminal', (per.), and *English Criminal Law*; Nye, *Crime*. In the view of W. D. Morrison in *Crime and its Causes* in 1891, habitual criminals were unfit to take part in the working of the modern industrial machine: 'no State will ever get rid of the criminal problem unless its population is composed of healthy and vigorous citizens. Very often crime is but the offspring of degeneracy and disease . . . stunted and decrepit faculties . . . either vitiate the character, or unfit the combatant for the battle of life.' (pp. vii–viii)
[26] See Radzinowicz and Hood, 'Habitual criminal', (per.), p. 1,315.
[27] Departmental Committee 1895, *Report*.

conceded to a positivist theory of crime in its stress upon the 'individual criminal' and its notion that irreclaimable individuals may exist 'just as some diseases are incurable'. These irreclaimable criminals were not conceived as presenting a direct revolutionary danger in 1895, but rather as a threat to the quality of civilisation: 'The retention of a compact mass of habitual criminals in our midst is a growing strain on our civilisation' (p. 5). Irreclaimable criminality threatened the utopia of internal unity in this age of empire. The notion of 'civilisation' was by now powerfully invested with the sense of imperial mission; what was 'strained' was exactly the viability of the ideology of a cohesive and unified ruling race.

Despite their view that '[r]ecidivism [was] the most important of all prisons questions', it was also found to be 'the most complicated and difficult' (p. 5). It was nearly a decade before a draft bill was presented in response to the Committee's recommendations, and thirteen years before they were actually translated into legislation. In 1908, Herbert Gladstone's Prevention of Crime Bill aimed at a diluted form of indeterminate sentencing in the case of 'hardened', 'incorrigible', 'professional' criminals. Rights of appeal and decision by jury were also included to allay liberal criticism.[28] Nevertheless the bill ran into opposition, regarding the fraught question of defining the habitual offender, and the very principles which were at stake in the new proposals (p. 1,367). The government gave way and settled for more modest proposals containing tougher curbs on the judge's discretion. But the introduction of the English 'dual track' system, with its new differentiation of categories of offender, was hailed as a land-mark.

In England's social and intellectual history, degeneration appears a less obvious issue than on the Continent; firstly, the notion of the degenerate as a clearly distinguishable being always tended to be diluted in the clash with a recalcitrant classical liberal conception of the individual; secondly, the prospect of the direct destruction, extinction or impotence of the state was on the whole seen to be implausible. Those who portrayed the social danger in such sensational terms were thus often effectively marginalised, coded as scare-mongers. The more-pervasive worries, as expressed by more 'sober' commentators, tended to qualify the alarmist picture; they tended to involve a slower, mediated process of decline in which a relative deterioration in the body of the city population in turn undermined the 'imperial race' with ensuing disintegrative effects upon the nation and empire.

Yet the language of degeneration continually returned, even as commentators overtly moved away from the most draconian measures of 'social

[28] See Radzinowicz and Hood, 'Habitual criminal', (per.), p. 1,364.

defence'. Views perceived as foreign and 'hysterical' were often refuted only in the name of a more refined version of the same language. Indeed the famous Inter-Departmental Committee on Physical Deterioration, (1904)[29] is a case in point. Established in the wake of a scandal, much canvassed by journalists and politicians, over the apparently exceptionally poor physique of large numbers of potential recruits for the army during the Boer War, the Committee is usually seen as a kind of English empiricist refutation of degenerationism. Certainly it did refuse to adopt the word 'degeneration' in the report's title and rejected the argument that the race as a whole was unfit or degenerate. The problem, they found, was not pervasive. It was bound geographically and socially to the poor of the slums, and the principle cause of 'deterioration' was overcrowding.[30] But even as a physically determinist anthropology appears to be abandoned in the name of environmentalism, its terms reappear in the report's assumption of a given 'type':

The evil is, of course, greatest in one-roomed tenements, the over-crowding there being among persons usually of *the lowest type*, steeped in every kind of degradation and cynically indifferent to the vile surroundings engendered by their filthy habits, and to the pollution of the young brought up in such an atmosphere.[31]

The Committee rejected degeneration in one sense, but its recommendations were based nevertheless upon a vision of an immutably feckless and

---

[29] Inter-Departmental Committee 1904, *Report*.

[30] See Searle, *Quest*, and *Eugenics and Politics*; Szreter, 'Decline', (diss.), pp. 100–4; Soloway, 'Counting the Degenerates', (per.); Barker, 'Curbing Fertility', (per.); Dwork, *War*, p. 12. On the Royal Commission on Physical Training (Scotland) which preceded the English inquiry see Soloway, 'Counting the Degenerates', (per.); cf. The Royal Commission on the Poor Law 1909: there is a class in our midst 'whose condition and environment are a discredit, and a peril to the whole community.' Society is all too easily 'hampered by an increasing load of this dead weight.' (p. 644). On the various witnesses to the Inter-Departmental Committee and the effective debunking of the more extreme hereditarian fears, see Szreter, 'Decline', (diss.), pp. 105–21. The eugenist Karl Pearson dismissed the Committee's rebuttal of degeneration, a problem, he suggested, which 'can only be attacked on purely academic lines; no real solution will be obtained unless it is studied in a manner wholly free of party bias and by those having no *responsibility either to the minister of a political party, or to a government department.*' Pearson's preface to Snow, *Intensity*, p. 2.

[31] Inter-Departmental Committee 1904, *Report*, p. 17, emphasis added. Or earlier, when taking the evidence of Charles Booth, the term 'undesirable class' is simply assumed (the term sliding from the undesirability of the conditions of a class, to the undesirability of the people themselves); it figures as an unproblematic expression, the shared language of the investigators, as though it were outside the specific issue and polemic of the inquiry: 'You have stated emphatically that it is the competition of the very poor that exercises the most depressing influence on the class immediately above them who if the very poor were eliminated, might maintain a more equal struggle for existence?' [Booth] 'I think that is true.' 'This undesirable class, which you describe as a dead loss to the State, is composed of the wastrels and ineffectives of society, those who, from whatever cause, have drifted into its dunghills and dustheaps?' [Booth] 'Yes.' (*Report*, pp. 47–8).

hopeless stratum of the poor; it proposed an eclectic series of measures to improve the environment, but also to survey constantly the body of 'this undesirable class': amongst the measures proposed, were the provision of a register of sickness, the inauguration of a permanent anthropometric survey, new medical officers of health, curbs on alcoholism, improved food and milk supply, special schools for 'retarded' children, controls on juvenile smoking, insanity, syphilis, the development of a mid-wife service;[32] or, as we are told more strategically, the need 'to take charge of the lives of those who, from whatever cause, are incapable of independent existence up to the standards of decency'.[33] In certain respects the language of degeneration, delineating classes and groups, circumscribed much of the argument in the very commissions and enquiries in the late-Victorian and Edwardian period which were set up to investigate and rule upon, precisely, the value of such concepts.

A further instance of this point is to be found in Goring's study of *The English Convict* (1913), commissioned and written under the auspices of the Home Office to investigate, amongst other issues, the validity of Cesare Lombroso's claims on the biological constitution of the criminal.[34] By the turn of the century, Lombroso's specific form of positivism was under heavy attack in Italy, and in the International Congresses of Criminal Anthropology, as has already been indicated earlier. Nevertheless the very establishment of Goring's project in the 1900s could be seen as evidence of Lombroso's lingering discursive importance, at least in framing central issues of debate.

Goring wrote that 'our appeal must be made, not to the opinions of descriptive psychologists, sociologists, and criminologists, but to the facts and calculus of the statistician'. Statistics, he went on, can have the accuracy of an 'exact science'.[35]

Goring certainly provided a powerful critique of Lombroso. But often it is the fact of this refutation alone which has found its way into the secondary literature, rather than the alternative account provided in its place. In fact, Goring counterposed Lombroso to English biometrics – those were the poles of the choice he offered. He insisted that he did not attack Lombroso's conclusions, but only his statistically crude methods (p. 18). The Italian doctor, he argued, had conflated the 'legal criminal' (the offender who got caught and sentenced), with the biological criminal, and

---

32 Inter-Departmental Committee 1904. *Report*, pp. 84–92.

33 Inter-Departmental Committee 1904, *Report*, p. 85.

34 The object of the project, begun in 1902 was to check the various criminological hypotheses and especially those of 'the Italian School' (*English Convict*, p. 6). Goring was not the first to offer a critique in English of Lombroso. For an earlier attack on Lombroso's methodology in the United States, see Kellor, *Experimental Sociology*.

35 *English Convict*, p. 374.

both of these with the unverifiable 'historical criminal' (p. 21). The stigmata which Lombroso had tabulated from the criminal body, argued Goring, were in fact a result of the generally smaller stature of criminals and their defective intelligence. But Goring rejected any primarily environmental explanation of crime, in favour of a supposedly statistically sophisticated hereditarianism:

relatively to its origin in the constitution of the malefactor, and especially in his mentally defective constitution, crime is only to a trifling extent (if to any) the product of social inequalities, of adverse environment or of other manifestations of what may be comprehensively termed the force of circumstances. (p. 371)

One needs to attend carefully to what was being rejected and what condoned in this report. Thus it stated categorically 'there is no such thing as an anthropological criminal type' but there was a physical and moral type who was predisposed to crime:

[there is] a physical, mental, and moral type of normal person who tends to be convicted of crime . . . on the average, the criminal of English prisons is markedly differentiated by defective physique – as measured by stature and body weight; by defective mental capacity – as measured by general intelligence; and by an increased possession of wilful anti-social proclivities – as measured, apart from intelligence, by length of sentence to imprisonment. (p. 370)

Whilst no anthropology of crime was deemed possible in the terms which Lombroso had established, Goring did not rule out the presence of some peculiar constitutional 'essence' in the delinquent and thus of the potential efficacy of a biological science or legal theory based on the differentiation of the population in its physical aspects, mental capacity, intelligence, anti-social proclivities. Moreover, since inheritance was the key to understanding the criminal's difference, there were, he argued, three crucial aspects to the crusade against crime. First, to modify the inherited tendency by appropriate educational means. Second, to segregate and supervise the unfit. Third, to attack the 'evil at its very root' by regulating reproduction (p. 373).

Steering between the danger of environmentalism on the one side and a crude hereditarian determinism on the other, Goring had always insisted on the valency both of nature and nurture. He had made his point by an analogy to bodily disease:

The most rabid of the infectionist school would not dispute that the vulnerability of the tissues to the attacks of the bacillus is a heritable quality . . . [but] he believes that, in hygienic conditions of life, the bacillus is warred against and killed or that, at any rate, it may be avoided.[36]

[36] *Inheritance*, p. 18.

In the opposite camp, he pointed out, were those who argued that 'heredity counts for everything' (pp. 18–19). What is remarkable both in the choice of analogy, and in the conceived opposition between English biometrics and Italian positivism, is the shared focus on the constitutional inheritance of the criminal as the key to comprehension and control. Goring had discovered no absolute difference between the criminal and the law-abiding body, but nevertheless he had found striking differences of degree in both 'physique and mental capacity'. As the preface to *The English Convict* put it, 'criminality is not a morbid state akin to physical disease which can be diagnosed and established by pure observation', but nevertheless 'the hereditary diatheses' play a key role in the make-up of the delinquent (p. 7). Thus whilst Lombroso's and Nordau's theses could be summarily dispatched ('a mass of imperfect and unclassified observations linked together by untested hypotheses', p. 8), the perceived central problem of the criminal as a constitutional being remained central.

From the 'sober works' of Maudsley, of Ribot, Richet and of Janet, to the 'extravagant though luminous books' of Lombroso and Nordau, Vernon Lee (pseudonym of Violet Paget) had observed in the *Fortnightly Review* in 1896, modern science has produced work of 'invaluable practical suggestiveness'.[37] The idea of degeneration in modern science, she went on, must cause us all to call into question our sanity and our health:

Hence most of us – all of us who have received no strong religious bias – prepare to go through life on the supposition that we are sound because we are *we* . . . [in fact] it is just as likely as not that we may be developing, in our innermost self, tendencies to habits destructive, if not to others directly, then indirectly through the impairing of our own physical and spiritual efficiency; we may be allowing ourselves to become through the pressure of external circumstances, semi-maniacs and semi-criminals, where we might, had we known, remained [sic] sane and harmless. (pp. 940–1)

Nordau's symptomatology, she pointed out, has taught us to become the detectives of degeneration, tracing the hidden configurations of disorder in contemporary culture: 'Eccentricity, Suspiciousness of evil, Egotism, *Idées Fixes*, Obsession by the Thought of Impurity, Lack of human sympathy, Confusion of Categories, Unbridled Violence of Hatred, Indiscriminate Destructiveness; he has taught us to recognise all these as the *stigmata of degeneracy*' (p. 928).[38]

---

[37] 'Deterioration', (per.), p. 929. Violet Paget (1856–1935) was a novelist and essayist who spent most of her life in Italy.
[38] Lee, 'Deterioration', (per.), p. 928. Cf. Isabel Foard's endorsement of Lombroso in an article entitled, 'The criminal: is he produced by environment or atavism?', in *The Westminster Review*.

The eleventh edition of the *Encyclopaedia Britannica* also took note of current developments in criminology. In an entry on Lombroso, it was observed that despite the fact that his work had been 'gravely criticised', it contained 'a substratum of truth', at least in so far as it proved that the punishment of 'born criminals' must be distinguished from that of criminals by circumstances. The high incidence of physical, mental, moral anomalies in the criminal, is 'due partly to degeneration, partly to atavism. The criminal is a special type of the human race, standing midway between the lunatic and the savage'.[39] In a separate article on crime, however, the Encyclopaedia was more critical:

In England [Lombroso's typology of crime] stands generally condemned, because it gives no importance to circumstance and passing temptation, or to domestic and social environment . . . (VII, p. 465)

Nevertheless, the article welcomed the development of a science of criminology in general which had 'strengthened the hands of administrators . . . emphasised the paramount importance of child rescue and judicious direction of adults . . . and insisted upon the desirability of indefinite detention for all who have obstinately determined to wage perpetual war against society by the persistent perpetration of crime' (VII, p. 465).

Hereditarian theories of crime and madness, and degenerationist theories of civilisation were not then confined to a few 'cranks', but neither were they to lead to a systematic change in the law. They were not assimilated as the terms of an obvious answer, but they were continually disseminated as the question.

'CENTRES OF DECAY'

Whereas in part I I stressed the importance of revolution in French degenerationism and in part II I emphasised the context of unification politics in Italian positivist theories of crime and social pathology, here I stress the interaction in England of a set of critical perceptions concerning the supposedly over-optimistic resonances of Darwin and Spencer, the viability of liberalism, mass democracy and the fate of the body in the city. Concern about internal bio-medical degeneration emerged for the first time not in the 1880s, in the context of the crisis of unemployment, riots and the formation of the Social Democratic Federation,[40] but rather in the late 1850s and 1860s.

It was during the 1850s that *The Lancet* first emphasised the word

---

[39] *Encyclopaedia Britannica*, 11th edn., 1910–1911, XVI, p. 936.
[40] See Stedman Jones, *Outcast London*.

'degeneration' to describe an internal deterioration which might earlier have been studied under the heading of 'decomposition' and to describe the decadence of certain races.[41] *The Lancet* was one of several journals which took account of the highly charged French medical and anthropological debate about racial degeneration and sought to relate it to an English intellectual and social context.

In the 1860s the question of the 'degeneration of the race' was entertained in the journal with references to Darwinian and Spencerian evolution, and with dark thoughts about the future of the cities and more specifically about the capital as a literal breeding ground of decay. In 1861 the deleterious effects of inbreeding amongst particular geographical and social groups was fiercely and persistently debated in the correspondence columns. As one writer gloomily acknowledged, it was not only the lower orders who were afflicted by morbid conditions which they then passed on to their children:

Are not the aristocracy and the care-worn denizen of the city, anxious, eager, depressed, with soul and body intent on business, and breathing all day long pestilential exhalations, subject to them too? And how can the unhealthy semen of such produce healthy offspring?[42]

In 1866, in an article entitled 'Race Degeneration', *The Lancet* was asking whether the topic was not becoming rather overblown, especially in the work of Morel across the Channel:

We have just read an account of an eminent example of this school of latitudinarian philanthropy. An enthusiastic Darwinian has been recently soliciting the pecuniary aid of the king of Prussia on behalf of 'arresting the degeneration of mankind', which according to some recent writers like M. MOREL is unequivocally progressing.[43]

But in the same year another article addressed rather less flippantly the question of urban degeneration, wondering whether there was an inherent contradiction in the evolution of cities:

If the consequences then of this social agglomeration be, on the one hand, increase of political power, of wealth, of commercial and social prosperity, and successful

---

41 Compare for instance *The Lancet*, 2 (July 1839), 597, and 1 (April 1857), 382. In *The Lancet* of the late 1850s and 1860s, we find a wide range of discussion of degeneration and decline; from clinical questions of 'gelatiniform degeneration of the right half of the stomach' (1 [April 1857], 382) and 'the nature of the waxy, lardaceous or "amyloid" degeneration' (1 [February 1867], 239–41) to the 'decadence of races': the Maori people show all the characteristics of 'an effete and debile stock' (2 [October 1860], 396).

42 K. Corbet, 'The degeneration of the race', letter in reply to S. Anderson Smith, *The Lancet*, 2 (August 1861), 170. For the full correspondence see 1 (February 1861), 202–3; 2 (September 1861), 232; 2 (October 1861), 360.

43 'Race degeneration', *The Lancet*, 1 (February 1866), 180.

competition with other nations, they are, on the other, an overtaxing of the physical and mental energies of national life-blood.[44]

The article noted the want of stamina, the flabby heart and undeveloped musculature of the urban poor. What we begin to see is an insistent cross-referencing of social preoccupations about the city with the specifically physical description of an impoverished nervous system and circulation: 'the blood is proved to be impoverished, and the nervous system devoid of that well-balanced tension on which the easy and harmonious working of the whole system depands'.[45] The process of decline, we are told, is primarily brought about by the effects of toxins like alcohol and tobacco, together with urban overcrowding, poor ventilation, diet and sexually transmitted diseases. But the processes of decay exceeded the 'vicious', coming to threaten the 'innocent' too:

though originating in the vicious course of individuals, [degenerations] are not confined in their consequences to the guilty sufferers, but are passed on to the offspring, and thus become year by year more generally diffused among the great mass of the people.[46]

Bodily degeneration was conflated with discussion of social and urban crisis:

He who would find the centres of decay in a nation, still on the whole robust and active, must seek for them at the points of social tension. The proofs of pressure, starvation, and atrophy, of vice and of brutal reversion, and of their results are all to be found there.[47]

In his later years, even the author of *The Origin of Species* (1859), Charles Darwin, worried about such 'brutal reversion'; questions

---

[44] 'The deterioration of race', *The Lancet*, 1 (June 1866), 691. Note that the article comments on the poor quality of military recruits: 'nearly four out of five fail to come up to [the] standard of bodily fitness'. Cf. Galton, *Hereditary Genius*, on modern civilisation's tendency to draw the best bodies into the city where they are systematically corrupted, '[s]o the race gradually deteriorates, becoming in each successive generation less fitted for a high civilization, although it retains the external appearances of one, until the time comes when the whole political and social fabric caves in, and a greater or less relapse to barbarism takes place, during the reign of which the race is perhaps able to recover its tone', p. 362; cf. Headley, *Problems*, ch. 9, 'The question of physical degeneration'; e.g. 'to go from west to east in London keeping one's mind on the subject of physique ... is a melancholy experiment. It brings out too painfully how a strong race can be crushed and dwarfed by vice, bad diet, bad housing and all that goes to make up a vile environment' (p. 237). Cf. Szreter, 'Decline', (diss.), p. 132, and Soloway, 'Counting the Degenerates', (per.), p. 156 which notes how apparent evidence suggesting that physique was declining in the countryside as well, was generally ignored.

[45] *The Lancet*, 1 (June 1866), 691.

[46] *The Lancet*, 1 (June 1866), 691.

[47] 'Degeneration amongst Londoners', *The Lancet*, 1 (February 1885), 264. Further discussion and reviews of degeneration can be found in the same journal at: 2 (1863), 643–6; 1 (1895), 48; 1 (1899), 33–4; 2 (1900), 1, 149; 1 (1904), 1, 133; 1 (1905), 369, 890.

remained to be answered about the future of 'the race' in a 'compassionate' era and a morbid urban milieu where the unfit did not perish. But when pressed by his cousin Francis Galton in the 1870s, he was not easily to be drawn into support for any particular legislative proposals. Galton had become unhappy with the implied equation of fitness with fecundity, given that the poorer classes of the city were the most fertile. He was puzzled with Darwin's idea that 'civilized men' were more prolific than 'wild men'.[48] The struggle for existence, Galton suggested, 'seems to me to spoil and not improve our breed', a view he had already expressed in a series of letters to Darwin in the 1860s.[49]

Darwin remained interested in, but uneasy about, the implications of degeneration and the proposal for racial regeneration as explored by some of his own followers. 'I venture to advise you not to carry the degradation principle too far', he wrote to Anton Dohrn.[50] Dohrn, a friend of Lankester and Huxley, was convinced that degeneration was a vital law which had to be incorporated into Darwinian zoology. The theme of 'descent' had of course long pre-occupied Darwin. Yet the critical response which greeted Robert Chambers' anonymous speculations on human evolution in the

---

[48] Darwin, *Descent of Man*, I, pp. 132–3; cf. Jones, *Social Darwinism*, p. 100.

[49] On this correspondence see Himmelfarb, *Victorian Minds*, pp. 326–7, and the extensive discussion in the chapters on Galton in Durant, 'Meaning of Evolution', (diss.). In *The Descent*, Darwin briefly responded to such issues and in particular 'the ingenious and original argument on this subject by Mr Galton' (*The Descent*, I, p. 177n): 'It has been urged by several writers that as high intellectual powers are advantageous to a nation, the old Greeks, who stood some grades higher in intellect than any race that has ever existed, ought to have risen, if the power of natural selection were real, still higher in the scale, increased in number and stocked the whole of Europe' (*The Descent*, I, pp. 177–8). This, he pointed out, was based on the fallacy that 'there is some innate tendency towards continued development in mind and body. But development of all kinds depends upon many concurrent favourable circumstances. Natural selection acts only in a tentative manner. Individuals and races may have acquired certain indisputable advantages and yet have perished from failing in other characters' (*The Descent*, I, p. 178). Cf. Darwin, *The Descent* (rev. ed.), p. 28, which speaks of the 'admirable labours of Mr. Galton' on inheritance and cites his *Hereditary Genius* (1869); cf. 'No one who has attended to the breeding of domestic animals will doubt that this must be highly injurious to the race of man. It is surprising how soon a want of care, or care wrongly directed, leads to the degeneration of a domestic race; but excepting in the case of man himself hardly any one is so ignorant as to allow his worst animals to breed' (ib., 134); if checks do not occur artificially or naturally in the propagation of the unfit and inferior 'the nation will retrograde, as has too often occurred in the history of the world' (ib., 140); cf. Jones, *Social Darwinism*, p. 100.

[50] Letter to Anton Dohrn (24 May 1875), in Dohrn, *Charles Darwin*, p. 63; cf. Dohrn's letter (31 May 1875) to Darwin, 'I regret to have added the exposition of my belief into a general degeneration throughout the whole organic world. But even that meets here and there with a partial approval, and will have some influence on the treatment of morphological investigation. I myself believe it very much' (pp. 64–5). On Dohrn's friendship with Huxley and Lankester see Dohrn, *Charles Darwin*, pp. 96, 98; on Dohrn's acquaintance with Darwin see pp. 93–4.

1840s had contributed to his decision to leave man almost entirely out of *The Origin*. (Darwin merely ventured the promise that one day 'light will be thrown on the origin of man and his history'.[51]) His *Notebooks*, however, had been full of such speculations on human heredity and its affiliations.[52]

By the time of *The Descent* in 1871 he could write explicitly that his object was to show solely 'that there is no fundamental difference between man and the higher mammals in their mental faculties'.[53] The tone as well as the subject had shifted in other ways. In *The Origin* he had declared it possible to 'look with some confidence to a secure future of equally inappreciable length'; he had insisted that 'natural selection works solely by and for the good of each being, all corporeal and mental developments will tend to progress towards perfection';[54] but in *The Descent* there were a number of ominous warnings about the direction of civilisation: 'Natural selection acts only in a tentative manner';[55] '[w]e must remember that progress is no invariable rule' (I, p. 177).

Certainly by the 1870s, one of the problems about Comtean positivism, in the view of Darwin and Huxley, was exactly its unwarranted political, religious and 'scientific' optimism.[56] What Comte shared with much of Victorian naturalism was an insistence on the absolute inter-connection of social units, the absurdity of classical political economy and individualism.[57] But his voluntaristic faith in the possibility of simply transcending competition by the will to unity and humanity ('Human catholicism' as Richard Congreve put it[58]) ran against the apparent emphases of evolutionism. The overtly 'religious' side of positivism developed above all by Congreve was anathema to most Darwinians, as was the political analysis which led sometimes to the endorsement of radical causes (not least the

---

51 *Origin*, p. 488.
52 'Our descent, then, is the origin of our evil passions!! – The Devil under form of Baboon is our grandfather!' ('M Notebook' [line ref. 123], Gruber, *Darwin on Man*, p. 289). 'The real argument fixes on hereditary disposition & instincts ... Verily the faults of the fathers, corporeal & bodily, are visited upon the children' ('M Notebook' [line ref. 73–4], *Darwin on Man*, p. 279). 'My theory would give zest to recent and fossil Comparative Anatomy: it would lead to study of instincts, heredity & mind heredity, whole of metaphysics – it would lead to closest examination of hybridity, – & generation, causes of change in order to know what we have come from & to what we tend' ('B Notebook' [line ref. B228], *Darwin on Man*, p. 447). 'Let man visit the Ourang-outang in domestication, hear expressive whine, see its intelligence when spoken, as if it understood every word sayd ... see its affection to those it knows ... see its passion & rage, sulkiness, & every action of despair ... & then let him dare to boast of his proud preeminence' ('C Notebook' [line ref. C79], *Darwin on Man*, p. 449).
53 *The Descent*, I, p. 35.   54 *Origin*, p. 489.
55 *The Descent*, I, p. 178.   56 See Wright, *Religion of Humanity*.
57 *Religion of Humanity*, p. 24.
58 Quoted in Wright, *Religion of Humanity*, p. 81.

enthusiasm some positivists showed for the Paris Commune[59]). Huxley spoke of his gratitude to Comte for leaving him 'with the conviction that the organisation of society upon a new and purely scientific basis is not only practicable, but is the only political object worth fighting for'; he dismissed positivism's religious pretensions, however, as 'Catholicism minus Christianity'.[60]

By the late 1850s and 1860s, something of Carlylean and Arnoldian social rhetoric had been displaced and re-invested in the image of the material body, its reproduction and evolution. Carlyle himself fought against Darwin's theories, but dreaded they might be true. Admittedly when he had examined criminals (members of what he called the 'Devil's regiments of the line') Carlyle saw bestial features: 'ape faces, imp faces, angry dog faces, heavy sullen ox faces . . . These abject ape, wolf, ox, imp and other diabolic-animal specimens of humanity, who of the very gods could ever have commanded them by love?'[61] Or again when he railed against the Irish, he saw 'squalid apehood'[62] and demanded that 'the Irish population must either be improved or else exterminated' (p. 183). But Carlyle's language was a far cry from the world of *The Descent* and its disturbing implication of even the scientist and the social commentator, in the simian realm.

To emphasise the startling nature of Darwinian descent in Victorian society and language is not in any way to deny that its discourse was always recuperable within religion and within familiar, socially hierarchical theories. Moreover one should not see the providentialism in Darwin himself as merely strategic – a mere subterfuge hiding his 'real' materialism. Historians of science have convincingly demonstrated the myriad continuities of language and faith running from the natural theological tradition of Paley through to Darwin and his followers.[63]

Yet Darwinism affiliated society, the body and reproduction in powerful new ways and certainly it was impossible for its followers to avoid

[59] See Wright, *Religion of Humanity*, pp. 110, 115.
[60] Huxley, 'Scientific aspects', (per.), pp. 656–7. Comtism had provided one answer to the Victorian crisis of belief – a new system of meaning and interpretation. As Harriet Martineau put it in 1853: 'The supreme dread of every one who cares for the good of the nation or race is that men should be adrift for want of an anchorage for their convictions. I believe that no one questions that a very large proportion of our people are now so adrift . . . The work of M. Comte is unquestionably the greatest single effort that has been made to obviate this kind of danger' (Martineau's introduction to Comte, *Positive Philosophy*, I, p. viii).
[61] 'Model prisons', pp. 55–6.   [62] 'Chartism', p. 182.
[63] See, for instance, Durant, 'Meaning of Evolution', (diss.), and Young, *Darwin's Metaphor*.

making links between the general issue of evolution and the 'chaos' of contemporary human reproduction. The *laissez-faire* of child-birth which in Darwin might be deemed beneficial, could also appear fearsome given the pathogenic conditions of the city. This view did not mean a return to Malthus, with the bleak assurance of death as nature's response to over-population, but rather the vision of a lingering degeneration in the individual, the procreation of a stunted race.

Heredity was thus perceived as an unresolved problem which demanded drastic social action. Moral exhortation or illumination alone (a 'good spirit' to take the rooftops off the houses of the poor, as Dickens had put it in *Dombey and Son*) was thus deemed incapable of resolving a crisis which was now evolving across generations. Alcoholism, say, was not only a cause but also an effect in a chain of degeneration. The individual might be born with a kind of inherited profligacy. In 1860, the *British and Foreign Medico-Chirurgical Review* cited Charles Kingsley to the effect that: 'I am one of those who cannot, on scientific grounds, consider drunkenness as a cause of evil, but as an effect. Of course it is a cause – a cause of endless crime and misery; but . . . to cure [it], you must inquire not what it causes, but what causes it.'[64] A few pages later the *Review* cited Morel, for whom

it is indispensable . . . that there should be a *predisposition*, in order that the particular cause may act in a special manner. It is necessary that various elements equally partaking of a physical and moral character should be brought into play under the influence of predisposition, and concur with the accidental cause in the factorship of a particular form of mental alienation . . . (p. 301)

In 'Nausicaa in London, or the Lower Education of Women' (1873), Kingsley described the admiration with which he viewed the physique of Greek Woman as enshrined in the statues of Antiquity. Walking away from the British Museum he was pained to remark the 'exceedingly small size of the average young woman'.[65] He exhorted physical activity and medical awareness, calling on young poor girls to 'copy in your person' that classical perfection, or 'at least learn to play at ball; and sing in the open air and sunshine' (p. 122) for this will increase 'the general strength of the upper torso without which full oxygenation of the blood and therefore general health is impossible' (p. 125). Kingsley's concern here was with the body, as though the whole social process could be grasped and analysed in its degradation and degeneration. The 'condition of England question' was now centrally concerned with the condition of the English body.

---

[64] *British and Foreign Medico-Chirurgical Review* (1860), 289.
[65] *Lectures and Essays*, p. 116.

Moreover the reader was alerted to the devastating reproductive effects of such an unhealthy milieu as the capital itself.[66]

As evolutionary theories entered ever more powerfully into the arena of public debate, Kingsley had paid increasing attention to the physical decrepitude of the race, as symptom, or perhaps even agent of its spiritual malaise and its future destiny. In a lecture and an essay in 1872, he seemed to echo a sentence from Carlyle's 'Chartism' ('The condition of the working-man in this country, what it is and has been, whether it is improving or retrograding'[67]); but the title of Kingsley's essay was 'The Science of Health' and the key words were 'race' and 'degeneration':

Whether the British race is improving or degenerating? What if it seem probably degenerating, are the causes of so great an evil? How can they be, if not destroyed, at least arrested? These are questions worthy attention, not of statesmen only and medical men, but of every father and mother in these isles.[68]

This bio-political nomenclature informed new critiques of various aspects of classical liberalism. A position emerged which grounded its criticism of *laissez-faire* neither in medievalism, evangelism, romanticism, nor in mere dark Carlylean hints of the dissolution to follow if the working classes were not better governed, but which, on the contrary, turned upon the central question of the race and the economy of its reproduction.

Not until the last quarter of the century in England did it become really compelling to attack contemporary capitalist society, within its own ideological terms, for its failure of growth, its performance in international competition, its relative demise.[69] The state-directed economy of Germany was now available as an alternative model of capitalist success and progress.[70] Critical social commentators might now point to the commercial advantage gained by the Prussians through their centralised bureaucracy,

---

[66] To take a later example, consider Havelock Ellis' intensifying preoccupation with the body, reproduction and sexology as a means to regeneration. A range of new scientific insights and disciplines were to be brought to bear on society in the pursuit of its revitalisation. By the turn of the century Havelock Ellis was supporting Galton's hereditarian work and its ominous findings about the future of the race. The unfit, he suggested, should be persuaded to be sterilised (see Grosskurth, *Havelock Ellis*, p. 410) and his own work increasingly involved the task of (as the introduction to one of his works put it) examining 'the disquieting signs of physical deterioriation', tracking the prevalence of vice, increase of insanity and feeblemindedness and their 'exhaustless drain upon free-flowing charity and the national purse' and the hideous congestion of slumdom 'with its irreparable loss of the finer sensibilities of beauty, sweetness and light' (*Race-Regeneration*, p. 7); cf. Ellis, *Social Hygiene*, pp. 38–9, and Ellis' introduction to Freeman, *Social Decay*.

[67] 'Chartism', p. 116.

[68] *Lectures and Essays*, p. 21.

[69] See Searle, *Quest*, pp. 11–12, 29; Harris, *Unemployment*, p. 46; Nye, *Crime*, p. 332.

[70] See Searle, *Quest*, pp. 5, 29, on the new mood of doubt in Britain during the 1865–1875 period when Bismarck's unification of Germany finally and irrevocably destroyed many blithe assumptions about Britain's permanent economic and diplomatic ascendancy.

system of education, tariffs and conscription.[71] In the social evolutionary language of many of Darwin's followers, inheritance was understood in a transformed language of political economy which refused a notion of the abstract and autonomous person and focussed on the capital of physiology, racial investment, the resources and capacities of the nervous system, growth and sexual expenditure. The body, it seemed, could not be left to itself since it was a crucial racial patrimony. As one commentator put it in 1890, summing up the potential bio-economic danger:

The lower strata of society, the great recruiting ground of the upper, are undergoing the same softening process. We are, in fact, using up our physiological capital very rapidly, and we should be very foolish to let the maintenance of stature or even an increase of the stature actualised blind us to the fact.[72]

When the medical-psychiatrist Henry Maudsley asked whether the reproductive material possessed 'in invested capital something of that which its parent laboriously acquired',[73] the answer was equivocal, but the labour/capital imagery was not by chance. The fate of capital and the body in 'the capital' were interfused. Only by applying biological and medical truths to the body, the nation and the empire, it was argued with increasing force, could the economy and society be sustained at all. When the supply of the supposedly healthier rural population ceased to supplement the jaded bodies of the third or fourth-generation city dweller, the so-called urban residuum might become ever more common.[74]

Economics were brought to bear on inheritance with a new detail and concentration. Francis Galton's long inquiry into heredity was perhaps the most striking example of the re-direction of questions of economic and social progress to the evolutionary problem of the body's reproduction. The labour value to be expected from future workers would be in jeopardy if, as Galton believed, the offspring of the working class reproduced and amplified in their bodies from birth, the degenerative effects of the urban, industrial life suffered by their parents. By the late-nineteenth century Galton had concluded that the really poor and destitute were doomed to social uselessness. Anyone who fell into the social investigator Charles Booth's lowest categories were an intolerable drain on the economy, indeed 'they create no wealth'.[75] In a section of his *Essays in Eugenics* entitled 'profit and loss' (pp. 29 ff.), he anticipated a time when the value of a prospective child could 'be estimated by an actuary, and consequently the

[71] *Quest*, p. 29.   [72] Headley, *Problems*, p. 242.
[73] *Hereditary Variation*, p. 29.
[74] See Searle, *Quest*; Stedman Jones, *Outcast London*; cf. for example Cantlie, *Degeneration Amongst Londoners*, and Bedford, 'Urban populations', (per.), p. 388.
[75] *Essays*, p. 19.

sum that it is appropriate to spend in favouring an X parentage' (p. 29). Eugenics counterposed itself to sentimental philanthropy and continually linked its social images with the recent 'evidence' of evolutionary zoology. Galton applied the image of the parasite (which was a primary instance of regression given by Lankester in his evolutionary theory of degeneration[76]) to society. There was, he argued, an absolute

contrariety of ideals between the beasts that prey and those they prey upon, between those of the animals that have to work hard for their food and the sedentary parasites that cling to their bodies and suck their blood . . .[77]

Darwin, it seemed to Galton, could not be left out of any adequate political or economic theory. The precise periodisation of this new emphasis on reproduction and degeneration is difficult to draw, but whilst when Galton first proposed his stark hereditarian ideas in the late 1860s they were still poorly received or even ignored, in the last three decades of the century there was growing enthusiasm for his work.[78]

Darwin's *Origin* had had an enormous emotional impact on Galton.[79] It had led him to re-direct his attention from geography and meteorology towards the quest for the very biological foundations of human society, a desperate search for a new philosophy of nature, a new theory of humanity and a new religion. Galton's quest ended in the ideal and the movement of eugenics, a word which he coined in 1883.[80] The role of eugenics in subjugating human selfishness, he wrote in a piece on 'The part of religion in human evolution', 'justly merits the name of religion'.[81] Galton's social-evolutionary politics stressed the inter-connectedness of society and hence the impossibility of classical liberalism (the endorsement of which had been in his view the deep error of Herbert Spencer).

Galton, it is true, had been interested in questions of race and its measurement before reading Darwin's *Origin*. In 1850, for instance, he had been in South West Africa where he reported how he had met the wife of a Hottentot at a mission station and since he '[professed] to be a scientific man' was 'exceedingly anxious to obtain accurate measurements of her

---

[76] See below, pp. 216–18.
[77] See Galton, *Essays*, p. 36; cf. Harris, *Unemployment*, p. 46, and on Beveridge's view of the unemployable and the parasitic, see p. 26. Cf. also Morel's similarly expressed view in France. If man through his isolation does not participate in the general progress, 'he becomes a useless and parasitical being' ['un être parasite et inutile'], who attacks society through 'the fatal consequences of a destructive egoism' (*Etudes Cliniques*, I, pp. 266–7).
[78] See Stepan, *Idea of Race*, p. 116.
[79] See Durant, 'Meaning of Evolution', (diss.), pp. 185, 199–200.
[80] See Galton, *Inquiries*; cf. Durant, 'Meaning of Evolution', (diss.), pp. 199–200.
[81] Galton, 'Religion', (per.); cf. Galton, *Essays*: 'it has indeed strong claims to become an orthodox religious tenet of the future, for Eugenics cooperates with the workings of Nature by securing that humanity shall be represented by the fittest races' (p. 42).

shape'.[82] This he effected, despite a certain amount of embarrassment, from a distance, with the aid of trigonometry. But Galton came home to England and turned his insatiable desire for numbers and measurements increasingly towards domestic 'problems' of inheritance and anthropometry informed by Darwinism. He suffered a succession of 'maladies prejudicial to mental effort', culminating in a breakdown in 1866 (p. 85); amongst other disappointments, it was in this period that it became apparent that his own marriage was likely to prove infertile; he became ever more fascinated by the question of evolution and inheritance at large, urging Britain's transformation from 'a mob of slaves, clinging together, incapable of self-government and begging to be led'[83] (Galton at his most Carlylean), into a new race of 'vigorous self-reliant men' (p. 357). In Galton's work, deeply troubling questions about the nation's level of social and political maturity, and specifically about the effects of a changing and widening electoral constituency after 1867, were deflected onto the problem of the racial body and mind; politics was dissolved into mathematics and biology.[84] Again we see that slide into biological idealism, that shift into a conception of degeneration as the imagined subject, cause and force of history. By the Edwardian period, Galton's endeavours had encouraged the formation of a new caste of eugenically orientated academics, journalists and doctors. An important grouping developed around the mathematician Karl Pearson, his journal *Biometrika* and University College, London, where he taught.[85] By 1912, London University played host to the first International Congress of Eugenics, with Leonard Darwin as president, Winston Churchill as vice-president.[86]

---

[82] Quoted in Forrest, *Francis Galton*, p. 45.

[83] Galton, 'Gregariousness', (per.), p. 357.

[84] Cf. for instance Geddes: 'we see how ... the dispute preceding the passing of the Factory Acts was not really at all a struggle between "economic science" on the one hand and "mere sentiment" on the other, but turned upon subordinating the lower idea of physical economics ... to the higher ideal of biological economics – that of maintenance and evolution of the population.' ('Application of biology', (per.), p. 1,166); cf. p. 1,167.) 'Again [in] the current dispute between individualist and socialist, we at once see that what the former has really taken his stand upon is simply the law of survival of the fittest, the principle of natural selection; while the socialist position has its base in the later but equally valid conception of the practicability of artifical selection.'

[85] University College was to be the intellectual base of the new theory and movement. Three of the figures discussed here, Galton, Maudsley and Lankester all had close connections with University College. On various items of correspondence between them, see the letters listed under Galton in the unpublished papers section of the bibliography below. On the foundation of Galton's fellowship and laboratory at University College, see Forrest, *Francis Galton*, p. 260. It should also be noted that Sir Cyril Burt, notorious key figure in the history of twentieth-century mental testing, continued the Galtonian tradition at the same institution. He occupied the important Chair of Psychology at University College from 1932–50; see Gould, *Mismeasure*, pp. 234–320.

[86] Foreign contributors included Sergi, Morselli, Loria, Michels and Magnan.

The Congress polarised opinion on the question of the eugenic implications of the rediscovery of Mendel's work. Indeed to many, Mendelism, as first championed by the Cambridge biologist William Bateson, appeared to have undermined certain key assumptions of traditional eugenics and biometrics – the utility, for instance, of measuring observable physical characteristics to make inferences regarding the laws of human variation (a practice which would eventually be dismissed as a radical confusion of genotype and phenotype). Controversy was aroused when an American eugenist, Dr Davenport, sought to use the idea of the dominant and the recessive, to justify marriage between a mentally vigorous man and a socially attractive and physically beautiful though defective woman. Pearson was totally appalled at this new line of argument, declaring that such a view 'passes my comprehension'.[87] He led something of a rearguard action against Mendelism. As one of his followers put it: 'we repudiate in the name of Eugenics any sanction for the enfeeblement of strong stocks by mating them with weak stocks on the basis of a theory which, even if true, declares that all the offspring will carry latent defect. The strong should mate with strength.'[88] What is remarkable, and what indeed must be stressed here, is precisely the endurance of a theory of degeneration and the degenerate beyond any specific technical demolition of its science, whether in medical psychiatry, criminal anthropology or eugenics.

The language of degeneration was elaborated by Galton, Pearson and various other anthropometrists, psychiatrists, anthropologists and lawyers within the London intelligentsia from the 1880s through the 1900s. They developed that mood of unease with the terms of evolutionary theory and its relation to social progress, already to be glimpsed in the 1850s and early 1860s. A certain image of degeneration had emerged to articulate in biological terms what was felt to be the widening political contradiction between national prosperity and empire on the one hand, and persistent urban poverty, criminal sub-culture and social pathology on the other.

The Victorian period did not, of course, witness a uniform shift in all social writing. Rather, a new widely shared agenda of questions about the body, the city and degeneration emerged, brought about in a complex late-nineteenth-century interaction of scientific theories and political perceptions. One could perhaps speak of 'the interest' of the medical and psychiatric profession in heightening the problem of health and reproduction in order to justify its own status and institutional expansion, but this

---

[87] *Mendelism*, p. 12.   [88] Heron, *Mendelism. A Criticism of Recent Work*, p. 7.

takes us only so far. My emphasis lies in a wider discursive context which was not merely 'controlled' as part of a project of medical professional-isation. The language of degeneration in *The Lancet* was sporadic, contra-dictory, eclectic – articulating fears and unknown possibilities rather than simply a policy for medical funding and recognition.

In 1885, *The Lancet* re-affirmed a diagnostically hopeful view of de-generation. It sought to stave off a pessimism which had even infiltrated the medical profession. 'We have good hope', declared the editors, 'that the national mind, recognising that there is degeneration and that it is curable, will continue to treat it with sympathy, as it has begun to do, and will direct upon it the fresh air of public discussion and the healthy exercise of a wisely corrective legislation.'[89] But the anxiety persisted. In 1888 under the title 'Are We Degenerating Physically?', *The Lancet* again rehearsed the arguments.

[Degeneration] . . . is undoubtedly at work among town-bred populations as the consequence of unwholesome occupations, improper [diet], and juvenile vice . . . while the optimistic view has most to urge in its favour, it would be wrong to ignore the existence of widespread evils and serious dangers to the public health. Amongst these evils and dangers are enumerated sexual indulgence in early life, premature marriages, over-pressure in education, improper food, increased tension . . . and the abuse of alcohol and tobacco.[90]

Degeneration then was a continuing theme from the 1850s to the 1880s and beyond. Yet the 1880s did witness a powerful intensification of theor-etical speculation. The problem was no longer merely academic or margin-al (reports or translations of Morel's work), but urgently tied to the crises of London society.

An important explanatory account of this language and its relation to metropolitan politics is to be found in Gareth Stedman Jones' *Outcast London* (1971). It traces significant shifts in the geography of industry and analyses the labour market, housing, poverty, casual work and unemploy-ment. These are mapped on to the changing language of social represen-tation in the last decades of the century and in particular to new forms of alarmism.

In the context of the birth of organised socialism on the one hand and of the re-occurrence of various demonstrations and riots in the 1880s on the other, many middle-class commentators represented and explained the life and economy of the city's casual poor in increasingly biological terms.[91] The language of 'demoralisation' gave way to 'urban degeneration'. Drink,

---

[89] 'Degeneration amongst Londoners', *The Lancet*, 1 (February 1885), 265.
[90] *The Lancet*, 2 (December 1888), 1,076.   [91] Stedman Jones, *Outcast London*, p. 313.

early marriage, improvidence, irreligion, idleness were increasingly seen as symptoms rather than simple causes in a process of physical and moral degeneration fostered and reproduced by the city itself. Displays of popular feeling, from the demonstrations of the unemployed of the mid-1880s to the riots of the Edwardian period, were read off in relation to the putative propensities of a new urban race. The very genesis of the 'welfare state', Stedman Jones argues, owed a great deal to middle class fear of the urban poor and their potential liaison with the (hitherto) 'respectable' working class, to the hyperbolic image of revolution and to the fear of the social revenge of the outcast. Although the debate, and the fear, can be traced back much earlier in the Victorian period, it is in the 1880s, Stedman Jones insists, that the theory of hereditary urban degeneration first received widespread support from the middle classes and found its authoritative backing in the work of Booth, Marshall, Langstaff and Llewellyn Smith (p. 128). And at the edge of the writings of those 'sober' commentators, there was a huge populist literature which saw the social problem in truly cataclysmic terms.[92]

The fears persisted in the 1900s. Amidst the early disasters of the Boer War and the scandal of an apparent deterioration in the average physique of potential recruits, the fear of urban degeneration found its apotheosis. The relatively reassuring findings of the Inter-Departmental Committee on Physical Deterioration in 1904 (already discussed earlier), at least in relation to the scale of biological degeneration, did little to allay the sensationalist fears of politicians and journalists.

During World War I, however, the phenomenon of casual labour and cyclical unemployment almost disappeared and the specific nexus between a supposed residuum of the unemployable and a wider evolutionary process involving the 'degeneration of the Londoner', receded from view. In Stedman Jones' words:

Once decent and regular employment was made available, the 'unemployables' proved impossible to find. In fact they had never existed, except as a phantom army called up by late-Victorian and Edwardian social science to legitimize its practice.[93]

If this was indeed the end of one 'phantom army', it was not the end of the wider bio-medical discourse of degeneration. Degeneration was certainly called up by various sciences for purposes of legitimation; but it was more

---

[92] *Outcast London*, ch. 6, and Keating (ed.), *Unknown England*.
[93] *Outcast London*, p. 336.

than simply an instrument of those sciences;[94] it could not easily be put back or abandoned even in the face of specific, powerful technical critiques, precisely because it remained for so many commentators an assumed common sense, an inevitable home truth.

HENRY MAUDSLEY

This section looks in some detail at the writings of the important Victorian medical-psychiatrist, Henry Maudsley (1835-1918), to develop this argument around periodisation and transition in the language of degeneration. His work signals a wider development within Victorian social commentary, the confluence of a medico-psychiatric theory of *dégénérescence*, a Darwinian theory of evolutionary regression and a positivist theory of criminal inheritance, all of which in their turn flowed into a wider current of concern about the pathology of the city and modernity. Maudsley's increasingly strident elitism and his pessimistic account of 'mass democracy' was mediated by the perception of society's organic degeneration. The subsumption of crime and madness within this broader preoccupation with the future viability of 'mass civilisation' marks a shift in the terms of social description. Just as the category of the degenerate began to recede from view in the years before and during World War I, the notion of the crowd as the inevitable scene of degeneration and regression was further consolidated in European thought.

Maudsley's early 'Tennysonian' optimism, observed the psychiatrist Aubrey Lewis in 1951, is 'startling from a man who is now remembered as a pessimist'.[95] In Maudsley's work in 1860

all is for the best in the evolutionary survival of the fittest; the degenerate and the primitive are being eliminated as [in his words] 'humanity in its progress upwards, fashions the supporting stem only by sacrificing the early branches. All observation proves that mankind is advancing.' (pp. 265–6)

---

[94] Cf. Searle, 'Eugenics and Class', who argues that eugenics was in some cases merely a rhetoric deployed 'tactically' by various different groups. Thus it would be wrong to tarnish fabianism with the same brush as full-blown eugenics because although they used the terms, they did not mean the same thing: 'A similar tactical use of eugenics was made by Webb in his pronouncements on the declining birth rate and his call for an "Endowment of Motherhood" to prevent the United Kingdom being over-run by the Irish, Jews and the Chinese. *The language was indeed the language of eugenics*, but the policies that Webb was advocating ... were precisely the kind of policies which most eugenists detested and predicted would cause racial degeneration' (pp. 231–2); cf. the assumption of 'interests' as an explanatory key in Mackenzie, *Statistics*, p. 46.

[95] Lewis, 'Henry Maudsley', (per.), p. 265.

But in terms of the periodisation we are tracing, this change is not so startling. Indeed Maudsley at once reflected and contributed to a deepening evolutionary pessimism in the late-nineteenth century which was accompanied, nevertheless, by a deep proselytising faith in the role of medicine as key to social and political theory.

There had always been more than a streak of the prophet in Henry Maudsley. In a lecture at University College, London in 1876, he had observed that medicine was in the process of triumphing over a great many physical scourges which had afflicted society. Bloody flux or dysentery, small pox, plague, scurvy, spotted fever are 'almost diseases of the past'.[96] Soon, he suggested, medicine would triumph over the other major diseases, and thus it should extend its scope. Insights into the body could be applied to a broader context:

one may hope that the medical science of the future . . . will have a great deal to say in the way of instruction respecting the highest concerns of man's nature and the conduct of his life; that he will enter a domain which has hitherto been given up exclusively to the moral philosopher and the preacher. (p. 20)

Maudsley's writing did have a religious, preaching role and his very appearance later in life matched that image of the seer. A man with a 'straggling beard and piercing eyes',[97] he wrote in 'a sombre and weighty style illuminated by vivid flashes of imagination' which deeply impressed many of his contemporaries, although his style of medical and social diagnosis continually risked provoking accusations of charlatanism.[98] He advocated the popularisation of medical knowledge and abhorred the vogue for classical terms whereby 'every cut the surgeon makes is a magniloquent *ectomy* or *ostomy*!'[99] In his view, medical theory should be widely disseminated; for only by advertising its utility and insight could it gain true recognition as the expert witness of the law court and the government inquiry. Medicine, he argued, had to teach the law to abandon its primitive desire for retribution.[100] Nevertheless, the populist tone of

[96] *Maudsley, Introductory Lecture*, p. 19.

[97] '[Maudsley] had a huge head, straggling beard and piercing eyes, a low quiet voice. He was inclined to suddenly fire a question at one, which was embarrassing at any rate to me! I thought he was rather abrupt in his manner to some of his old patients, but they liked him and looked forward to his visits' (R. J. Stilwell, letter to Lewis [25 January 1948] in Aubrey Lewis's file on Maudsley in the Royal Bethlem Hospital archives; see unpublished items section in bibliography).

[98] 'An artist as much as a man of science, master of a sombre and weighty style, illuminated by vivid flashes of imagination' (Havelock Ellis, of Henry Maudsley, quoted in Scott, 'Henry Maudsley', p. 145, no source given). 'I met [Maudsley] only once when he was called in consultation about a patient of mine about 45 years ago. He made an obviously wrong diagnosis and it is possible that this experience destroyed any interest I may have had in him' (W. H. B. Stoddart, letter to Lewis [5 January 1948] in Lewis file).

[99] Maudsley, *Hereditary Variation*, p. 192.

[100] See Maudsley, *Responsibility*: '[we should] get rid of the angry feeling of retaliation which may be at the bottom of any judicial punishment' (p. 28).

Maudsley's own pronouncements risked incurring charges of vulgar show-manship from the more technically-minded of his colleagues or from hostile reviewers.[101] Maudsley's career was perhaps vaguely shrouded in an aura of seamy secrecy, both because of the candour of some of his writing and certain questionable clinical judgements, even shady dealings (for instance the charges involving dubiously motivated confinements which were aired in the inquiry of the Select Committee on Lunacy in 1877).[102]

Yet Maudsley had many supporters and admirers. He was certainly the Victorian English psychiatrist most widely read and quoted in Italy, France and Germany at the time.[103] Darwin quoted him appreciatively for his sensible and sober views in *The Descent of Man*,[104] as did Bagehot in *Physics and Politics*.[105] But Maudsley was also a very self-effacing prophet and ambassador: he took a dim view of self-celebration and had lamented the vanity of famous people who discoursed *ad nauseam* on their own history.[106] Maudsley made very little effort to record his own past and perhaps may have gone so far as to destroy the bulk of his personal papers. Following a medical training at University College, he had hoped to

---

[101] A reviewer from Oxford, for instance, reviewing *Life in Mind and Conduct* (1902), observed that it was written from Maudsley's 'well-known standpoint of medical ma-terialism ... with a cocksureness and neglect of past and contemporary thinking which no one but a medical materialist would venture on'. Furthermore the dubious doctor was 'constantly indulging in the cynical pleasure of ripping up the seamy side of things': 'A favourite term of Dr Maudsley's is "lust", and he is fond of illustrating various points of experience from some of the least pleasing aspects of human nature in a way which hardly renders his work suitable for family reading.' Sturt, 'Review', (per.), p. 258. Maudsley's materialism was certainly expressed in extreme ways sometimes. Thus for instance 'It is certain ... that lunatics and criminals are as much manufactured articles as are steam-engines and calico-printing machines, only the process of the organic manufactory are so complex that we are not able to follow them.' (Maudsley, *Responsibility*, p. 28). '*Emotion* signifies that which emotion was always felt to be – namely an internal commotion or perturbation moving outwards to discharge itself. How then describe its qualities except in the language of physics?' (*Life in Mind and Conduct*, p. 13).

[102] See Select Committee 1877, pp. 203–8.

[103] See Turner, 'Henry Maudsley'. On the French edition of Maudsley's *Le Crime et la folie*, see Scott, 'Henry Maudsley', p. 145; cf. Smith, *Trial*, p. 52; Ellenburger, *Discovery of the Unconscious*, p. 756.

[104] See Darwin, *Descent of Man*, I, p. 24.

[105] In *Physics and Politics*, Bagehot quoted Maudsley's Lamarckian opinion that '[p]ower which has been laboriously acquired and stored up as statical in one generation manifestly in such case becomes the inborn faculty of the next' (Maudsley, *Physiology*, p. 73). Bagehot argued in Lamarckian terms that the 'body is charged with stored virtue' (*Physics*, p. 6). 'Stored up power [is] either innate or acquired' (p. 7). Bagehot then saw the nervous system as an important factor in the advance of the individual and the race. Conscious effort produced habit which in its turn became fixed as a reflex of the nervous system. Maudsley was Bagehot's 'authority' for this view; cf. Driver, 'Walter Bagehot', p. 263.

[106] See Maudsley, *Religion*, p. 58 (chapter 6 is entitled 'Vanity'). Maudsley writes of the vanity of eminent men who 'leave behind them carefully preserved letters' and 'elaborate mem-oirs': '[a]musing sometimes comical, almost pitiable at times, is the ludicrous display of vanity by men of great eminence and superior intellectual endowments'. Cf. the discussion of Maudsley's professional discretion in Turner, 'Henry Maudsley'.

become a surgeon and to travel to India in the service of the East India Company. A preparatory year spent as a medical superintendent at the Wakefield Asylum was, however, to arouse his interest in the field of mental medicine which occupied him for the rest of his career.

Between 1856 and 1857 he was an assistant medical officer at the West Riding County Asylum, Wakefield. In the following two years he had a post at Essex County Asylum, Brentwood, and from 1858 to 1861 was a superintendent at Cheadle Royal Hospital, Manchester where he received acclaim for improving the standing and fortunes of the hospital. In private practice in London from 1862, he was also a physician in mental diseases at the West London Hospital (1864–74), professor of medical jurisprudence at University College, London (1869–79) and a Fellow of the Royal College of Physicians. He was joint editor of the *Journal of Mental Science* from 1862 to 1878 and president of the Medico-Psychological Association (1871). He had married Ann Conolly, the daughter of the great early Victorian alienist, John Conolly, in 1866. There were no children. Maudsley's subsequent notoriety and fame has perhaps rested principally on two factors: first, he was a famous polemicist against the higher education of women (especially during the 1870s[107]). Second, in 1907, Maudsley, by then an old man, offered the London County Council £30,000 to establish a university psychiatric clinic on the German model. After many delays it opened as the Maudsley Hospital in 1915 (three years before Maudsley's death) and is now the teaching hospital in psychiatry for London University. As this suggests, Maudsley's private practice had been extremely lucrative.[108]

Maudsley was powerfully influenced by Darwin's theory of evolution and convinced that science would eventually decipher all the signs of mind in its evolution across time. Science would finally be able to construe the codes and imprints of body and mind.[109] The body, he suggested, was like a (family) tree whose age, history and health could be seen in cross-section. Materialism did not mean the rejection of the idea of 'immortality', but simply the relocation of its meaning in terms of heredity; as he insisted in 1860, 'the weightiest reason which operates in preventing man from recognising the importance of the body is the difficulty he has in conceiving its immortality'.[110] Past experience moved down through the generations and

---

[107] See Maudsley, 'Sex in mind', (per.); cf. Elizabeth Garret Anderson's reply, 'Sex in mind', (per.).

[108] Note how Maudsley had earlier pointed out to medical students in a lecture that they were very unlikely to make great fortunes in their hallowed career whose true object was 'the welfare and progress of mankind upon earth' (*Introductory Lecture*, pp. 6–7).

[109] As he put it in 1902: 'Without doubt the character of every mind is written in the features, gestures, gait, and carriage of the body, and will be read there, when, if ever, the extremely fine and difficult language is fully and accurately learnt' (*Life in Mind and Conduct*, p. 54).

[110] Maudsley, 'Correlation', (per.), p. 76.

was inscribed in the body. Experience passed beyond consciousness, eventually reaching the nervous system, the reflex, the organic. By using the term 'unconscious' to describe a realm of inherited desire and experience outside the agent's 'responsibility', Maudsley raised crucial issues about crime and its punishment, which were part of a wide and sustained dispute between medical psychiatry and the legal profession.[111]

Environment worked upon mental forms and was subsumed through reproduction as a given physiological and neurological condition. The conjectural time-scale for such processes varied, but was often short enough to engender very immediate anxieties about the effects of urban life on reproduction. This argument seemed to call into question the very notion of a coherent rational subject – all consciousness was inextricably enmeshed in a history, a socio-biological past, which determined it, but was always beyond its control. There was no absolute barrier between sanity and insanity, but rather an enormous borderland.[112] The cartesian *cogito*, it seemed, and all theories which emanated from it were pre-scientific, for as he put it in *Body and Will* (1883): '[The individual] is linked in a chain of causation which renders it impossible he should ever transcend himself. It is a chain too, which a little reflection will prove to reach an indefinitely long way back in an ancestral past.'[113]

But in fact the authority and the ideal identity of the speaking-observing subject in this psychiatry remained unchallenged. The discourse posed history, genealogy, inheritance as the key to understanding the insane and the criminal, but was absolutely indifferent to these questions in relation to its own language and constructions. Thus on the one hand Maudsley advanced the disturbing argument that everybody can be sure 'that he is living his forefathers essentially over again . . . and furthermore suspect that the vicious or virtuous ancestral quality, imbued as silent memory in his nature may leap to light on the occasion of its fit stimulus'.[114] On the other hand, the texts posited a perfectly unruffled subject – quintessentially unified and detached. Doctor Maudsley never discussed the presence of a Mr Hyde behind him, 'ready to leap to light on the occasion of its fit stimulus'.

Maudsley read widely in contemporary European psychiatry; he was

---

[111] See Smith, *Trial*.

[112] See for instance Maudsley's comment on Guiteau, the assassin of the US president, in a letter (27 September 1883): 'Whether Guiteau was a little on one side or the other of a line that nobody can draw between sanity and insanity' is not important. What is crucial, he wrote is 'the state of things which produced him and permitted such an extraordinary trial and execution' (*American Notes and Queries*, 8, no. 7 [Marsh 1970], 102).

[113] *Body and Will*, p. 26.   [114] *Organic to Human*, p. 267.

clearly familiar with the work of Morel and Lombroso. In *Physiology and Pathology of Mind* (1867) degeneration was discussed, but shown to pose no serious threat to social progress, precisely because it could engender only its own eventual extinction. The mad and the unfit were simply the inevitable spin-off in the stern and remorseless process of evolutionary struggle 'which there necessarily is where the claimants are many and the supplies are limited'.[115] It was decreed by nature that 'the weakest must suffer, and some of them break down into madness' (p. 202). The mad were the waste-matter, indeed the very proof of the vigour of a march of progress with which they were unable to cope:

They are the waste thrown up by the silent but strong current of progress; they are the weak crushed out by the strong in the mortal struggle for development; they are examples of decaying reason thrown off by vigorous mental growth, the energy of which they testify. (p. 202)

Since the explanation of how degeneration arose was Lamarckian,[116] this confidence had depended upon the belief that the dominant physical and moral conditions of society were not pathogenic, or at least that they were quickly reformable. There were many contradictions in Maudsley's account. The counter-positioning of a dominant progress and a residuum of degenerates went together rather uneasily with the simultaneous insistence that criminals were underdeveloped, the primitive past rather than the pathological cast-offs of civilisation. In 1870, the very year in which Lombroso found inspiration in the 'atavistic' skull of the brigand Vilella, Maudsley observed in *Body and Mind* that:

[There is] truly a brute brain within the man's; and when the latter stops short of its characteristic development as *human* – when it remains at or below the level of an orang's brain, it may be presumed that it will manifest its most primitive functions, and no higher functions . . . some very strong arguments in support of Mr Darwin's views might be drawn from the field of morbid psychology. We may, without much difficulty, trace savagery in civilization, as we can trace animalism in savagery; and in the degeneration of insanity, in the *unkinding*, so to say, of the human kind, there are exhibited marks denoting the elementary instincts of its composition. (pp. 52–3)

In the same work, he confirmed Morel's reassuring view that the process

115 *Physiology*, p. 202.
116 Even much later Maudsley explained his sympathy with Lamarck and his doubts about Weismann's theory of the indestructibility of the germ plasm. Character, he wrote 'grows by adaptation and gradual accumulation of increments through the ages' (*Hereditary Variation*, p. 29). Cf. p. 32 where he rejected anti-Lamarckianism as fantastical. On the discussion of Weismannism in the 1880s, see Searle, *Eugenics and Politics*, p. 6.

of degeneration in families led within a few generations to sterility. The crucial point here is that from the 1850s through to the early 1870s, despite numerous contradictions in the course of the exposition, degeneration led securely to extinction in Maudsley's Morelian formulation.[117] Moreover, degeneration could be grasped in its visual immediacy; its truth was grounded and confined in the image: 'An irregular and unsymmetrical conformation of the head, a want of regularity and harmony of the features and, as Morel holds, malformations of the external ear, are sometimes observed [in the insane].'[118] The degenerate was thereby distinguished from the healthy; indeed degenerates constituted a distinct if ominous grouping in the city. There was, declared Maudsley in 1874, 'a distinct criminal class of beings who herd together in our large cities . . . propagating a criminal population of degenerate beings'.[119]

By the time of *Body and Will* (1883), Maudsley expressed a very different view. Degeneration was no longer cast as a subsidiary stream veering off from the river of progress and leading nowhere, but a major current threatening to carry all before it. That version of *dégénérescence* in Morel which assured society of the eventual extinction of the degenerate line, was abandoned by Maudsley in the 1880s in favour of a conception of degeneration as the universal counter-force to evolution. Society indeed was now perceived to be constituted by

a double flux of movement, as it were, ascendant and descendant, the ways or modes of degeneration in the descendent line being almost as many and divers (sic) as the varieties of evolution in the ascendent line. Some persons are high on the upward, others low on the downward path; many are just entering upon the one or the other; but there is no one who is not himself going in the one or the other direction and making the way which he takes easier for others to follow in.[120]

He spoke ominously of the death of the sun and warned that decadence was as possible as progress, degeneration as evolution (p. 310). All organic structures were liable to disintegration: 'ceasing to aggregate to itself [the organism] begins to disintegrate, ceasing to progress begins to regress,

---

[117] As he had put it in his Annual Report at Cheadle Royal Hospital in 1859–1860: 'families, like trees, often grow till they have attained their greatest development, then begin to decay and ultimately die out. The family culminates, as it were, in its greatest or most successful member, his offspring is feeble and simple, and of the next generation some perish in infantile convulsions, some live on scofulous or die and others may become insane. Ultimately there is the incapability of producing offspring and then the end comes' (First Annual Report at Cheadle Royal [1859–60] p. 10).
[118] Maudsley, *Body and Mind*, pp. 62–3.
[119] Maudsley, *Responsibility*, p. 29.
[120] Maudsley, *Body and Will*, p. 245.

ceasing to develop begins to decline' (p. 239). The pathogenic environment of the city, it now seemed, could sabotage the 'survival of the best'.[121]

Degeneration, moreover, could occur from the top downwards. Thus the most advanced countries and classes ('the highest products of evolution'[122]) might collapse first. The fate of societies in Maudsley's account thus paralleled the theory of madness as 'dissolution' (Spencer, Jackson[123]) in which aetiology could be traced to the progressive disintegration of cortical layers.

In the 1895 edition of the *Pathology of Mind*, Maudsley reverted somewhat to the earlier confidence: 'there appears to be at work a silent tendency in nature to restore an insane stock to a sound type, if regeneration be possible, or to end it if its degeneration be such that it is too bad to mend.'[124] The change of tone perhaps owed something to a broader recovery of confidence within government, press and the metropolitan middle classes at large, regarding the crisis of 'outcast London', so keenly felt during the 1880s. But Maudsley's formulation was tentative; society, the body, reproduction were perceived as bound up in a highly precarious interaction.

That vision of precariousness intensified in Maudsley's final works. Indeed *Organic to Human* (1916), his penultimate text, tapped a broader social-organicist conception of the crisis of civilisation to be found in European thought from Spengler to Ortega Y Gasset. Maudsley's writing

---

121 As he warned: 'Survival of the fittest does not mean always survival of the best in the sense of the highest organism; it means only the survival of that which is best suited to the circumstances good or bad, in which it is placed – the survival of a savage in a savage social medium, of a rogue among rogues, of a parasite where a parasite alone can live. A decline from a higher to a lower level of being, a process that is to say, of degeneration is an integrant and active part of the economy of nature' (*Body and Will*, p. 237).

122 Maudsley, *Body and Will*, p. 320.

123 See Clarke, 'Rejection', pp. 283–4; Dewhurst, *Hughlings Jackson*; Smith, 'Evolution', (per.), pts. 1 and 2; Fullinwinder, 'Freud, Jackson and speech', (per.). The concept of 'dissolution' was specifically drawn from Jackson who had in turn borrowed and developed it from Spencer. Jackson used the term 'dissolution' as a name for the 'reverse of the process of evolution' (Jackson, 'Evolution and Dissolution', p. 45). He argued that mental dissolution worked from the most sophisticated layers of the brain to the more primitive layers beneath. Dissolution for Jackson meant a '"taking to pieces" in the order from the least organised ... most complex and most voluntary, towards the most organised, most simple and most automatic' (see Smith, 'Evolution', (per.), pt. 2). Jackson used the analogy of a brain to a highly developed bureaucracy or the command structure of a navy in which control passed down the line if the commanding officer was incapacitated. The organism or the navy always achieved the fittest state possible to it, given the limitations imposed upon it. Cf. Maudsley, *Body and Will*, in which the brain is described as a multitude of nerve centres 'of high and low dignity', myriad 'superimposed layers', which, like a railway guide, was for the uninitiated 'a multitude of seemingly unintelligible figures and hieroglyphics'. The brain had many 'stations, tracks, junctions and branch lines, its quick trains and slow trains of thought' (pp. 114–15). Degeneration, he argued, worked from the top downwards. The 'highest products of evolution', and the most complex nations would go first (p. 320).

124 *Pathology*, p. 57.

in 1916 seemed to appeal to the fact of the war, as though it constituted the crystallisation of all he had been predicting for several decades:

> That which has been everywhere is that which possibly shall be again somewhere. Organic degeneracy being the sequel of organic development, no social organization can feel surely exempt from the law of growth and decay.[125]

Working-class revolt, socialism and communism were disclosed not for the first time by Maudsley as imminent dangers:

> In scattered and recurring manifestations there is ample evidence of a deep feeling of revolt in the working-classes against the domination of capitalism, more instinctively brooding perhaps at present than intelligently articulate ... a crop of self-prizing and self-deceiving demagogues ... [will spring up to exploit] the selfish passions and ignorant prejudices of the mob who put them in power. (pp. 236–7)

Socialists, he complained, sought the perfect state, but never explained how it was to be achieved in a world of imperfect individuals (p. 240). They were usually ignorant, he argued, of the 'wise' principles of eugenics.[126] Politics today was in any case a sordid business: 'nothing can be accomplished save by the formation of cliques, leagues, parties, unions and like confederations' (p. 335). The individual, he lamented, 'is practically impotent by himself' (p. 335). The squalor of 'party politics' and of other confederations was counterposed to a higher political discourse guaranteed by science, ostensibly inspired by the truths of evolution and nature.

The hostility to socialism, and its figurative comparison with the overthrow of order in the body, was not a new theme in 1916. On the contrary, the whole interpretation of contemporary international disorder was read off in relation to a bio-political theory of degeneration already in place much earlier. In *Body and Will* (1883), Maudsley had likened the psychosomatic chaos of insanity to a world where present-day demands for democracy and socialism had been conceded in their entirety. He referred his reader back to the French Revolution and argued that any trace of Enlightenment optimism would constitute a dangerous doctrine in the troubled climate of late-nineteenth-century England. Society was caught in a double bind, he had argued, for if it conceded too many demands, there would be anarchy, but if it conceded too few, there would be revolutionary eruptions.[127]

---

[125] *Organic to Human*, p. 26.

[126] See *Organic to Human*, pt. 2, ch. 8: 'The moralisation of the reproductive instinct'.

[127] 'There will be a grim experience and a troubled future for the nation that has not known, before that hour comes, how to guide these forces in the right way, and to absorb and embody them in fitting forms of social and political organization. The French Revolution was momentous enough as an event, but is perhaps more so as an awful example teaching how silently the great social forces mature, how they explode at last in volcanic fury, if too much or too long repressed' (Maudsley, *Body and Will*, p. 292).

The individual had been defined as a social being but the social was conceived in terms of a determining physiological and neurological past ('infraconscious depths'[128]), a whole subterranean world of racial inheritance. Reproduction had been cast as an infinitely delicate and precarious matter. Maudsley's notoriously reactionary views on the education of women, masturbation and sexuality[129] need to be set within the context of this long-standing intellectual investment in the body as key to national progress. Any behaviour by adolescent or adult men and women which appeared to vitiate reproduction, or indeed to disjoin sexual pleasure in any way from procreation was judged harmful, pathological and even unpatriotic. Mental disorder in women was seen to follow any deviation from the sexual function of reproduction so critical to society's survival. When Maudsley described adolescence as a fraught and dangerous period full of psychosomatic commotion, we see once again the confluence of political and bodily language: 'a revolution of the entire mental being; and if the nerve centres are unstable, it easily happens that their equilibrium is overthrown'.[130] Women who did not have children were portrayed as being plagued by the 'unrest of organic dissatisfaction, a vague void of being, the dim craving of something wanting to full womanhood'.[131] The end of menstruation was also cast as a peculiarly dangerous period in a woman's life.[132]

By the early twentieth century Henry Maudsley's political and sexual-political thought was increasingly preoccupied with the question of 'the masses' who, in their apparently inalienable irrationality, were perceived to be fatally drawn to socialism. Yet the traditional ruling classes, we are ruefully told, were unfortunately no less short-sighted than the masses who were to overthrow them: 'What is to hinder power in the masses from

[128] *Body and Will*, p. 32.
[129] See Skultans, *Madness and Morals*, part 3, ch. 8; Gilbert, 'Masturbation', (per.); Showalter, *Female Madness*.
[130] Maudsley, *Body and Will*, p. 260.
[131] Maudsley, *Pathology*, p. 389.
[132] If the reproductive function was over, what purpose could there now be in 'pleasing', 'desire', 'sensation'? Consider once again the political terminology adopted to convey the ruinous anarchy of non-reproductive sexuality: 'the natural cessation of menstruation at the change of life is accompanied by a revolution in the economy which is often trying to the mental stability of those who have a predisposition to insanity. The age of pleasing is past, but not always the desire, which indeed sometimes grows then more exacting; there are all sorts of anomalous sensations of bodily distress, attesting the disturbance of circulation and of nerve functions; and it is now that an insane jealousy and a propensity to stimulants are apt to appear, especially when there have been no children. When positive insanity breaks out, it usually has the form of profound melancholia, with vague delusions of an extreme character, as that the world is in flames, that it is turned upside down, that everything is changed, or that some very dreadful but undefined calamity has happened or is about to happen' (Maudsley, *Body and Mind*, p. 90).

being as selfish, coercive and corrupt as it has been in the classes . . . ?'[133] At least 'the classes' had felt the fear of 'the masses' to restrain their cupidity and greed, 'whereas power in the masses will feel no curb from a sense of force in the classes whose revolt would be futile' (p. 201). Cynical and pathological 'socialist' demagogues would move increasingly to the fore, gratifying 'the predatory instinct of human nature' (p. 299), supplying 'articulate form and function to the uneasy fermentations of feeling and dumb aspiration of imagination in the masses' (p. 299).

Such views were in some respects close to those of new liberals like Masterman for whom the city was also the locus of a remorseless illness and degeneration. According to Masterman, the city was a place of terrible destruction, 'a disintegrative force, tearing the family into pieces'.[134] It was inhabited by 'a homogeneous substance: the City Dweller' (p. 160), a source of irresolvable mysteries, riddles, secrets. 'It is in the city Crowd, where the traits of individual distinction have become merged in the aggregate and the impression (from a distance) is of little white blobs of faces borne upon little black twisted or misshapen bodies, that the scorn of the philosopher for the mob, the cynic for humanity, becomes for the first time intelligible' (pp. 95–6). The crowd, like the degenerate patient, was characteristically portrayed here as absolutely detached from the observer: its 'twisted or misshapen bodies', its collective mind and its vulgarity always seen 'from a distance' even when the insistence was simultaneously that degeneration had spread everywhere.

But to link Maudsley specifically to early-twentieth-century new liberalism is also misleading. The 'two cultures' of Edwardian liberalism and toryism, it has been pointed out,[135] intersected in their common idealisation of Nature, their dream of rural regeneration and their rejection of the supposed rootlessness of the city. The enfranchised urban 'masses' were frequently taken by liberals and tories alike as a symptom of a dangerous historical tendency towards social disintegration. Maudsley's work connected with a wider political pessimism to be found across parties and programmes from the later-Victorian period, only one of whose corollaries was the rethinking of the language of the Liberal Party.

There are points in Bernard Shaw's *Man and Superman* (1903), for instance, where the same social and political fears were expressed in similar language. Although Shaw insisted that 'the bubble of Heredity has been pricked',[136] the 'terrors of the degeneracy mongers' (p. 25) demolished,[137] and the notion of 'hereditary hooliganism' or an 'hereditary "governing

---

[133] Maudsley, *Organic to Human*, p. 201.
[134] Masterman, *Condition of England*, p. 110.
[135] See Offer, *Property and Politics*, pp. 337–8.
[136] *Man and Superman*, p. 24.
[137] For Shaw's critique of Nordau, see Shaw, *Sanity of Art*.

class"' (p. 25) debunked, he acknowledged the genuine dangers of democracy in a dysgenic environment:

> We must either breed political capacity or be ruined by Democracy, which is forced on us by the failure of the older alternatives ... Being cowards, we defeat natural selection under cover of philanthropy; being sluggards, we neglect artificial selection under cover of delicacy and morality. (p. 25)

Procreation, he continued, would clearly need to be disjoined from marriage if the primary task of evolutionary advance was to be accomplished; conventional morality, just as much as decadent non-reproductive pleasure, was a tiresome and hypocritically-used obstacle to the progress of breeding techniques:

> The modern devices for combining pleasure with sterility, now universally known and accessible, enable these persons to weed themselves out of the race, a process already vigorously at work ... (p. 225)

That vigorously-working racial progress was threatened by degeneration, 'long-unnoticed retrogressions' (p. 235) in a democracy-orientated society of recalcitrant 'Yahoos' (p. 245). What was apparently needed was a 'State Department of Evolution' (p. 245) and a human stud farm for the production of healthy citizens: 'King Demos must be bred like all other kings, and with Must there is no arguing' (p. 249).

Just as animals and plants which had evolved over centuries could 'relapse precipitously into the wild type in a generation or two' (p. 235), so 'a civilization in which lusty pugnacity and greed have ceased to act as selective agents and have begun to obstruct and destroy, rushes downward and backwards with a suddenness that enables an observer to see with consternation the upwards steps of many centuries retraced in a single life-time' (p. 235).

There was not of course only *one* form of pessimism, *one* social analysis, *one* political programme over the long period here under discussion. But what I seek to describe across otherwise eclectic political writing is the emergence by the last decades of the nineteenth century, of a shared vision of society as an organic process; that process, it seemed, was seriously or even perhaps fatally hampered by illness, pathology, degeneration. Take a very different example. In the same year as Maudsley's *Body and Will* (1883), the ultra-conservative Marquis of Salisbury also clearly expressed the need for the development of a language of degeneration. In his celebrated anonymous article in the *Quarterly Review*, 'Disintegration', he gathered together many of his thoughts on the horrors of French history (epitomised by the Commune), the mediocrity of American democracy and the degradation of an increasingly democracy-ridden England.

Democracy was tearing at the heart of the empire, prompting the inevitable question: 'how long can the final disintegration of the Empire be postponed?'[138]

Whilst the later Conservative Arthur Balfour was able to refer somewhat more pointedly to the bio-medical language of degeneration when he lectured on the subject of 'Decadence' in 1908,[139] Salisbury offered only faint hints, as though he was struggling vainly to find a contemporary nomenclature in any way commensurate with the modern 'disintegration' he described. In Salisbury's view history had 'not yet furnished us with materials wide enough or minute enough for constructing anything like a science of the diseases and decay of States'.[140] Maudsley's social analysis, one might say, was conceived as an attempt to provide such a science of the decay of states, predicated on the models of evolution and degeneration. It was committed to surpassing the political and psychological 'logic' of classical liberalism and individualism.

The work of Maudsley and the conception of degeneration he articulated needs to be understood in relation to that widespread political redefinition in late-Victorian and Edwardian society. The notion of degeneration was used at once to signify the urgency of intervention and, still more alarmingly, the potential impossibility of constituting the nation from society in its entirety. 'Englishness' had to be defined in a double movement of inclusion and exclusion, ideological assimilation and expulsion. In the light of changing political circumstances, for instance the increasingly wide electoral constituency, the criteria for social 'fitness' changed. It was not a question of rejecting the whole urban working class as a 'rabble', nor of accepting it wholesale, but of constructing cross-class ideologies of patriotism shored up against the combined internal and external threat of degeneration. As Arnold White, one of the more extreme degenerationist scaremongers had put it in 1886, England could no longer act as the world's 'rubbish heap'.[141]

Edwardian legislation was characterised both literally and metaphorically by the dream of a national insurance: a desire to tighten the supervision and welfare of the national stock, to exclude and eliminate degenerate 'foreign bodies'. Indeed the Royal Commission on Alien Immigration in 1903 and the ensuing Act of 1905, should not be seen as a mere anomaly, nor, exclusively, as part of some timeless, centuries-old phenomenon of anti-semitism, but in relation to that wider contemporary attempt to construct a racial-imperial identity, excluding all 'bad blood' and 'path-

---

[138] Smith, *Salisbury on Politics*, p. 376.   [139] Balfour, *Decadence*.
[140] Smith, *Salisbury on Politics*, p. 356.   [141] White, *Problems*, p. 144.

ological elements', literally expelling anarchists, criminals, prostitutes, the diseased, and the hopelessly poor – all those now declared 'undesirable aliens'.[142]

DEGENERATION: A CHAPTER IN DARWINISM

The *Oxford English Dictionary* helps confirm the periodisation of the word 'degeneration' which has been outlined through this chapter. It tells us that in the 1850s medical definitions of degeneration had been introduced into the language, suggesting '[a] morbid change in the structure of parts consisting in disintegration of tissue or in a substitution of a lower for a higher form of structure'.[143] The *OED* quotes a further nuance in 1880 when the eminent Darwinian zoologist Edwin Ray Lankester stated that: 'Degeneration may be defined as a gradual change of the structure in which the organism becomes adapted to less varied and less complex conditions of life'.

Much of Lankester's book *Degeneration. A Chapter in Darwinism* (1880) was taken up with technical zoological and botanical discussion. Yet it noted the continuities with earlier more obviously social dimensions of the theme, for instance philological arguments about the decline of certain languages and societies.[144] An earlier conflict between a (degenerationist) religious model of the fall of civilisations (reiterated in influential terms in the mid nineteenth century by, for example, Richard Whately, Bishop of Dublin[145]) and (progressivist) evolutionary theory had not been forgotten

---

[142] Arnold White was again the most virulently xenophobic of the witnesses to the Royal Commission. He lamented the emigration of 'British bone and sinew from the rural districts, and from London' and the influx of 'foreigners of doubtful value'. (Royal Commission on Alien Immigration, Minutes, II, p. 15). In his view, the Jews were a particular 'poison', because they themselves apparently viewed everybody else as degenerate. They regarded inter-marriage as 'contamination', thereby creating a kind of unassimilable core in the cities and above all London: ' ... these people are in the nature of poison to the immediate interests of the nation' (p. 24). The 'scum of Europe' which now plagued the United States had to be removed from Britain too. Immigrants, he argued were not the victims of poor housing, but its cause: 'these immigrants from the housing point of view are the womb of slums – they make slums' (p. 27). The Commission and the resulting Act were more 'modest', seeking to differentiate the good and the bad Jew, the desirable and the undesirable alien in terms of criminality, insanity, sexual immorality, lack of economic self-sufficiency, ill-health and political immoderation (see Aliens Act 1905, p. 22); cf. Feldman, 'The importance of being English: social policy, patriotism and politics in response to Jewish immigration, 1885–1906', in Stedman Jones and Feldman (eds.), *Between Neighbourhood and Nation* (forthcoming).

[143] According to the *OED* the word *dégénérescence* was only assimilated later. A first example is listed for 1882: 'they have all ... acquired the same parasitic habits and ... exhibit different stages in the same process of degenerescence'.

[144] Lankester, *Degeneration*, p. 58. For a later view and endorsement of Lankester's work, see Thomson, *Bible of Nature*; *Gospel of Evolution*; *Great Biologists*.

[145] See Whately, *On the Origin of Civilisation*.

by Lankester. Indeed he argued that evolutionary theory now had to retract at least part of the argument it had advanced in that debate. It was only by virtue of 'an unreasoning optimism' that

we are accustomed to regard ourselves as necessarily progressing, as necessarily having arrived at a higher and more elaborated condition ... and as destined to progress still further ... it is well to remember that we are subject to the general laws of evolution, and are as likely to degenerate as to progress.[146]

The Spencerian equation of evolution and progress was thus called into question. Evolution, it seemed, did not self-evidently prove any particular social theory. Yet Lankester's agnosticism over the question of progress was proposed in order to insist that contemporary social evolution did suggest a definite conclusion: degeneration.

A. R. Wallace, co-founder with Darwin of the evolutionary theory of natural selection, wrote in 1880 an enthusiastic review of Lankester's book:

This [degeneration of England] is very suggestive; but we may I think draw a yet higher and deeper teaching from the phenomena of degeneration. We seem to learn from it the absolute necessity of labour and effort, of struggle and difficulty, of discomfort and pain, as the condition of all progress, whether physical or mental, and that the lower the organism the more need there is of these ever present stimuli, not only to effect progress, but to avoid retrogression. And if so, does not this afford us the nearest attainable solution of the great problem of the origin of evil? What we call evil is the *essential* condition of progress in the lower stages of the development of conscious organisms.[147]

Wallace's own work, however, had moved substantially away from the conventional implications of social Darwinism.[148] He rejected Galton's eugenic philosophy on the grounds of its impracticability, ineffectiveness and immorality.[149] The problem, he insisted in an article in 1890, was social: in contrast with 'the almost inconceivable wastefulness and extravagance of the wealthy', compare 'the terrible conditions of missions of workers' (p. 330). 'What a mockery' he wrote, 'to still further whiten the sepulchre of modern society, in which is hidden "all manner of corruption" with schemes for the moral and physical advancement of the race' (p. 330). Yet degeneration informed Wallace's critique of Galton and the teleological approach to evolution. Wallace objected to facile evolutionary progressivism and pointed to moral and physical degeneration to show that decline

---

[146] Lankester, *Degeneration*, pp. 59–60.   [147] Wallace, 'Review', (per.), p. 142.
[148] See Durant, 'Meaning of Evolution', (diss.), p. 252.
[149] Wallace, 'Human Selection', (per.), p. 330. Cf., however, p. 325: 'In one of my latest conversations with Darwin he expressed himself very gloomily on the future of humanity, on the ground that in our modern civilization natural selection had no play, and the fittest did not survive.'

was just as possible as advance in human history. Lankester's book, he seemed to believe, could prove his point.

Lankester considered himself a cautious and reputable scientist, but he could not help but direct biology into the vexed question of present-day society. He feared that the life-giving qualities of civilisation bore with it a certain evolutionary cost. In his *Encyclopaedia Britannica* article on zoology, Lankester noted the undue optimism of the first post-Darwinian theoreticians:

The assumption was made that (with the rare exception of parasites) all the change of structure through which the successive generations of animals have passed has been one of progressive elaboration ... this assumption is not warranted ... degeneration or progressive simplification of structure may have, and in many lines certainly has, taken place, as well as progressive elaboration and in other cases continuous maintenance of the *status quo*.[150]

In the same article, Lankester touched still more explicitly on the vexed matter of eugenics, a problem of 'an exceedingly difficult and delicate nature':

The most thrifty and capable sections of the people are not (it has been shown) in the overcrowded areas, producing offspring at such a rate as to contribute to the increase of the population. That increase it has been shown, is due to the early marriage and excessive reproduction of the reckless and hopeless, the poorest, least capable, least desirable members of the community. (p. 1039)

In Herbert Spencer, social evolutionary theory had provided a rationale for classical liberalism. In the last decades of the nineteenth century and early years of the twentieth century, it provided a rationale for a statist critique and redefinition of progress and liberalism.[151] There were of course some, like H. G. Wells and Karl Pearson, who described themselves as at once eugenists and socialists.[152] But their socialism was defined in relation to the necessary, imperial conflict of races in the international arena rather than between classes at home. What I aim to stress now is that the socio-biological theory of degeneration emerged in and beyond the 1880s most powerfully as a counter-theory to mass-democracy and socialism.[153]

---

[150] Lankester, 'Zoology', p. 1,032.
[151] See Freeden, *New Liberalism*.
[152] On eugenics and Fabianism, see Jones, *Social Darwinism*, pp. 112–14; on Pearson, see Kevles, *In the Name of Eugenics*.
[153] See, for instance, the discussion of degeneration in Headley, *Problems*, p. 276; cf. Maudsley, *Body and Will*; *Organic to Human*. Those who threatened to disrupt society, observed Maudsley, are 'naturally' viewed as anti-social (*Life in Mind and Conduct*, p. 387). Anarchism, of course, was *a priori* pathological; as Maudsley put it, '[the anarchist's] outbursts are symptoms of an ailing social constitution which calls for suitable remedies; for in a social as in a bodily organism, convulsion signifies disease' (*Organic to Human*, p. 204). Cf. Maudsley, *Pathology*, p. 77. The socio-biological difficulty for progressive government, he wrote, was to steer between 'stagnant conservatism' and 'innovations

It should be recalled that Henry George, the American radical, had caused much consternation in the 1880s by setting out to show the paradoxical inter-dependence of progress and poverty. The 'great enigma of our times', according to George, was that 'material progress does not merely fail to relieve poverty – it actually produces it'.[154] The language of degeneration in the 1880s also involved the perception of structural contradictions between progress and poverty. It conceded that there was a deep crisis in the existing social order, but sought to offer a de-politicised theory, which deflected the terms of the discussion into concepts of nature, biology and race.

Discussing shifting attitudes to Marx across the later nineteenth century, Eric Hobsbawm points out that vociferous criticism of Marx's work only really gathered pace in the 1880s with the development of a British socialist movement influenced by Marxism.[155] Of course, the sense of foreboding about the political reliability of 'the proletariat' was already there much earlier. Perhaps it was not by chance that Thomas Huxley echoed a phrase from Marx's *Eighteenth Brumaire of Louis Bonaparte* when, in a 'Sunday Lecture', 'On the Physical Basis of Life', in 1868, he had sought to argue that it was the fundamental truths of science which were really most edifying and politically pertinent to 'the physiology of the future':[156] 'The consciousness of this great truth weighs like a nightmare, I believe, upon many of the best minds of these days'.[157]

The Sunday Lectures Series to which this statement was addressed, and in which such figures as Carpenter, Clifford, Maudsley, Pearson, Romanes

---

which go beyond safe development and cause disintegration' (*Life in Mind and Conduct*, p. 64). Cf. *Pathology*: 'Destroy the social structure of a nation, as in the French Revolution, and then behold what monsters of apish deformity and tigrish ferocity the individuals are capable of becoming' (p. 2). Society had to restrain or repress 'its too ardent reformers who would disturb violently and perhaps overthrow its equilibrium ... A healthy instinct of self-conservation recoils naturally ... from change which is not beneficient reform but destructive revolution' (*Life in Mind and Conduct*, p. 64). If people failed to learn their 'diverse functions' and 'different stations', 'social harmony' would collapse 'as [it does] in a bodily organism if the kidney-cells, for example claimed to do the work of the braincell' (*Organic to Human*, p. 252). Cf. Cantlie's view that a 'democratic negativeness is what seems to be the aim and goal of the rising generation ...' It was not the effect of the system 'but rather something which has resisted it' (*Degeneration Amongst Londoners*, p. 47). Cf. Reaney, 'Outcast London', (per.), where socialism was cast as a dangerous microbe penetrating the disease-prone world of the poor: 'The red cap of continental revolutionary thought is passing along like a spectre of scenes not a century old'.

154 *Progress and Poverty*, p. 9.
155 Hobsbawm, 'Dr Marx'; see also Searle, 'Critics', p. 81, on mounting conservative apprehension about the rise of socialism.
156 Huxley, *Methods*, p. 159; cf. the *Eighteenth Brumaire*: 'The tradition of all the dead generations weighs like a nightmare on the brain of the living' (Marx, *Selected Writings*, p. 301).
157 *Methods*, p. 160.

and Wallace all participated, attempted to illuminate 'the masses' through the popularisation of science. Huxley had written in a letter in 1855:

I want the working classes to understand that Science and her ways are great facts for them – that physical virtue is the base of all other and they are to be clean and temperate and all the rest – not because fellows in black and white ties tell them so, but because these are plain and patent laws of nature which they must obey 'under penalties'.[158]

Huxley provides a particularly illuminating example in his desire to use biological theory to produce a putatively moderate and measured political understanding, especially as he is so frequently lauded as the Victorian scientist who really did succeed in separating 'evolution and ethics' (to borrow one of his titles[159]). What he in fact rebutted were certain political conclusions drawn from evolution by Herbert Spencer on the one hand and Francis Galton on the other.

In his essay 'Social Diseases and Worse Remedies' (1891), a polemic in the main against General Booth and the Salvation Army, Huxley advocated a scientifically objective middle way between 'two contradictory and extremely mischievous systems', namely 'Anarchic Individualism' and 'despotic or Regimental Socialism'.[160] He pronounced his view to be no 'sentimental rhetoric' (p. 32) but a perception based on the laws he had discovered 'as a naturalist' (p. 32).

Booth's project was, in Huxley's view, really a kind of veiled socialism ('mere autocratic Socialism masked by its theological character' p. 7), which could be rejected on biological grounds. The advance of 'ethical man', he said, has 'by no means abolished, perhaps has hardly modified, the deep-seated organic impulses which impel the natural man to follow his non-moral course' (p. 23). In addition, socialism ignored the urgent problem of population, or more particularly the differential birth rate between classes: 'It is the true riddle of the Sphinx; and every nation which does not solve it will sooner or later be devoured by the monster [it] has generated' (p. 29).

The problems of overcrowding in the modern city, argued Huxley, were caused by the rapid population increase amongst the poor; no socialist tinkering with the distribution of wealth could possibly resolve this fundamental eugenic problem. Socio-economic questions dissolved in the final analysis into the matter of the organism, its evolution and reproduction.

---

[158] Thomas Huxley, letter to Dyster (27 February 1855), Leonard Huxley, *Life and Letters*, I, p. 138.
[159] Huxley, *Evolution and Ethics*. For the attempt to exonerate Huxley, see Himmelfarb, *Victorian Minds*, pp. 328, 331, and *Darwin and Darwinian Revolution*, p. 407; for a useful critique see Helfand, 'Huxley's "Evolution and Ethics"', (per.). On Huxley's rebuttal of Spencer's evolutionary ethics, cf. Collini, *Liberalism and Sociology*, p. 158.
[160] 'Social Diseases and Worse Remedies', p. 7.

Moreover '[a]rgumentation can hardly be needful to make it clear that no society in which the elements of decomposition are thus swiftly and surely accumulating, can hope to win in the race of industries' (p. 33). Competition and inequality within English society had to give way to the primary fact of the struggle between nations, empires, economies (p. 29). Above all, he insisted, political ideologies had to face up to the inexorable law of evolution, a gloomier law than was first appreciated:

it is an error to imagine that evolution signifies a constant tendency to increased perfection . . . Retrogressive is as practicable as progressive metamorphosis. (p. 17)

But even when Thomas Huxley's criticism misconceived completely the actual terms of the social crisis of the 1880s and 1890s by evacuating politics into biological regression, it set the climate for the discourses to come in and beyond 1914. Indeed, far from disappearing, the language of degeneration, regression and atavism were to find, as it were, a new lease of life in the context of war, providing a continuing counterpoint to blithe, optimistic jingoism. That profuse pre-war imagery, intimating the death of the sun, the decline of the race and the degradation of civilisation prefigured the real catastrophe ahead and powerfully mediated its interpretation and representation.

If what the physical philosopher tells us [is true] . . . the time must come when evolution will mean adaptation to an universal winter, and all forms of life will die out, except such low and simple organisms as the Diatom of the arctic and antarctic ice and the protococcus of the red snow . . . the course of life upon [the earth's] surface must describe a trajectory like that of a ball fired from a mortar; and the sinking half of that course is as much a part of the general process of evolution as the rising. (p. 17)

8

◁ ════════════════════════════════ ▷

Concluding remarks

The language of degeneration should be understood in relation to a long and complex process of political definition and redefinition in European culture and society. Whilst stressing the specificity of various key debates, my aim has also been to show the general shift from notions of the individual degenerate (as sustained by nosological models of *dégénérescence*) towards a bio-medical conception of crowd and mass civilisation as regression; the 'individual' was reconceived in relation to the mesh of evolutionary, racial and environmental forces which, it was now insisted, constituted and constrained his or her condition. With the institutional consolidation of socialism in European political parties and with continuing pressure for universal suffrage, the crowd, apparently, had to be recognised as a socio-political reality which was more than the sum of its individuals. To anxious commentators, both liberal and conservative, the crowd, the mass and the elite constituted the object of a new and urgent potential science.

'Whence comes the feeling', asked the *Spectator* in 1886 that the mob:

will be specially wicked, more wicked than any of its compound individuals, more thievish, more cruel, more murderous? That idea, quite universal in Europe, and the first cause of the dread of mobs, is not born of terror only, but is more or less substantially true.[1]

'Every now and again', observed the same journal in 1891, 'the readers of the daily papers must come across stories that will make them disbelieve for the time in our vaunted moral progress, and almost despair of the possibility of raising a certain type of human nature to anything like a higher level.'[2] The subject of the article was not the individual, but 'the collective inhumanity of a great number of people', or, in short, 'the shameless cowardice of the crowd'. Degeneration and atavism in this text were not located in the criminal or the insane, but in the amorphous 'body' of the crowd itself: 'a whole body of men, collected at hazard, who on occasions will prove themselves more mercilessly cruel than the pack of wolves that

---

[1] *Spectator*, 'Fear of mobs', p. 219.   [2] *Spectator*, 'Cowardice of crowds', p. 376.

222

tears to pieces and devours the fallen or wounded of its number' (p. 376). *Blackwoods* made the point in 1893 that

we must remember that, however much society at large may have changed for the better, the lowest stratum of all has not changed, and that lawlessness, cupidity, and ruffianism are just as rife in it now as they were in the days of Sir Robert Walpole or Lord George Gordon. We see by what a very thin and precarious partition after all are we divided from the elements of violence which underlie all civilized societies.[3]

The lowest stratum was both a recognisable sector of the population and simultaneously the destination of all individuals when forced into crowds. Between culture and anarchy, safety and atavistic violence, there was only 'a very thin and precarious partition'. To enter the crowd was to regress, to return, to be thrown back upon a certain non-individuality, the lowest common denominator of a crowd of ancestors – a world of dangerous instincts and primitive memories. The city, democracy, socialism: all in their way, it appeared, fostered an illusion of the individual's capacity to survive the crowd intact.

These periodicals did not always represent the crowd in such terms. Articles had previously appeared praising the wonderful peacefulness of the English *en masse*.[4] The representation of the essentially benign or malign nature of aggregations shifted somewhat, of course, from year to year, in relation to changing perceptions of the general political 'health' of the society. But, crucially, what we begin to see in the last decades of the nineteenth century is the elucidation – beyond any perceived specific moment of high disorder – of the crowd as constant irrationality, permanent fact of degeneration and regression. The crowd becomes a sociological category in the understanding of society. This was no longer in response to a specific threat (some isolated strike or riot), but a commentary upon modernity itself and the supposed dangers of socialism and mass democracy.

Past turmoil (Peterloo, chartism, reform demonstrations in the 1860s) was thus re-surveyed in the journals quoted above with the aim of finding the crucial political or rather, anthropological, 'lessons'. Foreign history offered still more compelling truths; *Blackwoods* again: 'The three French Revolutions of 1789, 1830, and 1848 furnish perhaps the best-known illustration of the danger and the folly of allowing mobs to have their own way at first, in the vain hope that they will run their course and then subside';[5] 'The French Revolutions of 1830 and 1848 sprang from just as

---

[3] *Blackwoods*, 'Mobs', p. 122.
[4] See *Spectator*, 'Physical Force', p. 535, and, 'Charm of crowds', p. 757.
[5] *Blackwoods*, 'Mobs', p. 123.

small beginnings as the Social Democratic Federation and the meetings in Trafalgar Square' (p. 121). Whatever the 'progress' in other spheres of the polity, the crowd always had the same nature (primitive, volatile, savage) and composition (a mixture of 'honest enthusiasts, vagrant idlers, political adventurers, and occasional criminals', p. 120).

There was nothing new about 'the fear of the mob' or the anxious scrutiny of the 'dangerous classes', but the late nineteenth century witnessed a distinctive attempt to produce a positive science (a distillation of psychology, biology, racial anthropology) of the essential, transhistorical features of the crowd (scene of the elision of class difference) and its relation to 'civilisation'.

What has been attempted in the present study is an analysis and a demonstration of the pervasiveness of a particular kind of medical and evolutionist idealism. Politics here cannot be understood in a merely party political sense. We find liberals, conservatives and socialists deploying the term and the assumptions of degeneration – although with different inflections. Thus Engels too, for example, was impressed by the idea of degeneration; he noted the fallacy of unconditional evolutionary progressivism in the notes for *Dialectics of Nature*:

Selection [may result from] greater capacity of adaptation to altered circumstances, where survivors are better suited to these *circumstances*, but where this adaptation as a whole can mean regress just as well as progress (for instance adaptation to parasitic life is *always* regress). The main thing: that each advance in organic evolution is at the same time a regression, fixing *one-sided* evolution and excluding evolution along many other directions.[6]

The language of social evolution within the subsequent history of socialism has been the subject of some investigation, but degeneration has hardly been considered. There is no analysis of this model and its assimilation in the more positivistic communist and socialist views of capitalism.

Certainly there were British communist scientists writing in the interwar period who had more than a passing sympathy with the language of eugenics, despite their insistence on other occasions that biological evidence was of dubious political value. Returning from a visit to Russia, at the invitation of the geneticist Vavilov in 1928, J. B. S. Haldane declared that 'the test of the devotion of the Union of Socialist Soviet Republics to science will, I think, come when the accumulation of the results of human

---

[6] Engels, *Dialectics of Nature*, p. 236; cf. Timpanaro, *Materialism*, p. 95. On Marx's acquaintance with Lankester and some speculations on his view of degeneration, see Feuer, 'Friendship', (per.).

genetics, demonstrating what I believe to be the fact of innate human inequality, becomes important'.[7] Another communist scientist, J. D. Bernal, dreamed of a Soviet state which would see the political ascendancy of 'the scientist'; his dream is in certain respects remarkably reminiscent of the Saint-Simonians' proposals one hundred years earlier,[8] but more directly it still evidences a concern, so characteristic of the late nineteenth century, with the advance of the species, waste, the residuum, the sub-stratum:

In a Soviet state (not the state of the present, but one freed from the danger of capitalist attack), the scientific institutions would in fact gradually become the government, and a further stage of the Marxian hierarchy of domination would be reached. Scientists in such a stage would tend very naturally to identify themselves emotionally rather with the progress of science itself than with that of a class, a nation, or a humanity outside science ... From one point of view the scientists would emerge as a new species and leave humanity behind; from another, humanity – the humanity that counts – might seem to change *en bloc*, leaving behind in a relatively primitive state those too stupid or stubborn to change. The latter view suggests another biological analogy: there may not be room for both types in the same world and the old mechanism of extinction will come into play.[9]

To trace the fascination with degeneration in philosophy, politics or culture from the nineteenth to the twentieth century should not lead us to produce an undifferentiated encyclopaedia of examples. Writings on degeneration in Europe were sometimes markedly different. Morel, Lombroso and Maudsley, to take three central examples from this study, produced over-lapping but historically distinguishable discourses. But one must also note the fundamental difference between the deployment of degeneration by these doctors taken together and its exploration and

---

[7] Haldane, *Inequality*, p. 137; cf. 'The biological facts put forward by the Eugenics Society would be a very good weapon in the Socialist armoury, if biological arguments had any political value. But ... they have no political value' (p. 131). Cf. '[Haldane] was primarily a geneticist and was fond of shocking public opinion with his hard-headedness (not to say hard-heartedness) about the possibility of ... using scientific means to determine the rights and duties of individuals. ("Some day", he wrote, "it may be possible to devise a scientific method of assessing the voting power of individuals ... In the remote future mankind may be divided into castes like Hindus or termites")' (Rée, *Proletarian Philosophers*, p. 86). On Haldane, cf. Macintyre, *Proletarian Science*; Kevles, *In the Name of Eugenics*. On the general question of eugenics in the Soviet Union, see Graham, 'Science and value', (per.), pp. 1,144–63.

[8] See Manuel, *Prophets*; Leroy, *Histoire des idées*.

[9] Bernal, *World, Flesh and Devil*, pp. 93–4. Cf. Haldane, *Inequality*: 'It is possible at least to imagine a society into which about 98 per cent of the population of most civilized countries would fit. There are, however, a certain small proportion of born misfits. Most of these suffer from serious physical and mental defects' (p. 83).

representation in a wide range of new artistic, philosophical and psychological work. We have already looked at various novels in the period which disturbed and challenged the model of degeneration, shifting the point of focus and the terms of address. Thus even as Zola insisted on his allegiance to modern medicine, medico-psychiatry and biology, his narratives explored profound contradictions in their models of inheritance and degeneration. In, say, Nietzsche or Freud (to take very different examples), the term 'degeneration' was not reproduced, but probed, appropriated and disorientated; and in part this was because the position of the narrator was that much less stable, more open to self-doubt and investigation.

First, Nietzsche. The scandal of the 'mad philosopher' was not least that he took the science of degeneration *too* literally. On the one hand racial degeneration was cast as *substantial* and unequivocal; on the other hand everything seemed metaphorical and interminably allusive in his writing: his texts were full of contemporary science, yet science was part of the 'sickness' of the modernity Nietzsche deplored. Diagnosed as a degenerate himself,[10] Nietzsche was not averse to pointing the finger at the supposed pathologies of others.[11]

Nietzsche accepted a great deal of current criminological and eugenic theory,[12] but pushed the implications further than many of the 'prudent' scientists into a kind of extreme provocation. My point here is not that Nietzsche should be exculpated in some simple sense (his pronouncements on crime and degeneration *are* chilling), but that there are real complexities in knowing how to read these utterances and where to locate the writer. It is that sustained difficulty which blurs the language of degeneration, the relation of subjects and objects. Nietzsche railed against 'our detestable criminal codes with their shopkeeper's scales and the *desire to counterbalance guilt with punishment*'[13] and demanded that the criminal be treated as a mental patient.[14] Morality, he suggested, had to be perceived through the

---

[10] See Nordau, *Degeneration, passim.*

[11] 'Wagner's art is sick. The problems he brings onto the stage – nothing but the problems of hysterics – the convulsive nature of his emotion, his over-excited sensibility, his taste for sharper and sharper spices ... *Wagner est une névrose.* Nothing perhaps is better known today, at any rate nothing is better studied, than the Proteus nature of degeneration, here hidden within the chrysalis of art and artist. Our physicians and physiologists possess in Wagner their most interesting case, at least a very complete one' (*The Wagner Case*, 1888, in *Nietzsche Reader*, pp. 142–3).

[12] See Lea, *Tragic Philosopher*, pp. 310–12. On Nietzsche's reading of Galton cf. Thatcher, *Nietzsche in England*, pp. 112–13.

[13] *Daybreak* (1881), in *Nietzsche Reader*, pp. 157–8.

[14] 'there exists no essential difference between criminals and the insane' (*Nietzsche Reader*, p. 157).

optic of the physical, the biological, the racial.[15] According to Nietzsche, degeneration was to be welcomed as the catalyst for regeneration and the birth of the superman: 'the *levelling* of the mankind of Europe is the great process which should not be arrested; it should even be accelerated':[16] 'The Revolution made Napoleon possible: that is its justification. We ought to desire the anarchical collapse of the whole of our civilisation, if such a reward were to be its result.'[17] At once deadly serious and full of irony, Nietzsche could only be condemned by the scientists of degeneration despite his apparent enthusiasm for some of their views – Karl Pearson explicitly and anxiously distanced Galton's work from Nietzsche's 'doctrine of scorn and contempt for the feeble'[18] which had spoken so brazenly of the 'annihilation of declining races', castration of the degenerate and of the need for new penal rights to 'utilise the feeble in experimentation'.[19] Nietzsche exulted in 'this age of enormous internal decay and disintegration',[20] and strove to go forward across the final illness and atrophy of civilisation, 'that is to say, *step by step further into decadence*'.[21]

Second, consider this quotation from Freud's *Beyond the Pleasure Principle* (1920):

[It] is often merely a matter of opinion when we declare that one stage of development is higher than another, and on the other hand biology teaches us that higher development in one respect is very frequently balanced or outweighed by involution in another. Moreover there are plenty of animal forms from whose early stages we can infer that their development has, on the contrary, assumed a retrograde character . . .

It may be difficult, too, for many of us, to abandon the belief that there is an instinct towards perfection at work in human beings, which has brought them to their present high level of intellectual achievement and ethical sublimation and which may be expected to watch over their development into supermen. I have no

---

[15] 'The church and morality say: "A race, a people perishes through vice and luxury." My *restored* reason says: when a people is perishing, degenerating physiologically, vice and luxury . . . *follow* therefrom. A young man grows prematurely pale and faded. His friends say: this and that illness is to blame. I say: *that* he became ill, *that* he failed to resist the illness, was already the consequence of an impoverished life, an hereditary exhaustion . . . Every error of whatever kind, is a consequence of degeneration of instinct, disaggregation of will: one has thereby virtually defined the *bad*. Everything *good* is instinct – and consequently easy, necessary free' ('The Four Great Errors', in *Twilight of the Idols*, p. 165).

[16] *Will to Power*, II, p. 328 (ref. 898).

[17] *Will to Power*, II, p. 314 (ref. 877).

[18] Pearson, *Life*, II, p. 119. But cf. Sighele, *Letteratura e sociologia*, ch. 1, 'Nietzsche and modern biological theory'. Sighele cautiously admired Nietzsche for the 'moral value unleashed by his thought' (p. 35).

[19] See Lea, *Tragic Philosopher*, pp. 303, 312.

[20] *Will to Power*, I, p. 55 (ref. 57).

[21] *Twilight of the Idols*, p. 101 (ref. 43). Cf. the discussion of Nietzsche and civilization's illness in Ellenberger, *Discovery of the Unconscious*, p. 275.

faith, however, in the existence of any such internal instinct and I cannot see how this benevolent illusion is to be preserved.[22]

The dismay and outrage with which Freud's followers greeted the concept of the 'death drive' is well-known.[23] In *Beyond the Pleasure Principle*, Freud anticipated the hostility and perplexity he would arouse. There was thus a diffident, even apologetic tone, as he suggested the existence of a natural force, even a desire, of death's inertia. It is strange perhaps that some of Freud's followers and commentators accepted the idea that this was totally uncharted scientific territory, forgetting that the 'death drive' rejoined, although in new terms, not only classical mythology or German Romanticism, but a powerful theme within nineteenth-century evolutionary naturalism. *Beyond the Pleasure Principle* was certainly not the moment where the language of science was unequivocally surrendered to mythology, mysticism, the occult. Indeed this study has been centrally concerned with that conception of degeneration in later-nineteenth-century human science and the broader social and historical concerns to which it was assimilated. In the work of, say, Maudsley or Lombroso, that conception can appear tantalisingly close to Freud's speculations, yet in other ways there was an abyss between their earlier investigation and psychoanalytic writing. The question of degeneration and the degenerate were not one and the same. Freud, it could be said, rejected the latter, but returned to the former. In 'Thoughts for the Times on War and Death' (1915) he lamented the current partisanship of science where '[a]nthropologists feel driven to declare [the enemy] inferior and degenerate, [and] psychiatrists issue a diagnosis of his disease of mind or spirit'.[24] On the other hand, the War was itself conceived as the return of the repressed, regression, the 'imperishable' primitive mind: 'it may well happen that a later and higher stage of development, once abandoned, cannot be reached again. But the primitive stages can always be re-established; the primitive mind is, in the fullest meaning of the word, imperishable' (p. 286). It was not only the wildly speculative nature of Freud's proposal of a death force which caused astonishment and opposition within psychoanalytic circles, but also the fact that it appeared in some eyes to fly in the face of biology and specifically of evolutionary theory. Was not life precisely a struggle for survival? Was not suicide against the grain of 'natural' behaviour? Was not civilisation the product of evolutionary advance, cultural development, the accretion of knowledge? And thus was not the 'death drive' an unfortunate

---

[22] Freud, *Pleasure Principle*, pp. 41–2.
[23] See for instance the recent discussion in Rose, *Sexuality*, pp. 16–17. Cf. Sulloway, *Freud, Biologist*, pp. 393, 414.
[24] *Thoughts for the Times*, p. 275.

anomaly in the progressivist, ameliorative terms of psychoanalysis? What was the clinical status of so hyperbolic an idea as Thanatos, so bathetic a source of inspiration as a cotton-reel game? Freud did not suggest that the 'death drive' was the preserve of the psychotic; indeed it constituted a universal law of nature, functioning in and beyond humanity. Glimpsed in the play of his grandson as in the physical structure of organisms, Freud had produced a bizarre hypothesis – a vital trajectory towards death.

It was only too easy for hostile readers to 'interpret' the 'death drive' for Freud in ways which by-passed the abstract claim, relating it merely to the author's psycho-biography.[25] No doubt there are insights to be drawn from such a personalised focus, but no doubt too, those who have 'psycho-analysed' the 'death drive' out of existence, say by finding it merely indicative of Freud's depression, a depression for which palpable reasons could always be found, felt more comfortable in its absence. It was a disturbing concept to work with, especially for those who saw the professional task, in a quasi-medical sense, to be 'curative'. Some subsequent biographers have also explained the 'death drive' in psychoanalytic work between the wars, with a plethora of references to 'real' and immediate contexts of crisis for Freud and for the age as a whole: the course of the Russian Revolution, the economic depression, the rise of Nazism, the threat of renewed war, personal illness, family deaths, schisms in the analytic movement, or just the mournful lyricism, symptomatic of a tired and elderly intellectual, conscious of witnessing the degradation of a culture, even 'the decline of the West'.[26] But to see writing as simply 'mirroring' the disintegration of a social order, a set of beliefs, relations, certainties, is to ignore the productivity of language in the very vision of social crisis and dislocation, the dense history of words and images which mediates each 'sense of an ending'. Thus one must be, at the very least, wary of epithets which code an age as uniquely discontented, decadent and degenerate. What does it mean at a given time to perceive culture as 'bread and circuses' or gloomily to predict the imminent decline of civilisation?

The 'death drive' was both physical and biological for Freud. Once again he had sought the proof of material sciences, 'hard' sciences, as though they could afford the confirmation of his insights into mind: 'The deficiencies in our description would probably vanish if we were already in a position to replace the psychological terms by physiological or chemical ones'. Yet immediately, however, the security of that promise was undercut: 'It is

[25] See Sulloway, *Freud, Biologist*, p. 394.
[26] *Freud, Biologist*, p. 394.

true that they too are only part of a figurative language; but it is one with which we have long been familiar and which is perhaps a simpler one as well.'[27] Freud was caught up continually in a kind of 'fort/da'[28] game, throwing away and pulling back 'the reel' of natural science. Just as he hoped for the isolation of a hormone which would confirm the nature of his 'speculations' on sexuality, so the 'death drive' was to be cast as a material process. The unfinished neurological *Project* was far in Freud's past, but the project of finding physical equivalents to psychic patterns was never fully abandoned.

Psychoanalysis, however, unlike the psychiatry of a Morel, Lombroso or Maudsley, began with the abandonment of a founding, determining, stable 'original' subject outside the history, the ceaseless process of identity. Autobiography, one might say, was shown to be a constitutive process in, not merely a subsequent representation of, the 'individual'. Freud posed the doctor as both subject and object of investigation; the psychological resistance of medicine to psychoanalysis was itself frequently called into question.[29] Of course this is not to say that Freud's psychoanalysis did not also sometimes recuperate the secure identity of doctor as masterful subject and the treatment as a stable opposition – practitioner versus patient: but this was far more than the reproduction of nineteenth-century psychiatry; it was and remains in its potential radically different.

This research has not been centrally concerned with Freud – he is discussed here only briefly as one of several examples of the wake of nineteenth-century degeneration. But this study is indebted to and in part dependent on a culture of psychoanalysis which in crucial respects has helped move us beyond the languages of nineteenth-century positivism and a history of ideas concerned only to reconstruct authorial intentions.

Part of the difficulty in providing a full, historical account of degeneration stems from the plurality of its connotations. Degeneration involved at once a scenario of racial decline (potentially implicating everyone in the society) and an explanation of 'otherness', securing the identity of, variously, the scientist, (white) man, bourgeoisie against superstition, fiction, darkness, femininity, the masses, effete aristocracy. Degeneration flirted and flitted between the dreams of purity and danger but in socially and

---

[27] *Pleasure Principle*, p. 60.

[28] The words Freud's grandson uses in his symbolic game with the cotton-reel as recounted in *Beyond the Pleasure Principle*.

[29] For instance: 'The less repellant of the so-called sexual perversions are very widely diffused among the whole population, as every one knows except medical writers upon the subject. Or I should rather say, they know it too; only they take care to forget it at the moment when they take up their pens to write about it' (Freud, *Dora*, p. 51]. Cf. Gilman, 'Sexology and Psychoanalysis', in Gilman and Chamberlin (eds.), *Dark Side*, ch. 4.

historically specific ways. In the writings of scientists, doctors, anthropologists, one encounters again a kind of 'fort/da' game with the projected object of investigation, entertaining the potential pollution of purity, only to consolidate it against the 'dangerous classes, races and sex'. The reader is threatened with a world of entropy or some future dissolution of stable positions, but at the same time offered a guarantee of them – the degenerate has a definite physiognomy. My aim has been to suggest the continually problematic structure of that vision.

Psychoanalysis, we are told, begins with the abandonment of psychiatry's theatre and spectacle.[30] Certainly the speech of the degenerate was practically unheard in the work of medical-psychiatry beyond a function in simply confirming a degeneracy already diagnosed. Speech was ignored in so far as it could challenge decisively the corpus of scientific knowledge and the petrified relationships of doctor and patient (degenerate, neurasthenic, hysteric . . .). It is the language rather than the direct clinical practice of psychiatry which has been at issue in much of the present volume. But certainly, to read now of the methods routinely used after 1914 to restore the voice of patients struck dumb by war is enough to hint the world of difference which lay, potentially, between this medical-psychiatry and 'the talking cure':

Other methods included painful lumbar punctures and retinal examinations. However more often than not the preferred method was electrical faradization . . . Patients would be made to queue in the treatment room and watch the first in line receive painful electrical shocks to his larynx. Faradization would continue until the subject emitted a noise (presumably a scream) – whereupon the doctor would inform him that he had recovered his voice.[31]

World War I with its mass mobilisation crystallised a new concern with crowds and madness in many ways, not least by demonstrating the inadequacy of a sharp division of 'fighting men' into the hereditarily fit and unfit. The problem was shellshock. By late 1916 it was claimed that shellshock cases constituted up to forty per cent of the casualties from heavy fighting zones.[32] Victims displayed a bewildering range of disabilities – paralyses and muscular contractures of the arms, legs, hands and

---

[30] Thus in one formulation, 'Charcot sees. Freud will hear. Perhaps the whole of psychoanalysis is in that shift' (Heath, *Sexual Fix*, p. 38). Or in another: 'In [Freud's] obituary of Charcot, there are constant references to sight. Charcot the visual was unconsciously a voyeur, in whose presence the hysterics of the Salpêtrière gave free rein to their exhibitionism. His presentations of patients were veritable shows, attended by the cream of Parisian high society. The coordinates of Charcot's scientific and therapeutic method were corporal space and scenic space. Distance and listening, on the other hand, were what Freud strove for' (Anzieu, *Freud's Self-Analysis*, p. 48).
[31] Stone, 'Shellshock', p. 253.   [32] 'Shellshock', p. 249.

feet, loss of sight, speech and hearing, choreas, palsies and tics, catatonia and obsessive behaviour, amnesia, severe sleeplessness and terrifying nightmares. Many senior officers and doctors took the view that shellshock cases were either insane and thus to be locked away, or malingerers to be court-martialled and shot. But the very scale of the phenomenon produced a managerial and conceptual crisis. Army statistics revealed that officers were more than twice as likely to suffer from breakdown on the battle field as men of the ranks; the much vaunted fortifying ethos of the public schools seemed to be futile.

Attempts to trace a 'tainted heredity', or the exclusively organic 'commotional' effects of exploding shells on constitutionally weak systems became increasingly difficult to sustain. Earlier hereditarian ideas about degeneration collided with the quintessential 'nobility' attributed to the war volunteers. Thus the debate about the aetiology of the shell-shocked, was itself shockingly vexed and traumatic.[33] Shellshock, Martin Stone concludes in a recent essay, 'brought the neuroses into the mainstream of mental medicine and economic life and set psychiatry's field of practice squarely within the social fabric of industrial society'.[34] The problem of mental illness could no longer be conceived as that of a restricted realm of degenerates with weak hereditary constitutions.

In other ways, however, World War I merely consolidated perceptions of civilisation's degeneration. Maudsley provides just one instance of a much broader European preoccupation with 'civilisation and its discontents' whose powerful genealogy runs from before the turn of the century through to the inter-war decades. As one commentator was to put it in 1932, World War I 'revealed all too clearly how ferociously unchanged beneath the thin veneer of civilisation lurked the old *bête humaine*, and how illusory was the belief in moral progress'.[35] He asked whether contemporary civilisation had now reached a turning point in history, similar to the moment of the collapse of the Graeco-Roman world and demanded that the racial question be placed at the centre of the social debate. In the same year J. Arthur Thomson reminded the public of Lankester's book *Degeneration* and the crucial fallacy of assuming that evolution meant progress. He mentioned how 'thorough going parasites' were often successful survivors and insisted that 'we have to face the fact of *degeneration*. Sometimes in fact, there has been simplification of structure, a loss of ancestral gains, and, it may be, a remarkable retrogression'.[36]

After 1914 certain images of the degenerate had receded from view and

[33] 'Shellshock', p. 249.   [34] 'Shellshock', p. 266.   [35] Schiller, *Social Decay*, p. 2.
[36] Thomson, *Great Biologists*, p. 166; cf. Armstrong, *Survival*.

the fear of a working-class population explosion in Britain subsided;[37] furthermore the 'unemployable' were widely employed in the war effort. Degenerationism did not disappear, however, but refracted through a further range of European social representations. Indeed whilst the notion of 'internal degeneration' may have aroused less publicity, war-time propaganda often spoke of the biological degeneracy of the enemy. Thus, for instance, English and French war-time propagandists provided racial anthropological evidence for Prussian degeneracy.[38] This externalisation of the problem of degeneration in the war drive, however, was only one discursive permutation. Some philosophical voices concluded that war revealed not the strength of the one and the pathology of the other, but rather the incredible frailty of civilisation itself, the constant possibility of regression. The decline of the West, Spengler insisted in 1918, was not an historical problem limited in time and space, but rather a philosophical question which 'includes within itself every great question of Being'.[39] Civilisation was the moment of the organic climax and disintegration of culture, namely 'a conclusion, the thing become, succeeding the thing becoming, death following life, rigidity following expansion' (p. 31). Civilisation, he suggested, inevitably gathered life into the cities and consequently deprived the land of resources (p. 32). The triumph of the city dweller was always the death of the organic principle: 'unstable in fluid masses, the *parasitical* city dweller [is] traditionless, utterly matter of fact' (p. 32, emphasis added). The parasite, remember, was a prime example of degeneration given by late-nineteenth-century zoologists like Lankester.[40] Modern culture, argued Spengler, was simply a routine of 'bread and circuses', wage disputes and football matches (p. 34). The geographical arrangement of the world could be temporarily changed by European expansion, but the limited time of the West could never be overcome: 'The expansive tendency is a doom, something daemonic and immense' (p. 37). History was genetic: 'the endless uniform wave-train of the generations' (p. 106) subject to 'organic logic' (p. 26), the rhythm of the species. In short we read here one more displacement of that long organicist theorisation of degeneration which has been the subject throughout the present study.

---

[37] See Soloway, 'Counting the degenerates', (per.), p. 159; Stedman Jones, *Outcast London*, concluding pages; cf. Nye, *Crime*, p. 388, which makes the point that the destruction of millions in the First World War seemed to prove that Europe was not dying slowly of incurable illnesses, but, on the contrary, had the capacity to unleash immediate destruction programmatically upon itself. Cf. Hofstadter, *Social Darwinism*, pp. 121, 203, which suggests that social Darwinist individualism was eclipsed in the United States by other theories after the First World War.
[38] See for example Boule, 'La Guerre', (per.); Merrifield, 'Evolution in the Direction of Degeneration'.
[39] *Decline*, p. 3.   [40] See the discussion of Lankester in part III above.

The biological, medical and evolutionist agenda was still apparent long after World War I in some of the more famous European 'laments' for the crisis of civilisation. Thus Ortega Y Gasset would write in the 1930s: 'there is no certain progress, no evolution, without the threat of "involution" '.[41] The nomenclature of regression, degeneration and atavism were brought to bear in the perception of 'mass society': 'Mass man' was 'a primitive who has slipped through the wings on the age-old stage of civilization' (p. 90). The triumph of the masses whether in bolshevism or fascism was 'the greatest crisis that can afflict peoples, nations and civilizations' (p. 11). The contemporary calamity was conceived as ultimately neither social, economic nor political, but the effect of a timeless social psychology: 'the masses, by definition, neither should nor can direct their own personal existence' (p. 11); 'the mass, as a psychological fact, can be defined without waiting for individuals to appear in mass formation' (p. 14).

Degeneration had its place in many theories and fictions in the first forty years of the twentieth century. Its discursive descent cannot be tied exclusively to the roots of one ideology, Nazism, or one country, Germany. My aim has been to demonstrate the complexity of the conception of degeneration in other European countries and to contribute a 'case study' which might be useful in new thinking about cross-disciplinary research, intellectual history or 'ideas in context'.

This work has sought to show the convergences and contiguities of various kinds of representation, without reducing them to one another, or assuming a model of 'manipulation' or 'ideological adaptation', as though languages were simply there 'on the shelf', to be chosen freely at will by various professional groups. To speak of degeneration's function within the consolidation of psychiatric and criminological knowledge has tended to lead sometimes into a rather limited and limiting argument about the use of ideas in the self-interested advancement of a profession or an institution, assuming that 'self', 'interest' and 'advance' are all immediately evident, unproblematic terms.

The present study, then, has outlined some of the complex political ramifications of degeneration and suggested the powerful historical anxieties articulated in Italy, France and England, emphasising at the same time the distinctiveness of representation in different states and across forms of social representation. The material has been organised in various ways in the course of this exposition so as to highlight important changes of connotation; a substantial part of the volume has been concerned with reconstructing certain specific intellectual careers (Morel, Buchez, Lombroso, Maudsley); these are treated at some length not so much for the sake

[41] *Revolt*, p. 86.

of biography *per se*, as because I take these figures and *oeuvres* to epitomise strikingly and helpfully the important dilemmas, contradictions and shifts in representation with which this study is generally concerned. Thus the work of those individual doctors is combined with a broader survey, drawing on a range of sources, vignettes and analyses, suggesting some significant affiliations or complicities, and charting important transformations in the wider shared terms of socio-political description and understanding across and beyond the second half of the nineteenth century. I also considered it important to place the literary references and material amidst the discussion of social and political debates rather than to set them completely apart either at the beginning or the end of the book; the aim was to refuse any assumption that the novels were simply (and marginally) reflecting a language created elsewhere and to suggest the crucial interaction of different forms of knowledge and writing in the production, dissemination and transformation of what was, despite all the internal differences and nuances, an identifiable shared language of degeneration. That language was notably uneven, plural, never simply reproduced, or perfectly synchronised across the various debates. There is no single trajectory of such writings across time and place; nor can they be (reassuringly) confined within the history of any one political designation such as socialist, liberal, conservative or fascist. I have tried to explore the tensions between similarity and difference in various interlocking arguments and projects, the shared models and yet quite distinct discursive effects. It could be argued (after Foucault) that the discourse of degeneration should be understood in a longer history of the construction of the subject and in a wider 'regime' of discipline, surveillance and punishment. But to situate degeneration in a broader, unfolding Enlightenment process of psychiatrisation, pathologisation and medicalisation easily homogenises in fact rather distinct discussions and texts, and may obscure the specific later-nineteenth-century contexts in which such languages developed and to which they spoke.

Foucault's extraordinarily eloquent works on the constitution of madness, criminality and sexuality seem for all their innovative subtlety (and perhaps this is partly as a consequence of their implacable and reductive hostility to psychoanalysis) always to abstract the figure of 'power'; more specific to our purpose here, Foucault returns the question of degeneracy, whenever he touches on it, to a supposedly overriding strategic function, in relation to the bourgeois and professional medical 'will to power', which, it seems to me, begs a number of questions that I have tried to develop in the present account.

In the collection *Power/Knowledge*, Foucault alludes fleetingly to the 'vast theoretical and legislative edifice constructed around the question of degeneracy and degenerates'; in response to his own questions, 'what took place here?', '[c]an one talk of interests here?',[42] he hints only that degeneration at once supported and engendered various wider disciplinary strategies, various fields of power. Foucault's conception of power draws heavily on military and war imagery; as he puts it in one stark hypothesis, 'power is war, a war continued by other means' (p. 90). Power is not primarily to be seen in economic terms: 'power relations do indeed "serve", but not at all because they are in "the service of" an economic interest taken as primary, rather because they are capable of being utilised in strategies' (p. 142). This theorisation does not assume any overall conscious agency or design, but the answer Foucault gives to the problem of degeneration is in fact not dissimilar to the standard professionalisation argument. In this account there is nothing particularly mysterious or recalcitrant about the theory of degeneration; it is in fact clearly to be understood as a tool or weapon in the history of psychiatric institutional advance. I do not of course deny that degeneration was taken up strategically and served institutional interests. But at the same time something of the complexity of the crisis and anxiety articulated in the language of degeneration is too easily explained away by Foucault when he describes how the 'invisibility' of pathology as perceived by Morel and much later-nineteenth-century medical-psychiatry simply functioned to guarantee professional expertise, the penetrating gaze, the eye of power:

I would be tempted to say that there was a necessity here (which one doesn't have to call an interest) linked to the very existence of a psychiatry which had made itself autonomous but needed thereafter to secure a basis for its intervention by gaining recognition as a component of public hygiene. And it could establish this basis only through the fact that there was a disease (mental alienation) for it to mop up. . . . Now, how can it be proved that madness constitutes a danger except by showing that there exist extreme cases where madness, even though not apparent to the public gaze, without manifesting itself beforehand through any symptom except a few minute fissures, minuscule murmerings perceptible only to the highly trained observer, can suddenly explode into a monstrous crime . . . Only a doctor can spot it, and thus madness becomes exclusively an object for the doctor, whose right of intervention is grounded by the same token. (p. 205)

Responding to Foucault's substitution of words like 'problem' or 'necessity' for the term 'interest', one of his interviewers retorts not without some reason with regard to the passage above: 'The gain appears very slight, and things remain still very imprecise' (p. 206). I have sought to identify some of the social, political and cultural anxieties invested in degeneration which are not fully addressed in Foucauldian equations of power and knowledge.

[42] *Power/Knowledge*, p. 204.

Indeed that equation has often been suspended or displaced here; my attention has been rather to the drama of a felt historical and historiographical *powerlessness*. Degeneration functioned at once as a representation of that crisis, and a means, never wholly successful, of containing, covering over, mastering profound political confusion and historical disorientation.

During and after the Great War, commentators from the Allied states often sought to portray 'Darwinian militarism' or 'racially aggressive' doctrines as an exclusively German preserve. Of course it is true that German culture and science in the inter-war years were to become intensely preoccupied with the theme of evolutionary fitness and racial degeneration but this was widely although never universally endorsed elsewhere. When commenting on the theme of degeneration in the 1930s, the American *Encyclopaedia of the Social Sciences* looked to German work and acknowledged that:

The literature of Aryanism and Nordicism and of eugenics have stressed the probability of a present degeneration of racial quality among Western nations. The former writers base their views largely on belief in the gradual inundation of supposedly pure Nordic types by the Westward push of Slavic elements and the assumed deleterious effects of race mixture.[43]

'It is not impossible', the article conceded, 'that a rich and humane civilisation may permit the undue multiplication of defective and parasitic types' (p. 57). In the post-World War II edition of the encyclopaedia, the entry for degeneration had disappeared. It may well be that we have to look to 1945 rather than 1914 to find degeneration really in retreat, truly and consistently a matter of mainstream scientific disavowal and embarrassment. For by then degeneration appeared inextricably intertwined with the web of fascist-ideology, the evils of the Nazi doctors, the unfathomable full horror of 'The Final Solution'.[44]

In Germany, as in England, the 1900s had witnessed the production of a considerable body of eugenic literature. In 1899 a German doctor in government service, Paul Nacke, had described it as a 'sacred duty of the state' to introduce legislative measures to facilitate the sterilisation of certain classes of degenerates'.[45] In 1897, a Heidelberg gynaecologist carried out the first sterilisation to prevent the procreation of 'inferior' offspring – in breach of the existing penal code which defined such an act as an illegal attack upon the person. It was, however, the German industrialist Krupp who was to provide perhaps the biggest impetus to the debate at this point. In 1900 he offered a large prize for the best essay on the subject

---

[43] 'Degeneration', in *Encyclopaedia of the Social Sciences* (New York), 5 (1935), 57.
[44] See Lifton, *Nazi Doctors*.   [45] See Noakes, 'Nazism and Eugenics', p. 80.

'What can we learn from the principles of the theory of evolution in relation to domestic political developments and the legislation of states?' The winner was Dr Wilhelm Schallmeyer. His study, entitled *Heredity and Selection in the Life of Nations. A Study in Political Science on the Basis of the New Biology*, became a standard German work on eugenics until the 1920s.[46] By 1904, there was a major journal in German dealing with the relations between biology, race and politics, the *Archiv für Rassen und Gesellschaftsbiologie*. The Racial Hygiene Society, closely connected to the *Archiv*, was founded in Berlin in 1905.

The various Nazi measures, including the sterilisation laws, introduced during the 1930s to curb supposed degeneracy, were preceded by a significant array of earlier theories, institutions and practices.[47] In early-twentieth century Italy too, Lombroso's work may have been coming under sustained criticism, but eugenics was developing strongly, even before Mussolini's endorsement.[48] In the aftermath of World War I, numerous Italian obstetricians, gynaecologists and other doctors agreed that the primary problem of post-war society was eugenic.

There is now, however, a significant secondary literature available to discomfort those who would deny the existence of Anglo-American equivalents of Nazi discourses on race, eugenics and degeneration.[49] Whilst Nazi eugenics in the 1930s was certainly treated with suspicion and disapproval by many contemporary European commentators, it was only in and after the Second World War that it was generally anathematised as totally pathological, abhorrent and evil. Much Nazi ideology drew upon a far wider fund of socio-political positions and theories. Of course, there is a vast gulf between discourses about the elimination of degenerate peoples and the actual practice of racial engineering and eventual genocide. Yet even that division is in part misleadingly stark. The eugenic crimes of the Nazis *were* of a totally different scale and order than those committed elsewhere, yet it should not be forgotten, to take one of the more obvious examples, that in many of the American states, sterilisation laws had already been passed, and indeed the Nazis studied such earlier legislation. Thousands of people were sterilised in the first four decades of this century

---

[46] Noakes, 'Nazism and Eugenics', p. 76.
[47] Hitler's 1933 'law for the prevention of hereditarily diseased offspring' aimed to prevent 'lives unworthy of life' and stated that 'anyone who has a hereditary illness can be rendered sterile by a surgical operation if, according to the experience of medical science, there is a strong probability that their offspring will suffer from serious hereditary defects of physical or mental nature.' Between 1933 and 1939 about 320,000 persons were sterilised under the terms of the law. For the details of this legislation and its earlier history, see Bock, 'Racism and Sexism', (per.), pp. 408, 413–14; Noakes, 'Nazism and Eugenics', pp. 85, 86.
[48] See Pogliano, 'Scienza e stirpe', (per.), p. 66.
[49] See for instance Hofstadter, *Social Darwinism*; Haller, *Eugenics*; Chase, *Legacy*; Gould, *Mismeasure*; Kevles, *In the Name of Eugenics*.

in the United States, and many more have been even since 1945, as a consequence of the 'triumph' of degenerationist anxieties.[50]

The period 1939–45 may then appear as the realisation, the crystallised evidence, of all that been sinister in the Victorian and Edwardian literature on progress and decay, crime and social pathology. It seems easy to see with hindsight that those earlier and variegated pronouncements are far from innocuous or marginal to European history. But the question remains as to what conditions transformed that earlier available language into the precise social and political practice of the Third Reich. In any event, it is clear that no simple continuity of the German tradition, or of earlier ideas, can alone account for Nazism; one must look rather to the complex political, economic, cultural and ideological conjuncture in the decades beyond 1918.[51]

Particular configurations and emphases can be found in the German debates on progress and degeneration which were less marked elsewhere, just as there were pronounced difference between the French, Italian and English perspectives on these questions. But the analysis of texts alone is not enough to *explain* the differing historical power of the language of degeneration in a variety of contexts. The ideas focussed in the present account cannot be seen in some philosophically idealist sense as the direct cause of either World War I or II much as Shaw seemed to do when he wrote: 'Neo-Darwinism in politics *has produced* a European catastrophe of a magnitude so appalling, and a scope so unpredictable, that as I write these lines in 1920, it is still far from certain whether our civilization will survive it' (emphasis added).[52] Nor can the emergence of the theory of degeneration be explained as the direct effect of nineteenth-century economic changes; rather it must be grasped as part of a continuing reciprocal process in which language, politics, economy and society shape, mediate and intersect, yet are irreducible to, one another.

The aftermath of Nazism and World War II have produced *inter alia* two very conspicuous historiographical tendencies: either the Third Reich is taken as emblematic of a deeper Western or capitalist historical totalitarianism, stretching as far back as the Enlightenment or even earlier; for the Frankfurt School for instance at its bleakest moments in the 1930s and 40s, '[E]nlightenment is totalitarian'.[53] Or conversely the ideology of

---

[50] See Chase, *Legacy*. On the debate around the Brock Report and the numerous calls in Britain through the 1930s for compulsory sterilisation legislation, and the continuing resistance, see Sutherland, *Ability*, pp. 40, 87–8.
[51] This point is forcefully made in Eley, *Unification to Nazism*.
[52] Shaw, *Back to Methuselah*, p. 9.
[53] Adorno and Horkheimer, *Dialectic*, p. 6. For a new version of this tendency to draw Nazism out into a much wider and ultimately undifferentiated history of Western culture, literature and politics, see Theweleit, *Male Fantasies*. For a critique of the 'anti-Enlightenment' position of certain texts in so-called 'anti-psychiatry', see Doerner, *Madmen*.

Nazism is spuriously confined to German-speaking culture, taken as part of the peculiarity of that history alone,[54] purged from the vision of a generally upright, decent European-wide anti-fascist society, the heir of the true Western tradition: as though Germany were simply aberrant or degenerate, a kind of cancer in the healthy body of the Continent. This drive to confine and to forget intensifies the sense of profound cultural consternation, repeated over and over again, when a particular event, trial or scandal rekindles the debate on the history of resistance and collaboration in so many war-time European societies.

Poliakov has observed more generally about the history of racism that '[a] vast chapter of Western thought [has been] ... made to disappear by sleight of hand'.[55] Assumptions of social organic degeneration, it might be said, still inflect politics and culture, even if the explicit theories of racial, biological, criminal and psychiatric degeneration are now buried or repressed in Western mainstream debate. Further research on the representation of degeneration and the degenerate in European culture since World War II would necessarily involve very difficult and unresolved theoretical questions about presence and absence, conscious and unconscious repressions, sleights of hand, the meta-narratives of political discourses. Such a study would certainly still find some explicit rhetorical appeals to the vision of evolutionary arrest and organic collapse, for instance, in the language of population studies. It would necessarily trace the uses of the past in contemporary representations of regression and decline, and the shifting 'places' of each national memory (to borrow from the title of a recent collection of essays on France[56]). But it would also need to trace the significance of an apparent *volte face*, a clouding over of the idea of degeneration within European social commentary in the aftermath of Nazism; to locate those intricate displacements, repressions and vanishing points could contribute to a wider political history of forgetting since 1945. Moreover, analysis and reflection on degenerationist languages from the past are surely opportune if we are to reformulate less mythologically the terms of our current crises.

[54] See Blackbourn and Elie, *Peculiarities*.   [55] Poliakov, *Aryan Myth*, p. 5.
[56] Nora (ed.), *Les Lieux de mémoire*.

BIBLIOGRAPHY

Primary literature

Unpublished items

Galton, Francis, Galton Papers, University College. London, Ref. 133/6 (correspondence with E. R. Lankester); 122/1M (correspondence on insanity in twins with Maudsley, Tuke, Gilchrist etc.).

Lewis, Aubrey, File of papers and correspondence on Henry Maudsley, in the archives of the Bethlem Royal Hospital, Kent. (No reference).

MacDonald, Arthur. Correspondence with the Home Office, 1906–1912, Public Records Office, Kew, Ref. HO 45/10563.172511/1: HO 45/10563.172511/2.

Books

Actes du premier congrès international d'anthropologie criminelle, biologie et sociologie (Rome, November 1885), Turin, 1886–7.

Actes du deuxième congrès international d'anthropologie criminelle, biologie et sociologie (Paris, August 1889), Paris, 1890.

Actes du troisième congrès international d'anthropologie criminelle (Brussels, August 1892), Brussels, 1893.

  Further congresses were held under the same auspices in Geneva (August 1896), records publ. 1897; Amsterdam (September 1901) 1901; Turin (April–May 1906), 1908; Heidelberg (1911), 1912.

Actes du congrès pénitentiaire international de Rome (November 1885), 3 vols., Rome, 1887.

Aliens Act, London, 1905.

Alongi, Giuseppe, *La Mafia. Fattori – manifestazioni – rimedi* (1886), Milan, 1904.

Angioliella, Gaetano, *Delitti e delinquenti politici: appunti*, Milan, n.d.

Anon., *Regeneration: A Reply to Max Nordau*, London, 1895.

Antonini, G., *I precursori di C. Lombroso*, Turin, 1900.

Armstrong, Charles Wickstead, *The Survival of the Unfittest*, London, 1927; revised edn, 1931.

Arndt, Rudolf, *Biologische Studien. II. Artung und Entartung*, 2 vols., Greifswald, 1892–5.

Arnold, Matthew, *Culture and Anarchy. An Essay in Political and Social Criticism*, London, 1869.

Bagehot, Walter, *Physics and Politics*, London, 1872.

Balfour, Arthur James, *Decadence* (Henry Sidgwick Memorial Lecture delivered at Newnham College, 25 January 1908), Cambridge, 1908.

Ball, Benjamin, *Leçons sur les maladies mentales*, 2nd edn, Paris, 1890.

Balzac, H. de, *The Country Doctor* (*Le Médecin de campagne*, 1833), translated by Ellen Marriage, London, 1895.

241

Barrès, Maurice, *La Terre et les morts (sur quelles réalités fonder la conscience française)*, Paris, 1899.

Amori et dolori sacrum – La mort de Venise, Paris, 1903.

Barzini, L., *Nel mondo dei misteri con Eusapia Paladino. Preceduto da uno studio di C. Lombroso*, Milan, 1907.

Beccaria, Cesare, *Dei delitti e delle pene* (1764), Livorno, 1824.

Bentham, Jeremy, *The Works of Jeremy Bentham*, edited by John Bowring, 11 vols., Edinburgh, 1838–43.

Collected Works, edited by J. H. Burns and H. L. A. Hart, London, 1968–.

An Introduction to the Principles of Morals and Legislation (1789), London, 1982.

Bergson, Henri, *Creative Evolution*, authorised translation by Arthur Mitchell, London, 1911.

An Introduction to Metaphysics, authorised translation by T. E. Hulme, London, 1913.

Bernal, J. D., *The World, the Flesh and the Devil. An Enquiry into the Future of the Three Enemies of the Rational Soul*, London, 1929.

Berthet, M., *Les Dégénérés dans les écoles primaires*, Grenoble, 1906.

Bertillon, A., *La Photographie juridicaire avec une appendice sur la classification et l'identification anthropométrique*, Paris, 1890.

Bianchi, A. G., Ferrero, G. and Sighele, Scipio, *Mondo criminale italiano*: vol. I. 1889–92, Milan, 1893; vol. II, 1893–4, Milan, 1894.

Billiet, Alexis, *Observations sur le recensement des personnes atteintes du goitre et de cretinisme dans les dioceses de Chambéry et de Maurienne*, Chambéry, 1851.

Brugia, Raffaele, *I problemi della degenerazione*, preface by E. Morselli, Bologna, 1906.

Boulland, J. F. A. Auguste, *Essai d'histoire universelle, ou exposé comparatif des traditions de tous les peuples*, 2 vols., Paris, 1836.

Brumke, Oswald, *Ueber Nervöse Entartung*, Berlin, 1912.

Buchez, P. J. B., *Introduction à la science de l'histoire*, 2nd edn, 2 vols., Paris, 1842.

Histoire de la formation de la nationalité française, 2 vols., Paris, 1859.

Traité de politique et de science sociale, published by his executors, L. Cerise and A. Ott, with a note on his life and work by A. Ott, Paris, 1866.

Buchez, P. J. B. and Roux, P. C., *Histoire parlementaire de la révolution française*, 40 vols., Paris, 1834–8.

Buffon, Count George Louis Le Clerc de, *Natural History General and Particular* (1749–88), A new edition, corrected and enlarged by William Wood, 20 vols., London, 1812.

Burke, Edmund, *Reflections on the Revolution in France* (1790), Harmondsworth, 1983.

Cantlie, James, *Degeneration amongst Londoners* (lecture delivered at the Parkes Museum of Hygiene 27 January 1885), London, 1885.

Carlyle, Thomas, 'Chartism' (1839), in *Critical and Miscellaneous Essays*, 7 vols., London, 1872, VI, pp. 109–86.

'Model Prisons', in *Latter-Day Pamphlets*, *The Works*, 30 vols, London, 1898, XX.

Carpenter, Edward, *Civilization: Its Cause and Cure and other Essays*, London, 1889.

Carrara, Francesco, *Programma del corso di diritto criminale* (1859), 2 vols., Florence, 1924.

Carrara, M., *Antropolgia criminale*, Milan, 1908.

Cerise, L. A. P., *Des Fonctions et des maladies nerveuses dans leurs rapports avec l'éducation sociale et privée, morale et physique*, Paris, 1842.

Chambers, Robert, *Vestiges of the Natural History of Creation* (1844), London, 1884.

Charcot, J.-M., *Leçons du Mardi à la Salpêtrière. Notes de Cours de MM. Blin, Charcot et H. Colin*, 2nd edn, Paris, 1892, I.

Charpentier, R., *Dégénérescence mentale et hystérie. Les empoisonneuses*, Paris, 1906.

Comte, Auguste, *The Positive Philosophy*, freely translated and condensed by Harriet Martineau, London, 1853.

Conrad, Joseph, *The Secret Agent* (1907), Harmondsworth, 1981.
Victory (1915), Harmondsworth, 1984.

Conway, Martin, *The Crowd in Peace and War*, London, 1915.

Dallemagne, J., *Dégénérés et déséquilibrés*, Brussels, 1895.

Danel, Louis, *La Notion de dégénérescence, particulièrement dans l'étude du mouvement littéraire et artistique contemporain*, Arras-Paris, 1907.

Darwin, Charles. *On the Origin of Species* (1859), a facsimile of the first edition, introduced by Ernst Mayr, Cambridge, Mass., 1964.
The Descent of Man and Selection in Relation to Sex, 2 vols., London, 1871.
The Expression of the Emotions in Man and Animals, London, 1872.
The Descent of Man, and Selection in Relation to Sex, 2 vols., 2nd edn. (1874), revised and augmented, London, 1883.

De-Filippi, F., *L'uomo e le scimie*. 3rd edn, Milan, 1865.

De Meis, A. C., *Il sovranno. Saggio di filosofia politica con riferenza all'Italia* (1868), edited by B. Croce, Bari, 1927.

Demoor, Jean *et al.*, *Evolution by Atrophy in Biology and Sociology* (1894), translated from the original by Mrs Chalmers Mitchell, London, 1899.

Departmental Committee on prisons, *Report* and *Minutes of evidence*, London, 1895.

De Sanctis, Francesco, *L'arte, la scienza e la vita*, edited by Maria Teresa Lanza, in *Opere*, 24 vols, Turin, 1972, XIV.

Desjardins, Albert, *La Méthode expérimentale appliquée au droit criminel en Italie*, Paris, 1892.

Dohrn, Anton, *Charles Darwin. Anton Dohrn. Correspondence*, edited by Christine Groeber, Naples, 1982.

Doyle, Arthur Conan, *The Lost World* (1912), London, 1977.
'The Adventure of the Empty House', in *The Return of Sherlock Holmes* (London, 1905), reprinted in *The Penguin Complete Sherlock Holmes*, Harmondsworth, 1985, pp. 483–666.
'The Adventure of the Creeping Man', in *The Case Book of Sherlock Homes* (London, 1927), reprinted in *The Penguin Complete Sherlock Holmes*, pp. 983–1,122.

Durkheim, Emile, *Le Suicide. Étude de sociologie* (1897), Paris, 1930.

Encyclopaedia of the Social Sciences, New York, 1935.

Ellis, Henry Havelock, *The Criminal*, London, 1890.

Man and Woman: A Study of Human Secondary Sexual Characters (1894), London, 1904.

The Problem of Race-Regeneration. New Tracts for the Times series, London, 1911.

The Task of Social Hygiene (1912), London, 1927.

Engels, Frederick, *Dialectics of Nature* (written 1873–83, first published 1925), translated by C. Dutt, London, 1940.

Féré, Charles, *Dégénérescence et criminalité. Essai physiologique*, Paris, 1888.

La Pathologie des émotions, Paris, 1892.

L'Instinct sexuel. Évolution et dissolution, Paris, 1899.

La Famille neuropathique. Théorie tératologique de l'hérédité et de la prédisposition morbide et de la dégénérescence, 2nd edn, Paris, 1899.

Ferrero, Gina Lombroso, *Cesare Lombroso. Storia della vita e delle opere narrata dalla figlia*, Turin, 1915.

Ferri, Enrico, *Socialismo e criminalità*. Turin, 1883.

Discordie positiviste sul socialismo. Ferri contro Garofalo, Palermo, 1895.

Criminal Sociology, translated with a preface by W. D. Morrison, New York, 1897.

'Ricordi liceali', in *Nel 70° Anniversario di Roberto Ardigò*, edited by G. Negri *et al.*, Turin, 1898, pp. 249–52.

Contro la marina militare. Discorsi alla camera dei deputati, Rome, 1901.

Contro il militarismo. Discorsi alla camera dei deputati, Rome, 1901.

Autobiografia preceduta da uno studio intimo, Milan, 1903.

Socialism and Positive Science. Darwin – Spencer – Marx, translated by Edith C. Harvey from the French edn of 1896, London, 1905.

Contro la piu grande guerra e per la sincerità parlamentare. Discorso parlamentare, Rome, 1916.

Enrico Pessina e il pensiero italiano sulla giustizia penale, Milan, 1917.

Difese penali. Studi di giurisprudenza penale. Arringhe civili, 2nd edn, 2 vols., Turin, 1923.

I delinquenti nell'arte, (1886), 2nd edn, Turin, 1926.

Mussolini uomo di stato, 2nd edn, Mantua, 1927.

Il fascismo in Italia e l'opera di Benito Mussolini, Mantua, 1927.

Sociologia criminale. 5th edn, 2 vols., Turin, 1929.

Arringhe e discorsi, edited and introduced by Bruno Cassinelli, Milan, 1979.

Ferriani, Lino, *Delinquenti che scrivono. Studio di psicologia criminale*, Como, 1899.

Flaubert, Gustave, *Bouvard and Pécuchet [1881] with the Dictionary of Received Ideas*, translated by A. J. Krailsheimer, Harmondsworth, 1976.

Fourier, Charles, *Epilogue (renvoyé). La politique rétrograde, faussée par 16 dégénérations* (1841), in *Oeuvres complètes*, Paris, 1966, v.

Franchi, Bruno, *Enrico Ferri. Il noto, il mal noto e l'ignorato*, Turin, 1908.

Freeman, Austin, *Social Decay and Regeneration*, introduced by Havelock Ellis, London, 1921.

Frégier, H. A., *Des Classes dangereuses de la population dans les grandes villes et des moyens de les rendre meilleures*, Paris, 1840.

Freud, Sigmund, *Dora, Fragment of an Analysis of a Case of Hysteria* (1905), in *The Standard Edition of the Complete Psychological Works of Sigmund Freud* (hereafter SE), translated from the German under the general editorship of James Strachey, VII.

Thoughts for the Times on War and Death (1915), SE, XIV.

Beyond the Pleasure Principle (1920). SE, XVIII.

Group Psychology and the Analysis of the Ego (1921). SE, XVIII.

Medusa's Head (1922), SE, XVIII.

Fetishism (1927), SE, XXI.

Civilization and its Discontents (1930). SE, XXI.

Galton, Francis, *Hereditary Genius. An Inquiry into its Laws and Consequences* (1869), introduced by H. J. Eysenck, London, 1978.

Inquiries into Human Faculty and its Development, London, 1883.

Essays in Eugenics, London, 1909.

Gaspare, Virgilio, *Passanante e la natura morbosa del delitto*, Rome, 1888.

Sulla natura morbosa del delitto. Saggio di ricerche, Turin, 1910.

Gaume, J.-J., *La Révolution. Recherches historiques sur l'origine et la propagation du mal en Europe depuis la Renaissance jusqu'a nos jours*, 6 vols., Paris, 1856–9.

Gemelli, Agostino, *Le dottrine moderne della delinquenza. Critica delle dottrine criminali positiviste*, Florence, 1908.

Cesare Lombroso. I funerali di un uomo e di una dottrina. 3rd edn, Florence, 1911.

George, Henry, *Progress and Poverty: An Inquiry into the Causes of Industrial Depressions and of Increase of Want with Increase of Wealth. The Remedy*, New York, 1880.

Gissing, George. *Demos. A Story of English Socialism* (1886), Brighton, 1972.

The Nether World (1889), Brighton, 1974.

Goncourt, Edmond and Jules de, *Journal. Mémoires de la vie littéraire*, published under the direction of the Academy Goncourt, 22 vols., Monaco, 1956.

Goring, Charles. *On the Inheritance of the Diatheses of Phthisis and Insanity. A Statistical Study based upon the Family History of 1500 Criminals*. Drapers' Company Research Memoirs. Studies in National Deterioration, Department of Applied Mathematics, University College, London, London, 1909.

The English Convict. A Statistical Study, London, 1913.

Greenwood, James. *The Wilds of London*, London, 1874.,

Low Life Deeps. An Account of the Strange Fish to be Found There, London, 1876.

The Seven Curses of London, London, n.d.

Griesinger, Wilhelm, *Mental Pathology and Therapeutics*, a facsimile of the English translation of 1867, introduced by Erwin H. Ackerknecht, New York, 1965.

Griffiths, Arthur, *Report to the Secretary of State for the Home Department on the Proceedings of the Fourth Congress of Criminal Anthropology Held at Geneva in 1896*, London, 1896.

Haeckel, Ernst, *The Evolution of Man. A Popular Scientific Study*, translated by J. McCabe, 2 vols, London, 1906.

Haldane, J. B. S., *The Inequality of Man and Other Essays*, London, 1932.

Hardy, Thomas, *Late Lyrics and Earlier*, London, 1922.

Harvey, Charles, *The Biology of British Politics*, London, 1904.

Haussman, G. E., *Mémoires*. 2nd edn, 3 vols., Paris, 1890–3.

Haycraft, John Berry, *Darwinism and Race Progress*, London, 1895.

Headley, F. W., *Problems of Evolution*, London, 1900.

Hegel, Georg Wilhelm Friedrich, *Lectures on the Philosophy of World History* (1822–30), translated by H. B. Nisbet, introduced by D. Forbes, Cambridge, 1980 (1975).

Heron, David, *Mendelism and the Problem of Mental Defect: A Criticism of Recent Work*, London, 1913.

Hertwig, Oscar, *The Biological Problem of To-day. Preformation or Epigenesis? The Basis of a Theory of Organic Development*, translated by P. Chalmers Mitchell, London, 1896.

Hirsch, William, *Genie und Entartung*, Berlin, 1894.

Holmes, S. J., *Studies in Evolution and Eugenics*, London, 1923.

Horace, *The Odes, Epodes, Carmen Seculare, and the First Satire*, translated by C. Hughes, with the Latin text. London, 1867.

Huxley, Leonard, *Life and Letters of Thomas Henry Huxley*, 2 vols., London, 1900.

Huxley. T. H., *Social Diseases and Worse Remedies. Letters to The Times on Mr Booth's Scheme*, London, 1891.

Methods and Results. Essays, London, 1894.

Evolution and Ethics. Collected Essays, London, 1894, IX.

Huysmans, J.-K., *A Rebours* (1884), Paris, 1895.

Against Nature (1884), Harmondsworth, 1979.

Inter-Departmental Committee on Physical Deterioration, Report (1904), in *Reports from Commissioners, Inspectors and other Series*, 41 vols., XXXII.

Jackson, John Hughlings, 'Remarks on Dissolution of the Nervous System as Exemplified by Certain Post-Epileptic Conditions' (1881), in *Selected Writings*, edited by James Taylor, 2 vols., London, 1932, II, pp. 28.

'On Some Implications of Dissolution of the Nervous System' (1882), in *Selected Writings*, II, pp. 29–44.

'Evolution and Dissolution of the Nervous System' (1884), in *Selected Writings*, II, pp. 45–75.

'Remarks on Evolution and Dissolution of the Nervous System' (1887), in *Selected Writings*, II, pp. 76–91, 92–118.

Jefferies, John Richard, *After London* (1885), London, 1939.

Joyce, James, *Finnegans Wake*, London, 1939.

Kellor, Frances A., *Experimental Sociology Descriptive and Analytical*, New York, 1901.

Kingsley, Charles, *Sanitary and Social Lectures and Essays*, London, 1880.

Krafft-Ebing, R. V., *Psychopathia Sexualis with especial reference to antipathetic sexual instinct*, authorised English tr. of 10th German edn, tr. Francis J. Rebman, London, 1899.

Kurella, Hans, *Cesare Lombroso. A Modern Man of Science*, translated from the German by M. Eden Paul, London, 1911.

Labriola, Antonio, *Lettere a Engels*, Rome, 1949.

Lankester, Edwin Ray, *Degeneration. A Chapter in Darwinism*, London, 1880.

'Biology and the State', The President's Address to the Biological Section of the British Association (at Southport, 1883), published in Lankester, *The Advancement of Science*, London, 1890, pp. 63–117.

'Zoology', in *Encyclopaedia Britannica*, 11th edn, 1910–11, XXVIII, pp. 1,022–39.

Larousse, Pierre, *Grand Dictionnaire universel du XIXe siecle*, Paris, 1866–8.

Le Bon, Gustave, *Physiologie de la génération de l'homme et des principaux êtres vivants*, Paris, 1868.

　The Crowd. A Study of the Popular Mind (Paris, 1895), translated from the French, London, 1896.

　The Psychology of Socialism (Paris, 1898), translated from the French, London, 1899.

　La Révolution française et la psychologie des révolutions, Paris, 1912.

　The Psychology of Revolution, translated by Bernard Miall, London, 1913.

　The World Unbalanced (Paris, 1923), translated from the French, London, 1924.

Lee, Gerald Stanley, *Crowds. A Study of the Genius of Democracy and of the Fears, Desires and Expectations of the People*, London, 1913.

Legrain, M., *Hérédité et alcoolisme. Etude psychologique et clinique sur les dégénérés buveurs et les familles d'ivrognes*, Paris, 1889.

　Dégénérescence sociale et alcoolisme, Paris, 1895.

Lombroso, Cesare, *L'uomo bianco e l'uomo di colore. Letture sull'origine e le varietà delle razze umane*, Padua, 1871.

　L'uomo delinquente studiato in rapporto alla antropologia, alla medicina legale ed alle discipline carcerarie, Milan, 1876.

　Sull'incremento del delitto in Italia e sui mezzi per arrestarlo, Turin, 1879.

　Genio e follia in rapporto alla medicina legale, alla critica ed alla storia, Turin, 1882.

　Lettere politiche e polemiche sulla pellagra in Italia, Rome, 1885.

　Studi sull'ipnotismo, 2nd edn, Rome, 1886.

　Palimsesti del carcere. Raccolta unicamente destinata agli uomini di scienza, Turin, 1888.

　Pazzi ed anomali. Saggi, 2nd edn, Città di Castello, 1890.

　The Man of Genius, London, 1891.

　Gli anarchici, Turin, 1894.

　L'antisemitismo e le scienze moderne, Turin, 1894.

　L'Homme criminel, 2nd edn, 2 vols., Paris, 1895.

　Gli anarchici, 2nd edn, Turin, 1895.

　Grafologia, Milan, 1895.

　Genio e degenerazione. Nuovi studi e nuove battaglie, Milan–Palermo–Naples, n.d. [1897?].

　In Calabria (1862–1897) (1898), reprinted with an introduction by Pasquino Crupi, Studi Meridionali series, Reggio Calabria, 1973.

　Le Crime: causes et remèdes, Paris, 1899.

　Delitti vecchi e delitti nuovi, Turin, 1902.

　La perizia psichiatrico-legale, Turin, 1905.

　Ricerche sui fenomeni ipnotici e spiritici, Turin, 1909.

　After Death – What? Spiritistic Phenomena and their Interpretation, translated by William Sloane Kennedy, Boston, 1909.

　Crime: Its Causes and Remedies, translated by H. P. Horton. Modern Criminal Science series, Boston, 1911.

　Criminal Man According to the Classification of Cesare Lombroso, briefly summarised by his daughter Gina Lombroso Ferrero, with an introduction by Cesare Lombroso, New York, 1911.

Lombroso, Cesare, *L'uomo alienato. Trattato clinico sperimentale delle malattie mentali*, Turin, 1913.

La donna delinquente, la prostituta e la donna normale, 3rd edn, 1915.

Lombroso, Cesare *et al.*, *La vita italiana durante la rivoluzione francese e l'impero*, Milan, 1897.

Lombroso, Cesare and Ferrero, E. G., *La donna delinquente, la prostituta e la donna normale*, Turin, 1893.

Lombroso, Cesare and Ferrero G., *The Female Offender*, translated from the Italian, introduced by W. Douglas Morrison, London, 1895.

Lombroso, Cesare, Ferri, Enrico, Garofalo, R., and Fioretti G., *Polemica in difesa della scuola criminale positiva*, Bologna, 1886.

Lombroso, Cesare and Laschi, R., *Il delitto politico e le rivoluzioni*, Turin, 1890.

Lombroso, Gina, *The Soul of Woman: Reflections on Life*, London, 1924.

Lombroso, Paola and Carrara, Mario, *Nella penombra della civiltà. (Da un inchiesta sul pensiero del popolo)*, Turin, 1906.

Lombroso, Paola and Lombroso, Gina, *Cesare Lombroso. Appunti sulla vita*, Turin, 1906.

London, Jack, *The People of the Abyss*, London, 1903.

Lucas, Prosper, *Traité philosophique et physiologique de l'hérédité naturelle*: vol. I, Paris, 1847; vol. II, Paris, 1850.

Macaulay, Thomas Babington, *The History of England from the Accession of James the Second* (1849–55), 6 vols, London, 1913–15.

MacDonald, Arthur, *Emile Zola. A Study of his Personality with Illustrations*, Washington D.C., 1898.

McDougall, William, *The Group Mind. A Sketch of the Principles of Collective Psychology with some Attempt to Apply them to the Interpretation of National Life and Character* (1920), 2nd edn, Cambridge, 1927.

McKenzie, F. A., *Famishing London. A Study of the Unemployed and Unemployable*, London, 1903.

Mallock, W. H., *Classes and Masses or Wealth, Wages and Welfare in the U.K. A Handbook of Social Facts for Political Thinkers and Speakers*, London, 1896.

Manci, Filippo, *La folla. Studio di psicologia collettiva e di diritto penale*, Milan, 1924.

Mandalari, Lorenzo, *La degenerazione nella pazzia e nella criminalità*, Turin, 1901.

Martineau, Henri, *Le Roman scientifique d'Emile Zola*, Paris, 1907.

Marx, Karl, *Selected Writings*, edited by David McLellan, Oxford, 1977.

Marx, Karl and Engels, Friedrich, *The Holy Family or Critique of Critical Critique* (1844), Moscow, 1956.

Masterman, C. F. G., *The Condition of England* (1909), London, 1960.

Maudsley, Henry, *Annual Report* as resident medical superintendant at Manchester Royal Lunatic hospital (near Cheadle), 1858–9 and 1859–60.

The Physiology and Pathology of the Mind, London, 1867.

Body and Mind. An Inquiry into their Connection and Mutual Influence Especially in Reference to Mental Disorders. The Gulstonian Lectures, 1870, delivered at the Royal College of Physicians, London, 1870.

Responsibility in Mental Disease, London, 1874.

Introductory Lecture Given by the Professor of Medical Jurisprudence at UCL, London, 1876.

Body and Will, London, 1883.

'Lessons of Materialism', a lecture delivered before the Sunday Lecture Society, 6 April 1879, in *A Selection of Lectures*, published by the Sunday Lecture Society, fourth selection, London, 1886.

'The Physical Basis of Will', a lecture delivered before the Sunday Lecture Society, 15 February 1880, in *A Selection of Lectures*, London, 1886.

'Common Sources of Error in Seeing and Believing', a lecture delivered before the Sunday Lecture Society, 27 February 1881, in *A Selection of Lectures*, London, 1886.

The Pathology of Mind, London, 1895.

The Pathology of Mind (1895), introduced by Aubrey Lewis, London, 1979.

Life in Mind and Conduct: Studies of Organic in Human Nature, London, 1902.

Hereditary Variation and Genius with Essay on Shakespeare, London, 1908.

Organic to Human, Psychological and Sociological, London, 1916.

Religion and Realities, London, 1918.

Mearns, Andrew, *The Bitter Cry of Outcast London* (1883), edited and introduced by Anthony S. Wohl, Leicester, 1970.

Merrifield, F., 'Human Evolution in the Direction of Degeneration with Especial Reference to Prussianised Germany' (pamphlet reprinted with some additions from the *Sussex Daily News*, 13 January 1915), London, 1915.

Mill, John Stuart, *Correspondance inédite avec Gustav D'Eichthal*, Paris, 1898.

Mobac, Domingo, *Genio, scienza ed arte e il positivismo di Max Nordau*, Turin, 1899.

Möbius, Paul Julius, *Ueber Entartung*, Wiesbaden, 1900.

Moreau (de Tours), J. J., *La Psychologie morbide*, Paris, 1859.

Morel, B. A., *Etudes cliniques. Traité théorique et pratique des maladies mentales*, 2 vols., Paris, 1852.

Traité des dégénérescences physiques, intellectuelles et morales de l'espèce humaine, Paris, 1857.

Swedenborg: sa vie, ses écrits, et leur influence sur son siècle, ou coup d'oeil sur le délire religieux, Rouen, 1859.

Traité des maladies mentales, Paris, 1860.

Le Non-Restreint ou de l'abolition des moyens coercitifs dans le traitement de la folie, Paris, 1860.

De la Formation du type dans les variétés dégénérées ou nouveaux éléments d'anthropologie morbide, Paris, 1864.

Traité de la médecine légale des aliénés, Paris, 1866.

Morel. B. A. and Billiet, Alexis (Archbishop of Chambéry) *Influences de la constitution géologique du sol sur la production du crétinisme. Lettres de Mgr Alexis Billiet. Réponses de M. Le Dr Morel*, Paris, 1855.

Morrison, William Douglas, *Crime and its Causes*, London, 1891.

Morselli, Enrico, *Il magnetismo animale, la fascinazione e gli stati ipnotici*, 2nd edn, Turin, 1886.

Nazari, Giulio, *Il Prof. Cesare Lombroso e il valore scientifico delle sue opere*, Oderzo, 1887.

Niceforo, Alfredo, *L'Italia barbara contemporanea. Studi ed appunti*, Milan-Palermo, 1898.

La mala vita a Roma, Turin, 1898.

Niceforo, Alfredo, *Richerche sui contadini. Contribuito allo studio antropologico ed economico delle classi povere.* Milan-Palermo, n.d.
Italiani del Nord e Italiani del Sud, Turin, 1901.

Nicotri, Gaspare, *Rivoluzioni e rivolte in Sicilia. Studi di sociologia storica,* 3rd edn, Turin, 1910.

Nietzsche, Friedrich, *The Will to Power* (1888), in *The Complete Works,* edited by Oscar Levy, 18 vols, London, 1909–1910, xiv–xv.
The Twilight of the Idols (1889) in *The Complete Works,* xvi.
A Nietzsche Reader, selected and translated with an introduction by R. J. Hollingdale, Harmondsworth, 1981.

Nordau, Max, *De la Castration de la femme,* Paris, 1882.
Degeneration (1892), translated from the 2nd German edition, New York, 1895.
Conventional Lies of our Civilization, translated from the 7th German edn, London, 1895.

Ortega Y Gasset, José, *The Revolt of the Masses* (1930), authorised translation from the Spanish, London, 1932.

Ott, A., *Manuel d'histoire universelle,* 2 vols., Paris, 1840.

Parliamentary Papers, London, 1919, xxvi.

Pearson, Karl, *Mendelism and the Problem of Mental Defect,* London, 1914.
The Life, Letters and Labours of Francis Galton, 2 vols., Cambridge, 1924.

Penta, Pasquale, *Rare anomalie di un cranio di delinquente,* Rome, 1889.
Giovanni Passannante pazzo e gli errori giudiziarii in fatto di alienazioni mentali, 2nd edn, Naples, 1890.
Le degenerazioni criminali communicazione, Naples, 1890.

Plato, *The Republic,* translated by A. D. Lindsay, London, 1950 (1935).

Poe, Edgar Allan, 'The Murders in the Rue Morgue' (1841) and 'The Facts in the Case of M. Valdemar' (1845), in *Selected Writings.* Harmondsworth, 1982.

Problems in Eugenics. Papers Communicated to the First International Eugenics Congress (held at the University of London 24–30 July 1912), London, 1912.

Rádl, E., *The History of Biological Theories,* translated and adapted from the German by E. J. Hatfield, London, 1930.

Raubot, M., *De la Décadence de la France,* 2nd edn, Paris, 1850.

Renan, Ernest, *L'Avenir de la science. Pensées de 1848,* Paris, 1890.

Report of the Royal Commission on Alien Immigration with Minutes of Evidence and Appendix, 2 vols., London, 1903.

Report of the Royal Commission on the Poor Law, London, 1909.

Report from the Select Committee on Lunacy Law, Together with the Proceedings of the Committee. Minutes of Evidence and Appendix, London, 1877.

Report upon the Physical Examination of Men of Military Age, Parliamentary Papers, London, 1919, xxvi .

Ribot, Theodule, *Heredity. A Psychological Study of its Phenomena, Laws, Causes and Consequences,* translated from the French, London, 1875.

Ritchie, David G., *Darwinism and Politics,* London, 1889.

Robin, Paul, *Dégénérescence de l'espèce humaine, causes et remèdes, communication à la Société d'anthropologie,* Paris, 1896.

Rossi, Pasquale, *L'animo della folla,* Cosenza, 1898.

Rousseau, Jean-Jacques, *Emile* (1762), London, 1974.
Discourse on the Origin of Inequality (1755), Harmondsworth, 1984.

Ruskin, John, *Fors Clavigera*, in *The Complete Works* (1903–12), edited by E. T. Cook and Alexander Wedderburn, 39 vols., London, 1907, xxvii–xxix.

Russo, F. and Serao, E., *La Camorra*, Naples, 1907.

Schiller, F. C. S., *Social Decay and Eugenical Reform*, London, 1932.

Select Committee on Transportation, Parliamentary Papers, London, 1856, xvii.

Seeley, J. R., *The Expansion of England. Two Courses of Lectures*, London, 1883.

Sergi, G., *L'evoluzione umana individuale e sociale, fatti e pensieri*, Turin, 1904.

Sernicoli, E., *Gli attentati contro sovrani, principi, presidenti e primi ministri*, Milan, 1894.

Sernicoli, E., *L'anarchia e gli anarchici*, 2 vols., Milan, 1894.

Shaw, George Bernard, *Man and Superman. A Comedy and a Philosophy* (1903), Harmondsworth, 1982 (1946).

   The Sanity of Art: An Exposure of the Current Nonsense about Artists being Degenerate, London, 1908.

   Back to Methuselah. A Metabiological Pentateuch (1921), Harmondsworth, 1977 (1939).

Sighele, Scipio, *Il delitto politico*, Bologna, 1891.

   La folla delinquente, Turin, 1891.

   La teoria positiva della complicità, 2nd edn, 1894.

   La delinquenza settaria. Appunti di sociologia, Milan, 1897.

   La donna nova, Rome, 1898.

   'Le Crime collectif', in *Actes du cinquième congrès international d'anthropologie criminelle*, Amsterdam, 1901, pp. 68–78.

   L'intelligenza della folla, Turin, 1903.

   Letteratura tragica, Milan, 1906.

   Letteratura e sociologia. Saggi postumi, Milan, 1914.

   I delitti della folla, 5th edn, Turin, 1923.

Simms, J., *Physiognomy Illustrated*, New York, 1872.

Snow, E. C., *The Intensity of Natural Selection in Man*, preface by Karl Pearson, Drapers' Company Research Memoirs/Studies in National Deterioration vi, London, 1911.

Sorel, Georges, *Les Illusions du progrès* (1908), Paris, 1921.

   The Illusions of Progress (1908), translated by John and Charlotte Stanley, Berkeley, 1969.

   Reflexions on Violence (1908), authorised translation by T. E. Hulme, London, 1925.

   Réflexions sur la violence (1908), Paris, 1950.

Spencer, Herbert, *Life and Letters*, edited by David Duncan, 1908.

Spengler, Oswald, *The Decline of the West* (1918), London, 1934.

Stevenson, Robert Louis, *The Strange Case of Dr Jekyll and Mr Hyde* (1886), Harmondsworth, 1984.

   The Works, Skerryvore edn, London, 1926, xxviii.

Stoker, Bram, *Dracula* (1897). The World's Classics, Oxford, 1983.

   Famous Imposters, London, 1910.

Taine, H. A., *Les Origines de la France contemporaine. La Révolution*, 3 vols., Paris, 1878–85.

   The Revolution, 3 vols., translated by John Durand, London, 1878–85.

   History of English Literature (Paris, 1863), translated by H. Van Lawn, New York, 1870.

Taine, H. A., *Life and Letters of H. Taine*, translated by R. L. Devonshire and E. Sparvel-Barley, 3 vols., London, 1902–8.

Talbot, Eugene S., *Degeneracy: Its Causes, Signs and Results*. The Contemporary Science series, edited by Havelock Ellis, London, 1898.

Developmental Pathology. A Study in Degenerative Evolution, Edinburgh, 1921.

Tarde, Gabriel, *L'Opinion et la foule*, Paris, 1901.

Tayler, J. Lionel, *Social life and the Crowd*, London, 1923.

Tennyson, A., *The Poems of Tennyson*, edited by C. Ricks, London, 1969.

Thiers, L. A., *Discours parlementaires*, Paris, 1880, ix.

Thomson, J. Arthur, *The Bible of Nature* (The Bross Lectures 1907), New York, 1908.

The Gospel of Evolution, London, n.d.

The Great Biologists, London, 1932.

Thulie, H., *La Lutte contre la dégénérescence et la criminalité*, 2nd edn, Paris, 1912.

Tocqueville, Alexis de, *Recollections* (*Souvenirs*, 1893), translated by George Lawrence, London, 1970.

Tolstoy, Leo, *Resurrection* (1900), Harmondsworth, 1985 (1966).

Toulouse, Edouard, *Emile Zola. Enquête médico-psychologique sur la supériorité intellectuelle*, Paris, 1896.

Tressell, Robert, *The Ragged Trousered Philanthropists* (1914), London, 1987 (1965).

Trotter, Wilfred, *Instincts of the Herd in Peace and War*, London, 1916.

Tuke, D. Hack, *A Dictionary of Psychological Medicine*. 2 vols., London, 1892.

Turati, Filippo, *Il delitto e la questione sociale* (1883), in *Turatti giovane. Scapigliatura, positivismo, Marxismo*, edited by Luigi Cortesi, Milan, 1965, pp. 138–213.

Verce, Ettore Fornasari di, *La criminalità e le vicende economiche d'Italia dal 1873 al 1890*, preface by C. Lombroso, Turin, 1894.

Virchow, Rudolf, *Cellular Pathology as Based upon Physiological and Pathological Histology* (1859), London, 1959.

Wells, H. G., *Selected Short Stories*, Harmondsworth, 1982.

Whately, Richard, *On the Origin of Civilization. A Lecture by his Grace the Archbishop of Dublin to the Young Men's Christian Association*, London, 1855.

White, Arnold, *The Problems of a Great City*, London, 1886.

Efficiency and Empire (1901), edited and introduced by G. R. Searle, Society and Victorians series, xv, Brighton, 1973.

Wilde, Oscar, *The Works of Oscar Wilde*, ed. G. F. Maine, London, 1948.

The Picture of Dorian Gray (1890), Harmondsworth, 1982.

Wilson, Albert, *Unfinished Man. A Scientific Analysis of the Psychopath or Human Degenerate*, introductory preface by Arnold White, London, 1910.

Zocioli, Ettore, *L'anarchia: Gli agitatori – le idee – i fatti*, Turin, 1907.

Zola, Emile, *Le Roman expérimental*, Paris, 1880.

The Experimental Novel, in *Modern Continental Literary Criticism*, edited by O. B. Hardison, London, 1964.

L'Assommoir (Paris, 1877), translated and introduced by Leonard Tancock, Harmondsworth, 1984.

Nana (Paris, 1880), translated and introduced by George Holden, Harmondsworth, 1983.

Germinal (Paris, 1885), translated and introduced by Leonard Tancock, Harmondsworth, 1982.

The Earth (Paris, 1887), translated and introduced by Douglas Parmée, Harmondsworth, 1980.

La Bête humaine (Paris, 1890), translated and introduced by Leonard Tancock, Harmondsworth, 1977.

The Debacle (Paris, 1892), translated and introduced by Leonard Tancock, Harmondsworth, 1972.

Doctor Pascal, or Life and Heredity (Paris, 1893), translated by Ernest A. Vizetelly, London, 1893.

Periodicals/articles

Periodicals cited in the text but not listed here under specific authors/articles are listed under their general title. This applies in those cases where a journal is mentioned only in passing or where (as in the case of *The Lancet*) numerous miscellaneous items have been recorded in footnotes.

Allan, J. M., 'On the real differences in the minds of men and women', *Anthropological Review*, 7 (1869), cxcv-ccxvi.

Anderson, Elizabeth Garret, 'Sex in mind and education: a reply', *Fortnightly Review*, 15 (1874), 582–94.

Annales médico-psychologiques, 'Note sur un cas de dégénération ganglieuse des nerfs de la moelle épinière', 3 (1844), 126–7.

Annales Médico-Psychologiques, 'Mort de Morel', séance 31 March 1873, 293–4.

Archivio di psichiatria, antropologia criminale e scienza penale, Turin, 1880–.

Artom, E., 'Il conte di Cavour e la questione napoletana', *Nuova antologia*, 4th series, 94 (Nov–Dec 1901), 144–52.

Baillarger, M., 'Influence de la menstruation sur la transformation de la manie en délire aigu', *Annales médico-psychologiques*, 2 (1885), 46–9.

Ball, Benjamin, 'Les Frontières de la folie', *Revue scientifique de la France et de l'étranger*, no. 1, 1–5 (6 January 1883).

Ball, Robert S., 'How long can the earth sustain life?', *Fortnightly Review*, 51 (1892), 478–90.

Bedford, R. C., 'Urban populations', *Fortnightly Review*, 53 (1893), 388–93.

Blackwoods, 'Mobs', 153 (1893), 109–25.

Bouchereau, Gustave, and Magnan, Valentin, 'Statistique des malades entrés en 1870 et en 1871 au bureau d'admission des aliénés de la Seine', *Annales médico-psychologiques*, 8 (1872), 342–86.

Boule, Marcellin, 'La Guerre', *L'Anthropologie*, 25 (1914), 575–80.

Boutny, Emile, 'La Jeunesse de Taine', *Revue politique et littéraire. Revue bleue*, 18 (1902), 257–64.

Bridges, J. H., 'Influence of civilization on health', *Fortnightly Review*, 6 (1869), 140–61.

British and Foreign Medico-Chirurgical Review, 21 (1858); 49 (1872).

Buchez, P., 'Rapport fait à la société médico-psychologiques sur le *Traité des dégénérescences physiques, intellectuelles et morales de l'espèce humaine et des causes qui les produisent*', *Annales médico-psychologiques*, 3 (1857), 455–67.

Cobb, Frances Power, 'What is progress and are we progressing?', *Fortnightly Review*, 1 (1867), 357–70.

Corbet, W. J., 'The increase of insanity', *Fortnightly Review*, 53 (1893), 7–19; 59 (1896), 431–42.

Cullèrre, A., 'Les Difformités osseuses de la tête et la dégénérescence', *Annales médico-psychologiques*, 1 (1895), 52–61.

Le Décadent, 1 (1886).

Dickens, Charles, 'Idiots', *Household Words*, 7 (1853), 313–17.

Digby, E., 'The extinction of the Londoner', *Contemporary Review*, 86 (1904), 115–26.

Drapes, Thomas, 'Is insanity increasing?', *Fortnightly Review*, 60 (1896), 483–93.

The Economist, 'Progress in political, civil and religious freedom', 8 February 1851, 138–9.

Féré, Charles, 'L'Hérédité morbide', *Revue des deux mondes*, 126 (1894), 436–52.

Foard, Isabel, 'The criminal: is he produced by environment or atavism?', *Westminster Review*, 150 (1898), 90–103.

Forster, W. E., 'Disintegration', *Quarterly Review*, 156 (1883), 559–95.

Galton, Francis, 'Gregariousness in cattle and men', *Macmillan's Magazine*, 23 (1871), 353–7.

'Statistical inquiry into the efficacy of prayer', *Fortnightly Review*, 68 (1872), 125–35.

'The part of religion in human evolution', *The National Review*, 23 (1894), 755–63.

Geddes, Patrick, 'On the application of biology to economics', *Report of the Fifty Fifth Meeting of the British Association for the Advancement of Science*, 1886, 1,166–7.

Gentile, Giovanni, 'Cesare Lombroso e la scuola italiana di antropologia criminale', *La Critica*, Anno vii. Fasc. iv. (20 July 1909), 262–74.

Halipre, A., 'Morel', *La Revue médicale de Normandie*, 1 (1900), 58–61.

Hazeltine, M. W., 'Nordau's theory of degeneration', *North American Review*, 160 (1895), 743–52.

Hogarth, Janet E., 'Literary degenerates', *Fortnightly Review*, 57 (1895), 586–92.

Hospital, 'Souvenirs rétrospectifs de 1871', *Annales médico-psychologiques*, 13 (1875), 11–18.

Huxley, T. H., 'The scientific aspects of positivism', *Fortnightly Review*, 5 (1869), 653–70.

Ireland, W. M., 'Degeneration: a study in anthropology', *The International Monthly*, 1 (1900), 235–79.

The Lancet (miscellaneous items cited from 1839–1905).

Lasègue, C., 'Morel. Sa vie médicale et ses oeuvres'. *Archives générales de médecine*, 1 (1873), 589–600.

Lasègue, C., and Morel, B. A., 'Études historiques sur l'aliénation mentale. École Psychique Allemande – Stahl'. *Annales médico-psychologiques*, 3 (1844), 40–52; 'Etudes historiques sur l'alienation mentale. Ecole Psychique Allemande – Heinroth', *Annales médico-psychologiques*, 4 (1844), 1–10.

Le Bon, Gustave, 'Psychologie de la Révolution française', *Revue politique et littéraire. Revue bleue*, January–June 1912, 651–3.

Lee, Vernon (pseudonym of Violet Paget), 'Deterioration of soul', *Fortnightly Review*, 59 (1896), 928–43.

Lombroso, Cesare, 'Saggio sullo studio della republica romana' (*Collettore dell' Adige*, 1852), reprinted in Lombroso, *Laboratorio di Pavia* (bound collection of early papers), n.d., in the library of the Museum of Criminal Anthropology, Turin.

'Schizzi di un quadro storico dell'antico agricoltura in Italia', *Collettore*, 1853.

'Ricerche sul cretinismo in Lombardia. *Gazetta medica italiana*, 31 (1859).

'Studi per una geografia medica d'Italia', *Gazetta medica italiana*, series 5, vol. 4 (1865); reprinted in Lombroso, *Laboratorio di Pavia* (bound collection of early papers), n.d.

'The physical insensibility of women', *Fortnightly Review*, 51 (1892), 354–7.

Lunier, L., 'Influences des événements de 1870–1871 sur le mouvement de l'aliénation mentale en France. *Annales médico-psychologiques*, 8 (1872), 161–84.

'De L'Influence des grandes commotions politiques et sociales sur le développement des maladies mentales', *Annales médico-psychologiques*, 11 (1874), 2–59, 350–93.

Magnan, Valentin, remarks at meeting of Medico-Psychological Society, 27 July 1885, *Annales médico-psychologiques*, 3 (1886), 99.

'The degenerate', *American Journal of Insanity*, 52 (1895), 193–8.

Maudsley, Henry, 'On the correlation of mental and physical force: or man a part of nature', *Journal of Mental Science*, 6 (1860), 50–78.

'Sex in mind and education', *Fortnightly Review*, 15 (1874), 466–83.

'Heredity in health and disease', *Fortnightly Review*, 39 (1886), 648–59.

'Criminal responsibility in relation to insanity', *Journal of Mental Science*, 41 (Oct 1895), 657–65.

Morel, B. A., 'Pathologie mentale' series in *Annales médico-psychologiques*, 1845–7: 'En Belgique, en Hollande et en Allemagne', 6 (1845), 196–222 and 350–8; 'En Italie', 7 (1846), 45–83; 'En Italie, en Allemagne et en Suisse', 7 (1846), 168–80 and 363–87; 'En Belgique, en Allemagne, en Italie et en Suisse', 8 (1846), 18–41; 'En Angleterre', 10 (1847), 96–122.

'Rapport médico-légal sur l'état mental d'un aliéné homicide avec des considérations sur ce que l'on doit entendre par la monomanie homicide', republished extract from *L'Union médicale* (December 1852), Paris, 1853.

'An analysis of a treatise on the degenerations, physical, intellectual and moral of the human race, and the causes which produce their unhealthy varieties with notes and remarks by the translator Edwin Wing M.D.', *Medical Circular*. 10–12 (1857–8).

'Du Délire panophobique des aliénés gémisseurs: influence des événements de guerre sur la manifestation de cette forme de folie', *Annales médico-psychologiques*, 6 (1871), 321–67.

Motet, A., 'Éloge de Morel', *Annales médico-psychologiques*, 12 (1874), 85–111.

Peck, H. T., 'Degeneration and regeneration', *The Bookman*, 3 (1896), 403–7.

Reaney, George Sale, 'Outcast London', *Fortnightly Review*, 239 (1886), 687–95.

Remusat, Charles de, 'Du Pessimisme politique', *Revue des deux mondes*, 28 (1860), 730–43.

Revue blanche, 'Quelques Opinions sur l'oeuvre de H. Taine', 13 (1897), 263–95.

La Revue médical de Normandie, 'Éloge de Morel', 1 (1900), 45.

Rivista penale (first series, 1874–1929).

Saturday Review, 'Ticket-of-leave men', 14 (1862), 241–2.

Review of Nordau's *Paradoxes* and Nietzsche's *Thus spoke Zarathustra*, 82 (1896), 89–91.

La Scuola positiva (first series, 1891–1920).

Sorel, Georges, 'La Position du problème de M. Lombroso', *Revue scientifique*, 51 (1893), 206–10.

'La Crime politique d'après M. Lombroso', *Revue scientifique*, 51 (1893), 561–565.

'La Femme criminelle d'après M. Lombroso', *Revue scientifique*, 52 (1893), 463–7.

Spectator, 'The fear of mobs', 59 (1886), 218–19.

'The physical force of the mob', 62 (1889), 535–6.

'The control of crowds', 62 (1889), 756–7.

'The charm of crowds', 64 (1890), 756–7.

'The cowardice of crowds', 66 (1891), 376–7.

Sturt, Henry, review of Maudsley's *Life in Mind and Conduct*, *International Journal of Ethics*, 14 (1904), 257–8.

Toulouse, E., discussion of recent research on Zola. Séance, 29 March 1897, *Annales médico-psychologiques*, series 8, vol. 6 (1897), 119–31.

Vasto, P., 'Il contagio delittuoso nelle masse', *Rivista di discipline carcerarie*, 10 (1898), 481–93.

Wallace, Alfred R., Review of Lankester's *Degeneration*, *Nature*, 22 (1880), 142.

'Human selection', *Fortnightly Review*, 48 (1890), 325–37.

[? Wells, H. G.], 'The extinction of man', *Pall Mall Gazette* (25 September 1894), 3.

Wilson, H. Schultz, 'Carlyle and Taine on the French Revolution', *Gentleman's Magazine*, 274 (1894), 341–9.

Zimmern, Helen, 'Professor Lombroso's new theory of political crime', *Blackwood's Magazine*, 49 (1891), 202–11.

The Zoist. A Journal of Cerebral Physiology and Mesmerism (founded 1843, ceased publication 1856).

Secondary literature

Books

Ackerknecht, Erwin H., *A Short History of Psychiatry*, translated from the German by Sulammith Wolff, London, 1959.

Adorno, Theodor W., and Horkheimer, Max, *Dialectic of Enlightenment* (1944), translated by John Cumming, London, 1979.

Agulhon, Maurice, *Marianne into Battle. Republican Imagery and Symbolism in France, 1789–1880*, translated from the French by Janet Lloyd, Cambridge, 1981.

Agulhon, Maurice, *The Republican Experiment 1848–1852*, translated from the French by Janet Lloyd, Cambridge, 1983.

Allen, Francis A., 'Raffaele Garofalo', in *Pioneers in Criminology*, edited and introduced by H. Mannheim, London, 1960, pp. 254–76.

Allum, Peter A., *Italy – Republic without Government?*, London, 1973.

Altavilla, E. *et al.*, *Enrico Ferri e la scienza penale italiana*, Quaderni di criminalità series, edited by Anselmo Crisafulli, Milan, 1940–3.

Andreucci, Franco, and Detti, T., 'Enrico Ferri', *Il movimento operaio italiano. Dizionario biografico 1853–1943*, Rome, 1976, II, pp. 342–6.

Anzieu, Didier, *Freud's Self-Analysis*. The International Psychoanalytic Library, translated from the French by Peter Graham, London, 1986.

Asor Rosa, Alberto, 'La cultura', *Storia d'Italia*, Turin, 1975, IV, pt. 2.

Avineri, Shlomo, *The Making of Modern Zionism. The Intellectual Origins of the Jewish State*, London, 1981.

Babini, V. P., Cotti, M., Minuz F., Tagliavini A., *Tra sapere e potere. La psichiatria italiana nella seconda metà dell'ottocento*. Bologna, 1982.

Babini, V. P., Minuz F., Tagliavini A., *La donna nelle scienze dell'uomo. Immagini scientifiche del femminile nella cultura italiana di fine secolo*, Milan, 1986.

Baker, Keith Michael, *Condorcet. From Natural Philosophy to Social Mathematics*, Chicago, 1975.

Baldick, Robert (editor and translator), *Pages from the Goncourt Journal*, Oxford, 1978.

Barrows, Susanna, *Distorting Mirrors. Visions of the Crowd in Late Nineteenth-Century France*, New Haven and London, 1981.

Barthes, Roland, 'Textual analysis of Poe's "Valdemar"', in *Untying the Text. A Post-Structuralist Reader*, edited by Robert Young, London, 1981, pp. 133–61.

Beer, Gillian, *Darwin's Plots, Evolutionary Narrative in Darwin, George Eliot and Nineteenth-Century Fiction*, London, 1983.

'Darwin's Reading and the Fictions of Development', in *The Darwinian Heritage*, edited by David Kohn, Princeton, 1986, pp. 543–88.

Bellamy, Richard, *Modern Italian Social Theory. Ideology and Politics*, Cambridge, 1987.

Benjamin, Walter, *Charles Baudelaire. A Lyric Poet in the Era of High Capitalism*, London, 1973.

Bergonzi, Bernard (ed.), *H. G. Wells. A Collection of Critical Essays*. Twentieth Century Views series (general editor Maynard Mack), New Jersey, 1976.

Blackbourn, David and Elie, Geoff, *The Peculiarities of German History. Bourgeois Society and Politics in Nineteenth-Century Germany*, Oxford, 1984.

Bleuel, Hans Peter, *Strength through Joy. Sex and Society in Nazi Germany*, translated from the German by J. Maxwell Brownjohn, London, 1973.

Blok, Anton, *The Mafia of a Sicilian Village, 1860–1960. A Study of Violent Peasant Enterpreneurs*, Oxford, 1974.

Bolt, Christine, *Victorian Attitudes to Race*, London, 1971.

Borie, Jean, *Zola et les mythes ou de la nausée au salut*, Paris, 1971.

Mythologies de l'hérédité au XIXe siècle, Paris, 1981.

Bosworth, Richard, *Italy and the Approach of the First World War*, London, 1983.

Bowler, Peter J., *Theories of Human Evolution. A Century of Debate, 1844–1944*, Oxford, 1986.

Brantlinger, Patrick, *Bread and Circuses. Theories of Mass Culture as Social Decay*, Ithaca, 1983.

Briggs, Asa, 'The Language of "Mass" and "Masses" in Nineteenth-Century England', in *Ideology and the Labour Movement. Essays Presented to John Saville*, edited by David E. Martin and David Rubinstein, London, 1979, pp. 62–83.

Brush, Stephen, *The Temperature of History. Phases of Science and Culture in the Nineteenth-Century*, New York, 1978.

Bulferetti, Luigi, *Le ideologie socialistiche in Italia nell'età del positivismo evoluzionistico (1870–1892)*, Florence, 1951.
Lombroso, Turin, 1975.

Burrow, J. W., *A Liberal Descent. Victorian Historians and the English Past*, Cambridge, 1981.

Bury, J. B., *The Idea of Progress. An Inquiry into its Growth and Origin* (1920), New York, 1955.

Butler, Rohan D'Olier, *The Roots of National Socialism, 1783–1933* (1941), New York, 1968.

Bynum, W. F., Porter, R. and Shepherd, M. (eds.), *The Anatomy of Madness. Essays in the History of Psychiatry*, 3 vols., London, 1985–8.

Calò, Emmanuele, *Enrico Ferri. Discorso pronunciato in occasione delle onoranze ad Enrico Ferri nel 50° anniversario della morte*, Mantua, 1979.

Castella, Gaston, *Buchez historien. Sa théorie du progrès dans la philosophie de l'histoire*, Fribourg, 1909.

Cecchi, Orfeo, *Un maestro dimenticato. Nel decimo anniversario della morte di Enrico Ferri*, repr. from the journal *Responsibilità civile e previdenza*, Milan, 1937.

Charlton, D. G., *Positivist Thought in France during the Second Empire 1852–1870*, Oxford, 1959.

Chase, Allan, *The Legacy of Malthus. The Social Costs of the New Scientific Racism*, Urbana, 1980.

Chevalier, Louis, *Labouring Classes and Dangerous Classes in Paris During the First Half of the Nineteenth Century* (Paris, 1958), translated from the French by Frank Jellinek, London, 1973.

Clark, Linda L., *Social Darwinism in France*, Alabama, 1984.

Clark, Martin, *Modern Italy 1871–1982*, London, 1984.

Clarke, Michael, 'The Rejection of Psychological Approaches to Mental Disorder in Late-Nineteenth-Century British Psychiatry', in *Madhouses, Mad-Doctors and Madmen. The Social History of Psychiatry in the Victorian Era*, edited by Andrew Scull, London, 1981, pp. 271–312.

Coleman, William, *Death is a Social Disease. Public Health Policy and Political Economy in Early Industrial France*, Madison, 1982.

Collie, Michael, *Henry Maudsley: Victorian Psychiatrist. A Bibliographical Study*, Winchester, 1988.

Collin, Fernand, *Enrico Ferri et l'avant projet de code penal italien de 1921*, Brussels, 1925.

Collini, Stefan, *Liberalism and Sociology. L. T. Hobhouse and Political Argument in England*, Cambridge, 1979.

Colombo, Giorgio, *La scienza infelice. Il Museo di Antropologia Criminale di Cesare Lombroso*, Turin, 1975.

Colp, R. Jnr., *To Be an Invalid: The Illness of Charles Darwin*, Chicago, 1977.

Conry, Yvette, *L'Introduction du Darwinisme en France au XIXe siècle*, Paris, 1974.

Corsi, P. and Weindling P., 'Darwinism in Germany, France and Italy', in *The Darwinian Heritage*, edited by D. Kohn, Princeton, 1986, pp. 683–729.

Cosmacini, Giorgio, 'Problemi medico-biologici e concezione materialistica nella seconda metà dell'ottocento', *Scienza e tecnica*, edited by Gianni Micheli, *Storia d'Italia*, Annali 3, Turin 1980, pp. 815–61.

Curtis, Michael, *Three Against the Third Republic. Sorel, Barrès and Maurras*, Princeton, 1959.

Curtis, L. Perry, *Apes and Angels. The Irishman in Victorian Caricature*, New York and Newton Abbot, 1971.

Cuvillier, Armand, *P. J. B. Buchez et les origines du socialisme chretien*, Paris, 1948.

Dansette, Adrien, *Religious History of Modern France*, translated from the French by John Dingle, 2 vols, London, 1961.

Davis, Jennifer, 'The London Garotting Panic of 1862. A Moral Panic and the Creation of a Criminal Class in Mid-Victorian England', in *Crime and the Law: The Social History of Crime in Western Europe since 1500*, edited by V. A. C. Gatrell, Bruce Lenman and Geoffrey Parker, The European Social History of Human Experience series, London, 1980, pp. 190–213.

De Peri, Francesco, 'Il medico e il folle: istituzione psichiatrica, sapere scientifico e pensiero medico fra otto e novecento', *Storia d'Italia*, Annali 7, Turin, 1984, pp. 1,059–140.

Derrida, Jacques, *Dissemination*, translated with an introduction by Barbara Johnson, London, 1981.

Dewhurst, Kenneth, *Hughlings Jackson on Psychiatry*, Oxford, 1982.

Didi-Huberman, Georges, *Invention de l'hystérie. Charcot et l'iconographie photographique de la Salpêtrière*, Paris, 1982.

Digeon, Claude, *La Crise allemande de la pensée française (1870–1914)*, Paris, 1959.

Doerner, Klaus, *Madmen and the Bourgeoisie. A Social History of Insanity and Psychiatry* (1969), translated by Joachim Neugroschel and Jean Steinberg, Oxford, 1981.

Donzelot, Jacques, *The Policing of Families*, translated from the French by Robert Hurley, London, 1979.

Douglas, Mary, *Purity and Danger. An Analysis of Concepts of Purity and Danger*, London, 1966.

Dowbiggin, Ian, 'Degeneration and Hereditarianism in French Mental Medicine, 1840–90: Psychiatric Theory as Ideological Adaptation', in W. F. Bynum, Roy Porter and Michael Shepherd (eds.), *The Anatomy of Madness. Essays in the History of Psychiatry*, 3 vols, Tavistock, 1985–8, i, ch. 8, pp. 188–232.

Drescher, Seymour *et al.* (eds.), *Political Symbolism in Modern Europe. Essays in Honour of George L. Mosse*, New Brunswick, 1982.

Driver, C. H., 'Walter Bagehot and the Social Psychologists', in *The Social and Political Ideas of some Representative Thinkers of the Victorian Age,* edited by F. J. C. Hearnshaw, London, 1933, pp. 194–221.

Driver, Edwin D., 'Charles Buckman Goring', in *Pioneers in Criminology*, edited by H. Mannheim, London, 1960, pp. 335–48.

Durant, John R. (ed.), *Darwinism and Divinity*, Oxford, 1985.

Dwork, Deborah, *War is Good for Babies and other Young Children. A History of the Infant and Child Welfare Movement in England 1898–1918*, London, 1987.

Edwards, Owen Dudley, *The Quest for Sherlock Holmes. A Biographical Study of Sir Arthur Conan Doyle*, Harmondsworth, 1983.

Eley, Geoff, *From Unification to Nazism. Reinterpreting the German Past*, Boston, 1986.

Ellenberger, Henri F., *The Discovery of the Unconscious. The History and Evolution of Dynamic Psychiatry*, New York, 1970.

Eyler, John M., *Victorian Social Medicine. The Ideas and Methods of William Farr*, Baltimore and London, 1979.

Fabian, Johannes, *Time and the Other. How Anthropology Makes its Object*, New York, 1983.

Farolfi, Bernardino, 'Antropometria militare e antropologia della devianza (1876–1908)', *Malattia e medicina, Storia d'Italia*, Annali 7, edited by Franco Della Peruta, Turin, 1984, pp. 1,181–219.

Feldman, David, 'The Importance of Being English: Social Policy, Patriotism and Politics in Response to Jewish Immigration', in *Between Neighbourhood and Nation. Histories and Representations of London since 1800*, edited by D. Feldman and G. Stedman Jones, forthcoming.

Forrest, D. W., *Francis Galton. The Life and Work of a Victorian Genius*, London, 1974.

Foucault, Michel, *Discipline and Punish*, Harmondsworth, 1977.

  Power/Knowledge: Selected Interviews and Other Writings 1972–1977, edited by Colin Gordon, New York, 1980.

Freeden, Michael, *The New Liberalism. An Ideology of Social Reform*, Oxford, 1978.

Furet, F., *Interpreting the French Revolution*, Cambridge, 1978.

Gallini, Clara, *La sonnambula meravigliosa. Magnetismo e ipnotismo nell'ottocento italiano*, Milan, 1983.

Garbari, Maria, *L'età giolittiana nelle lettere di Scipio Sighele*, Trent, 1977.

Garland, David, *Punishment and Welfare. A History of Penal Strategies*, London, 1985.

Gasman, Daniel, *The Scientific Origins of National Socialism. Social Darwinism in Ernest Haeckel and the German Monist League*, London, 1971.

Gay, Peter, *The Bourgeois Experience. Victoria to Freud*; vol. 1, *Education of the Senses*, Oxford, 1984.

  Freud: A Life for our Time, London, 1988.

Genil-Perrin, Georges Paul Henri, *Histoire des origines et de l'évolution de l'idée de dégénérescence en médecine mentale*, Paris, 1913.

George, Wilma, *Darwin*, London, 1982.

Giacobini, Giacomo and Panattoni, Gian Luigi (eds.), *Il Darwinismo in Italia. Filippo De Filippi, Michele Lessona, Paolo Mantegazza, Giovanni Canestrini*, Turin, 1983.

Gibaudan, René, *Les Idées sociales de Taine*, Paris, 1928.

Gilman, Sander, *Seeing the Insane*, New York, 1982.

  On Blackness without Blacks. Essays on the Image of the Black in Germany, Boston, 1982.

  Difference and Pathology. Stereotypes of Sexuality, Race, and Madness, Ithaca, 1985.

Gilman, Sander and Chamberlin, J. Edwards (eds.), *Degeneration. The Dark Side of Progress*, New York, 1985.

Glaser, Hermann, *The Cultural Roots of National Socialism*, London, 1978.

Glick, Thomas F. (ed.), *The Comparative Reception of Darwinism*, Austin, Texas, 1972.

Goldstein, Jan, *Console and Classify. The French Psychiatric Profession in the Nineteenth Century*, Cambridge, 1987.

Gould, S. J., *Ontogeny and Phylogeny*, Cambridge, Mass., 1977.
The Mismeasure of Man, London, 1981.

Granet, Michel, *Le Temps trouvé par Zola dans son roman le Docteur Pascal*, Paris, 1980.

Grosskurth, Phyllis, *Havelock Ellis. A Biography*, London, 1980.

Gruber, Howard E., *Darwin on Man. A Psychological Study of Scientific Creativity together with Darwin's Early and Unpublished Notebooks*, London, 1974.

Grupp, Stanley E. (ed.), *The Positive School of Criminology. Three Lectures by Enrico Ferri*, Pittsburgh, 1968.

Haley, Bruce, *The Healthy Body and Victorian Culture*, Cambridge, Mass., 1978.

Haller, Mark H., *Eugenics: Hereditarian Attitudes in American Thought*, New Brunswick, 1963.

Hamburger, Joseph, *Macaulay and the Whig Tradition*, Chicago, 1976.

Harris, José, *Unemployment and Politics: A Study in English Social Policy 1886–1914*, Oxford, 1972.

Harris, Ruth, 'Murder under Hypnosis in the Case of Gabrielle Bompard: Psychiatry in the Courtroom in Belle Époque Paris', in *The Anatomy of Madness*, edited by Bynum, Porter and Shepherd, London, 1985, ii, ch. 10.

Harrison, Ross, *Bentham*, The Arguments of the Philosophers series (edited by Ted Honderich), London, 1983.

Heath, Stephen, *The Sexual Fix*, London, 1982.

Hertz, Neil, *The End of the Line. Essays on Psychoanalysis and the Sublime*, New York, 1985.

Hilleges, Mark R., *The Future as Nightmare. H. G. Wells and the Anti-Utopians*, New York, 1967.

Himmelfarb, Gertrude, *Victorian Minds* (1952), London, 1968.
Darwin and the Darwinian Revolution, London, 1959.

Hirst, Paul Q., *Durkheim, Bernard and Epistemology*, London, 1975.

Hobsbawm, Eric, 'Dr Marx and the Victorian Critics', in *Labouring Men. Studies in the History of Labour*, London, 1964.
Bandits, Harmondsworth, 1969.

Hofstadter, Richard, *Social Darwinism in American Thought* (1944); revised edition, New York, 1955.

Houghton, Walter E., *The Victorian Frame of Mind 1830–1870*, New Haven, 1957.

Hughes, H. Stuart, *Consciousness and Society. The Reorientation of European Social Thought 1890–1930*, London, 1958.

Hulin, Jean-Paul and Coustillas, Pierre (eds.), *Victorian Writers and the City*, Lille, 1979.

Hunter, Allan, *Joseph Conrad and the Ethics of Darwinism*, The Challenges of Science series, London, 1983.

Isambert, François-André, *De la Charbonnerie au Saint-Simonisme. Étude sur la jeunesse de Buchez*, Paris, 1966.

Jean-Aubry, G., *Joseph Conrad. Life and Letters*, 2 vols, London, 1927.

Jennings, J. R., *Georges Sorel. The Character and Development of his Thought*, foreword by Theodore Zeldin, London, 1985.

Joll, James, *The Anarchists*, London, 1964.

Jones, Ernest, *Sigmund Freud. Life and Work*, 3 vols, London, 1953–7.

Jones, Greta, *Social Darwinism and English Thought*, Brighton, 1980.

Jones, R. A., 'Taine and the Nationalists', in *The Social and Political Ideas of some Representative Thinkers of the Victorian Age*, edited by Hearnshaw, London, 1933, pp. 222–50.

Jordanova, L. L., *Lamarck*, Oxford, 1984.

Keating, Peter (ed.), *Into Unknown England, 1866–1913: Selections from the Social Explorers*, London, 1976.

Kellner, Sven, '"*Le Docteur Pascal*" de Zola: rétrospective des Rougon-Macquart, livre de documents*, Lund, Sweden, 1980.

Kemp, Peter, *H. G. Wells and the Culminating Ape*, London, 1982.

Kevles, Daniel J., *In the Name of Eugenics. Genetics and the Uses of Human Heredity*, Harmondsworth, 1986.

Kohn, David (ed.), *The Darwinian Heritage*, Princeton, 1986.

Kolakowski, Leszek, *Bergson*, Oxford, 1985.

Landucci, Giovanni, 'Darwinismo e nazionalismo', *La cultura italiana tra '800 e '900 e le origini del nazionalismo*, Biblioteca dell'archivio storico italiano, XXII, Florence, 1981, pp. 103–87.

Landolfi, Enrico, *Scipio Sighele. Un Giobertiano tra democrazia nazionale e socialismo tricolore*, Rome, 1981.

Lea, F. A., *The Tragic Philosopher. A Study of Friedrich Nietzsche*, London, 1957.

Leith, James (ed.), *Images of the Commune*, Montreal, 1978.

Leonard, Jacques, *La Médecine entre les savoirs et les pouvoirs. Histoire intellectuelle et politique de la médecine française au XIXe siècle*, Paris, 1981.

Leroy, Maxime, *Histoire des idées sociales en France*, new edn, 3 vols, Paris, 1946–54.

Levra, Umberto (ed.), *La scienza e la colpa. Crimini criminali criminolgi: un volto dell'ottocento*, Milan, 1985.

Lidsky, Paul, *Les Écrivains contre la Commune*, Paris, 1970.

Lifton, Robert J., *The Nazi Doctors: Medical Killing and the Psychology of Genocide*, London, 1986.

Lukes, Steven, *Emile Durkheim: His Life and Work. A Historical and Critical Study*, London, 1973.

McClelland, J. S., *The French Right from De Maistre to Maurras*, London, 1970.

McGovern, William, *From Luther to Hitler. The History of Fascist-Nazi Political Philosophy*, Cambridge, Mass., 1941.

Macintyre, Stuart, *A Proletarian Science. Marxism in Britain 1917–1931*, Cambridge, 1980.

Mackenzie, Donald A., *Statistics in Britain 1865–1930*, Edinburgh, 1981.

Mack Smith, Denis, *Italy. A Modern History* (1959) new revised edition, London, 1969.

    Victor Emanuel, Cavour and the Risorgimento, London, 1971.

Manuel, Frank E., *The Prophets of Paris*, Cambridge, Mass., 1962.

Martin, Kingsley, *French Liberal Thought in the Eighteenth Century. A Study of Political Ideas from Bayle to Condorcet* (1929), edited by J. P. Mayer, London, 1962.

Millar, Ronald, *The Piltdown Man. A Case of Archaeological Fraud*, St Albans, 1974.

Minuz, Fernanda, 'Gli intellettuali socialisti e la scienza', in N. Urbinati *et al.*, *Studi sulla cultura filosofica italiana fra ottocento e novecento*, Bologna, 1982, pp. 223–51.

Mola, Aldo A., *L'imperialismo italiano. La politica estera dall'unita al fascismo*, Rome, 1980.

Monachesi, Elio, 'Cesare Beccaria', in *Pioneers in Criminology*, edited by H. Mannheim, London, 1960, pp. 36–50.

Morton, Peter, *The Vital Science. Biology and the Literary Imagination, 1860–1900*, London, 1984.

Moscovici, Serge, *L'Âge des foules: un traité historique de psychologie des masses*, Paris, 1981.

Mosse, George, *The Crisis of German Ideology. Intellectual Origins of the Third Reich*, London, 1964.

Mosse, George L., *Toward the Final Solution. A History of European Racism*, London, 1979.

Mucchi, Faina A., *L'abbraccio della folla. Cento anni di psicologia collettiva*, Bologna, 1983.

New Catholic Encyclopaedia, 15 vols, New York, 1967.

Nicasi, Stefania, 'Il germe della follia. Modelli di malattia mentale nella psichiatria italiana di fine ottocento' in *L'età del positivismo*, edited by Paolo Rossi, Bologna, 1986, pp. 309–32.

Nisbet, Robert, *History of the Idea of Progress*, London, 1980.

Noakes, Jeremy, 'Nazism and Eugenics: The Background to the Nazi Sterilisation Law of 14 July 1933', in *Ideas into Politics. Aspects of European History 1880–1950*, edited by R. J. Bullen *et al.*, London, 1984.

Nora, Pierre (ed.), *Les Lieux de mémoire*, Paris, 1984–.

Nouvelle Biographie generale, Paris, 1855.

Nye, Robert A., *The Origins of Crowd Psychology. Gustave Le Bon and the Crisis of Mass Democracy in the Third Republic*, Studies in Twentieth Century History series, London, 1975.

  The Anti-Democratic Sources of Elite Theory: Pareto, Mosca, Michels, Contemporary Political Sociology series, edited by Richard Rose, London, 1977.

  'Degeneration and the Medical Model of Cultural Crisis', in *Political Symbolism in Modern Europe*, edited by Seymour Drescher *et al.*, New Brunswick, 1982, pp. 19–41.

  Crime, Madness and Politics in Modern France. The Medical Concept of National Decline, Princeton, 1984.

Offer, Avner, *Property and Politics 1870–1914. Landownership, Law, Ideology and Urban Development in England*, Cambridge, 1981.

O'Hanlon, Redmond, *Joseph Conrad and Charles Darwin. The Influence of Scientific Thought on Conrad's Fiction*, Edinburgh, 1984.

Olmsted, J. M. D. and Olmsted, E. Harris, *Claude Bernard and the Experimental Method in Medicine*, New York, 1952.

Oxford English Dictionary, 1933.

Pancaldi, Giuliano, 'Darwinismo ed evoluzionismo in Italia 1860–1900', *Charles Darwin: 'storia' ed 'economia' della natura*, Florence, 1977, pp. 161–206.

  Darwin in Italia. Impresa scientifica e frontiere culturali, Bologna, 1983.

Paul, Harry W., 'Religion and Darwinism. Varieties of Catholic Reaction', in *The*

Comparative Reception of Darwinism, edited by Thomas Glick, Austin, Texas, 1972, pp. 403–36.

Pearson, Geoffrey, *Hooligan. A History of Respectable Fears*, London, 1983.

Peel, J. D. Y., *Herbert Spencer. The Evolution of a Sociologist*, London, 1971.

Petri, Barbara, *The Historical Thought of P.-J.-B. Buchez*, Washington D. C., 1958.

Pogliano, Claudio, 'L'utopia igienista (1870–1920)', in *Malattia e medicina*, edited by Franco Della Peruta, *Storia d'Italia*, Annali 7, Turin, 1984, pp. 589–631.

Poliakov, L., *The Aryan Myth. A History of Racist and Nationalist Ideas in Europe*, translated by E. Howard, London, 1974.

Pollard, Sidney, *The Idea of Progress. History and Society*, Harmondsworth, 1968.

Popper, Karl, *The Open Society and its Enemies* (1945), 2 vols, London, 1952.

Praz, Mario, *The Romantic Agony* (1933), translated from the Italian by Angus Davison, Oxford, 1951.

Preti, Luigi, *I miti dell'impero e della razza nell'Italia degli anni '30*, Rome, 1965.

Procter, Robert N., *Racial Hygiene: Medicine under the Nazis*, Cambridge, Mass., 1988.

Radzinowicz, Leon and Hood, Roger, *A History of English Criminal Law*, vol. 5, *The Emergence of Penal Policy*, London, 1986.

Rée, Johnathan, *Proletarian Philosophers. Problems in Socialist Culture 1900–1940*, Oxford, 1984.

Ronsin, Francis, *La Grève des ventres. Propagande neo-malthusienne et baisse de la natalité française*, Paris, 1980.

Rose, Jacqueline, *Sexuality in the Field of Vision*, London, 1986.

Rose, Stephen, Kamin, Leon J., Lewontin, R. C., *Not in our Genes. Biology, Ideology and Human Nature*, Harmondsworth, 1984.

Rossi, Paolo (ed.), *L'età del positivismo*, Bologna, 1986.

Said, Edward, *Orientalism*, New York, 1978.

Salomone, A. William, *Italian Democracy in the Making. The Political Scene in the Giolittian Era 1900–1914*, Philadelphia, 1945.

Salvadori, Massimo L., *Il mito del buongoverno. La questione meriodionale da Cavour a Gramsci*, Turin, 1963.

Sasso, Gennaro, *Tramonto di un mito. L'idea di 'progresso' fra ottocento e novecento*, Bologna, 1984.

Schiller, Francis, *Paul Broca: Founder of French Anthropology, Explorer of the Brain*, Berkeley and Los Angeles, 1979.

Schoenberner, Gerhard (ed.), *Artists against Hitler. Persecution, Exile, Resistance*, Bonn, 1984.

Schorske, Carl E., *Fin-de-siècle Vienna. Politics and Culture* (1961), Cambridge, 1981.

Scott, Peter, 'Henry Maudsley', in *Pioneers in Criminology*, edited by H. Mannheim, London, 1960, pp. 144–67.

Searle, G. R., *The Quest for National Efficiency. A Study in British Politics and Political Thought 1899–1914*, Oxford, 1971.

Eugenics and Politics in Britain 1900–1914, Science in History series, Leyden, 1976.

'Critics of Edwardian Society: The Case of the Radical Right', in *The Edward Age: Conflict and Stability 1900–1914*, edited by Alan O'Day, London, 1979, pp. 79–96.

'Eugenics and Class', in *Biology, Medicine and Society 1840–1940*, edited by Charles Webster, Cambridge, 1981, pp. 217–42.

Sellin, Thorsten, 'Enrico Ferri', in *Pioneers in Criminology*, edited by H. Mannheim, London, 1960, pp. 277–300.

Semmel, Bernard, *Imperialism and Social Reform. English Social–Imperial Thought 1895–1914*, London, 1960.

The Governor Eyre Controversy, London, 1962.

Seton-Watson, Christopher, *Italy from Liberalism to Fascism 1870–1925*, London, 1967.

Showalter, Elaine, 'Victorian Women and Insanity', in *Madhouses, Mad-Doctors and Madmen. The Social History of Psychiatry in the Victorian Era*, edited by A. Scull, London, 1981, pp. 313–36.

The Female Madness. Women, Madness and English Culture, New York, 1985.

Simon, Walter M., *European Positivism in the Nineteenth Century*, Ithaca, 1963.

Sinai, I. Robert, *The Decadence of the Modern World*, Cambridge, Mass., 1978.

Skultans, Vieda, *Madness and Morals, Ideas on Insanity in the Nineteenth Century*, London, 1975.

Smith, F. B., 'Health', in *The Working Class in England 1875–1914*, edited by John Benson, London, 1985, pp. 36–62.

Smith, Paul (ed.), *Lord Salisbury on Politics. A Selection from his Articles in the Quarterly Review, 1860–1883*, Cambridge, 1972.

Smith, Roger, *Trial by Medicine. Insanity and Responsibility in Victorian Trials*, Edinburgh, 1981.

Smith, Woodruff D., *The Ideological Origins of Nazi Imperialism*, Oxford, 1986.

Soffer, Reba N., *Ethics and Society in England. The Revolution in the Social Sciences 1870–1914*, Berkeley and Los Angeles, 1978.

Soloway, Richard Allen, 'Feminism, Fertility and Eugenics in Victorian and Edwardian England', in *Political Symbolism in Modern Europe*, edited by Seymour Drescher *et al.*, New Brunswick, 1982, pp. 121–45.

Soltau, Roger, *French Political Thought in the Nineteenth Century*, London, 1931.

Spirito, Ugo, *Storia del diritto penale italiano da Cesare Beccaria ai nostri giorni*, 2nd edn, Turin, 1932.

Stedman Jones, Gareth, *Outcast London. A Study in the Relationship Between Classes in Victorian Society* (1971). Harmondsworth, 1984.

Languages of Class. Studies in English Working-Class History 1832–1982, Cambridge, 1983.

Steiner, George, *The Death of Tragedy* (1961), Oxford, 1982.

On Difficulty and other Essays, Oxford, 1980.

Stepan, Nancy, *The Idea of Race in Science: Britain, 1800–1960*, London, 1982.

Stocking, George W. Jnr., *Race, Culture and Evolution*, New York, 1968.

Stone, Martin, 'Shellshock and the Psychologists', in *The Anatomy of Madness*, edited by Bynum, Porter and Shepherd, London, 1985, ii, pp. 242–71.

Stone, Norman, *Europe Transformed 1878–1919*, Fontana History of Europe series, Glasgow, 1983.

Sulloway, Frank J., *Freud, Biologist of the Mind. Beyond the Psychoanalytic Legend*, New York, 1979.

Sutherland, Gillian, in collaboration with Stephen Sharp, *Ability, Merit and Measurement. Mental Testing and English Education 1880–1940*, Oxford, 1984.

Swart, Koenraad W., *The Sense of Decadence in Nineteenth-Century France*, The Hague, 1964.

Taylor, Ian, Young, Jock and Walton, Paul, *The New Criminology: For a Social Theory of Deviance*, London, 1973.

Ternois, René, *Zola et ses amis italiens. Documents inédits*, Paris, 1967.

Thatcher, David S., *Nietzsche in England 1890–1914: The Growth of a Reputation*, Toronto, 1970.

Therborn, Goran, *Science, Class and Society. On the Formation of Sociology and Historical Materialism*, London, 1976.

Theweleit, Klaus, *Male Fantasies I: Women, Floods, Bodies, History*, Cambridge, 1987.

Timms, Edward, *Karl Kraus, Apocalyptic Satirist*, New Haven, 1987.

Timms, Edward and Collier Peter, *Visions and Blueprints. Avant-Garde Culture and Radical Politics in Early Twentieth Century Europe*, Manchester, 1988.

Timpanaro, Sebastiano, *On Materialism* (1970), translated from the Italian by Lawrence Garner, London, 1975.

Turner, Trevor, 'Henry Maudsley – psychiatrist, philosopher and entrepreneur', *Psychological Medicine*, 18 (1988), 551–74. Reprinted in *The Anatomy of Madness. Essays in the History of Psychiatry*, edited by Bynum, Porter and Shepherd, London, 1988, III.

Ungari, Paolo, *Alfredo Rocco e l'ideologia giuridica del fascismo*, Brescia, 1963.

Venturi, Franco, 'Cesare Beccaria and Legal Reform', in *Italy and the Enlightenment*, translated from the Italian by Susan Corsi, London, 1972, ch. 6.

Verwey, Gerlof, *Psychiatry in Anthropological and Bio-Medical Context. Philosophical Presuppositions and Implications of German Psychiatry 1820–1970*, translated from the German by Lynne Richards, Studies in the History of Modern Science series, vol. 5, Dordrecht, 1985.

Vidler, A. R., *A Century of Social Catholicism, 1820–1920*, London, 1964.

Villa, Renzo, 'Scienza medica e criminalità nell'Italia unita', *Malattia e medicina*, edited by Franco Della Peruta, *Storia d'Italia*, Annali 7, Turin, 1984, pp. 1,143–78.

Il deviante e i suoi segni. Lombroso e la nascita dell'antropologia criminale, Milan, 1985.

Waller, Gregory A., *The Living and the Undead: From Stoker's Dracula to Romero's Dawn of the Dead*, Urbana and Chicago, 1986.

Weber, Eugen, *The Nationalist Revival in France, 1905–1914*, Berkeley, 1959.

Peasants into Frenchmen. The Modernization of Rural France 1870–1914, Stanford, 1976.

Weindling, Paul, 'Theories of the Cell State in Imperial Germany', in *Biology, Medicine and Society 1840–1940*, edited by Charles Webster, Cambridge, 1981, pp. 99–155.

Health, Race and German Politics between National Unification and Nazism, 1870–1945, Cambridge, forthcoming.

Weiner, J. S., *The Piltdown Forgery* (1955), New York, 1980.

Whitford, Frank, 'The Triumph of the Banal: Art in Nazi Germany', *Visions and Blueprints. Avant-garde Culture and Radical Politics in Early Twentieth Century Europe*, edited by E. Timms and P. Collier, Manchester, 1988, pp. 252–69.

Williams, Raymond, *Culture and Society* (1958), Harmondsworth, 1961.

'Social Darwinism', in *The Limits of Human Nature*, edited and introduced by Jonathan Benthall, London, 1973, pp. 115–30.

The English Novel from Dickens to Lawrence (1970), London, 1984.

Williams, Roger L., *The Horror of Life*, London, 1980.

Winter, Jay, and Teitelbaum M., *The Fear of Population Decline*, New York, 1985.

Wise, Edward M., *The Italian Penal Code*, The American Series of Foreign Penal Codes, Colorado, 1978.

Wolfgang, Marvin E., 'Cesare Lombroso', in *Pioneers in Criminology*, edited by H. Mannheim, London, 1960, pp. 168–227.

Wright, T. R., *The Religion of Humanity. The Impact of Comtean Positivism on Victorian Britain*, Cambridge, 1986.

Young, Robert M., *Mind, Brain and Adaptation in the Nineteenth Century. Cerebral Localization and its Biological Context from Gall to Ferrier*, Oxford, 1970.

Darwin's Metaphor. Nature's Place in Victorian Culture, Cambridge, 1985.

'Darwinism is Social', in *The Darwinian Heritage*, edited by David Kohn, Princeton, 1985, pp. 609–38.

Zeev, Sternhell, *La Droite révolutionnaire, 1885–1914. Les origines françaises du fascisme*, Paris, 1978.

Zeldin, Theodore, *France, 1848–1945*: vol. 1, *Ambition, Love and Politics*, Oxford, 1973; vol. 2, *Intellect, Taste and Anxiety*, Oxford, 1977.

Dissertations

Alexander, Marc Daniel, 'The administration of madness and attitudes toward the insane in nineteenth-century Paris', Ph.D. dissertation, Johns Hopkins University, 1976.

Clarke, M. J., 'The data of alienism: evolutionary neurology, physiological psychology and the reconstruction of British psychiatric theory c. 1850–1900', D.Phil. dissertation, Oxford University, 1984.

Constant, Françoise, 'Introduction à la vie et à l'oeuvre de B.A. Morel (1809–1873)', Medical thesis, Paris, 1970.

Drusch, Jacques Jean Gaston, 'Entre deux discours. Aspects anthropologiques et organiques des dégénérescences de Morel et Magnan', Ph.D. dissertation, Paris, 1981.

Durant, John R., 'The meaning of evolution: post-Darwinian debates on the significance for man of the theory of evolution, 1858–1908', Ph.D. dissertation, Cambridge, 1977.

Farrall, Lyndsay Andrew, 'The origins and growth of the English eugenics movement 1865–1925', Ph.D. dissertation, University of Indiana, 1970.

Friedlander, Ruth, 'Bénédict-August Morel and the development of the theory of degenerescence (the introduction of anthropology into psychiatry)', Ph.D. dissertation, University of California at San Francisco, 1973.

Goldstein, Jan, 'Console and classify: the French psychiatric profession in the nineteenth century', Ph.D. dissertation, University of Chicago, 1977.

Harris, Ruth, 'Murders and madness. Legal psychiatry and criminal anthropology in Paris, 1880–1910', D.Phil. dissertation, Oxford University, 1984.

Lindemann, Dirk Henry, 'Intellectual roots of nazism. A study of interpretations', Ph.D. dissertation, University of Boston, 1983.

McClelland, J. S., 'Aspects of a political theory of mass behaviour in the works of H. Taine, G. Le Bon and S. Freud, 1870–1930', Ph.D. dissertation, Cambridge University, 1969.

Martin, Claude, 'La Dégénérescence dans l'oeuvre de B. A. Morel et dans sa postérité', 2 vols, Ph.D. dissertation, Paris, 1985.

Szreter, Simon, 'The decline of marital fertility in England and Wales 1870–1914', Ph.D. dissertation, Cambridge University, 1984.

Periodicals/articles

American Notes and Queries.

Barker, David, 'How to curb the fertility of the unfit: the feeble-minded in Edwardian Britain', *Oxford Review of Education*, 9 (1983), 197–211.

Beer, Gillian, 'Plot and the analogy with science in later nineteenth-century novels,' *Comparative Criticism*, 2 (1980), 131–49.

Bernart, Elena de, and Tricarico, Marcello, 'Per una rilettura dell'opera di C. Lombroso', *Physis*, 18 (1976), 179–84.

Bock, Gisela, 'Racism and sexism in Nazi Germany: motherhood, compulsory sterilization, and the state', *Signs*, 8, no. 3 (1983), 400–21.

Bonuzzi, Luciano, 'Economia politica e fisica sociale in Cesare Lombroso', *Acta Medicae Historiae Patavina*, 22 (1975–6), 21–31.

Cantor, Nathaniel, 'Recent tendencies in criminological research in Germany', *American Sociological Review*, 1 (1936), 407–18.

Castel, Francoise, 'Dégénérescence et structures. Réflexions méthodologiques à propos de l'oeuvre de Magnan', *Annales médico-psychologiques*, 1, no. 4 (1967), 521–36.

Crook, D. P., 'Darwinism – the political implications', *History of European Ideas*, 2, no. 1 (1981), 19–34.

Dupeu, Jean-Marc, 'Freud and degeneracy: a turning point', *Diogenes*, 97 (1977), 43–64.

Durant, John, 'Scientific naturalism and social reform in the thought of Alfred Russel Wallace', *British Journal for the History of Science*, 12 (1979), 31–58.
  'Biology as a social weapon', *Radical Science Journal*, 8 (1979), 105–8.
  'Exploring the roots of sociobiology', *British Journal for the History of Science*, 13, (1980).

Falnes, Oscar J., 'European progress and the "superior" races: as viewed by a fin-de-siècle liberal, Charles H. Pearson', *Journal of the History of Ideas*, 15 (1954), 312–21.

Feuer, Lewis S., 'The friendship of Edwin Ray Lankester and Karl Marx', *Journal of the History of Ideas*, 40 (1979), 633–48.

Freeden, Michael, 'Eugenics and progressive thought: a study in ideological affinity', *Historical Journal*, 22 (1979), 645–71.
  'Eugenics and ideology', *Historical Journal*, 26 (1983), 959–62.

Fullinwider, S. P., 'Sigmund Freud, John Hughlings Jackson, and speech', *Journal of the History of Ideas*, 44 (1983), 151–8.

Garbari, Maria, 'Il pensiero politico di Scipio Sighele', *Rassegna storica del Risorgimento*, 61 (1974), 523–61.

Gilbert, Arthur N., 'Masturbation and insanity: Henry Maudsley and the ideology of sexual repression', *Albion*, 12 (1980), 268–82.

Gold, Milton, 'The early psychiatrists on degeneracy and genius', *Psychoanalysis and the Psychoanalytic Review*, 47 (1960–1), 37–55.

Graham, Loren R., 'Science and values: the Eugenics Movement', *The American Historical Review*, 82, no. 5 (Dec. 1977), 1,133–64.

Hacking, Ian, 'The taming of chance by an army of statistics', *Times Higher Educational Supplement*, 30 October 1981.

Hammen, Oscar J., 'The spectre of communism in the 1840s', *Journal of the History of Ideas*, 14 (1953), 404–20.

Heath, Stephen, 'Psychopathia sexualis: Stevenson's strange case', *Critical Quarterly*, 28 (Spring–Summer 1986), 93–108.

Helfand, Michael S., 'T. H. Huxley's "Evolution and ethics": the politics of evolution and the evolution of politics', *Victorian Studies*, 20, no. 2 (Winter 1977), 159–77.

Hemmings, F. W. J., review of new volume of Zola's correspondence, *Times Literary Supplement*, 11 April 1986, 396.

Jones, Greta, 'Eugenics and social policy between the wars', *Historical Journal*, 25 (1982), 717–28.

Kershner, R. B., 'Degeneration: the explanatory nightmare', *The Georgian Review*, 40, no. 2 (Summer 1986), 416–44.

Lewis, Aubrey, 'The twenty-fifth Maudsley Lecture: Henry Maudsley: his work and influence', *Journal of Mental Science*, 97 (1951), 260–77.

Martindale, Colin, 'Degeneration, disinhibition and genius', *Journal of the History of Behavioural Sciences*, 7 (1971), 177–82.

Monachesi, Elio D., 'Trends in criminological research in Italy', *American Sociological Review*, 1 (1936), 396–406.

Moore, Jim, 'Socialising Darwinism', in *Science as Politics*, edited by Les Levidow, Radical Science series, 20 (1986), 38–80.

Nye, Robert, 'Degeneration, neurasthenia and the culture of sport in *Belle Époque* France', *Journal of Contemporary History*, 17 (1982), 51–68.

'Heredity, pathology and psychoneuroses in Durkheim's early work', *Knowledge and Society*, 4 (1982), 103–42.

'The bio-medical origins of urban sociology', *Journal of Contemporary History*, 20, no. 4 (Oct. 1985), 659–75.

Pogliano, Claudio, 'Scienza e stirpe: eugenica in Italia (1912–1939)', *Passato e presente*, 5 (1984), 61–97.

Radzinowicz, L., 'L'antropologia criminale e l'esecuzione delle sanzioni detentive', *Rivista di diritto penitenziario*, 13 (1935), 3–14.

'Lombroso', *The Saturday Book* (1945), 103–8.

'Ideology and crime: the deterministic position', *The Columbia Law Review*, 65 (1965), 1,047–60.

Radzinowicz L., and Hood, Roger, 'Incapacitating the habitual criminal, the English experience', *Michigan Law Review*, 78 (1980) 1,305–89.

Radzinowicz, L., and Turner J. W. C., 'The language of criminal science', *Cambridge Law Journal*, 7 (1939–41), 224–37.

Romantisme: revue du dix-neuvième siècle, Sangs, 31 (1981).

Said, Edward W., 'Representing the colonized: anthropology's interlocutors', *Critical Inquiry*, vol. 15, no. 2 (Winter 1989), 205–25.

Saveson, John E., 'Conrad, *Blackwood's* and Lombroso', *Conradiana*, 6 (1974), 57–62.

Schneider, William, 'Toward the improvement of the human race: the history of eugenics in France', *Journal of Modern History*, 64, no. 2 (1982), 268–91.

Sekula, Allan, 'The body and the archive', *October*, 39 (Winter 1986), 3–64.

Smith, C. U. M., 'Evolution and the problem of mind: part I, Herbert Spencer', *Journal of the History of Biology*, 15 (1982), 55–88.

'Evolution and the problem of mind: part II. John Hughlings Jackson', *Journal of the History of Biology*, 15 (1982), 241–62.

Soffer, Reba N., 'New elitism: social psychology in pre-war England', *Journal of British Studies*, 8 (1969), 111–40.

'The revolution in English social thought, 1880–1914', *American Historical Journal*, 75 (1970), 1,938–64.

Soloway, Richard, 'Counting the degenerates: the statistics of race deterioration in Edwardian England', *Journal of Contemporary History*, 17 (January 1982), 137–64.

Tanner, Tony, 'Joseph Conrad and the last gentleman', *Critical Quarterly*, 28 (Spring–Summer 1986), 109–42.

Walk, Alexander, 'Medico-psychologists, Maudsley and the Maudsley', *The British Journal of Psychiatry*, 128 (Jan. 1976), 19–30.

Walter, Richard D., 'What became of the degenerate? A brief history of a concept', *Journal of the History of Medicine and Allied Sciences*, 10 (1956), 422–9.

Weber, Eugen, 'Pierre de Coubertin and the introduction of organised sport in France', *Journal of Contemporary History*, 5 (1970), 1–30.

Zaloszic, Armand, 'La dégénérescence', *Ornicar? Bulletin périodique du champ freudien*, 7 (1976), 61–74.

INDEX

Agulhon, Maurice, 40, 41–2, 89–90n
anarchism, 95, 130–1, 161
anti-semitism: in *Dracula*, 173; and Royal
  Commission on Alien Immigration,
  215–16
Ardigò, R., 131, 146
Arnold, Matthew, 30
Asor Rosa, Alberto, 115

Bagehot, Walter, 13, 205
Bakunin, Alexander, 130
Balfour, Arthur, 215
Ball, Benjamin: critique of *dégénérescence*,
  101–2; on increase in insanity, 43
Balzac, H. de, *The Country Doctor*, 46
Barrès, Maurice, 99
Baudelaire, Charles, 14, 75
Beccaria, Cesare, 112, 136, 137, 138
Bentham, Jeremy, 136, 137, 138
Benthamism, 177
Bergson, Henri, 102–4
Bernal, J. D., 225
Bernard, Claude, 45, 82n
Billliet, A. (Archbishop of Chambèry), 47
Bonald, Vicomte de, 98
Booth, Charles, 185n, 197
Brantlinger, Patrick, *Bread and Circuses*,
  18
Broca, Paul, 51, 135
Buchez, Philippe, 4, 49, 62–7, 234; on
  Morel's *Treatise*, 59–61
Buffon, Count Georges Louis Le Clerc, 61
Burke, Edmund, 94
Burt, Cyril, 199n

Carlyle, Thomas, 30, 67–8, 159, 194, 196
Carpenter, Edward, 173
Carrara, Francesco, 146
Cerise, L. A. P., 45
Chambers, Robert, 11–12, 192
Charcot, J.-M., 55, 90, 100, 169
Chevalier, Louis, 53
Churchill, Winston, 199
Comte, Auguste, 42, 62, 81n, 131, 193
Congreve, Richard, 193
Conrad, Joseph: on heat death of sun, 160;

The Secret Agent, 109–10, 160–1;
  Victory, 161–2
cretinism, 15, 45–8, 172
crime: and alien invasion, 216; and
  degeneracy, 27–8; and punishment, 181;
  and recidivism, 182–4; classical theory
  of, 136–8, 146; Galton's composite
  photography of criminals, 163–5; in
  Conrad, 160–1; supposed increase of in
  19th century, 11; in Stevenson, 165–7;
  Marx and Engels on literature of, 21–2;
  political, 141–2, 144; positivist theory of,
  136–8, 189: Talbot on, 23; urban crime,
  21–2, 60, 209; Victorian preoccupation
  with, 178; Zola's representation of, 84–5
criminal anthropology: in Italy, 4, 7,
  109–11, 119–22, 126, 128, 133, 138–9;
  international congresses of, 4, 106, 109,
  120, 139–43, 178, (Franco-Italian debate)
  139–43
crowds, images and theories of, 4, 90–6,
  105, 150, 213, 222–4, 235
Cullèrre, A., 8
Curtis, Michael, 104

Dallemagne, J., 142
Dansette, Adrien, 57–8
Darwin, Charles, 6, 11, 178; and Galton,
  191–2, 198; and Maudsley, 205; as
  over-optimistic, 174, 189, 190; *Descent
  of Man*, 171, 192n, 193, 194; *Expression
  of Emotions*, 150; *Notebooks*, 193n;
  Origin of Species, 193
Darwin, Leonard, 199
Darwinism: Lombroso's version of, 100;
  politics of, 6, 158, 194–5, 197, 216–18,
  237, 239; reception of, (in France) 100–1;
  (in Italy) 112; social Darwinism and
  imperialism, 39
Davenport, C. B., 200
decadence, literature of, 14, 41–2
degenerate art exhibition (Munich), 27n
Degeneration: and alcoholism, 87, 195; and
  appeals to science, 2, 230; and art, 27,
  117; and cretinism, 47–8; and 'dangerous